UNCOMMON DISSENT

UNCOMMON DISSENT

Intellectuals Who Find Darwinism Unconvincing

Edited by William A. Dembski

ISI BOOKS

WILMINGTON, DELAWARE

Cataloging-in-Publication Data:

Uncommon dissent : intellectuals who find Darwinism unconvincing / edited by William A. Dembski. — 1st ed. — Wilmington, Del. : ISI Books, c2004.

p. ; cm.

Includes index.
ISBN: 1932236309 (cloth)
ISBN: 1932236317 (paper)

1. Evolution (Biology)—Religious aspects. 2. Intelligent design (Teleology)
3. Creationism. 4. Religion and science. 5. Darwin, Charles, 1809–1882—Criticism and interpretation. I. Dembski, William A., 1960–

BL263 .U53 2004   2004102726
213—dc22   CIP

Published in the United States by:

ISI Books
Post Office Box 4431
Wilmington, Delaware 19807
www.isibooks.org

Cover design by Kevin van der Leek

Book design by Kara Beer

Manufactured in the United States of America

To the memory of Michael Polanyi,
for freeing inquiry from ideology

"The purpose of freedom is to create it for others."

— Bernard Malamud, *The Fixer*

CONTENTS

PART II: DARWINISM'S CULTURAL INROADS

PART III: LEAVING THE DARWINIAN FOLD

PART IV: AUDITING THE BOOKS

ACKNOWLEDGMENTS

The contributors to this volume are to be commended for a provocative and illuminating set of pieces. All but three were specifically commissioned for this collection. The exceptions are the essays by Phillip Johnson and David Berlinski and the interview with Marcel-Paul Schützenberger.

Thanks are due Fr. Richard John Neuhaus and the editors at *First Things* for permission to reprint the Johnson essay (which appeared in the October/November 1990 issue) as well as for opening the pages of that journal to dissent from Darwinism.

Thanks are also due Dennis Wagner, head of Access Research Network (ARN), for permission to reprint the Schützenberger interview. ARN orginally published the interview through its journal *Origins & Design* (in the spring of 1996, volume 17, number 2). Paul Nelson, the editor of that journal, arranged for David Berlinski to do the translation.

I must thank the editors at *Commentary* for permission to reprint Berlinski's essay "The Deniable Darwin" (which appeared in June 1996) along with his responses to critics in "Denying Darwin" (the title given by *Commentary* to the correspondence that Berlinski's essays elicited and which was published in September 1996).

Also to be thanked are the following letter-writers, who gave permission to have their letters critical of Berlinski's essay to be reprinted here: H. Allen Orr, Richard Dawkins, Daniel C. Dennett, Arthur M. Shapiro, Paul R. Gross, and Eugenie C. Scott.

In addition, thanks are due to John Wilson, the editor of *Books & Culture,* for writing a foreword that helpfully situates the pieces collected here within the broader cultural conversation. *Books & Culture,* like *First Things* and *Commentary,* provides a model for how the debate surrounding Darwinism should be handled: informed discussion without censorship.

Finally, Jeremy Beer, editor in chief at ISI Books, is to be commended for first envisioning this project, for seeing it to completion, and above all for having the courage to face the opposition that invariably arises when Darwinism is questioned.

In the April 7, 2003, issue of the *Harvard Crimson,* Richard T. Halvorson, then an undergraduate, wrote, "We must refuse to bow to our culture's false idols. Science will not benefit from canonizing Darwin or making evolution an article of secular faith. We must reject intellectual excommunication as a valid form of dealing with criticism: the most important question for any society to ask is the one that is forbidden." With this volume, the Intercollegiate Studies Institute continues its long and celebrated tradition of asking the forbidden questions and thereby refusing to bow to our culture's false idols.

John Wilson

FOREWORD

For years now, the *New York Review of Books* has been sending a di-
rect-mail letter that asks—in bright red letters—"Are you an intellectual?" I was glad to see that the subtitle of *Uncommon Dissent* is *Intellectuals Who Find Darwinism Unconvincing.* "Intellectual" is a perfectly
good noun that has fallen on hard times, particularly among conservatives, where it is almost always used pejoratively.

An intellectual may be, but is not necessarily, a specialist. Not all
academics are intellectuals; not all intellectuals are academics. To be an
intellectual is to possess a hungry mind and a willingness to question
received opinion. But, contrary to a fashionable perversion of the
intellectual's calling, *intellectual* is not a synonym for *skeptic.* Healthy
skepticism is indeed essential to the intellectual life, but it must not become an end in itself. There is a reality to which we are all accountable,
a reality that invites our understanding.

Since you have picked up *Uncommon Dissent,* there's a good chance
that you would have to answer yes to the *NYRB*'s question. And you
may already know that the book you're holding is dangerous; it may get
you into trouble. By questioning Darwinism, you place yourself in the
company of all the cranks who have violated the taboos enforced by our
current opinion-makers.

In many settings, the contempt of the enlightened won't affect
you. If, however, you are teaching at a college or university, the costs
may be considerable. (False dramatics? Not at all. The art of blackball-
ing is practiced with great skill and ruthlessness in academia.)

Of course, the ferocity of resistance merely underlines the need for
informed dissent. The almost comically hyperbolic arrogance of the
Darwinian establishment, well documented in William Dembski's in-

troduction to this volume, is representative of a larger malaise. As Steve Fuller observes in his new book, *Kuhn vs Popper: The Struggle for the Soul of Science,*

> Popper's view that a non-scientist might criticize science for failing to abide by its own publicly avowed standards is rarely found inside academia today. For those who have inherited Kuhn's Cold War belief that normal science is a bulwark in a volatile world, it comes as no surprise that philosophers today would sooner criticize creationists for violating evolutionary strictures than evolutionists for violating more general scientific norms—an activity for which Popper had been notorious.

But there's another, subtler danger to which almost every reader of this book is potentially vulnerable. The role of dissenter can be costly, but it can also be powerfully seductive. How easy it is, after reading a book such as this, to puff oneself up with pride, to wax dogmatic about the "crumbling edifice of evolutionary theory," and to fall into the very arrogance that is characteristic of Darwinism at its worst.

If you really are an intellectual, and not what Solzhenitsyn calls a "smatterer," you will finish this book with more questions than answers. You won't simply accept the assertions of the authors gathered here, themselves a very diverse bunch; you'll subject them to the same sort of searching critique they have brought to bear on Darwinism.

You will wonder, for starters, what precisely is meant by "Darwinism"—or "evolution," for that matter, a notoriously slippery word. Is it the notion that life is merely a cosmic accident, the product of chance and natural selection? If so—and that is an essential aspect of the doctrine of some of the most visible proponents of Darwinism—there's no reason not to toss it overboard.

But what about common descent? "Evolution," Richard Dawkins writes in his introduction to *The Best American Science and Nature Writing 2003,* "is one of the most securely established facts in all science. The knowledge that we are cousins to apes, kangaroos, and bacteria is beyond all educated doubt." Isn't there abundant evidence that—in this limited but hardly insignificant sense—evolution is real, however open to dispute the adequacy of natural selection as its engine may be? (Even Richard Dawkins is right once in a while.)

What about scientists like Simon Conway Morris, the distinguished Cambridge paleobiologist whose book *Life's Solution: Inevitable Hu-*

mans in a Lonely Universe argues that the evolution of life reveals a pattern, an underlying direction, in which he finds "the richness of a Creation"? Nothing of this "complexity and beauty," he adds, "presupposes, let alone proves, the existence of God, but all is congruent." Is he right? If so, why? If not, why not? Part of your job as a reader of *Uncommon Dissent* is to read it in dialogue with books such as *Life's Solution* or *Perspectives on an Evolving Creation*, a newly published collection of essays edited by Keith B. Miller.

Since I have given you the beginnings of a reading list, let me conclude with one of my favorite books on Darwinism—one that is unfairly neglected in the literature. It is a small children's book, *Yellow and Pink,* written and illustrated by William Steig, who died in the fall of 2003 at the age of ninety-five. Steig, whose cartoons appeared in the *New Yorker* from 1930 on, was best known for his children's books (including *Shrek!,* the basis for the hit movie).

Yellow and Pink was first published in 1984 and was reissued in 2003 just a few months before Steig's death. It is the story, as the opening lines tell us, of "two small figures made of wood, . . . lying out in the sun one day on an old newspaper. One was short, fat, and painted pink; the other was tall, thin, and painted yellow." They are wondering how they came to be there—indeed, how they came to exist in the first place.

Pink looks at his companion—"He found Yellow's color, his well-chiseled head, his whole form, admirable"—and he decides: "Someone must have made us."

Not so, counters Yellow: "I say we're an accident, somehow or other we just happened." And they begin a debate, each forcefully pressing his case.

I don't want to reveal the rest of the plot and spoil it for you. But I will say this: on the issue at stake, Steig's little fable is far more penetrating than whole stacks of books that have accumulated in my study. I hope you will put it on your own bookshelf, not far from *Uncommon Dissent.*

William A. Dembski

INTRODUCTION
The Myths of Darwinism

Immodest ideas have a way of gathering mythologies, and Darwinism is no exception. Darwinism's primary myth is the myth of invincibility: all of Darwinism's other myths follow in this myth's train. Darwinism, its proponents assure us, has been overwhelmingly vindicated. Any resistance to it is futile and indicates bad faith or worse. Thus Richard Dawkins has charged those who resist Darwin's grand evolutionary story with being "ignorant, stupid or insane (or wicked, but I'd rather not consider that)."[1] Nor has Dawkins mitigated his position over time. More recently he added: "I don't withdraw a word of my initial statement. But I do now think it may have been incomplete. There is perhaps a fifth category, which may belong under 'insane' but which can be more sympathetically characterized by a word like *tormented, bullied,* or *brainwashed.*"[2]

The myth of invincibility recurs in the writings of philosopher Daniel Dennett who, in *Darwin's Dangerous Idea*, describes Darwinism as a universal acid that eats away every idea it touches. Dennett is so smitten with Darwinian evolution that he regards it as the greatest idea ever conceived, far ahead of the ideas of Newton and Einstein. This awe of Darwinism has now worked its way into the popular culture. Thus, novelist Barbara Kingsolver will describe Darwin's idea of natural selection as "the greatest, simplest, most elegant logical construct ever to dawn across our curiosity about the workings of natural life. It is inarguable, and *it explains everything.*"[3]

Given such sentiments, it's not surprising that discipline after discipline is now being "Darwinized." Cosmology has its self-reproducing black holes governed by cosmological natural selection (see Lee Smolin's *The Life of the Cosmos*). Ethics and psychology have now become evolutionary ethics and evolutionary psychology (see Robert Wright's *The*

Moral Animal and Steven Pinker's *How the Mind Works*). Even the professional schools are being overtaken, so that we now have books with titles like *Evolutionary Medicine* (medicine), *Managing the Human Animal* (business), *Economics as an Evolutionary Science* (economics), and *Evolutionary Jurisprudence* (law). And let's not forget religious studies, in which God genes (i.e., genes that cause us to believe in God irrespective of whether God exists) and the Darwinian roots of religious belief have become a growth industry (see, for instance, Pascal Boyer's *Religion Explained: The Evolutionary Origins of Religious Thought*).

Such enthusiasm for Darwinism might be endearing except that its proponents are deadly earnest. For instance, in *Darwin's Dangerous Idea* Daniel Dennett views religious believers who dissuade their children from believing Darwinian evolution as such a threat to the social order that they need to be caged in zoos or quarantined (both metaphors are his).[4] Because of the myth of invincibility that now surrounds it, Darwinism has become monopolistic and imperialistic. Though often associated with "liberalism," Darwinism as practiced today knows nothing of the classical liberalism of John Stuart Mill. The proponents of "Darwinian liberalism" tolerate no dissent and regard all criticism of Darwinism's fundamental tenets as false and reprehensible.

Yet according to Mill, "We can never be sure that the opinion we are endeavouring to stifle is a false opinion; and even if we were sure, stifling it would be an evil still." Mill expanded:

> First, if any opinion is compelled to silence, that opinion may, for aught we can certainly know, be true. To deny this is to assume our own infallibility. Secondly, though the silenced opinion be an error, it may, and very commonly does, contain a portion of truth; and since the general or prevailing opinion on any object is rarely or never the whole truth, it is only by the collision of adverse opinions that the remainder of the truth has any chance of being supplied. Thirdly, even if the received opinion be not only true, but the whole truth; unless it is suffered to be, and actually is, vigorously and earnestly contested, it will, by most of those who receive it, be held in the manner of a prejudice, with little comprehension or feeling of its rational grounds. And not only this, but, fourthly, the meaning of the doctrine itself will be in danger of being lost, or enfeebled, and deprived of its vital effect on the character and conduct: the dogma becoming a mere formal profession, inefficacious for good, but cumbering the ground,

and preventing the growth of any real and heartfelt conviction, from reason or personal experience.[5]

Charles Darwin was Mill's contemporary and fully accepted Mill's
classical liberalism. In the *Origin of Species,* Darwin wrote: "A fair result can be obtained only by fully stating and balancing the facts and
arguments on both sides of each question."[6]

By contrast, many of Darwin's contemporary disciples have turned
stifling dissent into an art form. Because the myth of invincibility must
be preserved at all costs, it is not acceptable to place doubts about Darwinism on the table for vigorous discussion. Rather, the doubts must be
disqualified and repressed. To see this, consider the response by Darwinists to Senator Rick Santorum's "Sense of the Senate" amendment
to the Elementary and Secondary Education Act:

> It is the sense of the Senate that (1) good science education
> should prepare students to distinguish the data or testable
> theories of science from philosophical or religious claims that
> are made in the name of science; and (2) where biological
> evolution is taught, the curriculum should help students to
> understand why this subject generates so much continuing
> controversy, and should prepare the students to be informed
> participants in public discussions regarding the subject.[7]

An eminently reasonable amendment, no doubt. Indeed, the U.S.
Senate voted overwhelmingly for it (91-8). Even Senator Ted Kennedy,
rarely an ally of Santorum's, voted for it. What's more, by merely reflecting the "sense of the Senate," this amendment was nonbinding. And
yet, the American Association for the Advancement of Science, the National Center for Science Education, and the American Civil Liberties
Union (to name but a few) were up in arms over this amendment. Why?
Because evolution was singled out for special treatment and opened to
critical scrutiny. Why, detractors of the amendment demanded, wasn't
general relativity or the atomic theory of matter singled out for similar
treatment?

Comparisons of evolutionary theory with well-established theories of physics and chemistry display wishful thinking. The reason those
theories were not singled out for critical scrutiny is, of course, because
they are well established and evolutionary theory is not. This book will
detail the weaknesses of Darwinian evolutionary theory and, going even
further, argue that the preponderance of evidence goes against Darwin-

ism. Regardless of one's point of view, it's actually quite easy to see that Darwinism is not in the same league as the hard sciences. For instance, Darwinists will often compare their theory favorably to Einsteinian physics, claiming that Darwinism is just as well established as general relativity. Yet how many physicists, while arguing for the truth of Einsteinian physics, will claim that general relativity is as well established as Darwin's theory? Zero.

Once Darwinism becomes a target for critical scrutiny, its proponents change the target. Thus, when David Berlinski criticized Darwinism in his December 2002 article in *Commentary* (titled "Has Darwin Met His Match?"), biologist Paul Gross took him to task for making "Darwinism" the topic of controversy. According to Gross, only "those who do not know much evolutionary biology" refer to something called "Darwinism."[8] Evolutionary biology, we are assured, is far richer than the caricature of it called Darwinism.

Despite such protestations, Darwinism is in fact the right target. It is no accident that in debates over biological evolution Darwin's name keeps coming up. Repeated references to Darwin and Darwinism are not made simply out of respect for the history of the subject, as though evolutionary biology needed constantly to be reminded of its founder. Darwin's theory constitutes the very core of evolutionary biology; he therefore looms larger than life in the study of biological origins. Indeed, nothing in evolutionary biology makes sense apart from Darwinism.

To see this, we need to understand Darwinism's role in evolutionary biology. Darwinism is really two claims. The less crucial claim is that all organisms trace their lineage back to a universal common ancestor. Any two organisms are n-th cousins k-times removed where n and k depend on the two organisms in question. This claim is referred to as "common descent." Although evolutionary biology is committed to common descent, that is not its central claim.

Rather, the central claim of evolutionary biology is that an unguided physical process can account for the emergence of all biological complexity and diversity. Filling in the details of that process remains a matter for debate among evolutionary biologists. Yet it is an in-house debate, and one essentially about details. In broad strokes, however, any unguided physical process capable of producing biological complexity must have three components: (1) hereditary transmission, (2) incidental change, and (3) natural selection.

Think of it this way: We start with some organism. It incurs some change. The change is incidental in the sense that it doesn't anticipate future changes that subsequent generations of organisms may experience (neo-Darwinism, for instance, treats such changes as random mutations or errors in genetic material). What's more, incidental change is heritable and therefore can be transmitted to the next generation. Whether it actually is transmitted to the next generation and then preferentially preserved in subsequent generations, however, depends on whether the change is in some sense beneficial to the organism. If so, then natural selection will be likely to preserve organisms exhibiting that change.

This picture is perfectly general. As I already noted, it can accommodate neo-Darwinism. It can also accommodate Lamarckian evolution, whose incidental changes occur as organisms, simply by putting to use existing structures, enhance or modify the functionalities of those structures. It can accommodate Lynn Margulis's idea of symbiogenetic evolution, whose incidental changes occur as different types of organisms come together to form a new, hybrid organism. And it can also accommodate other forms of incidental change, including genetic drift, lateral gene transfer, and the activity of regulatory genes in development.

Evolutionary biologists debate the precise role and extent of hereditary transmission and incidental change. The debate can even be quite sharp at times. But evolutionary biology leaves unchallenged Darwinism's holy of holies—natural selection. Darwin himself was unclear about the mechanisms of hereditary transmission and incidental change. But whatever form they took, Darwin was convinced that natural selection was the key to harnessing them. The same is true for contemporary evolutionary biologists. That's why to this day we hear repeated references to Darwin's theory of natural selection but not to Darwin's theory of variation or Darwin's theory of inheritance.

Apart from design or teleology, what could coordinate the incidental changes that hereditary transmission passes from one generation to the next? To perform such coordination, evolution requires a substitute for a designer. Darwin's claim to fame was to propose natural selection as a designer substitute. But natural selection is no substitute for intelligent coordination. All natural selection does is narrow the variability of incidental change by weeding out the less fit. What's more, it acts on the spur of the moment, based solely on what the environment at present deems fit, and thus without any foresight of future possibilities. And yet this blind process, when coupled with another blind process (incidental change), is supposed to produce designs that exceed the capacities of any designers in our experience.

Leaving aside small-scale evolutionary changes, such as insects developing insecticide resistance (which no one disputes), where is the evidence that natural selection can accomplish the intricacies of bioengineering that are manifest throughout the living world (such as producing insects in the first place)? Where is the evidence that the sorts of incidental changes required for large-scale evolution ever occur? The evidence simply isn't there. Robert Koons (chapter 1) helps us appreciate what's at stake by imagining what would happen to the germ theory of disease if scientists never found any microorganisms or viruses that produced diseases. That's the problem with Darwinism: In place of detailed, testable accounts of how a complex biological system could realistically have emerged, Darwinism offers just-so stories about how such systems might have emerged in some idealized conceptual space far removed from biological reality.

Why, then, does Darwinism continue to garner such a huge following, especially among the intellectual elite? There are two reasons: (1) It provides a materialistic creation story that dispenses with any need for design, purpose, or God (which is convenient for those who want to escape the demands of religion, morality, and conscience). (2) The promise of getting design without a designer is incredibly seductive—it's the ultimate free lunch. No wonder Daniel Dennett, in *Darwin's Dangerous Idea*, credits Darwin with "the single best idea anyone has ever had."[9] Getting design without a designer is a good trick indeed.

But all good tricks need some sleight of hand to deflect critical scrutiny. With Darwinism, that sleight of hand takes the form of myths. Darwinism depends on several subsidiary myths to prop its primary myth—the myth of invincibility. Artfully invoked and applied, these subsidiary myths have been enormously successful at censoring all doubts about Darwinism. Altogether, there are four subsidiary myths, and it is instructive to see how they work in detail:

(1) *The myth of fundamentalist intransigence*. According to this myth, only religious fanatics oppose Darwinism. What else could prevent the immediate and cheerful acceptance of Darwinism except fundamentalist intransigence? Darwinism, to the convinced Darwinist, is a self-evident truth. Biologist Paul Ewald, for instance, writes: "You have heritable variation, and you've got differences in survival and reproduction among the variants. That's the beauty of it. It has to be true—it's like arithmetic. And if there is life on other planets, natural selection has to be the fundamental organizing principle there, too."[10] If Darwin's theory is as sure as arithmetic, what could prevent people from seeing its truth?

Perhaps the failure of people to accept Darwinian evolution is a failure of education. One frequently gets this sense from reading publications by the National Academy of Sciences, the National Center for Science Education, and the National Association of Biology Teachers. If only people could be made to understand Darwin's theory properly, they would readily sign off on it. But since Darwinists hold a monopoly on biology education in America, something else must be hindering Darwinism's acceptance. Accordingly, a mindless fundamentalism must reign over the minds of a vast majority of Americans, leading them to dig in their heels and resist Darwinism's truth, which otherwise would be plain for all to see.

Thus, what many Darwinists desire is not just more talented communicators to promote Darwinism in America's biology classrooms, but an enforced educational and cultural policy for total worldview reprogramming, one that is sufficiently aggressive to capture and convert to Darwinism even the most recalcitrant among "religiously programmed" youth. That's why Darwinists like Daniel Dennett, to all appearances a participant in and advocate of democracy, fantasize about quarantining religious parents. It seems ridiculous to convinced Darwinists like Dennett that the fault might lie with their theory and that the public might be picking up on faults inherent in that theory.

For the Darwinist, the myth of fundamentalist intransigence justifies all forms of character assassination, ad hominem attacks, guilt by association, and demonization. An increasing cultural groundswell against Darwinism has meant that Darwinists are no longer able to simply ignore their critics. Instead, they routinely begin their responses to critics by labeling them as creationists, which in the current intellectual climate is equivalent to being called a holocaust denier, a flat-earther, or a believer in horoscopes. Creationism, properly speaking, refers to a literal interpretation of Genesis in which God through special acts of creation brings the biophysical universe into existence in six literal twenty-four-hour days, somewhere in the last several thousand years. When Richard Dawkins replies to David Berlinski's criticisms of Darwinism (see chapter 14), he will call Berlinski, who is a secular Jew, a "creationist." This is not only name-calling, it is also incorrect. Recently Berlinski remarked: "I have no creationist agenda whatsoever and, beyond respecting the injunction to have a good time all the time, no religious principles, either."[11] If Berlinski can be branded a creationist, then woe to those who actually have religious convictions and oppose Darwinism.

(2) *The Myth of Prometheus.* This myth is the flipside of the previous one. If only religious crazies oppose Darwinism, then it is only

the intelligent and courageous who embrace Darwinism and fully accept its consequences. In the original myth, Prometheus brought fire to humanity and thus gave human beings control over nature (a power previously reserved to the gods). Prometheus did this at great personal cost, incurring the wrath of the gods, who chained him to a mountaintop and decreed that birds of prey should forever tear and consume his liver. By opposing arbitrary limitations that the gods imposed on humanity, Prometheus symbolized liberation from ignorance and superstition. In place of comforting myths that assure us of a special place in the great scheme of things, Prometheus teaches us to spurn the gods and stare the ultimate meaninglessness of reality in the eye without flinching.

Darwinists enjoy styling themselves as Prometheus's heirs. Accordingly, they are humanity's benefactors, conferring scientific insights that tell us the grim truth about our biological origins and thereby liberate us from our benighted fundamentalist past. Darwinism views the organic world as a great competition for life in which all living forms are ultimately destined for extinction. This is a bitter pill, but it is the best medicine we have. Fundamentalism, by contrast, is an opiate that causes us to sleepwalk through life, accepting fairy tales about our biological origins as well as fairy tales about any life beyond death. (Conflating the language of fairy tales with the language of ordinary religious belief is a favorite among more extreme Darwinists such as Steven Weinberg.)

The myth of Prometheus has been a public relations bonanza for Darwinists, helping them to score some of their best propaganda points. Take, for instance, the movie *Inherit the Wind*, a fictional portrayal of the Scopes monkey trial in which the forces of reason in the guise of Darwinism struggle against the mindless fundamentalism of a backwater town. The movie portrays Darwinism as the defender of scientific truth and intellectual honesty and also as the great liberator from religious bigotry. Given only this movie, who in their right mind would not support Darwinism? Notwithstanding, the actual Scopes trial, as Edward Sisson recounts in chapter 5 of this book, provided a quite different picture. Clarence Darrow, the Darwinist attorney who defended Scopes, carefully arranged the trial so that Darwinism was never subjected to cross-examination.

Although the myth of Prometheus has lofty pretensions, for many Darwinists it provides an excuse for elitism and snobbery. Accordingly, they divide the world into the moronic masses who reject Darwinism and its consequences, and the smart people (themselves) who believe it. Take Richard Dawkins and Daniel Dennett's latest attempt to make atheism more alluring to the wider culture. They propose the word "bright" to serve the same role with respect to atheism as the word "gay" serves with respect to homosexuality. Dawkins writes:

> Paul Geisert and Mynga Futrell, of Sacramento, California, have set out to coin a new word, a new "gay." Like gay, it should be a noun hijacked from an adjective, with its original meaning changed but not too much. Like gay, it should be catchy. . . . Like gay, it should be positive, warm, cheerful, bright. Bright? Yes, bright. Bright is the word, the new noun. I am a bright. You are a bright. She is a bright. We are the brights. Isn't it about time you came out as a bright? Is he a bright? I can't imagine falling for a woman who was not a bright. The website www.celeb-atheists.com suggests numerous intellectuals and other famous people are brights. . . . A bright is a person whose world view is free of supernatural and mystical elements. The ethics and actions of a bright are based on a naturalistic world view. . . . You can sign on as a bright at www.the-brights.net.[12]

Since an atheistic worldview is best nourished on Darwinism (it was Dawkins, after all, who said that Darwin made it possible to be an intellectually fulfilled atheist), it follows that "brights" are also Darwinists. Perhaps in the future we shall see articles and books about "Darwin's Bright Idea."

(3) *The myth of victory past.* A scene in the Marx Brothers movie *Duck Soup* illustrates this myth. Groucho Marx, president of Freedonia, presides over a meeting of the cabinet. The following exchange ensues between Groucho and one of Freedonia's ministers:

Groucho: "And now, members of the Cabinet, we'll take up old business."

Minister: "I wish to discuss the Tariff!"

Groucho: "Sit down, that's new business! No old business? Very well—then we'll take up new business"

Minister: "Now about that Tariff . . ."

Groucho: "Too late—that's old business already!"

This exchange epitomizes Darwinism's handling of criticism. When a valid criticism of Darwinism is first proposed, it is dismissed without an adequate response, either on a technicality or with some irrelevant point, or is simply ignored. As time passes, people forget that Darwinists never adequately met the criticism. But Darwinism is still calling the shots. Since the criticism failed to dislodge Darwinism, the criticism itself must have been discredited or refuted somewhere. Thereafter the criticism becomes known as "that discredited criticism that was refuted a long time ago." And, after that, even to raise the criticism betrays an outdated conception of evolutionary theory. In this way, the criticism, though entirely valid, simply vanishes into oblivion. With the internet and an emerging intellectual community that refuses to be cowed by Darwinist bullying, that scenario is beginning to change, but historically that is how Darwinists have handled criticism.

Michael Behe's challenge to Darwinian evolution provides a recent case study in the myth of victory past. Certain biochemical systems are molecular machines of great sophistication and intricacy whose parts are each indispensable to the system's function. Such systems are, as Behe defines them in his 1996 book *Darwin's Black Box, irreducibly complex*. What's more, as Behe also notes, such systems resist Darwinian explanations. Indeed, the biological community has no detailed, testable proposals for how irreducibly complex systems might have arisen through Darwinian means, only a variety of wishful speculations. Biologists like James Shapiro and Franklin Harold, who have no "creationist" or "intelligent design" agenda, admit that this is so.[13] Nevertheless, it is routine among Darwinists to declare that Behe's ideas have been decisively refuted and even to provide references to the biological literature in which Behe's ideas are supposed to have been refuted.

But what happens when one tracks down those references in the biological literature that are said to have refuted Behe? David Ray Griffin, a philosopher with no animus against Darwinism or sympathy for Behe's intelligent design perspective, remarks:

> The response I have received from repeating Behe's claim [that the evolutionary literature fails to account for irreducible complexity] is that I obviously have not read the right books. There are, I am assured, evolutionists who have described how the transitions in question could have occurred [i.e., how, contra Behe, Darwinian pathways could lead to irreducibly complex biochemical systems]. When I ask in which books I can find these discussions, however, I either get no answer or else some titles that, upon examination, do not in fact contain the promised accounts. That such accounts exist seems to be something that is widely known, but I have yet to encounter someone who knows where they exist.[14]

It will help to see how this Darwinist technique of "passing the buck" actually plays out in practice. The National Center for Science Education is now the premier watchdog group for keeping concerted criticism of Darwinism outside the public arena. At the time of this writing, the Public Broadcasting Service is airing a Nova-style video program titled *Unlocking the Mystery of Life*. This program is critical of Darwinism and features Michael Behe's ideas about irreducible complexity. The National Center for Science Education has a critical response to this program on its website (www.ncseweb.org) written by Andrea Bottaro, an immunologist on the faculty of the University of Rochester Medical Center. Here is what Bottaro says about irreducible complexity:

> The crucial argument . . . widely discussed in the video is the concept of "irreducibly complex" systems, and the purported impossibility of conventional evolutionary mechanisms to generate them. Although it was quickly rejected by biologists on theoretical and empirical grounds, [ref#6] "irreducible complexity" has remained the main staple of [Intelligent Design] Creationism. Ironically, this argument was just recently delivered a fatal blow in the prestigious science journal *Nature*, where a computer simulation based entirely on evolutionary principles (undirected random mutation and selection) was shown to be able to generate "irreducibly complex" outputs. [ref#7][15]

This all sounds quite impressive and damning until one follows the paper trail. Indeed, what are the references #6 and #7 that Bottaro cites? Reference #6 refers to the articles on Kenneth Miller's evolution website.[16] What's on this website? Prominently displayed is Miller's 1999 book, *Finding Darwin's God*. Despite Miller's promises to the contrary, don't look for a refutation of irreducible complexity there. None of Miller's arguments against irreducible complexity withstands scrutiny. Behe claimed that the biological literature is bereft of *detailed* Darwinian explanations for the origin of *irreducibly complex* biochemical machines. Miller refers his readers to "four glittering examples of what Behe claimed would never be found." Go to the articles that Miller cites, however, and you'll find that Miller's four glittering examples not only fail to be detailed but also fail to be irreducibly complex. Miller isn't even in the right ballpark. Behe shows this clearly in his article "Irreducible Complexity and the Evolutionary Literature: Response to Critics."[17]

What about the rest of Miller's website? Miller lists several articles critical of Behe: "Design on the Defensive" (actually a collection of four articles directed at Behe), "A Review of *Darwin's Black Box*," "Answering the Biochemical Design Argument," and Miller's most recent essay, "The Flagellum Unspun: The Collapse of 'Irreducible Complexity.'" Ironically, Miller wrote this last article for a book that Darwinist Michael Ruse and I are editing together for Cambridge University Press (*Debating Design: From Darwin to DNA*). What's more, Behe is a contributor to the book.

"The Flagellum Unspun" was Miller's big chance to put his best foot forward and wipe the floor with irreducible complexity. And yet Miller's entire argument consists not in providing a detailed Darwinian pathway to the irreducibly complex system that has become the mascot of the intelligent design movement (i.e., the bacterial flagellum), but in pointing out that such pathways are not logically impossible because irreducibly complex systems (like the flagellum) include subsystems (like the type III secretory system) that perform functions in their own right and therefore could be acted on by natural selection.

Four years after the publication of *Finding Darwin's God*, Miller's core argument against Behe is that the subsystems within irreducibly complex systems might, or could logically, be acted on by natural selection. He repeats this argument in the other articles critical of Behe on his website (the biological systems change from article to article, but the core argument remains unchanged). According to Miller, the parts of an irreducibly complex system are never totally functionless. Rather, those parts have functions and thus are grist for selection's mill. Accordingly, selection can work on those parts and thereby form irreducibly complex systems.

For the Darwinian faithful, such a handwaving argument is all that's required to refute irreducible complexity. The unconverted, however, want to know not why nothing is stopping natural selection from producing irreducible complexity but why we should think that natural selection can actively foster irreducible complexity (as it must if Darwinism is true—the biology of the cell, after all, is chock-full of irreducibly complex biochemical machines). To understand the difference, imagine yourself randomly sampling Scrabble pieces from an urn. Nothing is stopping the pieces from spelling the first few lines of Hamlet's soliloquy. But if they do spell the first few lines of Hamlet's soliloquy, something more than chance was involved. Likewise, with irreducibly complex systems, their emergence implicates more than just Darwin's selection mechanism.

To sum up, Bottaro's reference #6 purports to justify the rejection by the biological community of Behe's work on irreducible complexity. In fact, all it does is point the reader to the rationalizations employed by the biological community for sidestepping the challenge posed by irreducible complexity. Reference #6 is therefore an exercise in misdirection.

What about reference #7? This reference is to Richard Lenski et al.'s May 8, 2003 paper in *Nature* titled "The Evolutionary Origin of Complex Features."[18] This paper describes a computer simulation and thus contains no actual biology. Go to the discussion section, and you'll read: "Some readers might suggest that we 'stacked the deck' by studying the evolution of a complex feature that could be built on simpler functions that were also useful. However, that is precisely what evolutionary theory requires. . . ." In other words, the computer programmers built into the simulation what they thought evolution needed to make it work. The validity of this study therefore depends on whether the simulation faithfully models biological reality.

Unfortunately, the simulation presupposes the very point at issue. It therefore begs the question and doesn't prove a thing about real-life biological evolution. The Lenski simulation requires that complex systems exhibiting complex functions can always be built up from (or decomposed into) simpler systems exhibiting simpler functions. This is a much stronger assumption than merely allowing that complex systems may include functioning subsystems. Just because a complex system can include functioning subsystems doesn't mean that it decomposes into a collection of subsystems each of which is presently functional or vestigial of past function and thus amenable to shaping by natural selection.

The simulation by Lenski et al. assumes that all functioning biological systems are evolutionary kludges of subsystems that presently have function or previously had function. But there's no evidence that real-life irreducibly complex biochemical machines, for instance, can be decomposed in this way. If there were, the Lenski et al. computer simulation would be unnecessary. Without it, their demonstration is an exercise in irrelevance. Bottaro's "fatal blow" against irreducible complexity is nothing of the sort. Behe's ideas about irreducible complexity, and in particular the criticism they raise of Darwinism, remain very much alive and discussed among biologists.

(4) *The myth of the scientific juggernaut.* Despite all the propaganda to the contrary, science is not a juggernaut that relentlessly pushes back the frontiers of knowledge. Rather, science is an interconnected web of theoretical and factual claims about the world that are constantly

being revised. Changes in one portion of the web can induce radical changes in another. In particular, science regularly confronts the problem of having to retract claims that it once boldly asserted.

Consider the following example from geology. In the nineteenth century the geosynclinal theory was proposed to account for the origination of mountain ranges. This theory hypothesized that large trough-like depressions, known as geosynclines, filled with sediment, gradually became unstable, and then, when crushed and heated by the earth, elevated to form mountain ranges. To the question "How did mountain ranges originate?" geologists as late as 1960 confidently asserted that the geosynclinal theory provided the answer. In the 1960 edition of Clark and Stearn's *Geological Evolution of North America*, the status of the geosynclinal theory was even favorably compared with Darwin's theory of natural selection. Whatever became of the geosynclinal theory? An alternative theory, that of plate tectonics, was developed. It explained mountain formation through continental drift and sea-floor spreading. Within a few years, it had decisively replaced the geosynclinal theory. The history of science is filled with such turnabouts in which confident claims to knowledge suddenly vanish from the scientific literature.

The geosynclinal theory was completely wrong. Thus, when the theory of plate tectonics came along, the geosynclinal theory was overthrown. Often, however, theories are not completely wrong but offer some legitimate insights. Nevertheless, upon further investigation it is evident that they need to be revised, frequently by being contracted. When theories are first proposed, their originators try to push them to account for as much as possible—indeed, for too much. Only later do the limitations of the theory become evident.

It is always a temptation in science to think that one's theory encompasses a far bigger domain than it actually does. This happened with Newtonian mechanics. Physicists thought that Newton's laws provided a total account of the constitution and dynamics of the universe. Maxwell, Einstein, and Heisenberg each showed that the proper domain of Newtonian mechanics was far more constricted than scientists first believed. Newtonian mechanics works well for medium sized objects at medium speeds, but for very fast and very small objects it breaks down. In the latter case, we need to invoke, respectively, relativity and quantum mechanics. So, too, the proper domain of the Darwinian selection mechanism is far more constricted than most Darwinists would like to admit. In particular, large-scale evolutionary changes in which organisms gain novel, information-rich structures cannot legitimately be derived from the Darwinian selection mechanism.

Sometimes, as in the geosynclinal case, theories are replaced in their entirety by completely new theories. At other times, as with Newtonian mechanics, theories prove inadequate outside a certain range of phenomena and need to be supplemented. No one any longer learns geosynclinal geology, but all freshman physics students still learn Newtonian mechanics, though later in their course of study they also learn about quantum mechanics and relativity theory. In both these instances, however, defective theories give way to new and improved theories. But that's not always the case. It's also possible for theories to be overthrown or contracted without offering a replacement theory.

Consider the case of superconductivity. When the experimental evidence went against the existing theory, science did not require that a replacement theory be ready and available before establishing that the existing theory was inadequate. Such case studies are particularly important in the debate over evolution because they show that one may legitimately criticize Darwinism without having to argue for the adequacy of a replacement theory. Instead of trying to shoehorn recalcitrant data into theories that are empirically inadequate, science is regularly forced to give up overconfident claims that cannot be adequately justified. The rational alternative to Darwinism, therefore, need not be intelligent design but rather, as David Berlinski points out in chapter 14, intelligent uncertainty.

With regard to superconductivity, the Dutch physicist Kamerling Onnes discovered the phenomenon in 1911. Superconductivity refers to the complete disappearance of electrical resistance for materials at low temperatures. When Onnes made his discovery, however, there was no theory to account for superconductivity. Such a theory was not proposed until 1957. It was called the BCS theory after scientists Bardeen, Cooper, and Schrieffer, who received the Nobel Prize in physics for it in 1972. The first paragraph of the Nobel press release describes the BCS theory as providing "a complete theoretical explanation of the phenomenon."[19] But the theory didn't stay complete for long. In the 1980s Bednorz and Müller discovered superconductors at much higher temperatures than previously identified and explained by BCS. To date, no replacement theory for BCS has been found that extends to high-temperature superconductors. BCS, instead of being *the* theory of superconductivity," now merely explains a quite limited range of superconductors.

Science can get things wrong—indeed, massively wrong. What's more, sometimes we can tell that science has gotten something wrong without having to tell what the correct or true explanation is. Also, unlike religion, science has no prophets to tell us what course science must take or avoid taking. Different courses need to be tried, and only after they are tried does it become clear what was fruitful and what was fruitless.

*****

The aim of this book is to expose and unseat the myths that have gathered around Darwinism. Of course, by itself this book will not accomplish that end—Darwinism's myths are simply too entrenched in our intellectual culture for a single book to overturn them. As David Berlinski once remarked to me, "A shift in prevailing scientific orthodoxies will come only when the objections to Darwinism accumulate so forcefully that they can no longer be ignored." Think of this book, therefore, as ramping up the objections to Darwinism and its chapters as straws that, along with other straws, eventually will break Darwinism's back.

Why does Darwinism's back need to be broken? Because it is no longer merely a scientific theory but an ideology. Darwin's original proposal was actually quite modest: organisms adapt to their environments as a result of random variation and natural selection. Stated thus, Darwin's theory is incontrovertible and legitimately characterizes certain small-scale evolutionary changes. But this same theory is supposed to explain how the whole diversity and complexity of life came about. And having accounted for all of biology, it is supposed to account for just about everything else. As David Berlinski put it in the March 2003 issue of *Commentary*:

> The term "Darwinism" conveys the suggestion of a secular ideology, a global system of belief. So it does and so it surely is. Darwin's theory has been variously used—by Darwinian biologists—to explain the development of a bipedal gait, the tendency to laugh when amused, obesity, *anorexia nervosa*, business negotiations, a preference for tropical landscapes, the evolutionary roots of political rhetoric, maternal love, infanticide, clan formation, marriage, divorce, certain comical sounds, funeral rites, the formation of regular verb forms, altruism, homosexuality, feminism, greed, romantic love, jealousy, warfare, monogamy, polygamy, adultery, the fact that men are pigs, recursion, sexual display, abstract art, and religious beliefs of every description.[20]

Even such overweening ambitions would not be so bad if Darwin's theory were not held dogmatically. But it is held dogmatically and even ruthlessly. Darwinism has achieved the status of inviolable science, combining the dogmatism of religion with the entitlement of science. This is an unhappy combination. In consequence, critics encounter a ruthless dogmatism when challenging Darwin's theory. The problem isn't that Darwinists refuse to be tentative in holding their theory; no scientist with a career invested in a scientific theory is going to relinquish it easily. Typically, a scientist's affirmation of a scientific theory simply means that the scientist is convinced the theory is substantially correct. But scientists who hold their theories dogmatically go on to assert that their theories *cannot* be incorrect. Moreover, scientists who are ruthless in their dogmatism regard their theories as inviolable and portray critics as morally and intellectually deficient. (That's why most responses by Darwinists to critics begin with an ad hominem argument aimed at destroying the critic's credibility.)

How can a scientist keep from descending into dogmatism? There's only one way, and that's to look oneself squarely in the mirror and continually affirm: *I am a fallible human being. . . . I may be wrong. . . . I may be massively wrong. . . . I may be hopelessly and irretrievably wrong*—and mean it! It's not enough just to mouth these words. We need to take them seriously and admit that they can apply even to our most cherished scientific beliefs. Human fallibility is real and can catch us in the most unexpected places.

The problem with dogmatism is that it is always a form of self-deception. If Socrates taught us anything, it's that we always know a lot less than we think we know. Dogmatism deceives us into thinking we have attained ultimate mastery and that divergence of opinion is futile. Self-deception is the original sin because it deceives us into believing that self-deception is impossible. Richard Feynman put it this way: "The first principle is that you must not fool yourself, and you are the easiest person to fool." Feynman was particularly concerned about applying this principle to the public understanding of science: "You should not fool the laymen when you're talking as a scientist. . . . I'm talking about a specific, extra type of integrity that is [more than] not lying, but bending over backwards to show how you're maybe wrong."[21]

Sadly, Feynman's sound advice almost invariably gets lost when Darwin's theory is challenged. Richard Dawkins and Daniel Dennett are so over-the-top in their enthusiasm for Darwinism and in their animus against anyone who doesn't share their enthusiasm that they are easy targets. But what about the American Civil Liberties Union when it threatens to sue school boards and teachers for allowing criticism of Darwinian evolution to be taught? I'm not talking about teaching an alternative to Darwinism, like the theory of intelligent design. I'm simply talking about teaching criticisms of the theory as they appear in the peer-reviewed literature by recognized evolutionary biologists, such as the late Stephen Jay Gould (cf. the case of Roger DeHart, which was reported in the national press).[22] What about the National Center for Science Education when it pressures high schools to exclude books critical of Darwinism from their libraries (as happened in Melvindale, Michigan)?[23] Do we live in a society of rational discourse where controversial ideas like Darwinism can be reasonably disputed without fear of reprisal, or is this one of those topics for which uniformity of opinion has to be enforced?

We now face a Darwinian thought police that, save for employing physical violence, is as insidious as any secret police at ensuring conformity and rooting out dissent. To question Darwinism is dangerous for all professional scholars but especially biologists. As Michael Behe pointed out in an interview with the *Harvard Political Review*, "There's good reason to be afraid. Even if you're not fired from your job, you will easily be passed over for promotions. I would strongly advise graduate students who are skeptical of Darwinian theory not to make their views known."[24]

Although the Darwinian thought police has been hugely successful at quashing dissent among academics and the intellectual elites, they are having a much harder time ensuring conformity in the wider populace. Gallup poll after Gallup poll indicates that only about ten percent of the U.S. population accepts Darwinian evolution. The rest of the population is committed to some form of intelligent design (dividing fairly evenly between God-guided evolution and special creation).

It goes without saying that science is not decided by an opinion poll. Nevertheless, the overwhelming rejection of Darwinian evolution in the population at large is worth pondering. Given that Darwinism is the majority position among biologists, why has the biological community failed to convince the public that natural selection is the driving force behind evolution and that evolution so conceived (i.e., Darwinian evolution) can successfully account for the full diversity of life? This question is worth pondering because in most other areas of science, the public prefers to sign off on the considered judgments of the scientific community (science, after all, holds considerable prestige in our culture). Why not here? Steeped as our culture is in the fundamentalist-modernist controversy, the usual answer is that religious fundamentalists, blinded by their dogmatic prejudices, willfully refuse to acknowledge the overwhelming case for Darwinian evolution.

The problem with this explanation is that fundamentalism, in the sense of strict biblical literalism, is not nearly as common as Darwinists make out. Most religious traditions do not make a virtue out of alienating the culture. Despite postmodernity's inroads, science retains tremendous cultural prestige, and the religious world would like to live in harmony with the scientific one. Many religious believers accept that species have undergone significant changes over the course of natural history and therefore that evolution has in some sense occurred (consider, for instance, Pope John Paul II's 1996 endorsement of evolution). The question for religious believers and the public more generally is the extent of evolutionary change and the mechanism underlying evolutionary change—in particular, whether material mechanisms alone are sufficient to explain all of life.

The real reason the public continues to resist Darwinian evolution is that the Darwinian mechanism of incidental change and natural selection seems utterly inadequate to bear the weight that Darwinists place on it. Specifically, the claim that the Darwinian mechanism can generate the full range of biological diversity strikes people as an unwarranted extrapolation from the limited changes that the mechanism is known to effect in practice. The hard empirical evidence for the power of the Darwinian mechanism is in fact quite limited and includes such things as finch beak variation, changes in flower coloration, and bacteria developing antibiotic resistance. For instance, finch beak size does vary according to environmental pressure; the Darwinian mechanism does operate here and accounts for the changes we observe. But that same Darwinian mechanism is also supposed to account for how finches arose in the first place. This is an extrapolation. Strict Darwinists see it as perfectly plausible. The public remains unconvinced.

As this book shows, the public is right to remain unconvinced. This book divides into four parts. The first part shows why Darwinism faces a growing crisis of confidence. Robert Koons starts the ball rolling with his chapter "The Check Is in the Mail." In this chapter Koons details how Darwinism substitutes theft for honest labor by insulating Darwinian theories from all possible criticism. Koons argues that the real motivation for Darwinism is to be found in a thoroughgoing metaphysical attack on the idea of agency, both human and divine, that has been ongoing for two hundred years. He also suggests that by undermining the idea of reasonable and responsible agency, Darwinism helped prepare the way for a variety of destructive experiments in social engineering.

Next comes Phillip Johnson's well-known essay "Darwinism as Dogma," which originally appeared back in 1990 in *First Things*. This essay masterfully disentangles Darwinism's interweaving with materialist philosophy. And finally, there is Marcel-Paul Schützenberger's 1996 interview with *La Recherche*, conducted shortly before his death, in which he recapitulates his ideas about functional complexity and the challenge this feature of biological systems poses to Darwinism. The original interview was in French and was translated into English by David Berlinski for the journal *Origins & Design*. It has been further edited here for style and clarity.

Part two focuses on Darwinism's cultural inroads. Nancy Pearcey starts things off with a sweeping overview. The effect of reading her essay is dizzying as she documents how Darwinism has inveigled itself into one academic discipline after another. Next comes Edward Sisson's brilliant analysis of how the professionalization of science has rendered science incapable of correcting itself in the case of Darwinism. Essentially, the critic of Darwinism faces a prisoner's dilemma in which perpetuating Darwinian falsehoods, either by actively promoting them or by silent complicity, is the best strategy for advancing one's career. J. Budziszewski's chapter on natural law is a much needed corrective to an emerging literature that seeks to combat postmodern ethical relativism with a distorted version of natural law based on Darwinism. And finally, Frank Tipler's chapter on refereed journals shows how the peer-review process increasingly stifles scientific creativity and enforces orthodoxies like Darwinism. Although the chapter was specifically commissioned for this volume, Tipler's analysis has such huge public policy implications for the practice and funding of science that his chapter has now also appeared as an article on the web.[25]

Part three examines the dynamics of converting to and deconverting from Darwinism. Often, in the writings of Darwinists (e.g., Ronald Numbers's book *The Creationists*), one gets the impression that the more educated people become, the more reasonable Darwinism seems. Part three shows that this is not the case. Michael Behe, raised as a Roman Catholic and trained as a biologist, accepted Darwinism as he began his scientific career. Only later, as he reflected on what he had been taught about evolution, did his doubts about Darwinism arise and finally lead to a full deconversion from Darwinism. Michael Denton, by contrast, never accepted Darwinism. Though early in his life he rejected Darwinism because of his religious faith, Denton continued to reject Darwinism even after he had shed his religious faith and learned an awful lot of biology. James Barham began as Christian fundamentalist, turned to a hardcore atheistic brand of Darwinism, and then, after thinking deeply about the nature of biological function, turned to a naturalized form of teleology at odds with both fundamentalism and Darwinism.

Finally, part four examines the nitty-gritty of why Darwinism is a failed intellectual project. After reviewing and overturning many of the key evidences used to prop Darwinism, Cornelius Hunter shows why Darwinism should properly be regarded not as a positive scientific research program but as a reactionary metaphysical program whose justification depends intrinsically on naive assumptions about what God would and would not have done in designing biological systems. Next Roland Hirsch overviews many of the recent advances in molecular biology and biochemistry, showing how Darwinism has failed either to anticipate or to explain them. After that, Christopher Langan carefully examines the nature of causality and shows how Darwinism depends on a superficial analysis of causality to hide its fundamental conceptual problems. Finally, we come to the chapter that inspired this book, David Berlinski's June 1996 *Commentary* essay, "The Deniable Darwin." In exposing Darwinism's failure to resolve biology's information problem, this essay provoked an enormous response (over thirty published letters pro and con). In addition to the essay, this chapter includes some of the key letters by Darwinists critical of Berlinski's essay. It also includes Berlinski's replies to these critics.

In commending this volume to the reader, I wish to leave Darwinists with this closing thought: *You've had it way too easy until now.* It is no longer credible to conflate informed criticism of Darwinism with ignorance, stupidity, insanity, wickedness, or brainwashing. Informed critiques of Darwinism have consistently appeared ever since Darwin published his *Origin of Species* (cf. the work of Louis Agassiz, St. George Mivart, Richard Goldschmidt, Pierre Grassé, Gerald Kerkut, and Michael Polanyi). Unfortunately, because Darwinism's myths are so entrenched, such critiques have until now been unable to reach a critical mass and actually overthrow Darwinism. That is now changing. We'll know that a critical mass has been achieved when it becomes widely acceptable among intellectuals to challenge Darwinism. When that happens—when it becomes acceptable to say that the emperor has no clothes—Darwin's actual theory will assume the modest role in science that it deserves and Darwinism's grandiose pretensions will become dissertation fodder for nineteenth- and twentieth-century intellectual history. In other words, Darwinism will be history.

PART ONE
A Crisis of Confidence

Robert C. Koons

1. THE CHECK IS IN THE MAIL

Why Darwinism Fails to Inspire Confidence

Darwinism owes its present dominance to the widespread misperception that it has refuted the design argument. In particular, it is thought to have refuted the ancient argument from the complexity of biological functions to the existence of an intelligent creator. Yet except for specifying a few minor adjustments in pre-existing functions (like those required for resistance to antibiotics), evolutionary biologists have failed to offer any detailed scenarios demonstrating that the Darwinian mechanism of accidental variations and natural selection is an adequate substitute for intelligent creation. The mere logical possibility that such scenarios might someday be found is not sufficient evidence to raise genuine doubts about the reality of creation, much less to provide solid grounds for denying it.

Methodological naturalism, the rule that the natural sciences must proceed without invoking intelligent causes, would be justified if Darwinists first provided adequate, independent grounds for believing that natural, unintelligent causes produced many of the sophisticated biological functions we observe. But no such grounds have been provided. Instead, the assertion of methodological naturalism has been used to substitute theft for honest labor, insulating Darwinian theories from all possible criticism. Darwinism has been part of a metaphysical attack on the very idea of agency, both human and superhuman, that has been ongoing for two hundred years. By undermining the idea of reasonable and responsible agency, Darwinism has facilitated a variety of experiments in social engineering.

TWO METAPHYSICAL MODELS

The evidence for evolution, at least the evidence available to a layperson like myself, is far from compelling. It seems compelling only to those with a prior commitment to metaphysical materialism, for whom Darwinism is practically the only reasonable explanation available for life as we know it. As is well known, the fossil record of the family tree of evolution is so gappy that it consists of a great deal more gap than tree. This is especially true where the record is most complete, as in the case of the invertebrates. The missing links that have been found, like the Archaeopteryx or Australopithecus, are better described as mosaics: recombinations of adaptations found in what are assumed to be related families. Given that the forms of life found in the fossil record are more numerous and variegated than those we find alive today, it is not at all surprising that we should find fossil forms that are "intermediate" in some vague sense between living forms. What we don't find is the kind of continuous, seamless web of transformation of adaptive structures that would be needed to confirm the truth of Darwinism.

Of course, if evolution is defined broadly enough, there's little doubt that it has occurred. We do find a gradual "unfolding" of life (the original meaning of "evolution"): invertebrates appear before vertebrates, coniferous before flowering plants, small primates before great apes, and so on. This fact was well known before Darwin's work appeared. Darwin's crucial contention was that he had found the underlying causal mechanism driving this unfolding: the culling of variation by the competition for survival. Since Mendel's work was not yet known, variation was considered to appear by means of some mysterious process, but it was a process that was hypothesized to be blind, purposeless, and subhuman. When the Darwinian idea was combined with Mendelian genetics, resulting in the neo-Darwinian synthesis, the defining differential element of the theory was this: the probability of the occurrence of any mutation is unrelated to its prospective contribution to the functionality of any structure, present or future. Contributions to function affect only the chances of the mutation's successful propagation, not its original appearance.

Such a theory was, of course, a direct challenge to a widely held alternative account: one that attributed the origin of complex adaptations in living things to some form of irreducible intelligent agency, whether of a divine providence outside nature or a pervasive purposiveness within it. This alternative had reached its fullest state of development in the late eighteenth and early nineteenth centuries in France and

England, especially. But this French and British natural theology was the culmination of a continuous tradition stretching back to the Greek philosophers, especially Plato, Aristotle, and the Stoics; and to the wisdom literature of the Hebrews, especially the Psalms, Job, the Wisdom of Solomon, and Ecclesiastes. It is true that, prior to William Paley's *Natural Theology* in 1803, which investigated the internal mechanics of biological organisms, traditional natural theology did not focus exclusively on that internal, watch-like order. The orderly operations of the heavens and the generosity of the earth's environment for the continuation of life were most often cited as proof of a divine artificer. However, it is by no means the case that the mutual adjustment of bodily organs was overlooked.

The author of *Job* directs our attention to the biological world: "But now ask the beasts, and they will tell you; and the birds of the air, and they will tell you; or speak to the earth, and it will teach you; and the fish of the sea will explain it to you. Who among all these does not know that the hand of the Lord has done this?" (Job 12:7–9). Of course, Job is not recommending literal conversations with the animals. Instead, his point is that a careful study of the forms of animal life leads inescapably to the conclusion that they are the creatures of God. In *Ecclesiasticus*, the functionality and interdependency of natural forms is taken as proof of God's wisdom in crafting the world: "He hath garnished the excellent works of his wisdom. O how desirable are all his works. . . . All things are double against another, and he hath made nothing imperfect. One thing establisheth the good of another; and who shall be filled with beholding his glory?" (Ecclesiasticus 42:21–25).

Among the Greeks, the tendency was to find a kind of intelligence or wisdom immanent within the world, rather than embodied in a transcendent creator. Greeks and Hebrews were, however, at one in insisting that the world could be understood only in terms of the unfolding of an intelligent purpose. Pre-Socratic philosophers, like Anaximenes, Anaxagoras, Heraclitus and Xenophanes, thought that the order of the world required a mind (*nous*) or rational principle (*logos*) acting in a fundamental and pervasive agency. Plato's Socrates, in the *Phaedo*, gives voice to the conviction that science must give pride of place to the category of purposeful action. Socrates reports that his youthful enthusiasm for physicalistic explanations of natural phenomena disappeared when he encountered Anaxagoras's hypothesis that Mind directs and causes all things. This opened up a new way of explaining biological and other natural phenomena: "to find the cause of each thing . . . one had to find the best way for it to be" (*Phaedo* 97d).

Aristotle rejected the materialistic theory of evolution that was proposed by Empedocles and the atomists. He argued that we can make sense of biology only by taking purposiveness, final causation, to be an irreducible and primary reality. He repeatedly insisted that "nature does nothing in vain" (*De Caelo* 271a33, *Parts of Animals* 658a9, *Generation of Animals* 741b13) and that "nature invariably brings about the best arrangement of those that are possible" (PA 658a24). It is true that "nature" probably does not name (for Aristotle) a nature-transcending designer, but it does stand for an efficacious and fundamentally purposeful principle of explanation.

In both the *Laws* (Book X) and the *Timaeus*, Plato appealed to the order of the world as evidence for an intelligent creator, and this form of argument was sustained by the Stoics and by Cicero, bringing the Greek tradition even closer to the Hebrew. The synthesis of the Hebrew and Greek traditions appeared in the first century A.D. in the works of Hellenistic Jews like Philo, Josephus, and the apostle Paul. Augustine of Hippo in the fourth century argued that biological form had to be explained in terms of "rational seeds" implanted in matter at the very first moment of creation. For Augustine, the subsequent evolution of life through the remaining "six days" of creation, which he pointedly refrained from interpreting as a literal period of 144 hours, was a literal unfolding of a multitude of pre-established divine designs.[1]

Both Aristotle and Augustine illustrate the fact that challenges to Darwinism do not require the postulation of gaps or discontinuities in nature, or of ongoing interventions or intrusions from the supernatural. The crucial question is this: when novel forms of adaptation first appear, and before natural selection has had a chance to operate, is the probability of their emergence dependent on or independent of their functionality? Natural selection can explain only why functional forms persist and operate, not how they came to be there in the first place. For Plato, Aristotle, Augustine, and the other teleologists, the origin of biological function requires an irreducibly purposeful principle, or intelligent design.

The anti-teleological view that attempts to explain or explain away the appearance of design and purpose in nature did not originate with Darwin. Precursors of Darwin's theory of materialistic evolution through natural selection can be found in antiquity in Empedocles and Lucretius,[2] and in the eighteenth century in David Hume.[3] Naturalistic evolution is an approach that predates the birth of science and may well outlast it.

THE BURDEN OF PROOF

The Western philosophical tradition has thus bequeathed to us two competing metaphysical models: one in which everything is to be explained ultimately in terms of blind and purposeless forces (the materialistic model); and one in which purposefulness is a fundamental and irreducible reality (the teleological model). The most important question, from an epistemological point of view, is this: where should we locate the presumption of truth, and where the burden of proof? There are compelling grounds for placing the burden of proof on the materialistic model. Even stalwart Darwinists like Richard Dawkins admit that the defining task of biology is to explain the existence of things that appear to be designed.[4] Cicero, in *On the Nature of the Gods*, Book II, reports Aristotle's cave analogy: if a group of people had spent all of their lives underground and then emerged on the surface, they would be bound to think of the biologically rich world they discovered there to be the product of intelligence. Only familiarity dulls our sense of wonder at the craftsmanship of nature.[5]

In his *Essays on the Intellectual Powers of Man*, eighteenth-century Scottish philosopher Thomas Reid cites the capacity to recognize the signs of intelligent agency as part of the basic equipment of the human mind.[6] Without such a basic capacity, the means by which we recognize one another as intelligent and purposeful would remain mysterious. How we recognize intelligence even in our own behavior would be a mystery as well. When this basic faculty of intelligence-recognition considers the machinery of living things, the clear answer it delivers is yes, there is intelligence and purposefulness displayed in such machinery. If this was true 2,500 years ago, in the time of Aristotle, how much more true is it now that we know so much about the astonishingly superb design of the biomolecular machinery of the cell?

Nonetheless, the natural deliverances of our sense of intelligence can be defeated since, as in all other matters, our faculties are fallible on this question. It is therefore possible in principle for materialists to overcome the presumption of intelligence by means of a rationally compelling case. Still, there is an undeniable burden of proof that must first be assumed.

In *The Origin of Species*, Darwin recognized this fact. The argumentative structure of the book concedes that the presumption of reason lies with intelligent creation. Moreover, Darwin recognized that he could not yet shift the burden of proof. He was concerned, quite justifiably, with providing enough provisional evidence to create an atmosphere of open-mindedness. He hoped to convince biologists that his theory shouldn't be dismissed out of hand but should instead be given a fair chance by being given the chance to be fleshed out with specific hypotheses that could then be tested against the relevant evidence. At this task, I believe he was entirely successful. No reasonable person could, after reading the *Origin*, deny that this was a theory worthy of being taken seriously. At the least it justified an investigation into whether the evolutionary mechanism proposed was really adequate to its appointed task, and whether sufficient circumstantial evidence could be found substantiating that the mechanism of natural selection had in fact been at work.

To meet the burden of proof, there were two gaps that had to be filled: (1) Darwin's sketchy schema of variation and selection had to be filled out, in particular cases, with sufficient detail to verify that variation and natural selection could in fact be responsible for adaptations that had the appearance of being the product of intelligent design; and (2) particular hypotheses produced in this way had to be tested against the available evidence, both in the fossil record and in vestigial homologies, those remnants of organisms whose similarities indicated a common origin. Note that the second task presupposes success at the first: to attempt to test a vague, schematic model of "variation with selection" or "random mutations and selection" rather than specific scenarios is to attempt the impossible. Any evidence that is found can be made to accord with schematic Darwinism, and so can be counted as evidence "for" the theory. Only by replacing the schema with a specific sequence of possible mutations and selective pressures can we find something that is both falsifiable and confirmable by collateral evidence. But this is exactly what has never happened, no doubt because of the problems of intractability, the inability to manage or control the reconstruction of the genotypes of extinct and even unattested hypothetical ancestors. Whatever the reason, the burden of proof was never met, and the presumption of design never rebutted.

Take, for example, Richard Dawkins's attempts to prove that Darwinism is able to explain the emergence of the vertebrate eye.[7] Dawkins refers to a computer simulation by Nilsson and Pelger,[8] showing that one can gradually improve a light sensitive spot and reach, in 1800 steps or so, a fully functional, lens-bearing eye. This might be impressive, except that the computer simulation (like every single simulation referred to by Dawkins in the book) entirely omits the two crucial details about real biology: the genotype/phenotype distinction (the distinction between the genetic constitution of an individual or group as opposed to the properties produced by interaction with its environment) and the processes of embryological development. The steps in Nilsson and Pelger's program are phenotypical (that is, they concern changes in gross, morphological features in the fully formed adult). We are not given a model in which the successive forms of the eye are determined by successive trajectories of embryological development, nor are we given a model of how these successive trajectories are determined by successive, feasible mutations. Given these limitations, it is of course impossible to estimate the probabilities of the mutations required for each of the 1800 steps in the creation of the vertebrate eye. The model cannot be used to generate even a single prediction about present-day residues of the actual history of the eye. In other words, Dawkins's favorite model, the best now available, has not made even the smallest significant step beyond the bare speculations of Empedocles, Hume or Darwin.

FIVE STAGES IN THE CONFIRMATION OF DARWINISM

What would be required to move from a presumption of irreducible design to a reasonable certainty that the Darwinian mechanism is the actual cause of the forms of living things? We can reconstruct five stages:

Stage 0. The original, pre-Darwinian situation, in which the complex functionality of life triggered a natural human disposition to recognize intelligent agency, creating a strong presumption in favor of such agency as the cause of life.

Stage 1. An alternative mechanism is proposed, random variation culled by natural selection, and preliminary evidence in favor of the new hypothesis is gathered and systematized. As the upshot of this preliminary case, we must treat the hypothesis as representing a possibility, warranting further development and investigation. At this stage the presumption in favor of design has not been negated: intelligent agency seems still to be the presumptive cause, but there is an openness to the bare possibility that this presumption may one day be overwhelmed by compelling evidence in favor of the alternative.

Stage 2. In several paradigmatic cases, hypothetical Darwinistic pathways leading to actual adaptive forms are described in sufficient detail and with sufficient understanding of the underlying genetic and developmental processes that it seems virtually certain that these pathways represent genuine possibilities. These pathways must be possible, not only in the sense of involving no violation of physical or chemical laws, but also in the sense that every step in the path can be assigned an estimated probability that is sufficiently high for the joint probability of the entire pathway to be consistent with a reasonable belief that such a thing might really have happened. At this stage, we have, for the first time, grounds for some degree of doubt in the correctness of the presumption in favor of intelligent agency. The presumption is not yet cancelled: our attitude should continue to be one of assuming that the presumption is probably correct. We ought, however, to temper our certainty that it is correct to some significant degree. At this point, the Darwinian alternative has won the right to be taken seriously as a real possibility, not merely as a barely logical possibility, generating some doubt about the actuality of intelligent agency as the cause of life.

Stage 3. For a significant number of hypothetical pathways of the kind described in stage two, we are able to verify that the pathway was probably actualized in history. New evidence from fossils and homologies is found that conforms to our specific expectations, based on the hypothetical pathways, and few if any instances of evidence are found that cannot readily be explained in terms of these pathways. Each hypothetical pathway describes a large number of intermediate steps, leading from some known ancestral form lacking the adaptation in question to some known form possessing it. Each step should be fully described at both the genetic and the morphological level: that is, we should be specific about what mutations, lateral gene transfers, or other processes have occurred, and how the new genotype is expressed in morphology. For each step a hypothetical environment needs to be specified, and the tools of population genetics employed to show that the hypothetical new genotype would in fact be selected over its rivals in the hypothetical environment.

A pathway described in such detail should generate a vast number of specific predictions. First, the fossils that are discovered should match exactly the morphology of hypothetical steps. Second, the new forms of genetic vestiges and other homologies that are found should witness to the actual existence of the hypothetical genotypes. And third, the evidence of ancient ecosystems, including climate, geographical isolation, and presence of food sources, predators, and competitors, should be found—namely, evidence of the hypothesized selective environments. Once this kind of confirmation has been found for a significant number of specific Darwinian hypotheses, involving some of the biological forms that are paradigms of apparent purposiveness, the presumption in favor of design has been defeated, and we are in a position to believe, with a reasonable degree of certainty, that the Darwinian mechanism is probably responsible for all of life. Even at this stage, however, an apodeictic certainty would be inappropriate. We should remain open-minded about the possibility of discovering that some cases of apparent design will prove so resistant to Darwinian explanation that they may restore the presumption of design.

Stage 4. If nearly every case of apparent design has been successfully explained in Darwinian terms, and in each case we have found an overwhelming body of specific, confirming evidence, we are justified in treating Darwinism as established beyond a reasonable doubt.

Where are we today? Leading biologists assure us that we are at stage four. In fact, however, I believe that we are still in stage one. The task of stage two, of describing in sufficient detail specific Darwinian pathways leading to the origin of specific forms of biological function, remains an unfulfilled dream. This retardation in the progress of the Darwinian paradigm has not been caused simply by laziness or sloppiness on the part of its champions. The complexity of life makes the construction of stage-two hypotheses far more difficult in the case of Darwinism than in comparable cases from the physical or chemical sciences, such as Newtonian models of the solar system or quantum models of the electron orbits around a hydrogen atom. Our understanding of the genetic code, gene expression, and developmental processes are still rudimentary at best, and our powers of computation are still far too weak to be able to reverse-engineer a hypothetical phenotype into a corresponding genotype.

Nonetheless, the fact that stage two is extraordinarily difficult in the case of biology does not absolve Darwinists of the necessity of completing stage two before progressing to stage three or four. The latter stages presuppose, in an essential way, the completion of stage two, since without stage-two hypotheses, specific, testable predictions cannot be generated. In the absence of such predictions, any evidence in favor of evolution that can be gathered is only stage-one evidence: data that gives us grounds to put in the labor required for stage two, but that falls far short of what is needed even to qualify the presumption in favor of intelligent agency.

Nevertheless, preeminent biologists around the world assure us that we have reached stage four—that the Darwinian model of evolution is as certain as the sphericity of the earth, or the power of universal gravitation. Who am I as a mere layperson to challenge their claims? I am not the first, however. The essayist and cultural critic Richard M. Weaver faced this same question half a century ago. In an essay posthumously published in the collection *Visions of Order*, Weaver expressed the same worry:

I recognize that any layman's criticism of the theory of evolution will appear to most people today as reckless. The amount of study given the theory has been so extensive, the alleged proofs are from so many sources and are so massive in appearance, and the evolutionists have so much "liberal" opinion on their side that the average person who is still to reluctant to accept its implications feels that he may as well shrug in hopelessness and say, "I surrender."[9]

Nonetheless, as Weaver points out, although we must defer to the expert when he speaks credibly about facts with which he has special acquaintance, we must never delegate to the expert the right to think for us. Rational thought is an inalienable right and the responsibility of each human being: we would reach the depths of heteronomy and self-alienation if we surrendered to another the authority not only to discover the facts but also to evaluate their significance.

Indeed the layman must not presume to question the facts assembled by qualified scientists (although what constitutes a fact is itself sometimes debatable). Nevertheless, we need to look at the matter from greater perspective and remember that no science exists purely in the form of a collection of facts. The sciences are these facts plus structures of reasoning that are built upon them. The facts we are bound to receive if they come from sources that have given satisfactory evidence of their objectivity. But the reasoning that is done upon the basis of them is open to the inquiry of every man who has a rational faculty.[10]

We have, therefore, the right and even the duty to compare what Darwinian scientists have actually accomplished with what they still must accomplish if their strong claims of certainty are to be sustained. The evaluation of the arguments of biologists is within the competence of each person, as is the task of assessing the appropriate degree of doubt or certainty that attaches to their conclusions.

[I]f men are to be convinced that they are simply the products of evolution, the convincing must be done in accordance with the necessary laws of thought. This is merely saying that the layman has the right to ask about the connection between the factual evidence and the conclusion when that connec-

tion is not apparent to him. He has the right to ask philosophical questions about the way the facts have been handled
and even about whether all of the relevant facts have been
taken into consideration.[11]

How can we explain the fact that there has been such confusion
among evolutionary biologists about the current state of their own research program? A number of plausible hypotheses push to the fore. It
may be that Darwin did such a marvelous job of fulfilling the requirement of stage one in *The Origin of Species* that later biologists have
wrongly taken Darwin's preliminary survey of the evidence as the paradigm of a mature scientific program. Perhaps stage one seems so interesting and suggestive that the need to push beyond it to stages two and
three has been overlooked. Another possibility is that evolutionary biologists were simply impatient to claim the same level of maturity for
their program as had been attained by comparable programs in physics,
astronomy and chemistry. The vastly greater complexity of biology ne-
cessitates that progress through the stages must be excruciatingly slow;
envy over the far greater velocity sustained by physics surely creates tremendous pressure on biologists to exaggerate the extent of their accom-
plishments.

It is also hard to overlook the fact that the birth and growth of
Darwinism coincided with a very widespread cultural and political rebellion against religion and the authority of the church. An interest in
contributing to this movement—and in suppressing resistance to it—
has surely motivated the exaggeration of the epistemological status of
Darwin's theory, including absurd hyperboles comparing the status of
Darwin's theory to that of the heliocentric model or the model of the
spherical earth. The virtues of a number of nearly contemporaneous
theories of scientific materialism—Feuerbach and Freud in psychology,
Marx in political economy, Comte and Durkheim in sociology—were
the objects of similarly inflated claims, almost certainly because of the
same rebellion. The temptation to indulge in a "noble lie" is by no means
limited to the pious.

Darwin himself contributed to the illicit shift in the burden of proof
in his well known challenge to his critics in *The Origin*: "If it could be
demonstrated that any complex organ existed which could not possibly
have been formed by numerous, successive, slight modifications, my
theory would absolutely break down."[12] It is, of course, impossible to
"demonstrate" any such thing. How could it be proved that something
could not possibly have been formed by a process specified no more

fully than as a process of "numerous, successive, slight modifications"? And why should the critic have to prove any such thing? The burden is on Darwin and his defenders to demonstrate that it is really possible for at least some of the complex organs we find in nature to be formed in this way: that is, by some specific, fully articulated series of slight modifications.

In the twentieth century, the most important factor contributing to confusion about the epistemological status of Darwin's program has been the widespread adoption of "methodological naturalism," a dogmatic definition of the very essence of science that excludes by fiat any reference to any explanatory principle that doesn't pass muster within the materialistic, anti-teleological model of metaphysics. The term "methodological naturalism" is itself a rhetorical tour de force. First, by appropriating the label "natural" for the materialistic tradition it subtly excludes the Aristotelian and Augustinian view, which sees nature as intrinsically and irreducibly teleological. Second, it has seduced many who subscribe to the teleological worldview as a matter of private conviction into embracing a merely "methodological" naturalism that supposedly poses no threat to their teleological ontology. If one is absolutely committed to the materialistic model, then of course something like Darwinism must be the true explanation of life. However, this provides no reason whatsoever for those not so committed to limit the scope of scientific theorizing to models that would be acceptable to the committed materialist.

Critics of the Darwinian program, including Phillip E. Johnson, have often complained about the circular reasoning that such methodological naturalism encourages.[13] Richard Weaver also noted this flaw in the public presentation of the Darwinian case:

> First and most generally, the theory of evolution can be viewed as a form of the question-begging fallacy. It demands an initial acceptance of the doctrine of naturalism before any explanation is offered. Specifically, when the biologist is faced with the fact of the enormous differentiation and specialization in nature, he says that these were caused by the proximate method which nature would use, *assuming that nature is the only creative force that exists.* For example, it is admitted by biologists that complete empirical data for the descent of man from the lower animals is missing. The problem then becomes how to fit into a scheme where nothing is allowed to appear except through natural causation. Thus it is reasoned

that if man possesses the largest brain found in nature, it is because it must have been utilitarian for him to develop a large brain. But how can this be proved except by reference to the a priori postulate that nothing develops except through organic need? Again and again in the literature of evolution one finds that things are viewed as "necessary" because they come from this assumed natural cause rather than as proved because they come from a known cause. In other words the fact that things have come into being is used as evidence that nature must have used the evolutionary process to bring them into being. I submit that this reasoning does not prove evolution a fact: it rather assumes that evolution is a fact and then uses it as both cause and effect in describing the phenomena of nature.[14] (emphasis in original)

Methodological naturalism might be justified if either Darwinian biology or materialistic versions of cognitive psychology had successfully reached either stage three or stage four. A success of this order against either of the two pillars of the teleological model might well justify continued reliance on models with a similar materialistic commitment. Although it would take me beyond the scope of this essay to substantiate this fact, it is clear that materialistic cognitive psychology is also mired still in stage one. In fact, it is clear that the materialistic theory of the mind cannot possibly reach stage two, three or four ahead of Darwinian biology, since, without a materialistic explanation of the origin of the human brain, any ontological reduction of the mind to the functioning of the brain fails to count decisively against the teleological model. It would be plausible for the teleologist to claim that it is the very ordering of the structure of the brain to the tasks of rational thought that calls for an irreducibly teleological explanation. However, we are in any case a long way from stage two, even with respect to the more limited task of reducing explanations of consciousness and the mind to functions of the brain.[15]

It is often claimed that the progress of science is simply the progress of materialist philosophy, with the consequence that every new scientific discovery, in whatever field, confirms the soundness of methodological naturalism. I have argued elsewhere that this notion is historically uninformed and epistemologically naïve.[16] Ancient materialism (e.g., Democritean atomism) played only a minor role in the scientific revolution, a role that was dwarfed by that of Platonic and Neoplatonic influences.

Although the arteriosclerosis of Aristotelian orthodoxy did retard, for a time, the progress of physical science (as the Galileo episode illustrates), we must not overlook the positive contribution of the teleological approach to nature. In medicine and anatomy, the progress achieved by Andreas Vesalius and William Harvey depended not only on their willingness to go beyond Aristotle but also upon their continued efforts to build on the foundations that Aristotle had laid. Harvey discovered the circulation of the blood because he believed in a divine architect who had created all things "for a certain purpose, and to some good end."[17] Such teleological thinking has proved indispensable in biology until the present day.[18] To identify a protein as an "enzyme" or a DNA molecule as a "code" is to use irreducibly teleological concepts, as is any reference to adaptations or disease.

In fact, physics itself provides at least as much support to the teleological model as it does to the materialistic one. Teleological principles (in the form of least action principles) have been among the most fundamental and enduring components of our best physical theories for the last three hundred years. All of Newton's optics and mechanics can be derived from William Rowen Hamilton's formulation of least action. Both the Schrödinger equations of quantum mechanics and Einstein's equations for general relativity can be derived from simple least action principles.[19] Max Planck forcefully argued that we should recognize that it is the integral equations at this teleological level that are most fundamental within modern physics, with the differential equations describing force interactions and the various energy conservation laws being mere epiphenomena.[20]

TU QUOQUE?

Darwinists like Allen Orr have often accused defenders of the teleological model with exceptional chutzpah, on the grounds that they have no business complaining about the lack of specificity in the hypotheses of Darwinian biology when their own hypotheses, the appeals to the agency of some obscure "designer" or "artisan," suffer from a far greater lack of detail.[21] There is some merit in this accusation, since, as an incipient research program, intelligent design theory is likewise somewhere in the midst of something analogous to stage one. Shall we then call it a draw, and conclude that the appropriate attitude to take on the question of Darwinism vs. intelligent design in the present circumstances is simply one of agnosticism? Surprisingly, critics of intelligent design like Orr refuse to draw this admirably judicious conclusion.

As attractive as such agnosticism might be, this argument for epistemological equivalency seems to overlook the central fact that I have been trying to press home in this essay: that the natural presumption about the cause of life lies with the intelligent agency position. Darwinism must progress to stage three or four before this presumption can be overcome. The intelligent agency position faces no such imperative since the inference from complex, interdependent functionality to intelligent agency is the natural, default position. Darwinian biologists and their pupils overlook this fact at their own cognitive peril. The fact that the human mind is in some sense designed to draw inferences to design should be a matter of common ground. Both teleologists and Darwinists can recognize that this is simply a fact about the proper functioning of the natural equipment of the human mind, even if Darwinists will see this as a case, like that of our belief in the objectivity of ethical values, of nature's deceiving us for our own procreative good.[22] The premature acceptance of materialist explanations risks the stultification of the human cognitive faculty, and that might well entail further cognitive malfunction. The threat of cognitive stultification alone should recommend caution about the inclusion in our textbooks of intemperate assertions regarding the certainty of evolution.

The bare possibility that a non-teleological explanation of apparent design might exist is not by itself sufficient to warrant real doubt about the reality of design, any more than the bare possibility that you and I are only brains in a *Matrix*-like vat is sufficient to warrant skepticism about the deliverances of our five senses. As Wittgenstein argued so convincingly, reasonable doubt must be grounded in reasons.[23] Skepticism about our natural epistemic faculties is not self-warranting.

It is, however, important to recognize that the formation of a scientific research program based on intelligent agency as a fundamental cause is still a long way off. The difficulties of reaching something like stage two in this case are quite similar to the difficulties facing the Darwinists. In the Darwinian case, the computational demands of modeling a bottom-up generation of new biological order are daunting. In the intelligent agency case, we face the difficulty that the agent involved would enjoy intellectual powers at least many orders of magnitude above our own and must have employed means of a kind that we can barely imagine. In addition, we have little idea of the scope of the agent's activity: what we see in terrestrial biology may be only a small part of a much larger design, whose ultimate purpose is beyond our ken.

Nonetheless, the situation is not hopeless. In fact, a good case can be made for the claim that all of biology, with the single exception of evolutionary biology, has, from its very inception, depended on the de facto acceptance of an intelligent-agency paradigm. From Aristotle to Galen to Vesalius, Harvey and Linnaeus, biologists have in effect reverse-engineered living things in order to discover their hidden design plan. To this very day, most biologists spend most of their time reconstructing such designs and finding the place of each component within them. Pick up nearly any published paper in cell biology or physiology and this is what you will find, with a perfunctory paragraph or two containing the mandatory genuflection in the direction of Darwin that asks: "Isn't evolution wonderful?"

It may be virtually impossible to fathom the ultimate purposes for which living things were designed, but proximal purposes are well within our grasp. We may not know why human life was created, but we can surely make reasonably educated guesses that the heart was designed to pump blood and the eye to enable sight.

In addition, the intelligent-agency model can refocus our attention to facts that Darwinism has long suppressed, facts that have been dismissed as mere coincidences unworthy of theoretical explanation. The history of life provides many examples of the apparent working out of a kind of biological foresight, as Michael Denton has amply documented.[24] This fact was also well known in Weaver's day: "[S]pecies are found to contain mutants which are not related to their present need for adaptation. In other words, mutations may occur long (and in the timetable of evolution 'long' may mean a very long while) before there is any need for them to insure the survival of the species. What this suggests is a kind of preadaptation, with the species being armed far in advance for some crisis it will meet in the future."[25]

How to Clean Up a "Universal Acid" Spill

Daniel Dennett has described Darwinism as a "universal acid," an intellectual neutron bomb with the capacity of destroying all traditional ideas of the meaning and destiny of human life.[26] Dennett looks forward with eager anticipation to more enlightened days in which religious folk and other believers in outmoded metaphysics can be sequestered in permanent reservations and zoos, where they can at least provide entertainment to their better-educated compatriots.[27]

Although I doubt that Darwinism is quite as powerful as Dennett imagines, it has for 150 years been one of the weapons of choice of all those, both on the Left and Right, who have wanted to undermine and ultimately to annihilate the great tradition of religious humanism that has formed the foundation of Western civilization. Marx wanted to dedicate *Das Kapital* to Darwin. John Dewey appeals repeatedly to the fact of evolutionary flux as the ultimate justification for jettisoning traditional ideas of education, character formation, political theory, and religion. On the Right, the use of Darwinism by the robber barons of unnuanced capitalism, and by the promoters of militant nationalism and racism, are also well known.

However, a few voices have argued in recent years that Darwinism is in fact a friend of conservative ideals and prescriptions, most prominently political theorist Larry Arnhart[28] and law professor John O. McGinnis.[29] There are two ways in which the Darwinian model could be said to support conservative thought. First, at least a partial reconciliation between Darwinism and Aristotelian natural law is possible: although Darwinists deny that teleology is a fundamental feature of the world, they can recognize a kind of quasi-teleological category, the category of structures and patterns that nature has in fact selected for specific functions. The heart wasn't literally designed for the sake of pumping blood, but it is a trait that has survived the rigors of natural selection because it successfully pumps blood. A Darwinist can similarly recognize the existence of quasi-teleological moral functions within human communities and the individual human personality. Some virtues, including justice and peaceableness, could be genuinely grounded in nature. These Aristotelian virtues, together with the fact that humans are adaptively social and political, could be the basis for a Darwinian theory of natural right.

Second, more recent versions of Darwinian theory, especially the punctuated equilibrium view of Stephen Jay Gould and Niles Eldredge, have significantly qualified the Heraclitean "all is flux" corollary of classical Darwinism that was celebrated by radical progressivists like Dewey. Humanity presumably long ago reached a stasis point, which could be taken as defining a fixed, even eternal, concept of human nature. The fixity of human nature, in turn, would provide an insuperable obstacle to all utopian schemes and a corrective to dreams of man's infinite perfectibility. A static human nature should discourage the plans of progressive social engineers aiming to produce a heaven on earth by bringing the human personality itself within the scope of their technical prowess.

Conservative Darwinism of this kind, however, promises a great deal more than it can deliver. My colleague J. Budziszewski, in an essay in this collection, argues persuasively against any attempt to ground classical natural law theory in Darwinian biology. Humanity may have a natural end or *telos* in some sense, according to the Darwinian account, but this end is an ultimately vacuous one. Everything nature selects, she selects for one ultimate purpose: the successful replication of the trait in question. However, the replication of a trait has value only if the trait itself has value intrinsically. The intrinsic purpose of human life cannot consist wholly in its propensity to produce more human life, where the purpose of the latter consists wholly in its propensity to produce still more human life, and so on, ad infinitum.

Second, the fixity of human nature is only an approximate and relative constancy. The prospects for genetic engineering may, at the very least, reinvigorate efforts at the transformation of human nature into a new and supposedly higher state. Moreover, the resistance to social engineering of a fixed genetic endowment is by no means insuperable, as even E. O. Wilson has recognized.[30] Radical alterations in the roles of the sexes, the structure of the family, or the distribution of talents and privileges is still possible, despite the strongest claims of sociobiology or evolutionary psychology. In principle and given the right environment, any genotype can be made to express itself in any conceivable phenotype. At most Darwinists can only warn that the economic costs of such alterations may be higher than anticipated.

Moreover, Darwinian conservatives must anchor their natural law in the nature of the human species, which is itself only a passing phase in the history of life. No matter how modified by notions of temporary equilibria, there is no place in the Darwinian worldview for those "permanent things" that Russell Kirk postulated as the foundation of conservative thought.

Finally, the internal logic of Darwinism demands that we explain away not only the apparent design of biological systems but also the apparent teleology of human creativity and action. It is no coincidence that one of the leading champions of Darwinism has built much of his academic career upon the project of explaining away the reality of human agency and consciousness.[31] Unless individual human action can ultimately be explained, without remainder, in terms of blind physical processes, the fundamental rationale for Darwinism is wanting. If we begin by eliminating the anthropomorphic elements of our view of nature, we inevitably end by eliminating the anthropomorphic elements in our view of ourselves. Human agency, as fundamentally discontinuous from the blindness and irrationality of the subhuman, must be dismissed as every bit as mythological as the attribution of teleology or purpose to nature as a whole, if Darwinism is to succeed. This Darwinian effort to dehumanize the human has undermined our sense of personal responsibility, of the infinite dignity and irreplaceable value of each human being, and of the sanctity of human life and freedom.

STILL WAITING FOR THE EVOLUTIONARY NEWTON

Copernicus moved heliocentric astronomy into stage one: he provided adequate evidence to motivate the investigation of a new theory. However, it was Kepler and Newton who brought the Copernican model into stage two, and it was the painstaking testing of the Newtonian model by astronomers in the seventeenth, eighteenth and nineteenth centuries (for example, Halley's use of the model to predict the orbital period of his comet) that enabled it to reach stage four. We're still waiting for Darwin's Newton: for a theorist who can take Darwin's proposal and produce even one hypothesis about the origin of one interesting biological mechanism, a hypothesis which specifies, step by step, the genetic changes that had to take place, the embryological alterations that these changes produce, and the quantifiable selective pressures that enable each new step to reach a significant proportion of the population.

It is not necessary to use physics or chemistry as the comparison class. Compare, for example, the Darwinian theory of evolution with the germ theory of disease. The germ theory has generated thousands of specific hypotheses, linking specific microorganisms with specific communicable diseases, and explaining in each case how the microorganism is transmitted from subject to subject and how infection by the microorganism produces the symptoms associated with the disease. Such hypotheses are eminently testable: one can treat the disease with an antibiotic known to be fatal to the hypothesized infectious agent, or one can block the channels known to transmit the germ, and then observe whether the disease is cured or contained. Nothing remotely like this is available in the Darwinian case. To take a famous, even iconic, example, we still do not know what genetic factors are responsible for the varying size and shape of Galapagos finches, and so, of course, we cannot demonstrate that these could all have plausibly resulted by mutation from some ancestral form, nor can we show that measurable selective pressures would have promoted the spread of such hypothetical mutations.[32] If we have failed to produce a testable hypothesis in such a longstanding and relatively simple example, consider how far we are from having such hypotheses at hand for the emergence of blood clotting, the central nervous system, or multicellular body plans.

Darwin's so-called theory is not really a theory at all: it is a schema for future theories. By failing to distinguish between a theory and an abstract sketch of the form of possible theories, Darwinian biologists have lost sight of the goal of building a genuine science. Instead, they have indulged in the far less onerous enterprise of using evolution as a stipulated narrative by which to "make sense" of biological facts, whatever they may be.

With the publication of *The Origin of Species*, Darwin produced a stack of promissory notes for future theories. This stack, dusty and yellowing with age, has lain undisturbed and unredeemed for nearly 150 years. The time is past due for an independent audit of the Darwinian enterprise, one that can write off irredeemable debt and rebalance the ledger books, cutting through the self-serving boosterism of its official spokesmen. Are there still grounds, as there were in 1859, for hoping that Darwin's ideas might one day engender a genuinely scientific explanation of the apparent design of the biological world? These hopes are fading, but such progress will be absolutely beyond reach so long as the leaders of the evolutionary community continue to exaggerate the status they have so far achieved, and so long as the resulting dogmatism arbitrarily limits the range of theoretical options.

Phillip E. Johnson

2. EVOLUTION AS DOGMA
The Establishment of Naturalism

The orthodox explanation of what is wrong with creationism goes something like this:

> Science has accumulated overwhelming evidence for evolution. Although there are controversies among scientists regarding the precise mechanism of evolution, and Darwin's particular theory of natural selection may have to be modified or at least supplemented, there is no doubt whatsoever about the *fact* of evolution. All of today's living organisms, including humans, are the product of descent with modification from common ancestors, and ultimately in all likelihood from a single microorganism that itself evolved from nonliving chemicals. The only persons who reject the fact of evolution are biblical fundamentalists, who say that each species was separately created by God about 6,000 years ago, and that all the fossils are the products of Noah's Flood. The fundamentalists claim to be able to make a scientific case for their position but "scientific creationism" is a contradiction in terms. Creation is inherently a religious doctrine, and there is no scientific evidence for it. This does not mean that science and religion are necessarily incompatible, because science limits itself to facts, hypotheses, and theories and does not intrude into questions of value, such as whether the universe or mankind has a purpose. Reasonable persons need have no fear that scientific *knowledge* conflicts with religious *belief*.

Like many other official stories, the preceding description contains just enough truth to mislead persuasively. In fact, there is a great deal more to the creation-evolution controversy than meets the eye, or rather, than meets the carefully cultivated media stereotype of "creationists" as Bible-quoting know-nothings who refuse to face up to the scientific evidence. The creationists may be wrong about many things, but they have at least one very important point to argue, a point that has been thoroughly obscured by all the attention paid to Noah's Flood and other side issues. That is this: what the science educators propose to teach as "evolution," and label as fact, is based not upon any incontrovertible empirical evidence, but upon a highly controversial philosophical presupposition. The controversy over evolution is therefore not going to go away as people become better educated on the subject. On the contrary, the more people learn about the philosophical content of what scientists are calling the "fact of evolution," the less they are going to like it.

To understand why this is so, we have to define the issue properly, which means that we will have to redefine some terms. No one doubts that evolution occurs, in the narrow sense that certain changes happen naturally. The most famous piece of evidence for Darwinism is a study of an English peppered-moth population consisting of both dark- and light-colored moths. When industrial smoke darkened the trees that were the moths' habitat, the percentage of dark moths increased, because of their relative advantage in hiding from predators. When the air pollution was reduced, the trees became lighter and more light moths survived. Both colors were present throughout, and so no new characteristics emerged, but the percentage of dark moths in the population went up and down as changing conditions affected their relative ability to survive and produce offspring.

Examples of this kind allow Darwinists to assert as beyond question that "evolution is a fact," and that natural selection is an important directing force in evolution. If they mean only that evolution of a sort has been known to occur, and that natural selection has observable effects upon the distribution of characteristics in a population, then there really is nothing to dispute. The important claim of "evolution," however, is not that limited changes occur in populations because of differences in survival rates. It is that we can extrapolate from the very modest amount of evolution that can actually be observed to a grand theory that explains how moths, trees, and scientific observers came to exist in the first place.

*****

Orthodox science insists that we can make the extrapolation. The "neo-Darwinian synthesis" (hereafter Darwinism) begins with the assumption that small random genetic changes (mutations) occasionally have positive survival value. Organisms possessing these favorable variations should have a relative advantage in survival and reproduction, and they will tend to pass their characteristics on to their descendants. By differential survival a favorable characteristic spreads through a population, and the population becomes different from what it was. If sufficient favorable mutations show up when and where they are needed, and if natural selection allows them to accumulate in a population, then it is conceivable that by tiny steps over vast amounts of time a bacterial ancestor might produce descendants as complex and varied as trees, moths, and human beings.

That is only a rough description of the theory, of course, and there are all sorts of arguments about the details. Some Darwinists, such as Harvard Professor Steven Jay Gould, say that new mechanisms are about to be discovered that will produce a more complicated theory, in which strictly Darwinian selection of individual organisms will play a reduced role. There is also a continuing debate about whether it is necessary to "decouple macroevolution from microevolution." Some experts do not believe that major changes and the appearance of new forms (i.e., macroevolution) can be explained as the products of an accumulation of tiny mutations through natural selection of individual organisms (microevolution). If classical Darwinism isn't the explanation for macroevolution, however, there is only speculation as to what sort of alternative mechanisms might have been responsible. In science, as in other fields, you can't beat something with nothing, and so the Darwinist paradigm remains in place.

For all the controversies over these issues, however, there is a basic philosophical point on which the evolutionary biologists all agree. Some say new mechanisms have to be introduced and others say the old mechanisms are adequate, but nobody with a reputation to lose proposes to invoke a supernatural creator or a mystical "life force" to help out with the difficulties. The theory in question is a theory of *naturalistic* evolution, which means that it absolutely rules out any miraculous or supernatural intervention at any point. Everything is conclusively presumed to have happened through purely material mechanisms that are in principle accessible to scientific investigation, whether they have yet been discovered or not.

The controversy over how macroevolution could have occurred has been caused largely by the increasing awareness in scientific circles that the fossil evidence is very difficult to reconcile with the Darwinist scenario. If all living species descended from common ancestors by an accumulation of tiny steps, then there once must have existed a veritable universe of transitional intermediate forms linking the vastly different organisms of today, such as moths, trees, and humans, with their hypothetical common ancestors. From Darwin's time to the present, paleontologists have hoped to find the ancestors and transitional intermediates and trace the course of macroevolution. Despite claims of success in some areas, however, the results have been on the whole disappointing. That the fossil record is in important respects hostile to a Darwinist interpretation has long been known to insiders as the "trade secret of paleontology." The secret is now coming out in the open. New forms of life tend to be fully formed at their first appearance, as were the fossil remains in the rocks. If these new forms actually evolved in gradual steps from pre-existing forms, as Darwinist science insists, the numerous intermediate forms that once must have existed have not been preserved.

*****

To illustrate the fossil problem, here is what a particularly vigorous advocate of Darwinism, Oxford Zoology Professor and popular author Richard Dawkins, says in *The Blind Watchmaker* about the "Cambrian explosion," i.e., the apparently sudden appearance of the major animal forms at the beginning of the Cambrian era:

> The Cambrian strata of rocks, vintage about 600 million years, are the oldest ones in which we find most of the major invertebrate groups. And we find many of them in an advanced state of evolution, the very first time they appear. It is as though they were just planted there, without any evolutionary history. Needless to say, this appearance of sudden planting has delighted creationists. Evolutionists of all stripes believe, however, that this really does represent a very large gap in the fossil record, a gap that is simply due to the fact that, for some reason, very few fossils have lasted from periods before about 600 million years ago.

The "appearance of sudden planting" in this important instance is not exceptional. There is a general pattern in the fossil record of sudden

appearance of new forms followed by "stasis," i.e., absence of basic evolutionary change. The fossil evidence in Darwin's time was so discour-
aging to his theory that he ruefully conceded: "Nature may almost be
said to have guarded against the frequent discovery of her transitional
or linking forms." Leading contemporary paleontologists such as David
Raup and Niles Eldredge say that the fossil problem is as serious now as
it was then, despite the most determined efforts of scientists to find the
missing links. This situation (along with other problems I am passing
over) explains why many scientists would dearly love to confirm the existence of natural mechanisms that can produce basically new forms of
life from earlier and simpler organisms without going through all the
hypothetical intermediate steps that classical Darwinism requires.

Some readers may wonder why scientists won't admit that there
are mysteries beyond our comprehension, and that one of them may be
how those complex animal groups managed to evolve directly from pre-
existing bacteria and algae without leaving any evidence of their transition. The reason that such an admission is out of the question is that it
would open the door to creationism, which in this context means not
simply biblical fundamentalism, but *any* invocation of a creative intelligence or purpose outside the natural order. Scientists committed to philosophical naturalism do not claim to have found the precise answer to
every problem, but they characteristically insist that they have the important problems sufficiently well enough in hand that they can narrow
the field of possibilities to a set of naturalistic alternatives. Absent that
insistence, they would have to concede that their commitment to naturalism is based upon faith rather than proof. Such a concession could be
exploited by promoters of rival sources of knowledge, such as philosophy and religion, who would be quick to point out that faith in naturalism is no more "scientific" (that is, empirically based) than any other
kind of faith.

In his book, immediately following the above passage discussing
the Cambrian explosion, Dawkins adds the remark that, whatever their
disagreements about the tempo and mechanism of evolution, scientific
evolutionists all "despise" the creationists who take delight in pointing
out the absence of fossil transitional intermediates. That word "despise"
is well chosen. Darwinists do not regard creationists as sincere doubters
but as dishonest propagandists, persons who probably only pretend to
disbelieve what they must know in their hearts to be the truth of naturalistic evolution. The greater their apparent intelligence and education,
the greater their fault in refusing to acknowledge the truth that is staring them in the face. These are "dark times," Dawkins noted last year in

the *New York Times,* because nearly half of the American people, including many "who should know better," refuse to believe in evolution. That such people have any rational basis for their skepticism is out of the question, of course, and Dawkins tells us exactly what to think of them: "It is absolutely safe to say that if you meet somebody who claims not to believe in evolution, that person is ignorant, stupid, or insane (or wicked, but I'd rather not consider that)."

*****

Darwinists disagree with creationists as a matter of definition, of course, but the degree of contempt they express for creationism in principle requires some explanation beyond the fact that certain creationists have used unfair tactics, such as quoting scientists out of context. It is not just the particular things that creationists do that infuriate the Darwinists; the creationists' very existence is infuriating. To understand why this is so, we must understand the powerful assumptions that mainstream scientists find it necessary to make, and the enormous frustration they feel when they are asked to take seriously those who refuse to accept those assumptions.

What Darwinists like Dawkins despise as "creationism" is something much broader than biblical fundamentalism or even Christianity, and what they proclaim as "evolution" is something much narrower than what the word means in common usage. All persons who affirm that "God creates" are in an important sense creationists, even if they believe that the Genesis story is a myth and that God created gradually through evolution over billions of years. This follows from the fact that the theory of evolution in question is *naturalistic* evolution, meaning evolution that involves no intervention or guidance by a creator outside the world of nature.

Naturalistic evolution is consistent with the existence of "God" only if by that term we mean no more than a first cause which retires from further activity after establishing the laws of nature and setting the natural mechanism in motion. Those who say they believe in evolution, but who have in mind a process guided by an *active* God who purposely intervenes or controls the process to accomplish some end, are using the same term that the Darwinists use, but they mean something very different by it. For example, here is what Douglas Futuyma, the author of a leading college evolutionary biology textbook, finds to be the most important conflict between the theory of evolution and what he thinks of as the "fundamentalist" perspective:

Perhaps most importantly, if the world and its creatures developed purely by material, physical forces, it could not have
been designed and has no purpose or goal. The fundamentalist, in contrast, believes that everything in the world, every
species and every characteristic of every species, was designed
by an intelligent, purposeful artificer, and that it was made
for a purpose. Nowhere does this contrast apply with more
force than to the human species. Some shrink from the conclusion that the human species was not designed, has no purpose, and is the product of mere material mechanisms—but
this seems to be the message of evolution. *(Science on Trial:
The Case for Evolution)*

It is not only "fundamentalists," of course, but theists of any description who believe that an intelligent artificer made humanity for a
purpose, whether through evolution or otherwise. Futuyma's doctrinaire
naturalism is not just some superfluous philosophical addition to Darwinism that can be discarded without affecting the real "science" of the
matter. If a powerful conscious being exists outside the natural order, it
might use its power to intervene in nature to accomplish some purpose,
such as the production of beings having consciousness and free will. If
the possibility of an "outside" intervention is allowed in nature at any
point, however, the whole naturalistic worldview quickly unravels.

Occasionally, a scientist discouraged by the consistent failure of
theories purporting to explain some problem like the first appearance
of life will suggest that perhaps supernatural creation is a tenable hypothesis in this one instance. Sophisticated naturalists instantly recoil
with horror, because they know that there is no way to tell God when he
has to stop. If God created the first organism, then how do we know he
didn't do the same thing to produce all those animal groups that appear
so suddenly in the Cambrian rocks? Given the existence of a designer
ready and willing to do the work, why should we suppose that random
mutations and natural selection are responsible for such marvels of engineering as the eye and the wing?

*****

Because the claims of Darwinism are presented to the public as "science," most people are under the impression that they are supported by
direct evidence, such as experiments and fossil record studies. This im-

pression is seriously misleading. Scientists cannot observe complex biological structures being created by random mutations and selection, either in a laboratory or elsewhere. The fossil record, as we have seen, is so unhelpful that the important steps in evolution must be assumed to have occurred within its "gaps." Darwinists believe that the mutation-selection mechanism accomplishes wonders of creativity not because the wonders can be demonstrated, but because the Darwinists cannot think of a more plausible explanation for the existence of wonders without involving an unacceptable *creator*, i.e., a being or force outside the world of nature. According to Gareth Nelson, a senior zoologist at the American Museum of Natural History, "evidence, or proof, of origins—of the universe, of life, of all the major groups of life, of all the minor groups of life, indeed of all the species—is weak or nonexistent when measured on an absolute scale." Nelson wrote that statement in the preface to a recent book by Wendell Bird, the leading attorney for the creationist organizations. Nelson himself is no creationist, but he is sufficiently disgusted with Darwinist dogmatism that he looks benignly upon unorthodox challengers.

Philosophical naturalism is so deeply ingrained in the thinking of many educated people today, including theologians, that they find it difficult even to imagine any other way of looking at things. To such people, Darwinism seems so logically appealing that only a modest amount of confirming evidence is needed to prove the whole system, and so the evidence of something like the peppered-moth example seems virtually conclusive. Even if they do develop doubts about whether such modest forces can account for large-scale change, their naturalism is undisturbed. Since there is nothing outside of nature, and since *something* must have produced all the kinds of organisms that exist, a satisfactory naturalistic mechanism must be awaiting discovery.

The same situation looks quite different to people who accept the possibility of a creator outside the natural order. To such people, the peppered-moth observations and similar evidence seem absurdly inadequate to prove that natural selection can make a wing, an eye, or a brain. From their more skeptical perspective, the consistent pattern in the fossil record of sudden appearance followed by stasis tends to prove that there is something wrong with Darwinism, not that there is something wrong with the fossil record. The absence of proof "when measured on an absolute scale" is unimportant to a thoroughgoing naturalist, who feels that science is doing well enough if it has a plausible explanation that maintains the naturalistic worldview. The absence of proof is highly significant, however, to any person who thinks it possible that there are more things in heaven and earth than are dreamt of in naturalistic philosophy.

Victory in the creation-evolution dispute ultimately belongs to the party with the cultural authority to establish the ground rules that govern the discourse. If creation is admitted as a serious possibility, Darwinism cannot win; and if creation is excluded a priori, Darwinism cannot lose. The point is illustrated in the logic employed by the National Academy of Sciences to persuade the Supreme Court that "creation-scientists" should not be given an opportunity to present their case against the theory of evolution in science classes. Creation-science is not science, said the Academy, because "it fails to display the most basic characteristic of science: reliance upon naturalistic explanations. Instead, proponents of 'creation-science' hold that the creation of the universe, the earth, living things, and man was accomplished through supernatural means inaccessible to human understanding."

*****

Besides, the Academy's brief continued, creationists do not perform scientific research to establish the mechanism of supernatural creation, that being by definition impossible. Instead, they seek to discredit the scientific theory of evolution by amassing evidence that is allegedly consistent with the relatively recent, abrupt appearance of the universe, the earth, living things, and man in substantially the same form as they now appear: "'Creation-science' is thus manifestly a device designed to dilute the persuasiveness of the theory of evolution. The dualistic mode of analysis and the negative argumentation employed to accomplish this dilution is, moreover, antithetical to the scientific method."

The Academy's brief went on to cite evidence for evolution, even though evidence was unnecessary in terms of their argument. Creationists are disqualified from making a positive case because science by definition is based upon naturalism. The rules of science also disqualify any purely negative argumentation designed to dilute the persuasiveness of the theory of evolution. Creationism is thus ruled out of court—and out of the classroom—before any consideration of evidence. Put yourself in the place of a creationist who has been silenced by that logic, and you may feel like a criminal defendant who has just been told that the law does not recognize so absurd a concept as "innocence."

With creationist explanations disqualified at the outset, it follows that the evidence will always support the naturalistic alternative. We can be absolutely certain that the Academy will not say, "The evidence

on the whole supports the theory of evolution, although we concede
that the apparent abrupt appearance of many fully formed animal groups
in the Cambrian rocks is in itself a point in favor of the creationists."
There are *no* scientific points in favor of creation and there never will be
any as long as naturalists control the definition of science, because creationist explanations by definition violate the fundamental commitment
of science to naturalism. When the fossil record does not provide the
evidence that naturalism would like to see, it is the fossil record, and not
the naturalistic explanation, that is judged to be inadequate.

When pressed about the unfairness of disqualifying their opponents *a priori,* naturalists sometimes portray themselves as merely insisting upon a proper definition of "science," and not as making any
absolute claims about "truth." By this interpretation, the National Academy of Sciences did not say that it is *untrue* that "the creation of the
universe, the earth, living things and man was accomplished through
supernatural means inaccessible to human understanding," but only that
this statement is *unscientific.* Scientific naturalists who take this line
sometimes add that they do not necessarily object to the study of creationism in the public schools, provided it occurs in literature and social
science classes rather than in science class.

This naturalist version of balanced treatment is not a genuine attempt at a fair accommodation of competing worldviews, but a rhetorical maneuver. It enables naturalists effectively to label their own product as fact and its rival as fantasy, without having to back up the decision with evidence. The dominant culture assumes that science provides
knowledge, and so in natural science classes fundamental propositions
can be proclaimed as objectively true, regardless of how many dissent-
ers believe them to be false. That is the powerful philosophical meaning
of the claim that "evolution is a fact." By contrast, in literature class we
read poetry and fiction, and in social science we study the subjective
beliefs of various cultures from a naturalistic perspective. If you have
difficulty seeing just how loaded this knowledge-belief distinction is,
try to imagine the reaction of Darwinists to the suggestion that their
theory should be removed from the college biology curriculum and studied instead in a course devoted to nineteenth-century intellectual history.

*****

By skillful manipulation of categories and definitions, the Darwinists
have established philosophical naturalism as educational orthodoxy in

a nation in which the overwhelming majority of people express some form of theistic belief inconsistent with naturalism. According to a 1982 Gallup poll aimed at measuring nationwide opinion, 44 percent of respondents agreed with the statement that "God created man pretty much in his present form at one time within the last 10,000 years." That would seem to mark those respondents as creationists in a relatively narrow sense. Another 38 percent accepted evolution as a process guided by God. Only 9 percent identified themselves as believers in a naturalistic evolutionary process not guided by God. The philosophy of the 9 percent is now to be taught in the schools as unchallengeable truth.

Cornell University Professor William Provine, a leading historian of Darwinism, concluded from Gallup's figures that the American public simply does not understand what the scientist means by evolution. As Provine summarized the matter, "The destructive implications of evolutionary biology extend far beyond the assumptions of organized religion to a much deeper and more pervasive belief, held by the vast majority of people, that non-mechanistic organizing designs or forces are somehow responsible for the visible order of the physical universe, biological organisms, and human moral order." Provine blamed the scientific establishment itself for misleading the public about the absolute incompatibility of contemporary Darwinism with any belief in God, designing forces, or absolute standards of good and evil. Scientific leaders have obscured the conflict for fear of jeopardizing public support for their funding, and also because some of them believe that religion may still play a useful role in maintaining public morality. According to Provine, "These rationalizations are politic but intellectually dishonest."

The organizations that speak officially for science continue to deny that there is a conflict between Darwinism and "religion." This denial is another example of the skillful manipulation of definitions, because there are evolution-based religions that embrace naturalism with enthusiasm. Stephen Jay Gould holds up the geneticist Theodosius Dobzhansky, "the greatest evolutionist of our century and a lifelong Russian Orthodox," as proof that evolution and religion are compatible. The example is instructive because Dobzhansky made a religion out of evolution. According to a eulogy by Francisco Ayala, "Dobzhansky was a religious man, although he apparently rejected fundamental beliefs of traditional religion, such as the existence of God and of life beyond physical death. His religiosity was grounded on the conviction that there is meaning in the universe. He saw that meaning in the fact that evolution has produced the stupendous diversity of the living world and has progressed from primitive forms of life to mankind. . . . He believed that somehow

mankind would eventually evolve into higher levels of harmony and creativity." In short, Dobzhansky was what we would today call a New Age
pantheist. Of course evolution is not incompatible with religion when
the religion is evolution.

Dobzhansky was one of the principal founders of the neo-Darwinian synthesis. Another was Julian Huxley, who promoted a religion
of "evolutionary humanism." A third was the paleontologist George
Gaylord Simpson. Simpson explained in his book *The Meaning of Evolution* that "there are some beliefs still current, labeled as religious and
involved with religious emotions, that conflict with evolution and are
therefore intellectually untenable in spite of their emotional appeal."
Simpson added that it is nonetheless "self-evident . . . that evolution and
true religion are compatible." By true religion he meant naturalistic religion, which accepts that "man is the result of a purposeless and natural
process that did not have him in mind." Because efforts have been made
to obscure the point, it should be emphasized that Simpson's view is not
some personal opinion extraneous to the real "science" of Darwinism.
It is an expression of the same naturalism that gives Darwinists confidence that mutation and natural selection, Darwinism's "blind watchmaker," can do all the work of a creator.

*****

Against this background, readers may perceive the cruel irony in Justice
William Brennan's opinion for the Supreme Court majority, holding the
Louisiana "balanced treatment" statute unconstitutional because the
creationists who promoted it had a "religious purpose." Of course they
had a religious purpose, if by that we mean a purpose to try to do something to counter the highly successful efforts of the proponents of naturalism to have their philosophy established in the public schools as "fact."
If creationists object to naturalistic evolution on religious grounds, they
are admonished that it is inappropriate for religion to meddle with science. If they try to state scientific objections, they are disqualified instantly by definitions devised for that purpose by their adversaries.
Sisyphus himself, eternally rolling his stone up that hill in Hades, must
pity their frustration.

The Darwinists are also frustrated, however, because they find the
resurgence of creationism baffling. Why can't these people learn that
the evidence for evolution is overwhelming? Why do they persist in denying the obvious? Above all, how can they be so dishonest as to claim
that scientific evidence supports their absurd position? Writing the in-

troduction to a collection of polemics titled *Scientists Confront Creationism,* Richard Lewontin attempted to explain why creationism is doomed by its very nature. Because he is a dedicated Marxist as well as a famous geneticist, Lewontin saw the conflict between creation and evolution as a class struggle, with history inevitably awarding the victory to the naturalistic class. The triumph of evolution in the schools in the post-Sputnik era signaled that "the culture of the dominant class had triumphed, and traditional religious values, the only vestige of control that rural people had over their own lives and the lives of their families, had been taken away from them." In fact, many creationists are urban professionals who make their living from technology, but Lewontin's basic point is valid. The "fact of evolution" is an instrument of cultural domination, and it is only to be expected that people who are being consigned to the dustbin of history should make some protest.

Lewontin was satisfied that creationism cannot survive because its acceptance of miracles puts it at odds with the more rational perception of the world as a place where all events have natural causes. Even a creationist "crosses seas not on foot but in machines, finds the pitcher empty when he has poured out its contents, and the cupboard bare when he has eaten the last of the loaf." Lewontin thus saw creationism as falsified not so much by any discoveries of modern science as by universal human experience, a thesis that does little to explain either why so absurd a notion has attracted so many adherents or why we should expect it to lose ground in the near future.

Once again we see how the power to define can be used to distort, especially when the critical definition is implicit rather than exposed to view. (I remind the reader that to Lewontin and myself, a "creationist" is not necessarily a biblical literalist, but rather any person who believes that God creates.) If creationists really were people who lived in an imaginary world of continual miracles, there would be very few of them. On the contrary, from a creationist point of view, the very fact that the universe is on the whole orderly, in a manner comprehensible to our intellect, is evidence that we and it were fashioned by a common intelligence. What is truly a miracle, in the pejorative sense of an event having no rational connection with what has gone before, is the emergence of a being with consciousness, free will, and a capacity to understand the laws of nature in a universe which in the beginning contained only matter in mindless motion.

* * * * *

Once we understand that biologists like Lewontin are employing their scientific prestige in support of a philosophical platform, there is no longer any reason to be intimidated by their claims to scientific expertise. On the contrary, the inability of most biologists to make any sense out of creationist criticisms of their presuppositions is evidence of their own philosophical naiveté. The "overwhelming evidence for naturalistic evolution" no longer overwhelms when the naturalistic worldview is itself called into question, and that worldview is as problematical as any other set of metaphysical assumptions when it is placed on the table for examination rather than being taken for granted as "the way we think today."

The problem with scientific naturalism as a worldview is that it takes a sound methodological premise of natural science and transforms it into a dogmatic statement about the nature of the universe. Science is committed by definition to empiricism, by which I mean that scientists seek to find truth by observation, experiment, and calculation rather than by studying sacred books or achieving mystical states of mind. It may well be, however, that there are certain questions—important questions, ones to which we desperately want to know the answers—that cannot be answered by the methods available to our science. These may include not only broad philosophical issues such as whether the universe has a purpose, but also questions we have become accustomed to think of as empirical, such as how life first began or how complex biological systems were put together.

Suppose, however, that some people find it intolerable either to be without answers to these questions or to allow the answers to come from anyone but scientists. In that case science must provide answers, but to do this, it must invoke *scientism*, a philosophical doctrine which asserts arbitrarily that knowledge comes only through the methods of investigation available to the natural sciences. The Soviet Cosmonaut who announced upon landing that he had been to the heavens and had not seen God was expressing crudely the basic philosophical premise that underlies Darwinism. Because we cannot examine God in our telescopes or under our microscopes, God is unreal. It is meaningless to say that some entity exists if in principle we can never have knowledge of that entity.

With the methodology of scientism in mind, we can understand what it means to contrast scientific "knowledge" with religious "belief," and what follows from the premise that natural science is not suitable for investigating whether the universe has a purpose. Belief is inherently subjective, and includes elements such as fantasy and preference. Knowledge is in principle objective, and includes elements such as facts and laws. If science does not investigate the purpose of the universe, then in scientific terms the universe effectively has no purpose, because a purpose of which we can have no knowledge is meaningless to us. On the other hand, the universe does exist, and all its features must be explicable in terms of forces and causes accessible to scientific investigation. It follows that the best naturalistic explanation available is effectively true, with the proviso that it may eventually be supplanted by a better or more inclusive theory. Thus naturalistic evolution is a fact, and the fact implies a critical guiding role for natural selection.

Scientism itself is not a fact, however, nor is it attractive as a philosophy once its elements and consequences are made explicit. Those who want naturalistic evolution to be accepted as unquestioned fact must therefore use their cultural authority to enact rules of discourse that protect the purported fact from the attacks of unbelievers. First, they can identify science with naturalism, which means that they insist as a matter of first principle that no consideration whatever be given to the possibility that mind or spirit preceded matter. Second, they can impose a rule of procedure that disqualifies purely negative argument, so that a theory with a very modest degree of empirical support can become immune to being disproved until and unless it is supplanted by a better naturalistic theory. With these rules in place, Darwinists can claim to have proved that natural selection crafted moths, trees, and people, and point to the peppered-moth observation as proof.

*****

The assumption of naturalism is in the realm of speculative philosophy, and the rule against negative argument is arbitrary. It is as if a judge were to tell a defendant that he may not establish his innocence unless he can produce a suitable substitute to be charged with the crime. Such rules of discourse need protection from criticism, and two distinct rhetorical strategies have been pursued to provide it. First, we have already seen that the direct conflict between Darwinism and theism has been blurred, so that theists who are not committed to biblical inerrancy are led to believe that they have no reason to be suspicious of Darwinism. The remaining objectors can be marginalized as fundamentalists, whose purportedly scientific objections need not be taken seriously because "everybody knows" that people like that will believe, and say, anything.

The second strategy is to take advantage of the prestige that science enjoys in an age of technology by asserting that anyone who disputes Darwinism must be an enemy of science, and hence of rationality itself. This argument gains a certain plausibility from the fact that Darwinism is not the only area within the vast realm of science where practices such as extravagant extrapolation, arbitrary assumptions, and metaphysical speculation have been tolerated. The history of scientific efforts to explain human behavior provides many examples; in fact, some aspects of cosmology, such as its Anthropic Principle, invite the label "cosmo-theology." What makes the strategy effective, however, is not the association of Darwinism with the more speculative aspects of cosmology, but its purported link with technology. Donald Johanson put the point effectively, if crudely: "You can't accept one part of science because it brings you good things like electricity and penicillin and throw away another part because it brings you some things you don't like about the origin of life."

But why can't you do exactly that? That scientists can learn a good deal about the behavior of electrons and bacteria does not prove that they know how electrons or bacteria came into existence in the first place. It is also possible that contemporary scientists are insightful in some matters and, like their predecessors, thoroughly confused about others. Twentieth-century experience demonstrates that scientific technology can work wonders, of course. It also demonstrates that dubious doctrines based on philosophy can achieve an undeserved respectability by cloaking themselves in the mystique of science. Whether Darwinism is another example of pseudoscience is the question, and this question cannot be answered by a vague appeal to the authority of science.

For now, things are going well for Darwinism in America. The Supreme Court has dealt the creationists a crushing blow, and state boards of education are beginning to adopt "science frameworks." These policy statements are designed to encourage textbook publishers to proclaim boldly the fact of evolution—and therefore the naturalistic philosophy that underlies the fact—instead of minimizing the subject to avoid controversy. Efforts are also under way to bring under control any individual teachers who express creationist sentiments in the classroom, especially if they make use of unapproved materials. As ideological authority collapses in other parts of the world, the Darwinists are successfully swimming against the current.

*****

There will be harder times ahead, however. The Darwinist strategy depends upon a certain blurring of the issues, and in particular upon maintaining the fiction that what is being promoted is an inoffensive "fact of evolution," which is opposed only by a discredited minority of religious fanatics. As the Darwinists move out to convert the nation's school children to a naturalistic outlook, it may become more and more difficult to conceal the religious implications of their system. Plenty of people within the Darwinist camp know what is being concealed, and cannot be relied upon to maintain a discreet silence. William Provine, for example, has been on a crusade to persuade the public that it has to discard either Darwinism or God, and not only God but also such non-materialistic concepts as free will and objective standards of morality. Provine offers this choice in the serene confidence that the biologists have enough evidence to persuade the public to choose Darwinism, and to accept its philosophical consequences.

The establishment of naturalism in the schools is supposedly essential to the improvement of science education, which is in such a dismal state in America that national leaders are truly worried. It is not likely, however, that science education can be improved in the long run by identifying science with a worldview that is abhorred by a large section of the population, and then hoping that the public never finds out what is being implied. Such a project would require that the scientific establishment commit itself to a strategy of indoctrination, in which the teachers first tell students what they are supposed to believe and then inform them about any difficulties only later, when it is deemed safe to do so. The weakness that requires such dogmatism is evident in Philip Kitcher's explanation of why it is "insidious" to propose that the creationists be allowed to present their negative case in the classroom:

> There will be . . . much dredging up of misguided objections
> to evolutionary theory. The objections are spurious—but how
> is the teacher to reveal their errors to students who are at the
> beginning of their science studies? . . . What Creationists really
> propose is a situation in which people without scientific
> training—fourteen-year-old students, for example—are asked
> to decide a complex issue on partial evidence.

A few centuries ago, the defenders of orthodoxy used the same logic to explain why the common people needed to be protected from exposure to the spurious heresies of Galileo. In fairness, the creationists Kitcher had in mind are biblical fundamentalists who want to attack orthodox scientific doctrine on a broad front. I do not myself think that such advocacy groups should be given a platform in the classroom. In my experience, however, Darwinists apply the same contemptuous dismissal to any suggestion, however well informed and modestly stated, that in constructing their huge theoretical edifice upon a blind commitment to naturalism, they may have been building upon the sand. As long as the media and the courts are quiescent, they may retain the power to marginalize dissent and establish their philosophy as orthodoxy. What they do not have the power to do is to make it true.

Marcel-Paul Schützenberger

3. The Miracles of Darwinism
1996 Interview with La Recherche

Q: What is your definition of Darwinism?

S: Darwinists argue that the double action of chance mutations and natural selection explains evolution. This general doctrine accommodates two mutually contradictory schools—gradualists on the one hand and saltationists on the other. Gradualists insist that evolution proceeds by small successive changes; saltationists that it proceeds by jumps. Richard Dawkins has come to champion radical gradualism, [the late] Stephen Jay Gould a no less radical version of saltationism.

Q: You are known as a mathematician rather than a specialist in evolutionary biology . . .

S: Biology is, of course, not my specialty. But biologists themselves have encouraged the participation of mathematicians in the overall assessment of evolutionary thought, if only because they have presented such an irresistible target. Richard Dawkins, for example, has been fatally attracted to arguments that hinge on concepts drawn from mathematics and computer science—arguments which he then, with all his comic authority, imposes on innocent readers. Mathematicians are, in any case, epistemological zealots. It is normal for them to bring their critical scruples to the foundations of other disciplines. And finally, it is worth observing that the great turbid wave of cybernetics has carried mathematicians from their normal mid-ocean haunts to the far shores of evolutionary biology. There, up ahead, René Thom and Ilya Prigogine may be observed paddling sedately toward dry land, members of the Santa Fe Institute thrashing in their wake. Stuart Kauffman is among them.

An interesting case, a physician half in love with mathematical logic, burdened now and forever by having received a papal kiss from Murray Gell-Mann. This ecumenical movement has endeavored to apply the concepts of mathematics to the fundamental problems of evolution— the interpretation of functional complexity, for example.

Q: What do you mean by functional complexity?

S: It is impossible to grasp the phenomenon of life without that concept, the two words each expressing a crucial idea. The laboratory biologists' normal and unforced vernacular is almost always couched in functional terms: the function of an eye, the function of an enzyme, or a ribosome, or the fruit fly's antennae. Functional language matches up perfectly with biological reality. Physiologists see this better than anyone else. Within their world, everything is a matter of function, the various systems that they study—circulatory, digestive, excretory, and the like—all characterized in simple, ineliminable functional terms. At the level of molecular biology, functionality may seem to pose certain conceptual problems, perhaps because the very notion of an organ has disappeared when biological relationships are specified in biochemical terms. But appearances are misleading. Certain functions remain even in the absence of an organ or organ systems. Complexity is also a crucial concept. Even among unicellular organisms, the mechanisms involved in the separation and fusion of chromosomes during mitosis and meiosis are processes of unbelievable complexity and subtlety. Organisms present themselves to us as a complex ensemble of functional interrelationships. If one is going to explain their evolution, one must at the same time explain their functionality and their complexity.

Q: What is it that makes functional complexity so difficult to comprehend?

S: The evolution of living creatures appears to require an essential ingredient, a specific form of organization. Whatever it is, it lies beyond anything that our present knowledge of physics or chemistry might suggest. It is a property upon which formal logic sheds absolutely no light. Whether gradualists or saltationists, Darwinians have too simple a conception of biology, rather like a locksmith misguidedly convinced that his handful of keys will open any lock. Darwinians, for example, tend to think of the gene as if it were the expression of a simple command: do this, get that done, drop that side chain. Walter Gehring's work on the regulatory genes controlling the development of the insect eye reflects this conception. The relevant genes may well function this way, but the story on this level is surely incomplete, and Darwinian theory is not apt to fill in the pieces.

Q: You claim that biologists think of a gene as a command. Could you be more specific?

S: Schematically, a gene is like a unit of information. It has simple binary properties. A sequence of gene instructions resembles a sequence of instructions specifying a recipe. Consider again the example of the eye. Darwinists imagine that it requires—what? A thousand or two thousand genes to assemble an eye, the specification of the organ thus requiring one or two thousand units of information? That is absurd! Suppose a European firm proposes to manufacture an entirely new household appliance in a Southeast Asian factory. And suppose that for commercial reasons the firm does not wish to communicate to the factory any details of the appliance's function, like how it works or what purposes it will serve. With only a few thousand bits of information, the factory is not going to proceed very far or very fast. A few thousand bits of information, after all, yields only a single paragraph of text. The appliance in question is bound to be vastly simpler than the eye. Charged with its manufacture, the factory will yet need to know the significance of the operations to which they have committed themselves in engaging their machinery. This can be achieved only if they already have some sense of the object's nature before they undertake to manufacture it. A considerable body of knowledge, held in common between the European firm and its Asian factory, is necessary before manufacturing instructions may be executed.

Q: Would you argue that the genome does not contain the requisite information for explaining organisms?

S: It does not, according to the understanding of the genome we now possess. The biological properties invoked by biologists are in this respect quite insufficient. While biologists may understand that a gene triggers the production of a particular protein, that knowledge—that kind of knowledge—does not allow them to comprehend how one or two thousand genes suffice to direct the course of embryonic development.

Q: You are going to be accused of preformationism . . .

S: And of many other crimes. My position is nevertheless a strictly rational one. I've formulated a problem that appears significant to me: How is it that with so few elementary instructions the materials of life can fabricate objects that are so marvelously complicated and efficient? This remarkable property with which they are endowed—just what is its nature? Nothing within our actual knowledge of physics and chemistry allows us intellectually to grasp it. If one starts from an evolutionary point of view, it must be acknowledged that in one manner or another the earliest fish contained the capacity, and the appropriate neural wiring, to bring into existence organs which they did not possess or even need, but which would be the common property of their successors when they left the water for the firm ground, or for the air.

Q: You assert that, in fact, Darwinism doesn't explain much.

S: It seems to me that the union of chance mutation and selection has a certain descriptive value. But in no case does the description count as an explanation. Darwinism relates ecological data to the relative abundance of species and environments. In any case, the descriptive value of Darwinian models is pretty limited. Besides, as saltationists have indicated, the gradualist thesis seems totally ridiculous in light of our growing knowledge of paleontology. The miracles of saltationism, on the other hand, cannot discharge the mystery I have described.

Q: Let's return to natural selection. Isn't it the case that despite everything the idea has a certain explanatory value?

S: No one could possibly deny the general thesis that stability is a necessary condition for existence. This is the real content of the doctrine of natural selection. The outstanding application of this general principle is Berthollet's laws in elementary chemistry. In a desert, the species that die rapidly are those that require water the most. Yet that does not explain the appearance among the survivors of those structures whose particular features permit them to resist aridity. The thesis of natural selection is not very powerful. Except for certain artificial cases, we remain unable to predict whether this or that species or this or that variety will be favored or not as the result of changes in the environment. What we can do is establish the effects of natural selection after the fact—to show, for example, that certain birds are disposed to eat this species of snails less often than other species, perhaps because their shell is not as visible. That's ecology. To put it another way, natural selection is a weak instrument of proof because the phenomena subsumed by natural selection are obvious. They establish nothing from the point of view of the theory.

Q: Isn't the significant explanatory feature of Darwinian theory the connection established between chance mutations and natural selection?

S: With the discovery of genetic coding, we have come to understand that a gene is like a word composed in the DNA alphabet. Such words form the genomic text and tell the cell to make this or that protein. Either a given protein is structural, or it works in combination with other signals from the genome to fabricate yet another protein. All the experimental results we know fall within this scheme. The following scenario then becomes standard: A gene undergoes a mutation, one that may facilitate the reproduction of those individuals carrying it; over time, and with respect to a specific environment, mutants come to be statistically favored, replacing individuals lacking the requisite mutation. But evolution cannot simply be the accumulation of such typographical errors. Population geneticists can study the speed with which a favorable mutation propagates itself under these circumstances. They do this with a lot of skill, but these are academic exercises, if only because none of the parameters that they use can be empirically determined. In addition, there are the obstacles I have already mentioned. We know the number of genes in an organism. There are about one hundred thousand for a higher vertebrate. This we know fairly well. But this seems grossly insufficient to explain the incredible quantity of information needed to accomplish evolution within a given line of species.

Q: A concrete example?

S: Darwinists say that horses, which once were as small as rabbits, increased their size to escape more quickly from predators. Within the gradualist model, one might isolate a specific trait—increase in body size—and consider it to be the result of a series of typographic changes. The explanatory effect achieved is rhetorical, imposed entirely by the trick of insisting that what counts for an herbivore is the speed of its flight when faced by a predator. Now this may even be partially true, but there are no biological grounds that permit us to determine that this is in fact the decisive consideration. After all, increase in body size may well have a negative effect. Darwinists seem to me to have preserved a mechanistic vision of evolution, one that prompts them to observe merely a linear succession of causes and effects. The idea that causes may interact with one another is now standard in mathematical physics; it is a point that has had difficulty penetrating the carapace of biological thought. In fact, within the quasi-totality of observable phenomena, local changes interact dramatically. After all, there is hardly an issue of *La Recherche* that does not contain an allusion to the Butterfly Effect. Information theory is precisely the domain that sharpens our intuitions about these phenomena. A typographical change in a computer program does not change it just a little. It wipes the program out, purely and simply. It is the same with a telephone number. If I intend to call a correspondent by telephone, it doesn't much matter if I am fooled by one, two, three or eight figures in his number.

Q: You accept the idea that biological mutations genuinely have the character of typographical errors?

S: Yes, in the sense that one base is a template for another, one codon for another. But at the level of biochemical activity, one is no longer able properly to speak of typography. There is an entire grammar for the formation of proteins in three dimensions, one that we understand poorly. We do not have at our disposal physical or chemical rules permitting us to construct a mapping from typographical mutations or modifications to biologically effective structures. To return to the example of the eye: a few thousand genes are needed for its fabrication, but each in isolation signifies nothing. What is significant is the combination of their interactions. These cascading interactions, with their feedback loops, express an organization whose complexity we do not know how to analyze. It is possible we may be able to do so in the future, but there is no doubt that we are unable to do so now. Gehring has recently discovered a segment of DNA which is involved both in the development of the vertebrate eye and which can also induce the development of an eye in the wing of a butterfly. His work comprises a demonstration of something utterly astonishing, but not an explanation.

Q: But Dawkins, for example, believes in the possibility of a cumulative process.

S: Dawkins believes in an effect that he calls "the cumulative selection of beneficial mutations." To support his thesis, he resorts to a metaphor introduced by the mathematician Emile Borel—that of a monkey typing by chance and in the end producing a work of literature. It is a metaphor, I regret to say, embraced by Francis Crick, the co-discoverer of the double helix. Dawkins has his computer write a series of thirty letters, these corresponding to the number of letters in a verse by Shakespeare. He then proceeds to simulate the Darwinian mechanism of chance mutations and selection. His imaginary monkey types and retypes the same letters, the computer successively choosing the phrase that most resembles the target verse. By means of cumulative selection, the monkey reaches its target in forty or sixty generations.

Q: But you don't believe that a monkey typing on a typewriter, even aided by a computer . . .

S: This demonstration is bogus. Dawkins doesn't even describe precisely how it proceeds. At the beginning of the exercise, randomly generated phrases appear rapidly to approach the target; the closer the approach, the more the process begins to slow. It is the action of mutations in the wrong direction that pulls things backward. In fact, a simple argument shows that unless the numerical parameters are chosen deliberately, the progression begins to bog down completely.

Q: You would say that the model of cumulative selection, imagined by Dawkins, is out of touch with palpable biological realities?

S: Exactly. Dawkins's model lays entirely to the side the triple problems of complexity, functionality, and their interaction.

Q: You are a mathematician. Suppose that you try, despite your reservations, to formalize the concept of functional complexity.

S: I would appeal to a notion banned by the scientific community, but one understood perfectly by everyone else—that of a goal. As a computer scientist, I could express this in the following way. One constructs a space within which one of the coordinates serves in effect as the thread of Ariadne, guiding the trajectory toward the goal. Once the space is constructed, the system evolves in a mechanical way toward its goal. But look, the construction of the relevant space cannot proceed until a preliminary analysis has been carried out, one in which the set of all possible trajectories is assessed and their average distance from the specified goal is estimated. Such a preliminary analysis is beyond the reach of empirical study. It presupposes that the biologist (or computer scientist) knows the totality of the situation, the properties of the ensemble of trajectories. Yet in terms of mathematical logic, the nature of this space is entirely enigmatic. It is crucial to remember that the conceptual problems we face in trying to explain life, life has entirely solved. Indeed, the systems embodied in living creatures are entirely successful in reaching their goals. The trick involved in Dawkins's embarrassing example arises from his surreptitious introduction of a relevant space. His computer program calculates from a random phrase to a target, a calculation that corresponds to nothing in biological reality. The function that he employs flatters the imagination, however, because its apparent simplicity elicits naïve approval. In biological reality, the space of even the simplest function has a complexity that defies understanding, and indeed defies any and all calculations.

Q: Even when they dissent from Darwin, the saltationists are more moderate: they don't pretend to hold the key that would permit them to explain evolution.

S: Before we discuss the saltationists, however, I must say a word about the Japanese biologist Motoo Kimura. He has shown that the majority of mutations are neutral, without any selective effect. For Darwinians upholding the central Darwinian thesis, this is embarrassing. . . . The saltationist view, revived by Stephen Jay Gould, in the end represents an idea of Richard Goldschmidt's. In 1940 or so, Goldschmidt postulated the existence of very intense mutations, no doubt involving hundreds of genes, and taking place rapidly, in less than one thousand generations, thus below paleontology's threshold of resolution. Curiously enough, Gould does not seem concerned to preserve the union of chance mutations and selection. The saltationists run afoul of two types of criticism. On the one hand, the functionality of their supposed macromutations is inexplicable within the framework of molecular biology. On the other hand, Gould ignores in silence the great trends in biology, such as the increasing complexity of the nervous system. He imagines that the success of new, more sophisticated species, such as the mammals, is a contingent phenomenon. He is not in a position to offer an account of the essential movement of evolution, or at the least an account of its main trajectories. The saltationists are thus reduced to invoking two types of miracles: macromutations as well as the great trajectories of evolution.

Q: In what sense are you employing the word "miracle"?

S: A miracle is an event that should appear impossible to a Darwinian in view of its ultra-cosmological improbability within the framework of his own theory. Now, speaking of macromutations, let me observe that to generate a proper elephant, it will not suffice suddenly to endow it with a full-grown trunk. As the trunk is being organized, a different but complementary system—the cerebellum—must be modified in order to establish a place for the ensemble of wiring that the elephant will require in order to use the trunk. These macromutations must be coordinated by a system of genes in embryogenesis. If one considers the history of evolution, we must postulate thousands of miracles; miracles, in fact, without end. No more than the gradualists, the saltationists are unable to provide an account of those miracles. The second category of miracles are directional, offering instruction to the great evolutionary progressions and trends—the elaboration of the nervous system, of course, but the internalization of the reproductive process as well, and the appearance of bone, the emergence of ears, the enrichment of various functional relationships, and so on. Each is a series of miracles, whose accumulation has the effect of increasing the complexity and efficiency of various organisms. From this point of view, the notion of *bricolage* [tinkering], introduced by François Jacob, involves a fine turn of phrase, but one concealing an utter absence of explanation.

Q: The appearance of human beings—is that a miracle, in the sense you mean?

S: Naturally. And here it does seem that there are voices among contemporary biologists—I mean voices other than mine—who might cast doubt on the Darwinian paradigm, which has so dominated discussion for the past twenty years. Gradualists and saltationists alike are completely incapable of providing a convincing explanation of the near simultaneous emergence of a number of biological systems that distinguish human beings from the higher primates: bipedalism, with the concomitant modification of not only the pelvis but also the cerebellum; a much more dexterous hand, with fingerprints conferring an especially fine tactile sense; the modifications of the pharynx, which permit phonation; and the modification of the central nervous system, notably at the level of the temporal lobes, permitting the specific recognition of speech. From the point of view of embryogenesis, such anatomical systems are completely different from one another. Each modification constitutes a gift, a bequest from a primate family to its descendants. It is astonishing that these gifts should have developed simultaneously. Some biologists speak of a predisposition of the genome. Can anyone actually recover the predisposition, supposing that it actually existed? Was it present in the first of the fish? Confronted with such questions, the Darwinian paradigm is conceptually bankrupt.

Q: You mentioned the Santa Fe school earlier in our discussion. Do appeals to such notions as chaos . . .

S: What we have here are highly competent people inventing poetic but essentially hollow forms of expression. I am referring in part to the hoopla surrounding cybernetics. And beyond that, there lie the dissipative structures of Prigogine, or the systems of Varela, or, moving to the present, Stuart Kauffman's edge of chaos—an organized form of inanity that is certain soon to make its way to France. The Santa Fe school takes complexity and applies it to absolutely everything. They draw their representative examples from certain chemical reactions, the pattern of the seacoast, atmospheric turbulence, or the structure of a chain of mountains. The complexity of these structures is certainly considerable, but in comparison with the living world, they exhibit in every case an impoverished form of organization, one that is strictly non-functional. No algorithm allows us to understand the complexity of living creatures. These examples owe their initial plausibility to the assumption that the physico-chemical world exhibits functional properties that in reality it does not possess.

Q: Should one take your position as a statement of resignation, an appeal to have greater modesty, or something else altogether?

S: Speaking ironically, I might say that all we can hear at the present time is the great anthropic hymnal, with even a number of mathematically sophisticated scholars keeping time, as the great hymn is intoned, by tapping their feet. The rest of us should, of course, practice a certain suspension of judgment.

PART TWO
Darwinism's Cultural Inroads

Nancy R. Pearcey

4. Darwin Meets the Berenstain Bears
Evolution as a Total Worldview

Controversies over how to teach evolution in the public schools keep sprouting up like hardy wildflowers defying the power of natural selection. When Ohio debated the subject in 2002, the state Department of Education received more response than to any previous issue. Why does the public care so passionately about a theory of biology? Because people sense intuitively that there's much more at stake than a scientific theory. They know that when naturalistic evolution is taught in the science classroom, then a naturalistic view of ethics will be taught down the hallway in the history classroom, the sociology classroom, the family life classroom, and in all other areas of the curriculum. As one leader in the Ohio controversy put it, "A naturalistic definition of *science* has the effect of indoctrinating students into a naturalistic *worldview*."[1]

This is why the public cares so much about evolution. Darwinism functions as the scientific basis for an overall naturalistic worldview, and it is being promoted today far beyond the bounds of science, in virtually every field of study.[2]

Birds, Bees, and Bats

Even within biology itself, evolution depends more heavily on philosophical assumptions than most scientists might care to admit. Consider these words from the well-known science-popularizer Richard Dawkins: "*Even if there were no actual evidence* in favor of the Darwinian theory . . . we should still be justified in preferring it over all rival theories."[3] Why? Because it is naturalistic.

Stating the same idea from the opposite direction, a Kansas State University professor published a letter in the prestigious journal *Nature* that said: "*Even if all the data point to an intelligent designer*, such an hypothesis is excluded from science because it is not naturalistic."[4] The case thus appears to be closed from the outset: No matter where the evidence points, science is permitted to consider only naturalistic theories.

What this means is that science itself has been redefined in terms of naturalistic philosophy—in which case, something very much like Darwinism *has* to be true. After all, if nature is all that exists, then some purely naturalistic process must have generated life in all its diversity. "Anyone who believes [in materialism] must, as a matter of logical necessity, also believe in evolution," explains Tom Bethell:

> No digging for fossils, no test tubes or microscopes, no further experiments are needed. For birds, bats, and bees do exist. They came into existence somehow. Your consistent materialist has no choice but to allow that, yes, molecules in motion succeeded, over the eons, in whirling themselves into ever more complex conglomerations, some of them called bats, some birds, some bees. He 'knows' that is true, not because he sees it in the genes, or in the lab, or in the fossils, but because it is embedded in his philosophy.[5]

UNIVERSAL DARWINISM

Unless we grasp the crucial role played by philosophical assumptions, we will not engage the origins debate effectively. The influential cultural analyst Francis Schaeffer once wrote that the central reason religious believers have not been more effective in addressing modern culture is that they tend to see things in "bits and pieces." They worry about individual moral controversies, like family breakdown, decadent entertainment, abortion and the life issues, and so on. But they don't see the big picture that connects all the dots.

And what *is* that big picture? All these forms of cultural dissolution, Schaeffer writes, have "come about due to a shift in worldview . . . to a worldview based on the idea that the final reality is impersonal matter or energy shaped into its current form by impersonal chance."[6] In other words, long before there was an Intelligent Design movement, he understood that everything hangs on your view of origins. If you start with impersonal forces operating by chance (in other words, naturalistic evolution), then over time you will end up with naturalism in moral, social, and political philosophy.

Many evolutionists today would agree with Schaeffer. In fact, one of the fastest-growing disciplines today is the application of evolution to social issues, under the rubric of evolutionary psychology (an updated version of sociobiology). The argument is that if Darwinism is true in biology, then it must also explain every aspect of human behavior. Some even say we're entering an age of "Universal Darwinism," when it will be expanded into an overarching, all-encompassing worldview.

Already evolutionary psychology has become remarkably wide-ranging, as a quick survey of recent books will show. One of the topics tackled most frequently is morality. After all, if human behavior is ultimately programmed by "selfish genes" (as Richards Dawkins argues in *The Selfish Gene*), then it is enormously difficult to explain the origin of unselfish or altruistic behavior. Thus books keep appearing with titles like *The Moral Animal* and *Evolutionary Origins of Morality*, arguing that morality is not based on divine revelation; it is a product of natural selection. We learn to be kind and helpful only because it helps us survive and produce more offspring. "The basis of ethics does not lie in God's will," writes E. O. Wilson, the founder of sociobiology; ethics is "an illusion fobbed off on us by our genes to get us to cooperate."[7]

Religion is another favorite target, and recent books include *In Gods We Trust* and *Religion Explained: the Evolutionary Origins of Religious Thought*. The basic theme is that religion is merely an idea that appears in the human mind when the nervous system has evolved to a certain level of complexity. That is, a brain complex enough to imagine hidden predators, like saber-toothed tigers hiding in the bushes, may also malfunction by imagining unseen agents that are *not* real, like gods and spirits.[8]

For politicians, there's a book titled *Darwinian Politics: The Evolutionary Origin of Freedom*. For economists, there's *Economics as an Evolutionary Science*. For educators, there's *Origins of Genius: Darwinian Perspectives on Creativity*, which defines intelligence as a Darwinian process of generating a variety of ideas and then selecting those that are "fittest." In medicine, a slew of new books have appeared, with titles such as *Evolutionary Medicine*, and *Why We Get Sick: The New Science of Darwinian Medicine*.[9]

Evolution even offers insights for businessmen: *Executive Instinct: Managing the Human Animal in the Information Age*. The book asks, "How do we manage people whose brains were hardwired in the Stone Age?" For women, there's *Divided Labours: An Evolutionary View of Women at Work*. If you're a parent, there's *The Truth about Cinderella: A Darwinian view of Parental Love*.[10]

Of course, to really sell books you have to talk about the racier topics, and so there are titles such as *Evolution of Desire: Strategies of Human Mating,* and *Ever Since Adam and Eve: The Evolution of Human Sexuality,* and finally, *The Dangerous Passion: Why Jealousy Is as Necessary as Love and Sex.*[11] It seems science is descending to the level of soap opera.

DARWINIAN FUNDAMENTALISM

Despite the number of books being churned out on evolutionary psychology, some scientists remain skeptical. It's remarkably easy to come up with stories about how some form of behavior *might* be adaptive in some circumstances, then jump to saying it *was* adaptive—even if there is no actual evidence for the process. In other words, most of the scenarios offered are little more than "just-so" stories. The late Stephen J. Gould of Harvard denounced evolutionary psychology as "Darwinian fundamentalism"—a phrase suggesting that Darwinism itself has become a rigid orthodoxy.[12] "The ugly fact," says evolutionary geneticist H. Allen Orr, "is that we haven't a shred of evidence that morality did or did not evolve by natural selection."[13]

What we have to realize, however, is that once the evolutionary premise has been accepted, the evidence is all but irrelevant. Applying Darwinian explanations to human behavior becomes a matter of simple logic. After all, if evolution is true, then how else did the mind emerge, if *not* by evolution? How else did human behavior arise, if *not* through adaptation to the environment?

The force of sheer logic became clear a few years ago, when a book came out called *The Natural History of Rape.* The authors made the disturbing claim that rape is not a pathology, biologically speaking, but is an evolutionary adaptation for maximizing reproductive success. In other words, if candy and flowers don't do the trick, some men may resort to coercion to fulfill the reproductive imperative. The book calls rape "a natural, biological phenomenon that is a product of the human evolutionary heritage," akin to "the leopard's spots and the giraffe's elongated neck."[14]

The book aroused considerable public controversy, which the authors say took them by surprise. After all, it is simple logic that any behavior that survives today *must* have conferred some evolutionary advantage—otherwise it would have been weeded out by natural selection. One of the authors, Randy Thornhill of the University of New Mexico, appeared on National Public Radio, where he found himself on the receiving end of an avalanche of angry calls. Finally he said, in essence, that the logic is inescapable: for if evolution is true, then it must also be true, that "every feature of every living thing, including human beings, has an underlying evolutionary background. That's not a debatable matter."

In other words, *evolution* and *evolutionary psychology* are a package deal: If you accept the premise, you must accept the conclusion.

This explains why most criticisms of evolutionary psychology have proven ineffective: typically they focus on facts and numbers without questioning the underlying evolutionary assumption. For example, critics of the rape thesis argued that, statistically, rapists often attack women too old or too young to reproduce (or even men, e.g., prison rape). These facts clearly undercut the theory that rape is motivated by any kind of reproductive imperative.[15] Yet for the most part, these critics agreed with the underlying assumption that human behavior is ultimately a product of natural selection—which meant they had to grant the basic premise. The only area of actual disagreement was over the details. As Bethell put it elegantly, "The critics were disarmed by their shared worldview."[16]

This explains why evolutionary psychology continues to grow and gain new converts. In fact, the rape thesis itself has reappeared in a recent book by Steven Pinker of MIT, titled *The Blank Slate: The Modern Denial of Human Nature* (Viking, 2002). Pinker writes that rape is likely an adaptive strategy pursued by low-status males who are "alienated from a community" and "unable to win the consent of women." And since it is adaptive in these circumstances, a gene that predisposes such males to rape will spread.[17]

TELLING DARWINIAN STORIES

You might think that evolutionary accounts of behavior would kick in only *after* there is evidence that the behavior in question is actually inherited. Evolutionary theories might then be invoked to explain how and why it came to be inherited. But what happens is a curious inversion, where stories are spun out to explain why the behavior is adaptive, even in cases where there's no independent evidence that it is genetically based.

Consider another example. A few years ago, Pinker published an article in the *New York Times* applying evolutionary psychology to the topic of infanticide. This was shortly after the news media had reported the story of the "Prom Mom," a teenage girl who gave birth to a baby at a school dance and dumped the newborn in the trash. Around the same time, an unmarried teen couple killed their newborn as well. The public was shocked, and so Pinker reassured them that infanticide has been practiced in most cultures throughout history. Its sheer ubiquity suggests that it *must* have been preserved by natural selection—which in turn means it *must* have some adaptive function. "The emotional circuitry of mothers has evolved" to commit infanticide in situations where it is advantageous, Pinker wrote. "A capacity for neonaticide is built into the biological design of our parental emotions."[18]

There are several problems with this scenario, beginning with the fact that there is no evidence that neonaticide is a genetic trait to begin with, let alone one selected by evolution. "Where are the twin studies, chromosome locations, and DNA sequences supporting such a claim?" Orr demands. "The answer is we don't have any. What we do have is a story—there's an undeniable Darwinian logic underlying the murder of newborns in certain circumstances." It is this "Darwinian logic" that drives the theory, Orr says, not any set of facts: "And so the inversion occurs: the evolutionary story rings true; but evolution requires genes; therefore, it's genetic. This move is so easy and so seductive that evolutionary psychologists sometimes forget a hard truth: a Darwinian story is not Mendelian evidence. A Darwinian story is a story."[19]

The "Darwinian logic" is so compelling that Darwin himself was taken in by it. In *The Descent of Man* he argued that the "murder of infants has prevailed on the largest scale throughout the world, and has met with no reproach." Indeed, "infanticide, especially of females, has been thought to be good for the tribe."[20] More than a century ago, Darwin understood where the logic of his theory led.

Yet evolutionary psychology proves to be so elastic that it can explain just about anything. On one hand, evolution is said to account for mothers who kill their newborn babies. But, of course, if you were to ask why most mothers do *not* kill their babies, why, evolution accounts for that too. A theory that explains any phenomenon and its opposite, too, in reality explains nothing. It is so flexible that it can be twisted to say whatever proponents want it to say.

PETER SINGER'S PET PROJECT

Other examples abound. Not long ago, a Princeton University professor published an article defending, of all things, bestiality. Peter Singer was already notorious for favoring rights for animals and euthanasia for people. The article was called "Heavy Petting," and in it Singer makes it clear that his real target is the Judeo-Christian system of morality.

In the West, he writes, we have a "Judeo-Christian tradition" claiming that "humans alone are made in the image of God." Indeed, "in Genesis, God gives humans dominion over the animals." But evolution has thoroughly refuted the biblical account, Singer insists: Evolution teaches that "We are animals"—and the result is that "sex across the species barrier . . . ceases to be an offence to our status and dignity as human beings."[21]

These ideas do not stay neatly contained in academia, but trickle down into popular culture. A few years ago a song went to the top of the charts by a group called the Bloodhound Gang, which had a catchy refrain: "You and me baby ain't nothin' but mammals, so let's do it like they do on the Discovery Channel." The video featured band members dressed up as monkeys, simulating sex acts. Back in the 1940s Alfred Kinsey, himself a committed Darwinist, insisted that the only basis for moral norms is what other mammals do—whatever fits "the normal mammalian picture."[22] What Kinsey said half a century ago is now being recast in songs for teenagers.

In fact, Darwinian naturalism is being targeted to even younger children. A few years ago, I picked up a book for my little boy called *The Berenstain Bears' Nature Guide*. In it, the Bear family invites the reader on a nature walk, and after a few pages, we open to a two-page spread, glazed with the light of the rising sun, proclaiming in capital letters: "Nature . . . is all that IS, or WAS, or EVER WILL BE!"[23]

That line should be familiar to most Americans. It is an echo of Carl Sagan's PBS program *Cosmos* and his trademark phrase: "The Cosmos is all that is or ever was or ever will be." Those who attend a liturgical church may recognize that Sagan was mimicking the *Gloria Patri* (". . . As it was in the beginning, is now, and ever will be"). Now the authors of the Berenstain Bears are repackaging Sagan's naturalistic religion for small children.[24] The point is that when naturalistic evolution appears even in books for young children, then we can be sure that it has permeated the entire culture.

WHEN DARWINISTS "CHEAT"

In the past, social scientists sought to limit the implications of evolution by erecting a wall between biology and culture. Evolution creates the human body, they argued, but after that culture takes over. The claim that culture is autonomous was a common defense against biological determinism. But today that wall is crumbling. Scientists have begun to recognize that they can no longer impose an arbitrary limit on the "Darwinian logic." Proponents of evolutionary psychology are relentlessly applying evolution across the board to religion, morality, politics, and every other form of human behavior.

Yet so far, the main effect of evolutionary psychology seems to consist in debunking traditional moral and religious teachings—explaining, and in some sense justifying, things like rape, infanticide, and bestiality. If this is the only moral guide we can glean from nature, it's not a very attractive one. "Natural selection is, I agree, politically and morally unattractive," writes science writer Mark Ridley. "Natural selection contains a selfish, competitive element" that has inspired some nasty political theories, including, historically speaking, the Social Darwinism of the eugenics movement, the robber barons of early capitalism, and Hitler's Third Reich.[25]

At times, proponents seem to sense that the theory will not fly very well with the public unless it can come up with a more positive message. This explains why books and articles have begun to appear assuring us that, in the end, evolutionary psychology provides a basis for traditional ethical standards like altruism or two-parent families or some other Western moral ideal. Yet, since Darwinism does not actually provide an adequate basis for these values, the end result is a patch-up job, with the two elements stuck together incongruously.

A recent example is Daniel Dennett's new book, *Freedom Evolves*, which seeks to reconcile Darwinism with a belief in human freedom.[26] Though Dennett makes an impressive effort, says philosopher John Gray in a recent review, "the notion that humans are free in a way that other animals are not does not come from science. Its origins are in religion—above all, in Christianity." Thus, "despite all his impassioned protestations to the contrary, Dennett is seeking to salvage a view of humankind derived from Western religion." In other words, he is simply borrowing from the Christian heritage, without having an independent basis to support it. "The obsession with reconciling scientific determinism with freedom is characteristic of cultures that have shed Christianity but wish to retain the belief in the special standing of humans that Christianity once assured," Gray goes on.[27] In other words, evolutionary psychologists like Dennett are trying to uproot what they find attractive from the Christian worldview and transplant it into the alien soil of a Darwinian worldview.

We might say these Darwinists are "cheating" by borrowing from the Christian heritage in order to avoid facing squarely the bankruptcy of their own belief system. This is far more common than one might think. In another article, Gray says the whole of Western liberalism is actually parasitic on Christianity. Liberals' high view of the human person, he says, is derived directly from Christianity: "Liberal humanism inherits several key Christian beliefs—above all, the belief that humans are categorically different from all other animals." No other religion has given rise to the conviction that humans have a unique dignity.

Think of it this way: If Darwin had announced his theory of evolution in India, China, or Japan, it would hardly have made a stir, Gray says. "If—along with hundreds of millions of Hindus and Buddhists—you have never believed that humans differ from everything else in the natural world in having an immortal soul, you will find it hard to get worked up by a theory that shows how much we have in common with other animals." Thus liberal humanism borrows its high view of human dignity and human rights directly from Christianity. "The secular worldview is simply the Christian take on the world with God left out," Gray writes. "Humanism is not an alternative to religious belief, but rather a degenerate and unwitting version of it."[28]

A Virus of the Mind?

Not only is evolutionary psychology an incoherent patchwork, it is also ultimately self-refuting. Consider: If ideas are products of evolution, then that includes the idea of evolutionary psychology. Like all other ideas, it is not true but only useful for survival. Proponents of the theory are eager to use it to debunk traditional theism, but fail to see that it debunks itself.

Dennett's trademark metaphor is that Darwinism is a "universal acid," that "eats through just about every traditional concept" of religion or morality or social order.[29] And yet, it is the height of wishful thinking for Dennett to presume that the acid will dissolve only *other* people's views and not his own. As philosopher Mary Midgely writes, "This is, however, evidently a selective acid, trained to eat only other people's views while leaving Dennett's own ambitious project untouched."[30] When ideas are reduced to survival strategies, thus ruling out the very possibility of objective truth, then the idea of Darwinian evolution itself can hardly be regarded as objectively true.

This becomes even clearer if we consider one of the favorite concepts employed by evolutionary psychologists—the idea of "memes," proposed as a kind of mental analogue to genes. Just as genes are the carriers of physical traits, so memes are hypothetical units of culture that are said to be carriers of ideas. Some evolutionary psychologists speak of them almost as parasites that can "infect" people's minds, just as biological parasites infect their bodies—though instead of producing physical illness, they produce patterns of thought and behavior. Memes are entirely mythical entities, yet the idea has caught on and become widespread. You might even say the meme has multiplied rapidly. By analogy with genetics, the concept of "memetics" gives the illusion of providing a scientific way of explaining culture.[31]

Not surprisingly, evolutionary psychologists' favorite example of a meme is religion, and Richard Dawkins has even suggested that religion is nothing but a computer virus that infects the brain.[32] But of course, sauce for the goose is sauce for the gander, and we might reasonably ask how memetics applies to Dawkins's own convictions. His attachment to Darwinian evolution must likewise result from infection by a mental virus. As Midgely argues, accept the idea of memes, and you must conclude that the only reason Dawkins and others "campaign so ardently for neo-Darwinism must be that a neo-Darwinist meme . . . has infested their brains, forcing them to act in this way." After all, "if you propose the method seriously you must apply it consistently"—not only to other systems of thought but also to your own.[33] Thus evolutionary psychology undercuts itself.

HOW EVOLUTION CHANGED AMERICA

One beneficial effect of the rise of evolutionary psychology has been to make it unavoidably clear that the debate over Darwinism is not only over scientific facts but also over conflicting worldviews. "The Darwinian revolution was not merely the replacement of one scientific theory by another," the great zoologist Ernst Mayr once said, "but rather the replacement of a worldview, in which the supernatural was accepted as a normal and relevant explanatory principle, by a new worldview in which there was no room for supernatural forces."[34] This shift in worldview is actually much more significant than any particular scientific theories, for it has been taken as normative far beyond the bounds of science, thus reshaping American thought and social institutions.

As historian Neal Gillespie explains, the Darwinian revolution did not center on its mechanism of natural selection but on its definition of knowledge—its epistemology. The older epistemology assumed an open universe, in which concepts like design, purpose, and teleology made sense and were considered perfectly rational. But Darwin wanted to establish a positivistic epistemology, which assumed a closed system of cause and effect, ruling out the very concept of design and purpose. "Darwin's rejection of special creation was part of the transformation of biology into a positive science, one committed to thoroughly naturalistic explanations based on material causes and the uniformity of nature," explains Gillespie. And not only in biology, but in every other field as well.[35]

When Darwin's theory was accepted in biology, says historian Edward Purcell, its broader implication was understood to be a new theory of knowledge generally. People working in fields outside of science—the social sciences, law, and politics—came to see that Darwinism implied "a wholly naturalistic and empirically oriented world view." In this worldview, theological dogmas became "at worst totally fraudulent and at best merely symbolic of deep human aspirations." In other words, religion was demoted to either outright lies or merely symbols for human ideals.[36]

HOW DID THESE IDEAS AFFECT AMERICAN THOUGHT?

When Darwinism first arrived on American shores in the late nineteenth century, it was welcomed by a group of thinkers who founded an entire school of philosophy based on it called philosophical pragmatism. Key figures included John Dewey, William James, Charles Peirce, and Oliver Wendell Holmes Jr. The core of their thought was that if life has evolved, then the human mind has evolved as well—in which case, all the human sciences have to be rebuilt on the basis of evolution: philosophy, law, education, and theology. Let's look briefly at each of these in turn.

Philosophy: Does It Work?

The pragmatists began by asking: What does Darwinian naturalism mean for the way we understand the human mind? They answered: It means the mind is nothing more than a part of nature. As a result, it is incapable of reaching *beyond* nature to know a transcendent Truth or moral order; instead the mental world is a product of natural selection just as the physical world is. Concepts and ideas are nothing but chance variations that arise in the human brain, akin to Darwin's chance variations in biology. The ideas that survive to become beliefs and convictions are those that help us adapt to the environment. They are merely mental survival strategies, no different from the lion's teeth or the eagle's claws. William James held that even our knowledge of mathematical truths, such as $2 + 2 = 4$, arose as a variation in the minds of our ancestors, and was then selected for its usefulness in the struggle for existence and passed on as a heritable variation.[37]

John Dewey penned a famous essay called "The Influence of Darwin on Philosophy," where he announced that Darwinism had given rise to a "new logic to apply to mind and morals and life."[38] In this new evolutionary logic, ideas are not judged by a transcendent standard of divine Truth but only by their success in getting us what we want.

The new logic applies to every field, including religion. According to James, any system of thought is "true" insofar as it meets certain needs. Presented with a complex world, he wrote, humans naturally wonder what its ultimate nature is. "Science says molecules. Religion says God." How do we decide which is true? Well, on one hand, James said, "science can do certain things for us." (That is, scientific reasoning enables us to "deduce and explain" events). But on the other hand, "God can do other things" for us. (Religion can "inspire and console" us.) The question each person must ask is: "*Which things* are worth the most?"[39] Whatever you decide, that's your truth. Or, as James liked to say, truth is the "cash value" of an idea: If it "pays" off, then we call it true.

Now, James thought this was a good argument in favor of maintaining religious beliefs. In his view, religion makes a difference for the better, providing people with a fuller, more integrated life. It never occurred to him that his way of justifying religious beliefs might be used by someone else for opposite purposes—as a way of condemning religion. But that's exactly what Dewey did. He argued that naturalistic beliefs function more successfully than religious beliefs as integrative factors in human life. In short, naturalism works better.[40]

Theology: God Evolving in the World

In theology, the pragmatists asked: What kind of God is compatible with evolution? And they answered (at least those who retained any notion of the divine at all) that the only conception of God consonant with evolution is an immanent one—a finite deity evolving in and with the world.

James urged the notion of a finite God (or gods) as a solution to the problem of evil: Since God is neither omniscient (He does not know in advance what is going to happen) nor omnipotent (He does not have the power to prevent evil from happening), He is thereby absolved from any responsibility for evil. God struggles to overcome evil the best He can, just as humans do. By the end of his life, James viewed God as a cosmic consciousness, weaving all individual consciousness into a grand unity.[41]

Another of the pragmatists, Charles Peirce, embraced a kind of panpsychism (everything in the universe has at least a rudimentary mind or consciousness), and envisioned the entire cosmos evolving toward God or Mind or the Absolute in a teleological process he called "evolutionary love."[42]

These ideas, in turn, influenced Charles Hartshorne, the founder of Process Theology, which some say is the fastest-growing movement in mainline seminaries today.[43] It teaches that God is a divine spirit evolving in and with the world—the soul of the world, the evolving cosmic life of which our lives are a part. This is not, strictly speaking, *pantheism*, where God equals the universe ("All is God"). It is *panentheism* ("All in God"). Process Theology breaks sharply with traditional theism by holding that God is limited: God is neither omniscient nor omnipotent, but is a finite being who evolves together with the world through history.

Surprisingly, some of these themes have spilled over into evangelical circles as well, in what is known as Open Theism, which proposes that God cannot know or determine the future. The term itself is borrowed from the pragmatists, who emphasized that an evolving universe is an "open" universe—a world of novelty, innovation, emergence, and unpredictable possibilities, which cannot be known in advance, even by God.[44] Clearly, one reason for challenging evolutionary *science* is so that churches and seminaries will not feel constrained to accept evolutionary *theology*.

Law: When Judges Make Law

Oliver Wendell Holmes applied pragmatism to legal philosophy, calling it legal pragmatism.[45] Sprinkling Social Darwinist concepts throughout his writings, he spoke of the law as merely a product of the "survival of the fittest" among competing interest groups.[46] If Darwin is right, he said, then there is no transcendent principle of justice we can appeal to. Instead, laws are merely the product of evolving historical custom— they are completely relative to particular times and cultures, and are constantly changing.

Once we grasp this, Holmes said, judges will be liberated from the past, and free to *change* the law to reflect whatever social policy they think works best (there's the pragmatism). "History sets us free and enables us to make up our minds dispassionately" whether the old legal rules still serve any purpose.[47] And the way to make that determination is by consulting the findings of social science. Thus law is reduced to a tool for social engineering. The justification for law, Homes said, is "not that it represents an eternal principle" like justice, but "that it helps bring about a social end which we desire." Of course, in practice this means a social end that the *judge* desires. Holmes unabashedly agreed that judges do not merely interpret the law but make law.

Where are these ideas evident in our own day? Where do we see judges not just interpreting the law but making law, enacting their own social policies? The most significant example is the *Roe v. Wade* abortion decision. Even supporters agree that the court essentially legislated from the bench. In the majority opinion, Justice Harry Blackmun wrote that abortion has to be considered in relation to "population growth, pollution, poverty, and racial" issues. In other words, the justices made their decision not by what the *law* said but by the social outcomes they favored. This is the heritage of legal pragmatism. And it will shape the way the courts deal with a host of new bioethical issues on the legal horizon, unless the underlying Darwinian worldview is effectively challenged.

Education: "Liberating" Students from Ethics

John Dewey did more to shape educational philosophy than anyone else in the twentieth century, and is often called "father" of American education. He recast intellectual inquiry as a form of mental evolution and said it should proceed in the same way as biological evolution: by posing problems and then letting students construct their own answers based on what works best—a kind of mental adaptation to the environment. (In Dewey's words, evolutionary naturalism proves that "every distinct organ, structure, or formation" serves as "an instrument of adjustment or adaptation to a particular environing situation.")[48] Translated into educational theory, Dewey's method is sometimes called the inquiry method of teaching—where teachers are not instructors but "facilitators," guiding students as they try out various pragmatic strategies to discover what works for them.[49]

Moreover, Dewey said, since the world is evolving, ethical knowledge is constantly changing. In *The Study of Ethics: A Syllabus*, he wrote that "chastity, kindness, honesty, patriotism, modesty, toleration, bravery, etc., cannot be given a fixed meaning, because each expresses an interest in objects and institutions which are changing."[50] The task of schools, therefore, is not to pass on an enduring heritage, but to prepare students to manage novelty and change. For Dewey, that meant equipping each new generation with a method of inquiry for constructing new truths for their times.

How do we go about constructing moral knowledge? In his general theory of knowledge, Dewey had analyzed the process of inquiry into a series of steps—identifying the problem, proposing various hypothetical solutions, testing each one, and so on, until we finally accept the hypothesis that works best. Applied to moral education, this led to various methods that outline a series of steps for students to use in clarifying their own values. Sidney Simon's method of "values clarification," with its seven-step process, is the best known, but it has been followed by others that represent variations on the same theme. Despite important differences, what ties these methods together is the idea that any value is to be regarded as valid, as long as the student has gone through the prescribed series of steps. Teachers are rigorously instructed not to question the conclusions that students reach.

Step number one consists in identifying what the student already likes or values. Since naturalistic theories of ethics acknowledge no transcendent or absolute standard, the only standard available is what the individual in fact values. This may sound easy enough, but in reality, Dewey argued, identifying our authentic values may prove difficult, for our experience is often distorted by moral dogmas telling us what we *ought* to want or value. Thus it is imperative to begin by disentangling our desires from all pre-existing moral dogmas, in order to clarify what we genuinely want.

This explains why many programs of moral education present students with sometimes shocking moral dilemmas designed to jolt them out of their pre-existing moral frameworks (which in practice tend to be those taught by their parents and pastors). The classic example is the Lifeboat dilemma, where students are required to judge the relative value of various individuals, in order to decide which one shall be thrown out to drown. The goal is to present situations that cannot easily be interpreted in light of the adult morality students have been taught—which, according to the theory, prevents them from being in touch with their own genuine, authentic values.

As a result, according to critics, the main effect of the inquiry approach to values teaching is to "liberate" students from the moral standards they bring into the classroom from home and church. Moreover, the method offers students no alternative standard, leaving them with nothing higher than their own subjective likes and dislikes—or worse, the pressures of the peer group. One education professor, Thomas Lickona, relates the story of a teacher who used the values clarification strategy with a class of low-achieving eighth-graders. Having worked through the requisite steps, the students concluded that their four most popular activities were "sex, drugs, drinking, and skipping school." The teacher was hamstrung: Her students had clarified their values, and the method gave her no leverage for persuading them that these values were unhealthy, destructive, or morally wrong.[51] Thus the main legacy of pragmatism in moral education is that teachers no longer impart to students the great moral ideals that have inspired virtually all civilizations, but instead train them to probe their own subjective feelings and values.

Constructivism: Constructing Our Own Reality

Today the same method is being applied to other subject areas as well. One of the most popular trends in educational theory is called constructivist education. Its premise is that if knowledge is a social construction, as Dewey said, then the goal of education should be to teach students how to construct their own knowledge. As one proponent explains, "Constructivism does not assume the presence of an outside objective reality that is revealed to the learner, but rather that learners actively *construct their own reality.*"[52]

This sounds like a tall order: Before kids are big enough to cross the street by themselves, they're supposed to learn how to "construct their own reality"? Nor are teachers to indicate whether students' ideas are right or wrong, says another proponent; they are merely to encourage students "to clarify and articulate their own understandings."[53] This explains why we have classes where children are taught to construct their own spelling systems, their own punctuation rules, their own math procedures, and so on. In one state, the history standards say that by high school, students "should have a strong sense of how to *reconstruct history*"[54]—certainly an Orwellian phrase.

New educational methodologies are often taught to teachers as the latest teaching techniques, as though they were the result of empirical studies on effectiveness in the classroom. But they are nothing of the kind. Most are a direct application of a philosophy, and constructivism is no exception: It is a direct application of Dewey's evolutionary epistemology. As one prominent theorist writes: "To the biologist, a living organism is viable as long as it manages to survive in its environment. To the constructivist, concepts, models, theories, and so on are viable if they prove adequate in the contexts in which they were created."[55] In other words, constructivism is based on the assumption that we are merely organisms adapting to the environment, and thus the only test of an idea is whether it works.

Reconstructionism: Politicizing the Classroom

Another educational trend that emerged from philosophical pragmatism was reconstructionism. Its roots go back to the 1930s, when the influential educator George S. Counts published *Dare the Schools Build a New Social Order?* Some scientists had begun saying that with the rise of human intelligence, it was now possible to take charge of the course of evolution itself. Thus Counts called on teachers to begin "controlling the evolution of society." He urged them to stop being merely transmitters of the culture and to become "creator[s] of social values." In his view, educators should deliberately reach for power and become change agents, raising students' consciousness about social problems and encouraging them to come up with alternative ways of ordering society.[56] In other words, education should become politicized, helping to direct the future course of evolution.

In our own day, Counts's vision is certainly being fulfilled, probably beyond his dreams. Increasingly, classroom time is taken away from the classics of western culture and devoted to politically correct causes, based on a philosophy of multiculturalism that reduces all ideas to interests based on race, class, or gender. Most educators no longer even define pedagogy in terms of fostering the search for truth and transmitting a valued heritage, says Frederic Sommers of Brandeis University. Instead they regard education as a means to "empower students by alerting them to the need for struggle against patriarchy, racism, and classism."[57] The classroom is no longer an arena where students can learn to weigh conflicting ideas dispassionately, but a place where students are indoctrinated in political radicalism and enlisted in the culture wars.

Postmodernism: "Keeping Faith" with Darwin

If this is starting to sound like postmodernism in the classroom, that's exactly what it is. One of the most influential philosophers in America today is the postmodernist Richard Rorty, who calls himself a *neo*-pragmatist. He argues that the logic of pragmatism leads to a form of postmodernism akin to the thought of Derrida, Heidegger, and Foucault.

At the heart of neo-pragmatism, Rorty says, is the conviction that "truth is made, not found." In other words, truth is a human construction—not something "out there," objective, waiting to be discovered. Our beliefs are nothing more than human inventions, like the gadgets of modern technology. And they function the same way as commodities in the marketplace—we accept ideas when they "pay off," when we find them "profitable."[58] Rorty is echoing James's phrase about the "cash value" of an idea.

If postmodernism involves an update of pragmatism, then it is likewise rooted ultimately in Darwinism. In an autobiographical essay, Rorty reveals that as a young man he was attracted to Christianity. But finding himself "incapable" of "the humility that Christianity demanded," he says, he turned away from God and determined to work out a philosophy that would be consistent with Darwinism. That philosophy was postmodernism.[59] In a *New Republic* article, Rorty wrote that "Keeping faith with Darwin" (a telling phrase) means understanding that the human species is not oriented "toward Truth" but only "toward its own increased prosperity" and survival.[60]

Yet if "keeping faith with Darwin" means we have to deny the possibility of finding "Truth," then Darwinism undercuts itself. For if ideas are not true but only useful for survival, then Darwinism itself is not true either. Darwin recognized the problem and was troubled about it, calling it his "horrid doubt." He wrote: "With me, the horrid doubt always arises whether the convictions of man's mind, which has been developed from the mind of the lower animals, are of any value or at all trustworthy." But of course, Darwin's own theory was itself a "conviction of man's mind," so he was cutting off the branch he himself was sitting on. In short, Darwinian naturalism is self-refuting.[61]

This argument has been spelled out in greater detail by philosopher Alvin Plantinga: "What evolution guarantees is (at most) that we *behave* in certain ways—in such ways as to promote survival." But "it does not guarantee mostly true or verisimilitudinous beliefs." In other words, natural selection preserves behavior that promotes survival; whether that behavior is based on true beliefs is irrelevant.[62] This is the fatal weakness of any form of evolutionary epistemology, whether in the work of the pragmatists at the dawn of the twentieth century or in the latest books on evolutionary psychology.

The Cognitive War

It has become a commonplace to say that America is embroiled in a "culture war" over conflicting values. But we must remember that values are always derivative—they stem from an underlying worldview. Thus the *values war* reflects an underlying *cognitive war* over origins. Francis Schaeffer was right: The big picture that draws everything together is one's view of origins. In order to identify the direction in which American culture is developing, we need to learn how to connect the dots back to the beginning. Whether one begins with blind material forces, or with a personal, intelligent Agent, everything else flows from that crucial starting point.

A common tactic for sidestepping the cognitive war is to keep science completely separate from religion and ethics. For example, the late Harvard paleontologist Stephen Jay Gould, a trenchant critic of any and all notions of divine creation, nevertheless sought to reassure the public that he was ready to grant science and religion equal respect—as long as they remained in their places. "These two great tools of human understanding," he wrote, operate in "complementary not contrary fashion in their totally separate realms." Does this separation of realms provide a genuine resolution of the cognitive conflict? It all depends on where you draw the line. It turns out that in Gould's division of labor, science deals with objective truths, whereas religion deals only with subjective values. As he puts it, science involves inquiry about the "factual character of the natural world" while religion is about the "utterly different realm of human purposes, meanings, and values."[63]

To decode this terminology, we have to bear in mind that when sociologists talk about *fact* versus *value*, they are opposing rational, objective, public knowledge (the fact realm) over against irrational, subjective, private emotion (the value realm). As Allan Bloom writes, "Every school child knows that values are relative" and are not to be mistaken for objective truth.[64] In other words, Gould has drawn the line in a way that accords naturalistic science a monopoly on truth, while reducing religion to subjective hopes and wishes, or at best group prejudices.

Phillip Johnson diagnoses the strategy neatly: "Whenever the 'separate realms' logic surfaces," he writes, "you can be sure that the wording implies that there is a ruling realm (founded on reality) and a subordinate realm (founded on illusions which must be retained for the time being)."[65] Retained, that is, merely for the sake of public relations. The scientific elites know they must not press the anti-religious implications of scientific naturalism too explicitly, lest the natives grow restless and rebel. But by employing the fact/value distinction, they can reassure the public of their great respect for religion, while at the same time reducing it to noncognitive, subjective experience that need not be taken seriously in the public arena.

To quote Johnson again: The fact/value split "allows the metaphysical naturalists to mollify the potentially troublesome religious people by assuring them that science does not rule out 'religious belief' (so long as it does not pretend to be knowledge)."[66] And since religion does not actually offer cognitive explanations of events, then naturalistic explanations can be expanded at will. This explains why today Darwinian naturalism is being applied to virtually every area of human thought and behavior—including religion itself.

RECOVERING A PLACE AT THE TABLE

Surprisingly, there are Christians who do not perceive the dangers of the fact/value split, and have actually embraced it. A fifteen-year-old Christian high school student told a Delaware newspaper that taking a class on evolution had no bearing on her religious beliefs. "Religion is what you believe because of faith," the student said. "With science, you need evidence and need to back it up."[67] The implication, of course, is that faith is completely independent of evidence and reason.

Similarly, on the web site for the PBS "Evolution" series, two young people identified only as science students attending a conservative Christian college are quoted as saying: "Science deals with the material world of genes and cells, religion with the spiritual world of value and meaning."[68] Notice how the students have separated science and religion into hermetically sealed compartments. This is not even accurate: Like all religions, Christianity does make claims about the nature of the material cosmos, the character of human nature, and events in history such as the Resurrection. Yet these Christian students flatly denied that their faith had any cognitive content, reducing it to subjective questions of "value and meaning." When Christians themselves are willing to reduce their religion to noncognitive categories, unconnected to questions of truth or evidence, then they have already lost the battle.

This is why the debate over Darwin and Intelligent Design is so important. By uncovering evidence that natural phenomena are best accounted for by Intelligence, Mind, and Purpose, the theory of Intelligent Design reconnects religion to the realm of public knowledge. It takes Christianity out of the sphere of noncognitive *value* and restores it to the realm of objective *fact*, so it can once more take a place at the table of public discourse. Only when we are willing to restore Christianity to the status of genuine knowledge will we be able to effectively engage the "cognitive war" that is at the root of today's culture war. Worldview clashes are far too important to leave to scientists to adjudicate. We all need to understand the debate and equip ourselves to discuss it within our own personal spheres of influence, and in the public square.

Edward Sisson

5. Teaching the Flaws in Neo-Darwinism

What's at Stake?

Like most of the readers for whom this volume is intended, I am a layman interested in the debate over biological evolution. As I see it, the key question in this debate is whether at least *some* of the diversity of life on earth can be explained *only* through intelligent design, or whether *all* life is the result of chance events occurring in DNA (or perhaps elsewhere) that are then "selected" in some fashion without the need of any guiding intelligence. Advocates of neo-Darwinism, punctuated equilibrium, or of similar theories under other labels, all assert that chance combinations of atoms and molecules, primarily in DNA, given several billion years in which to operate and to be selected, not only can but in fact have given rise to all of the diversity of life we see today. This is the fundamental principle common to a variety of different theories that are sometimes labeled "naturalistic evolution" but might more usefully be labeled "unintelligent evolution." I use the phrase "unintelligent" evolution to accommodate the possibility that an intelligent designer (or designers) theoretically might generate new designs (and thus produce the diversity of life) by causing preexisting species to undergo designed changes in DNA, and thus to undergo "intelligent" evolution. My argument in this essay is with the proposition that *un*intelligent processes are the complete and sufficient explanation for all biodiversity.[1]

Over the past eight years I have read much on this topic, not only out of intellectual curiosity, but also because I am the father of two elementary school children. I have thought at length about how my children should be taught about these issues when they reach high school, and about how *I* will teach them, regardless of what the schools decide to teach.

I come to this debate as a commercial litigation partner in a 600-lawyer firm. As a litigator, I am accustomed to the techniques of rhetoric, spin, *ad hominem* arguments, and other methods of verbal persuasion and intimidation. My law degree is from Georgetown. I am also a graduate of M.I.T. (major in architecture) with some training in the evaluation of scientific theories (courses in physics, chemistry, astrophysics, calculus, and mathematical modeling of ecological systems). Lastly, I am a mainline Episcopalian who, aside from attending church from 1998 to 2001 to introduce my children to the faith, has not attended church regularly for the past thirty years.

The debate over biological evolution is wide-ranging, often vehemently prosecuted, and often deformed by personal and institutional interests and attitudes. The debate is multi-sided and usually carried on with a level of complexity and misdirection that can be quite frustrating. Observed data is asserted to be evidence for conclusions that, logically, do not necessarily follow from that data. Arguments are offered to support certain points; yet upon reflection the arguments support only a few, or perhaps none, of those points.

The deformed nature of this debate is unlike any other debate in the realm of science, which reflects the fact that a fundamental question, as old as human society itself, is at stake: whether there exists in our world an intelligence that we cannot directly perceive but which has an ability to affect us. As popular opinion, and ultimately government, with its money and power, shifts in the answer that it adopts to this question—yes, there is such an intelligence, or no, there is not—the relative social prominence, prestige, and power of two large social groups, scientists and clergy, tips back and forth.

In this debate, the advocates of unintelligent evolution have assumed much the greater burden. They have asserted to us, the general public, that they have *proven* (not merely that it is possible, but that it is *proven*) that *no* life form—not one—required the aid of a designing intelligence. Rather, blind and purposeless material processes alone were required. It is this claim—that the matter is proven or established by overwhelming evidence or settled beyond reasonable doubt—that is the foundation for their demand that the public schools must teach theories of unintelligent evolution.

But, contrary to their assertion, the unintelligent evolution hypothesis is *not* proven. In fact, I conclude that it has been *dis*proven, and that an intelligent cause is necessary to explain at least some of the diversity of life as we see it. The observed data, and the mathematical-statistical analysis of that data, establish at a minimum that at least some, and perhaps most, of the diversity of life must have occurred through intelligent direction. There is not enough space in this chapter to summarize all the relevant arguments; in fact, the purpose of this volume is to provide the reader with such summaries by the very authors of those arguments, and it would be redundant for me to do so here.

Still, I want to point to one aspect of the theory of intelligent design that I have found particularly persuasive. Design intelligence theorists, notably the editor of this volume, William Dembski, have developed techniques for intelligence detection, techniques useful in detecting intelligent design both in human-made artifacts as well as in biology. Having reviewed a variety of attempts to rebut their work on intelligence detection, I have found them all unpersuasive. They do not persuade, primarily, because as any parent, business manager, or detective knows, we often are confronted by events we are told are accidental but which we reasonably conclude were intentional. Moreover, those teachers and educational systems that administer standardized multiple-choice tests are also engaged in a form of "intelligence" detection that operates similarly to the intelligence detection "filter" developed by Dembski. Those who reject the intelligence theorists' work on intelligence detection also inadvertently reject our ability to make qualitatively similar judgments in a whole host of other situations having nothing to do with the origin and subsequent diversification of life. To use a phrase common in litigation, the rebuttals "prove too much" because the rebuttal arguments, if true, cannot be limited just to the origins debate; they necessarily deny our ability to reason about and judge matters that all of us agree we can reason about and judge.

A THOUSAND DOCTORS (OF PHILOSOPHY) CAN'T BE WRONG—OR CAN THEY?

The possibility that the reigning paradigm explanation of the diversity of life may be false is immensely intriguing, which is why I started to follow the issue. Could such an extraordinary thing really be true? In advertising, we are all familiar with claims that a particular medicine is good for us because "a thousand doctors" all attest to the product and they "can't be wrong." The proponents of unintelligent evolution can easily marshal a thousand Ph.D.s to attest the validity of their theory. The theory has spread like a dye through hundreds of textbooks at all levels of education. Can all these Ph.D.s really be wrong?

There are of course many precedents for the general proposition that the reigning theories of an era may be false. Witness Galen's theory of the four humors of the body, which led doctors to "bleed" patients in hopes of curing them; or Ptolemy's theory of the earth-centric universe. Thomas Kuhn in his famous book *The Structure of Scientific Revolutions* analyzes more examples of this sociological phenomenon.[2]

A more recent example of persistent belief in a theory unsupported by direct observation was the view that now-submerged land bridges once connected the continents, which were believed to be fixed and immobile.[3] The parallel between what is happening in evolutionary theory to what happened in the land-bridge theory is particularly apt.

For thousands of years, scientists had never seen the continents move, and the thought that they might move sounded fantastical. But by the 1920s, sufficient data had accumulated to suggest that the continents might once have been joined, and so must have since drifted to their present positions.

One class of such evidence was the distribution of certain fossils that appeared in both Africa and South America, which strongly suggested that the two continents had once been connected.[4] Proponents of continental drift suggested that a population occupying a single contiguous land area had been fossilized, and then the land in which they had been fossilized had separated into the two continents.

Religious leaders had a different explanation: the continents had always been separate, and God had placed similar creatures (or fossils that appeared to have once been living creatures) in the two widely distant locations. This religious theory violated the uniformitarian principle advocated by British geologist Sir Charles Lyell, that fossils had been created through processes still in operation today. Yet leading geologists of the time also feared that continental drift violated the uniformitarian principle, and that if this principle were not upheld, religion would regain unwarranted dominance in geology.[5]

As historian of science Naomi Oreskes states, "uniformitarianism was associated in many geologists' minds with the exclusion of religious arguments from geology and the consolidation of geology as a science."[6] In order to preserve uniformitarianism, exclude religious argument from geology, and yet reject the continental drift theory, the scientific establishment after 1920 needed to identify a mechanism whereby the creatures that produced the fossils could have crossed the South Atlantic between Africa and South America. From 1931 to 1933 American geologists Charles Schuchert and Bailey Willis developed a theory of an isthmian link, or land bridge, which had become submerged beneath the South Atlantic because of the subsidence of the land and the melting of the ice-age glaciers—an east-to-west ridge running between Africa and

South America. To explain other fossil data and data relating to patterns of ancient glaciation, Schuchert and Willis proposed other submerged isthmian links, connecting Africa to India, Vietnam to Australia, Australia to Antarctica, and Antarctica to South America.[7]

As Oreskes states, "This explanation was patently ad hoc—there was no evidence of isthmian links other than the paleontological data they were designed to explain (away). Nevertheless, the idea was widely accepted, and it undercut a major line of evidence of continental drift."[8]

The recently deceased Harvard evolutionist Stephen Jay Gould called the isthmian links a "deus ex machina . . . flung with daring abandon across 3,000 miles of ocean," and that "[t]he only common property shared by all these land bridges was their utterly hypothetical status . . . [but] to Willis, Schuchert, and any right-thinking geologist of the 1930s, one thing legitimately seemed ten times as absurd as imaginary land bridges thousands of miles long: continental drift itself."[9] Gould noted the "highly fertile imaginations" of Schuchert and Willis could explain away any observations that appeared to support continental drift, and stated that the lesson to be learned from the land-bridge episode was that "orthodoxy colors our vision of all data; there are no pure facts." Or, as a proverb puts it, "If I had not believed it, I would not have seen it."

But particularly after World War II, with the development of more advanced undersea research tools, science learned the topography of the ocean floor, and learned that there had never been any land bridges.[10] Schuchert and Willis and their elaborate inventions vanished. Simultaneously, other scientists developed an alternative naturalistic, unintelligent, non-religious theory to explain the data: plate tectonics, of which continental drift was a part. The scientific establishment adopted this new theory.

The parallel between the evolution debate and the continental drift debate is quite striking. In unintelligent evolution, it is assumed that there cannot be an intelligent designer since humans have never perceived one, just as it was assumed that continents can't move since humans had never seen them move. Thus, to establish the factual existence of the mechanism for change in species (the equivalent of the land bridge), it is necessary simply that a scientist *imagine* a non-intelligent solution. That imagined solution—sequential mutations to germ cell DNA resulting from unintelligent processes, followed by a take-over of the population by individuals possessing the mutations—necessarily becomes *a fact*, just as the land bridge became a "fact," regardless of the astounding odds against the occurrence of those events. Only its *details*—the specific genetic mutation processes by which this operates—await actual observation. This two stage presentation—the "fact" of common descent and the "theory" of the details of how common descent actually works—is exactly how biology textbooks describe the matter.[11]

I believe that anyone who reads the highly imaginative speculations of evolutionary scientists concerning how to generate the diversity of animal and plant features we see today, and who then reviews the highly imaginative speculations of Schuchert and Willis, will be struck by the similarity in the mental processes of, on the one hand, the evolutionists, and other the other, Schuchert and Willis and their followers. Both engaged in speculation (a) in defense of scientific orthodoxy and (b) in opposition to the feared ascendancy of alternative religious explanations. But as Oreskes put it with respect to the land bridges, the only "evidence" for these speculations is "the data they were designed to explain (away)."

The scientific establishment, casting its eye over the diversity of life on earth (the observed data), sees that data—the diversity itself—as "overwhelming" and "enormous" evidence proving the "fact" that all these species evolved from common ancestors. Descent with modifications resulting from unintelligent, natural processes caused the diversity. The most remarkable thing one learns by reading the works of the contributors to this volume is the discovery that the claim of "overwhelming" evidence does not stand. The scientific establishment is looking at the tangible facts on the ground—the data, the diversity of life forms on earth—and it sees in that data evidence of facts that it passionately wants to be true and that it feels need to be true. But the message they have, since Darwin, convinced themselves is there in the observed data is simply *not* in that data.

To the extent that the data that is supposed to be evidence for unintelligent evolution is simply the diversity of life itself—in other words, the data that the theory is supposed to explain (away)—it is not evidence for the unintelligent evolution theory. To say that diversity proves unintelligent evolution and therefore unintelligent evolution is the cause of diversity is plainly circular reasoning. Moreover, for hundreds of years prior to Darwin, excellent scientists such as the French naturalist Georges-Louis Leclerc, Comte de Buffon, looked at this exact same data—the diversity of life—and rejected the proposition that creatures can evolve across species boundaries as the explanation for that data.[12] Although the diversity of life was observed before Darwin, it is only since Darwin that it has been asserted to constitute evidence *only* for unintelligent evolution.

To address this problem, over the years since Darwin, the scientific establishment has asserted that, once investigated, different classes of data would demonstrate that an unintelligent natural mechanism caused living species to transform one to another. To repeat our analogy to the land bridge, these are theories that postulate where, how high, and how broad the "land bridge" of unintelligent evolution must be, and set out a program of exploration to operate as a kind of sonar, penetrating into the deeps to reveal which of the detailed unintelligent evolution theories was most likely to be correct.

The first way of identifying the "land bridge" of unintelligent evolution—the details of how descent from common ancestors actually worked, with modifications resulting from unintelligent, natural processes—was to be the identification of transitional evolutionary forms that would be documented in the fossil record. The "sonar" would be a worldwide program of archaeological digs. Science expected to find sequential layers of gradually changing forms, which would confirm the fact of descent with modification (although the fossils, being stone versions of hard body elements such as bones, would not provide direct proof of the genetic mutation process or that the process was unintelligent and natural).

But 150 years of investigation into the layers of the earth has *not* revealed the predicted transitional forms. In other words, the "sonar beams" have not found the "land bridge." Scientists looked beneath the "sea" (the dirt) but the "land bridge" (the transitional forms) was not there. (I know some evolutionists say that the fossil record is sufficient, and every month or so the popular press reports on some obscure fossil discovery that supposedly is evidence of unintelligent evolution. The other contributors to this volume have convincingly refuted that assertion, however—see, for instance, Michael Denton's *Evolution: A Theory in Crisis*.)[13]

Other kinds of "sonar" were proposed, and investigated, but each time they failed to reveal the existence of the proposed "land bridge," namely descent from common ancestors with modifications resulting from unintelligent, natural processes. There is no space here to discuss them, so I must refer you to the other contributors to this volume.[14]

Today, the "land bridge" most strenuously advanced as evidence that the generation of new species results from descent with modifications caused by natural, unintelligent, random processes is the mutation of germ cell DNA that supposedly causes beneficial changes in body forms and structures. Technologies sufficient to conduct the investigation into such mutations—the "sonar" that allows this theory to be tested—are fairly recent, but have been around long enough that of the trillions upon trillions of mutations said to have led to all of the genes in all living things, science should have found proof of a large number of such mutations by now. But it does not appear that even one such beneficial mutation in germ cell DNA *that caused a change in body form* has ever been identified.

The scientific establishment tells us regularly that evidence of beneficial genetic mutation is everywhere, that the development of pesticide resistance by insects, antibiotic resistance by bacteria, or beak-length changes in Galapagos finches caused by drought conditions are all examples of evolution, in which a few individuals develop new features in their DNA to combat a "selection event" that causes a mass die-off.

But all these processes are merely natural variants of breeding, such as that which has been conducted by humans for thousands of years. In every population under study, be it cockroaches under attack by the Orkin Man, bacteria under attack by a doctor, finches suffering because of a drought, or woolly sheep in a breeder's flock, an external event—be it pesticide, medicine, drought, or the preferences of human farmers—causes individuals that have certain traits to die without reproducing, letting others *that already have certain other traits* reproduce more offspring. Those offspring *that also have those traits* are in turn able to consume the available food and other necessities of life (whether provided by nature or by the breeders) that otherwise would have been denied to them (either because it was consumed by the offspring of the prematurely deceased individuals, or was withheld by the breeders).

What has happened in each instance is that a gene *that was present in a smaller proportion of the population before the environmental or breeding condition* occurred is now carried by proportionally more (and in total numbers more) offspring than would have been the case had the condition *not* occurred.[15] Further selective pressures—be they continual application of pesticides, medicine, drought, or breeding preferences—lead to a further focus on those particular traits—traits that are still, however, derived from genes *that already existed in the population prior to the first appearance of the condition* that caused the selection process to begin. From the perspective of the creatures, whether being bred or naturally selected, the operation of the process is identical. This process is often referred to as "microevolution" although there is no actual mutation of any gene at all.

The only difference is that in human-controlled breeding, we *know* that the beneficial gene was present in a minority of the population *before* the selection event (the controlled breeding) occurred—because that is the very trait that the breeders decide to select. By contrast, in natural selection occurring in prehistoric times, no human was present to observe the change, and thus there has been no human observation of the species to verify that the trait eventually "selected" was *absent* from the entire population *prior* to the selection event. But the fact that humans did not observe the trait in a minority, prior to the selection event, is not evidence that the trait was absent from the DNA of the species prior to that event.

Nor does the timing of the event that causes the die-off tell us anything about *when* or *how* the survivors of the die-off *first* came into possession of the genes that produced the traits that led to their fortuitous ability to increase their population after the die-off of their competitors. The survivors are evidence that a gene has become established in a much greater proportion of the population, but are not evidence that the gene arose at the time of the selection event, or that the gene arose by some random means.

The central problem for the theory of unintelligent evolution is that it asserts that the state of life on earth that existed billions of years ago exhibited very few genes, which the theory must connect with the current state of life, in which there are trillions of genes. The theory implies, but does not ever really try to prove, that the dates the supposed mutations occurred have some timing connection with the dates of population die-offs and the appearance in the fossil record of new body forms. But analysis of the prehistoric dates of die-offs and of population increases in fact tells us nothing about when the genes we see today first came into existence, nor of how they came into existence. The evidence of breeding disproves the assumption that there is any timing link at all between the date a gene (that produces a noticeable new body form) first appears in the gene pool of a species and the date by which creatures that exhibit the body form produced by that gene have become so numerous that science notices the appearance of that new body form in the fossil record.

Thus the startling fact is that *none* of the variations in body form seen in nature are evidence sufficient by themselves to prove that the beneficial mutation of genes is caused by natural, spontaneous, unintelligent causes, because the beneficial genes that step to the fore as a result of the process may have been present in an unobserved minority of the species *before* the selection process begins—and may have been in the genetic make-up of some of the members of the species no matter how far back one can trace that kind of creature through its ancestors.

Observations since before Darwin until today are consistent with the proposition that, to use another analogy, the genetic make-up of each organism is not like an infinitely malleable clay that can be shaped into the genes necessary for all living things; rather, the genetic make-up of each organism is like an erector set or model kit with a vast number of interchangeable pieces, from which a great variety of forms can be built, but which is ultimately limited by the *finite initial number of interchangeable parts* in the kit. Breed, or "naturally select," as you wish, but invariably every species runs into its limit when it runs out of interchangeable parts in its "kit." There is nothing new in this idea; in 1753 Buffon termed this "kit" the "interior mold" of a creature that allowed variations within certain limits, but was not so plastic as to permit one species to be transformed into another.[16]

It is interesting to speculate that the recent discovery of so-called "junk DNA" might be the discovery of unused (but potentially usable) parts in the genetic "kit" and that this DNA is not "junk" at all but is in fact the stuff of potentially beneficial changes in body form, which may have been used by the ancestors of the organism in the past and which may be used by the descendants of the organism in the future.

THE SCIENTIFIC ESTABLISHMENT AS LITIGATING COUNSEL FOR UNINTELLIGENT EVOLUTION

The support for the unintelligent evolution theory is so weak, and the challenges it must surmount so overwhelming, that I wondered how to explain the refusal of the scientific establishment to throw up its hands and confess that 150 years after Darwin, no data has been found that amounts to real evidence for unintelligent evolution as the explanation for the diversity of life, and that science is ignorant of how the diversity of life came to be. Here I believe that my experience as a litigator provides several useful insights.

One of the things I have observed in the practice of law is a particular mental process lawyers go through when they take a case. I think scientists, who often function as advocates, are consciously or unconsciously employing the same mental process.

Non-lawyers often wonder how a lawyer can advocate one position, while at the same time privately believing that a different position is true. The answer is that many lawyers employ a thought process that entirely avoids putting themselves into that dilemma. Upon receiving a case, a lawyer who uses this process immediately inquires what result the client wants, and asks himself first *not* "what are the facts" but "what facts must be true so that my side wins what it seeks?"

After determining what facts need to be true for the client to win, the lawyer *then* looks at the data and the applicable law and in every instance asks "can I understand this data, in light of the applicable law, to be evidence proving the facts that need to be true for my side to win?" The lawyer then, as much as possible, mentally adopts an understanding of the data as evidence for the facts that need to be true if the goal is to be achieved. The process is not unbounded; the lawyer's assessment of what the court might accept as a proper interpretation of the data bounds what the lawyer will believe and then advocate.

But the key point is that at no time does the lawyer need to step back and say "what is my assessment of this data *independent* of the interest of my client?" The lawyer's independent assessment of the facts is irrelevant to the client's goals, and usually is irrelevant to any other interest of the lawyer, so she or he need spend no effort developing such an assessment. Thus the lawyer never has in mind two conflicting understandings of the data; the lawyer only develops the understanding that is closest to a reasonable interpretation of the data as evidence for the facts that gain the goal the client seeks. In experienced lawyers, this mental process goes on entirely unconsciously. If the party on the other side of the case had retained the lawyer first, the lawyer, using the same mental process, would develop an entirely different understanding of the data.

I believe this process is even more strongly at work in the scientific community than it is among litigators. Each scientist also, in effect, has a client: her- or himself and by extension the scientific establishment itself, which controls the scientist's future career. The scientific establishment, like any client, has economic and sociological interests. The key, as far as this debate goes, is that broad public acceptance of unintelligent evolution leads the public to direct its greatest deference, respect, and attention to the leaders of the science establishment, and away from those whom the public sees as leaders in the area of understanding the supernatural, such as leaders of religious organizations. The prestige of science and scientists is enhanced and the prestige of religion and clergy reduced.

Sociologist Bernard Barber of Columbia University discusses the effect of such sociological pressures in the preface to a 1990 reprint of his 1961 *Science* magazine article "Resistance by Scientists to Scientific Discovery,"[17] in which he discusses the fact that, on occasion, the scientific establishment may resist evidence that challenges a prevailing theory. The resistance is not the result of the application of normal critical scientific scrutiny but is rather "due to the direct operation of cultural (e.g., received ideas) or social-structural (e.g., social-status differences) factors" that are "specifiable social-structural or cultural factors."[18] Or as Professor Sir Fred Hoyle of Cambridge University put it, "It is a mistake to suppose that science is an unswerving pursuit of objective truth. Partially it is, but only to the extent that the truth does not turn out to contradict what has already been taught in the educational process."[19]

Hoyle goes on to address a specific example: the theory of evolution. According to him, the things that are "wrong" with evolutionary theory have "never had a fair hearing" because "the developing system of popular education [in Darwin's day] provided an ideal opportunity for zealots who were sure of themselves to overcome those who were not, for awkward arguments not to be discussed, and for discrepant facts to be suppressed. This was because popular education created a body of students who . . . had of necessity [to earn their livings] and because it is only students from privileged backgrounds who can afford to adopt views contrary to what they are told."[20]

Now it is true, of course, that theories are often rejected. But almost never does this happen merely because the alleged evidentiary basis that led to the initial acceptance of the theory has been exposed by further investigation as being inadequate to justify the theory. Instead, as Gould put it, "The lesson of history holds that theories are overthrown by rival theories."[21] Kuhn makes the same point.[22] In other words, once science has claimed to have knowledge, it never afterwards confesses ignorance. It does not abandon a reigning paradigm until an acceptable replacement paradigm is offered. Thus, while the scientific establishment often admits that it is in ignorance of matters for which it has never had a reigning paradigm—indeed, the purpose of science is to investigate areas of admitted ignorance—the scientific establishment will *never* admit ignorance of any subject *for which it has adopted a reigning paradigm.* Once science has asserted that it has an answer to a question, it may later announce that it has changed its answer, but it will never admit that it was wrong and now has no answer. This principle is not compelled by any impartial principle of scientific investigation, but is instead a product of compelling sociological factors.

This is a serious structural flaw in the conduct of modern science that finds its most powerful expression in the debate over the origin and subsequent diversification of life. Preserving the preeminence of a naturalistic, non-intelligent, non-religious explanation for the origin and subsequent diversification of life serves the sociological function of privileging the scientific establishment as the group vested by our society with the right to pronounce fundamental truths about the world that affects our day-to-day lives. By so doing, it displaces and keeps in check the religious establishment (and any newly emerging religious groups) that formerly competed effectively for that social role. In short, acceptance by the public of the truth of unintelligent evolution gives to scientists a kind of power, prestige, and income. This sociological dynamic has been obvious ever since Huxley debated Bishop Wilberforce, and it found particular expression in the Scopes Monkey Trial. The result of the scientific establishment's success in this debate has been to humiliate and drive the clergy from the podium from which truths about the world are pronounced, leaving the podium for pronouncements of truth to be controlled by scientists.

For the scientific establishment to abandon *voluntarily* the unintelligent evolution paradigm and admit the possibility of intelligent design would be a remarkable event, in which a powerful social group voluntarily and seriously diminished its own authority, permitting a historically competing group (religious leaders both traditional, "new age," and other) that claims to have insight into the operation of such an intelligence to gain prestige at the expense of the science community. That is why the scientific establishment vigorously resists abandoning the unintelligent evolution paradigm. Instead, it may shift from one particular theory of unintelligent evolution to another—from neo-Darwinism to punctuated evolution to some other theory that might be developed—but it will never accept the concept that some form of intelligent designer must exist to explain some of the data we observe.

APPARENT SINCERITY VERSUS ACTUAL SINCERITY

There is also a unique reason why scientists are particularly averse to developing an opinion that the theory of unintelligent evolution cannot explain all of the diversity of life on earth, and that an intelligent-designer theory may be necessary to explain at least some of the diversity of life.

In litigation, even if a lawyer does develop an internal belief about the data that conflicts with the presentation he or she needs to make in court, the lawyer is expected to keep that belief private. The lawyer's obligation is not to be *actually* sincere but to *appear* sincere. Thus there is no danger to the lawyer's livelihood if the lawyer develops a private understanding of the data that conflicts with the understanding to be presented in court.

But in science the rule is different. Scientists are supposed to be *actually* sincere. They are supposed to develop genuine, individual opinions about the data and then *express* those opinions. Thus it is vital to a scientist's career *not* to develop opinions which, if expressed, will end that career, because opinions once developed are supposed to be expressed, not hidden in favor of expressing opinions the scientist does not sincerely believe. For brevity's sake, we may call this the "sincerity rule."

Because of the fear that to admit the presence of intelligent design would undermine the social predominance of science (and thus its funding and prestige), no leader of a major American scientific institution can publicly abandon the paradigm of unintelligent evolution and yet retain his position of leadership. As in any human organization, the people who most effectively advance the interests of the scientific establishment are the ones chosen to lead the establishment. Those who impede the achievement of the establishment's ends are rejected. Thus, there is simply no purpose for scientists to take the time to consider the challenges to the paradigm and develop an individual response, because if that response is a rejection of the paradigm, the scientist must either suppress it (and violate the rule that scientists should be sincere) or else express it (and likely end his career). Everyone below the top on the hierarchy ladder knows that to question unintelligent evolution will mean the end of career advancement; so for them, too, there is simply no incentive to consider that the challenges to unintelligent evolution might be valid. On the contrary, there are very strong incentives *not* to consider those challenges in any way that might lead to accepting them.

The "sincerity rule" means that if scientists develop a *dis*belief in *un*intelligent evolution, they must express it. Thus, preservation of career advancement opportunities is predicated on the maintenance of belief in unintelligent evolution. That is why challenges to the theory of evolution at best will receive a condescending hearing in forums dominated or controlled by the science establishment.

Finally, in judging the nature of the debate over the origin and subsequent diversity of life, there is another aspect of litigation that sheds light on why the debate is conducted as it is. A psychology that commonly operates in litigation is that opposing lawyers are primed to reject every statement by the other side—for there is no advantage in considering that the statements might be true. Lawyers are not engaged in a mutual search for truth. In comparing the writings of the science-trained advocates of intelligent design with the writings of their opponents, I see that psychology occurring again and again on just *one* side of the debate: the side of the science establishment. That psychology is *not* evident in the work of intelligent design proponents that I have read.

The fact that it is missing from their work is one reason why I have come to trust them more than their opponents in this debate. I think that the intelligent design advocates want to talk with me about looking for the truth. In sharp contrast, the science establishment is primarily engaged in using intimidation, ridicule, and innuendo against its critics.

The "Perry Mason" Burden of Proof: Having to Find the "Real Culprit"

A key issue in any litigation is who bears the burden of proof and just what that burden requires. Particularly with respect to the theory of unintelligent evolution, scientists do not approach challenges to the theory with the impartiality and sincerity that the scientific method is supposed to require of them. Instead, as noted above, scientists approach such challenges with the assumption that the reigning unintelligent evolution theory prevails if there is any reasonable understanding of observed data that can make the data consistent with the theory. This is the *same* mental process as that employed by a lawyer who seeks to interpret all of the data as evidence that supports a predetermined conclusion. The burden is on the challenger.

But this problem is small compared to the fact that in science, unlike law, a significant *new* element is added to that burden. As noted above, the science establishment will not abandon a theory unless some scientist shows not only that certain of the data *cannot* reasonably be understood as being consistent with the theory, but also that the data supports some new theory. To recall Stephen Jay Gould, "theories are overthrown by rival theories," not by demonstrations that the accepted theories ought never to have become accepted in the first place. This, too, is part of the sociology of science. The history of science demonstrates that because of career dynamics, individuals attain prominence, prestige, and position by advocating and convincing others in the scientific establishment of the validity of new or existing theoretical explanations, data, and observations. As sociologist Robert K. Merton stated almost fifty years ago, "On every side, the scientist is reminded that it is his role to advance knowledge" and to "have made genuinely original contributions to the common stock of knowledge."[23]

This burden of proof in science is far greater than the burden of proof in law. To analogize, the "reigning theory" is that advanced by the prosecution, while the defense counsel's job is to rebut that theory. But in law, unlike science, the defense counsel need not offer an alternate theory to explain the facts that led to the prosecution. While Perry Mason always exposes the real killer in the process of acquitting his client, real defense lawyers almost never provide the real culprit in order to get their clients off the hook. In law, a practitioner can have a very successful career as defense counsel by simply proving that prosecution theories are unsupported by the data; he need not go on to prove alternative theories. The defense lawyer can quite happily admit complete ignorance as to who is the real culprit.

Not so in science. No scientist sees a career advantage in proclaiming not only that the scientific establishment is ignorant of the truth, but that he or she is *also* ignorant. Indeed, as science writer Stephen Mihm commented in a March 9, 2003, *Washington Post Book World* review of the book *Rational Mysticism*, the "scientific community . . . is understandably reluctant to concede defeat (in general, it's a poor strategy for getting grants)." Thus, science thrusts upon challengers the burden of offering an alternative theory before it will abandon the prevailing theory, despite all mathematical, logical, and evidentiary challenges to that theory.

What this means is that not only is the burden of proof on challengers immeasurably higher in science than in law, but there are also distinct and powerful career disincentives for anyone to take on the "defense counsel" role of disproving the flawed paradigm. Why should anyone do it, when there is no reward even for success? The scientific establishment, by demanding that those who challenge its theories must produce workable alternatives, is demanding that the defense counsel either produce "the real culprit" or else the jury must accept the prosecution's case. This imposes an unfair burden of proof that, if it were applied in law, would require every defense lawyer to be as effective as the fictional Perry Mason. No wonder reigning scientific paradigms are so rarely abandoned.

This lopsided burden of proof amounts to a special immunity against rejection that stems not from impartial rules of scientific investigation, but is instead a product of careerism within science and of the larger sociological dynamic in which the science establishment maintains its position of dominance among those who pronounce what is true about the world we live in. But as laymen, we need not and ought not accept science's sociological rule. If data once believed to be evidence supporting a theory are now known *not* to be evidence for that theory, the proper and logical step is to withdraw our acceptance of that theory, regardless of whether any alternative theory is yet offered for our inspection.

ATTACKING THE MESSENGER

There is another characteristic element in litigation that also appears repeatedly in the evolution debates: the *ad hominem* denigration of the representatives of the other side, and the assertion that the opponent said things he or she didn't really say. In litigation, lawyers regularly seize upon any action by the other side's lawyers that can be characterized as evidence that the lawyer is deceitful, incompetent, confused, or acting in bad faith. The goal is to get the judge to discount the credibility of the other side's spokesman. Anyone who delves into the books, articles, and internet postings in the evolution debate will see instantly who employs these kinds of tactics and who does not. For example, the authors aligned with the scientific establishment *always* label skeptics of unintelligent evolution "creationists" in an attempt to box all doubters in with young-earth Christian fundamentalists, while adding sneering comments that denigrate their intellectual integrity. But if you read the advocates of intelligent design, you will find that these accusations are false.

OPENING BRIEF, OPPOSITION BRIEF, REPLY, AND SURREPLY

Yet another similarity between the conduct of litigation and the conduct of the origins debate is a pattern that is characteristic of the pattern in litigation: Party A submits an opening brief, party B submits an opposition, A offers a reply, and B submits a surreply. In litigation, these documents are all legal briefs subject to impartial court rules as to length and format, and the judge is expected to read all of them. Each side is treated equally. In the origins debate, we the lay public are the ultimate judges. But we are not required to read all the documents. Thus, a new strategy enters into the mix: the side drafting the Opposition tries to persuade us (the judges) not to bother reading the Opening Brief.

Typically, the process starts with a book critical of unintelligent evolution (the opening brief). The opposition brief takes the form of a book review in a magazine that likely favors unintelligent evolution in its own editorial policy. If the magazine permits the book author to pen a defense of the book, typically the space offered is quite limited in length. Sometimes the magazine will allow the critical reviewer to reply to the author's defense, and that reply may be longer than the space the magazine allowed the author for his defense of the book. This serves the magazine's interests because it assures that the critic will appear at his best, and the magazine's argument will appear correct. If the critic came off poorly in the exchange, or if readers came away thinking that the magazine's policy was unsound, the magazine itself would look bad for having advocated a flawed policy.

Now, in litigation, the judge is expected to read the opening brief. But in this debate, the lay public often decides whether or not to read the book based on reading the review (the opposition brief), the author's reply to the review, and the critic's rebuttal to that reply. The issue becomes not the merits of the theory of unintelligent evolution but instead whether the reader should take the time to read the book that criticizes those merits. The ability of the proponents of unintelligent evolution to manipulate *that* debate—giving *substantially* more space to those who denounce the book than to the author of the book—can clearly bias the process in ways that are unfair. For example, by printing a review that treats the book harshly, denying the author adequate space to reply, and then allowing the reviewer an extensive opportunity to trash the author's reply, more and more members of the public will be persuaded that the book is illogical and not worth reading—not because the magazine has fairly presented the merits of the book, but because the magazine has presented the merits *un*fairly. This is where the internet provides a vital corrective. I have often found that authors who challenge unintelligent evolution are able to effectively rebut their opponents when provided space on their own websites, space that the editors of magazines affiliated with the scientific establishment deny to them.

I have also found that those who promote unintelligent evolution often have a better grasp of the forensic opportunities than do the challengers of unintelligent evolution. One common technique used by critics when they reply to an author's defense of intelligent design is to claim that every comment in the original book review left unanswered by the author is a point the author "cannot rebut." But in reality the decision not to pen a defense to every point is compelled by the magazine's refusal to provide sufficient space, and by the author's judgment as to which of the points would be of most interest to the readers of the magazine. Here again, it is important to learn these forensic techniques and to discount whoever uses them. These techniques are not the mark of an impartial truth-seeker; they are the mark of a self-interested advocate.

THE SCOPES TRIAL AS REASON TO TEACH UNINTELLIGENT EVOLUTION'S FLAWS

The scientific establishment gains a tremendous social benefit from the widespread teaching of unintelligent evolution. As philosopher Daniel

Dennett of Tufts University wrote in his book *Darwin's Dangerous Idea: Evolution and the Meanings of Life*, Darwin's theory is a "universal acid" that corrodes "the fabric of our most fundamental beliefs."[24] The only belief that the theory does *not* corrode is the belief in the science establishment—and thus the belief that scientists are the persons in our society best qualified to make pronouncements on the fundamental truths of our physical existence.

It seems that it is in order to promote deference to scientists that the scientific establishment makes and distributes in our schools "Darwin's acid," corroding the allegiance of students to any other class of truth-pronouncers *except* scientists. That is the reason, I believe, that we are told high school students must learn this theory without being exposed to any of its weaknesses and inadequacies—so that deference to scientists becomes a foundational assumption of their mental make-up *before* they are old enough to question either the theory or the authority of the scientific establishment that is built on it, as they might if they were not exposed to the theory until college.

Whenever a challenge to the teaching of evolution in the high-schools arises, the scientific establishment and its allies trot out the Scopes Monkey Trial and attempt to cast the challengers as throwbacks to the Christian fundamentalists portrayed in the movie *Inherit the Wind*. It is their position that if the scientific establishment has ratified a science textbook, such as the book from which Scopes taught evolution, the state should not engage in "censoring" the material in that book.

The Scopes Monkey Trial plays such a prominent role in the debate that I decided, as part of my investigation of these issues, to purchase a copy of the Scopes trial transcript;[25] a copy of the textbook from which Scopes taught, *A Civic Biology*;[26] and a copy of the companion lab guide to that textbook.[27] Review of these source materials—very different from the biased picture presented in *Inherit the Wind*—was a real eye-opener.

In the Scopes trial, there was never any judgment or verdict that unintelligent evolution is true. (The prosecution argued and the judge agreed that the Tennessee statute in question barred the teaching of the theory even if it were true, so its truth was not an issue in the case.) Nor, notably, was the truth of the theory of unintelligent evolution and the supposed evidence for it ever subjected to cross-examination. Scopes's lawyers presented extensive written statements from seven scientists stating that evolution is the correct explanation for the diversity of life on earth.[28] The prosecution sought permission to cross-examine the five pro-Darwinian science experts whose statements had been read in open court, but Clarence Darrow and the other Scopes lawyers objected and the court refused to allow it.[29]

Nor, ironically, given the popular understanding of the case as a disproof of Christian fundamentalism, was fundamentalism technically an issue in the case. The Tennessee statute did not mandate the teaching of fundamentalism or of any other theory that might explain the origin and subsequent diversification of life on earth. The statute merely barred the teaching of evolution.

But Darrow and the entire defense team wished to make fundamentalism the issue, and they succeeded. Prosecution lawyer William Jennings Bryan agreed to be questioned by Darrow on his personal interpretation of the Bible (the famous examination shown in a false light in *Inherit the Wind*) *only* if Darrow agreed to be questioned on the evidence for evolution—and the judge agreed that Bryan could question Darrow after Darrow questioned Bryan.[30] The bargain by Bryan, submitting to examination so that he could examine Darrow, was a last-ditch attempt to place *some* criticism of unintelligent evolution into the Scopes trial record to counteract the one-sided, unchallenged presentation of the pro-evolution side.

But after his famous examination of Bryan, Darrow unexpectedly changed Scopes' plea to guilty, which closed the evidence and made it impossible for Bryan to call Darrow to the stand to question him on evolution.[31] Darrow could easily have changed the plea before his examination of Bryan; the fact that Darrow changed the plea only *after* he conducted his examination indicates that his intention all along was to use Bryan to challenge Christian fundamentalism and then to escape any challenge to the theory of unintelligent evolution. The result was that in the Scopes Monkey Trial, scientists presented their case for evolution without any challenge to the merits of their arguments that the data they offered was evidence for its truth.

Unintelligent evolution's escape from proper cross-examination is long-standing. Prof. Hoyle's comments to that effect bear repeating: the scientific challenges to unintelligent evolution have "never had a fair hearing" because "the developing system of popular education [from Darwin's day to the present] provided an ideal opportunity for zealots who were sure of themselves to overcome those who were not, for awkward arguments not to be discussed, and for discrepant facts to be suppressed."[32]

Those who invoke the Scopes trial whenever evolution is questioned are using a deceptive rhetorical tactic: attempting to cast today's modern questioners of unintelligent evolution back eighty years and paint them as the "bigots and ignoramuses" of 1925 whom Darrow denounced as trying to "control[] the education of the United States."[33] But those who would impute to today's challengers the attitudes of 1925 should take heed how this throwback technique applies to them. According to Harvard law professor Alan Dershowitz in his 1990 introduction to *The Scopes Trial*, those who advocated for evolution in 1925 included "racists, militarists, and nationalists" who used evolution "to push some pretty horrible programs," including the forced "sterilization of 'unfit' and 'inferior'" people; "the anti-immigration movement" that wanted to bar immigration of people of "inferior racial stock;" and "Jim Crow" laws that evolutionists "rationalized on grounds of the racial inferiority of blacks."

Just as today's modern evolutionists have advanced beyond these reprehensible positions and ought not be cast back eighty years as if they operated from those beliefs, so too today's intelligent design challengers of unintelligent evolution whom I have found persuasive are very different people from the fundamentalists of 1925. The proponents of intelligent design whom I find persuasive do not argue that evolution must be suppressed because of some conflict with the Bible. Instead, they argue that unintelligent evolution should be questioned because the scientific evidence offered to support it is weak.

Examination of Scopes's text book, *A Civic Biology*, demonstrates another important lesson about whether the scientific establishment should receive the great deference it demands from our school boards concerning what should be taught in our schools. *A Civic Biology* and its companion lab book both contain sections on eugenics—introduced by the statement that "[t]he science of being well born is called eugenics."[34] The scientific establishment of the time fully supported this "science" of eugenics. This endorsement by the scientific establishment meant that eugenics was taught in our schools.

Here is what the scientific establishment of that time caused schoolchildren to learn. As Dershowitz notes, Hunter's *A Civic Biology* divided humanity into five races and ranked them in terms of superiority, concluding with "the highest type of all, the Caucasians, represented by the civilized white inhabitants of Europe and America." In its discussion of the legacies of two families, *A Civic Biology* taught schoolchildren that the failure to apply eugenics forced the state of New York to bear the cost of "over a hundred feeble-minded, alcoholic, immoral, or criminal persons" and resulted in the births of "33 sexually immoral, 24 confirmed drunkards, 3 epileptics, and 143 feeble minded. . . . The evidence and the moral speak for themselves! Hundreds of families such as those described above exist today, spreading disease, immorality, and crime to all parts of this country. . . . [T]hese families have become parasitic on society." Hunter's textbook—the one that the science establishment of today says that the state should have given maximum deference in 1925—recommends that society "separat[e] the sexes in asylum . . . preventing intermarriage and the possibilities of perpetuating such a low and degenerate race."[35] Such was the position the science establishment promoted to the children of Tennessee at the time of the Scopes Monkey Trial. I think the state should have rejected this position *despite* the fact that the science establishment supported it.

The lab book, at Problem 160, asks students to use inheritance charts "[t]o determine some means of bettering, physically and mentally, the human race," so that students can answer the concluding question: "Should feeble-minded persons be allowed to marry?" A "Note to teachers" says that "[t]he child is at the receptive age and is emotionally open to the serious lessons here involved."[36] Ironically, the lab book contains nothing on evolution. Apparently the scientist who wrote the book, and the scientific establishment that applauded it, felt it was more important for the "receptive" young students to learn eugenics than evolution.

Of course, the scientific establishment of today would denounce all of this. Thus the very text book from which Scopes taught—the very book that the scientific establishment of today proclaims Scopes ought to have been able to use in 1925 without any interference by the state—includes material that today the scientific establishment rejects.

The real question is whether the rest of the world should wait for the science establishment to catch up before we decide to reject paradigms that have hung on in our textbooks for years, despite manifold and rapidly accumulating flaws, only because no one has yet developed an *alternative* paradigm that science will accept, one that will preserve for the scientific establishment its place of prominence as the preeminent truth-telling group in our society.

If we cast ourselves back to 1925 and ask ourselves whether it would have been proper for the State of Tennessee then to have adopted a law barring the teaching of eugenics, despite the scientific establishment's support at that time for that theory, would anyone today condemn the state for that law? If we imagine a milder hypothetical 1925 law—a law that permitted the teaching of eugenics as the scientific establishment demanded, but that required that challenges to the theory also be taught—would not everyone today applaud the foresight of the state in enacting such a law? Would we not all agree that *if* such a "science" of eugenics had to be taught in our schools because of the insistence of the scientific establishment, that it would be appropriate *also* to teach the flaws in that "science"?

The hypothetical example of a state law mandating that doubts about the "science" of eugenics be taught demonstrates that it is appropriate for the people who determine our school curricula not to be bound to adhere to whatever the scientific establishment espouses at any given time. Instead, the population at large—who are free from the institutional incentives and biases of the scientific establishment—are entirely within their rights to doubt and indeed to abandon a theory before the scientific establishment might decide to doubt or abandon that theory. The principle espoused by the scientific establishment—that ignorance is never admitted once a paradigm has been adopted—is part of the career dynamics of science, not a principle for determining the truth to be taught in schools.

Nor will it do to say the weaknesses in the various theories of unintelligent evolution must be kept hidden to avoid confusing students. The fact is, there is nothing confusing about stating that the theory of unintelligent evolution, which depends entirely on the supposed occurrence in history of trillions of germ cell DNA gene mutations *that beneficially affect body shape* (this qualifier is important, since it is variations in body shape that appear in the fossil record), has not identified *any* such mutations, let alone a sufficient number of mutations for it to be reasonable to infer that *all* of the trillions of mutations occurred because of unintelligent processes.

Recognizing that when it comes to the origins debate the scientific establishment is institutionally unable to adhere to the stated ideal of searching for truth regardless of material interests, school boards ought to give serious consideration to sharing with students the data and analysis that cast doubt on the truth of unintelligent evolution. To do so, of course, would require those in charge of school curriculae to publicly disagree with, and reject, the position vehemently advocated by the scientific establishment. Any such move might be challenged in the courts. If so, the courts ought to allow states and school boards to supersede and reject the positions of the scientific establishment when, in the good-faith judgment of those states and school boards, those positions serve more to protect the sociological interests of the scientific establishment than to advance an objective assessment of the observed data.

J. Budziszewski

6. Accept No Imitations
The Rivalry of Naturalism and Natural Law

In ethics, there are two ways to take human nature seriously. The first is to regard nature as the design of a supernatural intelligence; you take it seriously because you take God seriously. The other is to regard nature (in a physical or material sense) as all there is. Here you ascribe to matter—or to some process, property, or aspect of matter—the ontological position that theists ascribe to God. Natural lawyers follow the first way; naturalists follow the second. Similar name—radically different meaning.

Nature means something different to the naturalist than it does to the natural lawyer. It has to. The naturalist cannot view nature as a design because in his view there isn't anyone whose design it might be. What is, just is. If you accept the principle of sufficient reason, this is rather unsatisfactory, for no one seriously maintains that the universe had to be just the way it is. There might have been fewer stars, or more. There might have been creatures like us, or there might not. There might not have been a universe at all. Nature, then, is a contingent being, not a necessary being like God, and contingent beings need causes. The naturalist rejects this line of reasoning, or at least limits it. He might concede that each thing in nature needs a cause, but he denies that the entire ensemble of things needs a cause. This exception seems suspiciously arbitrary.

It is easy to see how the natural lawyer's approach can ground ethics. If God himself is the Good—the uncreated source of all being, all meaning, and all value in created things—then inasmuch as his intentions are reflected in our own design, in human nature, these intentions are normative for us.[1] Consider, for example, the inclination to associate in families. This is not the same as a mere desire to do so; indeed we have conflicting desires, and some people would rather be alone. It would be more accurate to say that we are made for family life; that fitness for family life is one of our design criteria. For humans, then, the familial inclination is a *natural* inclination. When we follow this inclination we are not acting in opposition to our design, but in accord with our design. Family is not a merely apparent good for us but a real one, and the rules and habits necessary to its flourishing belong to the natural law. Next consider the universal testimony of conscience against murder. This is more than a matter of guilty feelings; indeed no one always feels remorse for doing wrong, and some people never do. Nevertheless, the wrong of deliberately taking innocent human life is acknowledged at all times and everywhere, and this too belongs to the natural law. Notice that both examples concern design. The former concerns the design of the inclinations, as apprehended by the intellect. The latter concerns the design of the intellect itself, for we are so made that there are certain moral truths, things we *can't not know.*[2]

How the other view could ground ethics is hard to see. If material nature is all there is, then how could actions have non-material properties like right and wrong? Another puzzle is how there could be true moral "law" without a lawgiver. Perhaps it would be like the "law" of gravity—a pattern that we cannot help but enact, a force to which we cannot help but yield. But in that case, "you ought to" would mean the same thing as "you do." Stones do not deliberate about whether they "ought" to fall.

*****

Some naturalists concede the point, or as we must say here, the pointlessness. William Provine declares that "No purposive principles exist in nature. . . . No inherent moral or ethical laws exist, nor are there absolute guiding principles for human society. The universe cares nothing for us and we have no ultimate meaning in life."[3] Richard Dawkins opines, "The universe that we observe has precisely the properties we should expect if there is, at bottom, no design, no purpose, no evil and no good, nothing but blind, pitiless indifference."[4] According to E. O. Wilson, "Human behavior—like the deepest capacities for emotional response which drive and guide it—is the circuitous technique by which human genetic material has been and will be kept intact. Morality has no other demonstrable ultimate function."[5] Wilson and Michael Ruse write, "[O]ur belief in morality is merely an adaptation put in place to further our reproductive ends. . . . [E]thics as we understand it is an illusion fobbed off on us by our genes to get us to co-operate (so that human genes survive). . . . Furthermore, the way our biology enforces its ends is by making us think that there is an objective higher code to which we are all subject."[6] On the subject of conscience, Robert Wright chimes in, "It's amazing that a process as amoral and crassly pragmatic as natural selection could design [!] a mental organ that makes us feel as if we're in touch with higher truths. Truly a shameless ploy."[7]

From views like this, it is only a small step to the opinion that a truly authentic morality would be Promethean, setting itself *against* the shameless ploy. That's what Richard Dawkins thinks. First he sets the stage: "We are survival machines, robot vehicles blindly programmed to preserve the selfish molecules known as genes." Then he issues the call to arms: "Let us understand what our own selfish genes are up to, because we may then at least have the chance to upset their designs, something that no other species has ever aspired to."[8] *Écrasez l'infâme!* It is all very stimulating, but of course if we really are "blindly programmed" by our genes, then the call to revolt is worse than futile. One might as well expect a typewriter to revolt against the keys.

Perhaps Dawkins is setting his hopes on cultural evolution, for later he suggests that higher-level genetic programs are "open" and do not settle every detail of the way we live. Yet this is hardly a promising gambit, for his discussion of culture merely exchanges one form of determinism for another. As he sees things, our bodies are blindly programmed to preserve the self-replicating molecules called genes, and our cultures are blindly programmed to preserve the self-replicating ideas called "memes." If we take him at his word, then presumably the idea of revolt is merely another of the replicators. In this case he rails against blind destiny only because he is blindly destined so to rail.

Further complicating the story is that from time to time the very writers who say that naturalism destroys morality have sometimes propounded the view that it *implies* a morality. Wilson, for example, believes that we are *morally* obligated to preserve all extant living species. The reasoning seems to be that (1) whatever is, is lovable; (2) the preservation of whatever is, is right; and (3) if we fail to pay sufficient homage to whatever is, there will be retribution. This is not quite how Wilson puts it. Here is how he frames the idea in a newspaper column adapted from his 2002 book *The Future of Life*:

> "Don't mess with Mother Nature." The lady is our mother all right, and a mighty dispensational force as well. After evolving on her own for more than three billion years, she gave birth to us a mere million years ago, an eye blink in evo-

lutionary time. Ancient and vulnerable, she will not tolerate
the undisciplined appetite of her gargantuan infant much
longer.

Could it be that he is speaking poetically and does not intend his
words to be taken in a moral sense? On the contrary:

> The issue, like all great decisions, is moral. Science and tech-
> nology are what we can do; morality is what we agree we
> should or should not do. The ethic from which moral deci-
> sions spring is a norm or standard of behavior in support of
> a value, and value in turn depends on purpose. Purpose,
> whether personal or global, whether urged by conscience or
> graven in sacred script, expresses the image we hold of our-
> selves and our society. A conservation ethic is that which aims
> to pass on to future generations the best part of the nonhu-
> man world. To know this world is to gain a proprietary at-
> tachment to it. To know it well is to love and take responsibil-
> ity for it.[9]

The foregoing passage is rather cloudy. For starters, what does
Wilson mean by "moral"? Is there an "ought" in there—is he saying
anything more than "I have feelings of love, awe, and fear toward nonhuman nature, and I want you to have them too"? Plainly, one can *elicit*
such feelings on the part of other people without recourse to an "ought."
For example, I might get you to share my fear of environmental disaster
by conjuring an image of it. But can one recommend such feelings *as
moral* without recourse to an "ought"? To sharpen the point: One sees
that Wilson might regard people who fail to share his fear as deficient in
imagination, but it is hard to see how he could regard them as deficient
in *duty*. Duty doesn't look any more like a property of matter than right
and wrong.[10] From time to time Wilson notices the difficulty. On such
occasions he waves his hands and refers vaguely to "emergent" properties of matter—properties that appear only when matter is complexly
organized. But this is sleight of hand, because he has no idea how complexly organized matter could give rise to such properties either. Finding a property that he cannot account for, he calls it "emergent" and
says that he has explained it.

*****

A heterogeneous movement, variously styled "evolutionary ethics" and "evolutionary psychology," shares the goal of providing a naturalistic basis for moral judgments, but tries to be more systematic. This new naturalist fashion comes in three overlapping varieties.

The variety closest in spirit to Wilson's own work tries to demonstrate that a moral sense has evolved among human beings because it confers a selective advantage. Consider, for example, the human tendency to help out other people, even at some cost to oneself. At first it might seem that a genetic predisposition for such behavior could never have evolved by natural selection because unselfishness spends resources for nothing; every selfless act reduces the likelihood of passing on the genes that have made one act selflessly. But if the ancestors of human beings already lived in family groups, maybe not.[11] Under those circumstances, the ones most likely to receive aid would be relatives, and for each degree of relationship, there is a certain likelihood that the relative is carrying *the same* gene. So, even though an act of self-sacrifice reduces the likelihood that I will pass on my *own* copy of the gene, it increases the likelihood that my relatives will pass on theirs. If my act helps a sufficient number of such relatives, then the proliferation of the gene in question is assisted even more than it would have been by selfishness. This is called "kin selection."[12]

If kin selection really happens, then it might explain the tendency to help out other people. It might even explain why we approve of the tendency. The problem is that it can't explain whether we *ought* to approve of it. After all, the fact that we developed one way rather than another is an accident. We might have turned out like guppies, who eat their young instead of helping them. Someone might reply, "That we *might have* turned out differently is no concern of ours. The fact is that we didn't. Besides, natural selection has determined not only that we are the way we are, but that we're happy about the way we are. We don't need a justification for being pleased!" Not so fast. We may be pleased about our tendency to render aid, but we are not so pleased about its limits. As a matter of fact, many of our tendencies *dis*please us; consider how appalled we are by our propensity for territorial aggression. Now our tendency to territorial aggression and our propensity to be appalled by it must both belong to the genome. What sense could there be, then, in judging between them? Genes provide no basis for judging between gene and gene. The basis of morality must lie elsewhere.

The second variety of evolutionary ethics tries to show that by considering how we came to be, we will learn more about how we are. According to this view, Darwinism reveals the universal, persistent features of human nature. Why it should do so is very strange because Darwinism is not a predictive theory. It does not proceed by saying "According to our models, we should expect human males to be more interested in sexual variety than human females; let's find out if this is true." Rather it proceeds by saying "Human males seem to be more interested in sexual variety than human females; let's cook up some models about how this might have come to pass." In other words, the theory *discovers nothing*. It depends entirely on what we know already, and proceeds from there to a purely conjectural evolutionary history.

These conjectures are made to order. You can "explain" fidelity, and you can "explain" infidelity. You can "explain" monogamy, and you can "explain" polygamy. Best of all (for those who devise them), none of your explanations can be disconfirmed—because all of the data about what actually happened are lost in the mists of prehistory. In the truest sense of the word, they are myths—but with one difference. The dominant myths of most cultures encourage adherence to cultural norms. By contrast, the myths of evolutionary ethicists encourage cynicism about cultural norms. Robert Wright is remarkably candid about this effect:

> Our generosity and affection have a narrow underlying purpose. They're aimed either at kin, who share our genes, at nonkin of the opposite sex who can help package our genes for shipment to the next generation, or at nonkin of either sex who seem likely to return the favor. What's more, the favor often entails dishonesty or malice; we do our friends the favor of overlooking their flaws, and seeing (if not magnifying) the flaws of their enemies. Affection is a tool of hostility. We form bonds to deepen fissures. . . .
>
> It is safe to call this a cynical view of behavior. So what's new? There's nothing revolutionary about cynicism. Indeed, some would call it the story of our time—the by now august successor to Victorian earnestness.[13]

An evolutionary ethicist of this second sort does not claim that Darwinism itself provides the foundation for ethics. What it does provide, he thinks, are the general features of human nature with which ethics must come to terms. Wright's ethics, for example, are utilitarian; he holds that "the fundamental guidelines for moral discourse are pleasure and pain." Given a utilitarian ethics, here is how he explains the usefulness of Darwinism:

Of course, happiness is great. There's every reason to seek it.
There's every reason for psychologists to try to instill it, and
no reason for them to mold the kinds of people natural selection "wants." But therapists will be better equipped to make
people happy once they understand what natural selection
does "want," and how, with humans, it tries to get it. What
burdensome mental appliances are we stuck with? How, if at
all, can they be defused? And at what cost—to ourselves and
to others? Understanding what is and isn't pathological from
natural selection's point of view can help us confront things
that are pathological from our point of view.[14]

If we ask Wright why he *does* favor utilitarianism, he gives the
intriguing answer that once Darwinism gets loose in the world, we find
that it becomes harder and harder to find principles on which everyone
will agree. All the old ones have been destroyed. "[I]n a post-Darwinian
world" which "for all we know is godless," minimalism rules; fewer principles are better than more. Utilitarianism, of course, has only one—
pleasure good, pain bad. Does this *prove* the goodness of pleasure and
the badness of pain? No, but we do regard pleasure as good and we do
regard pain as bad. "Who could disagree with that?" Wright asks. Like
most utilitarians, he is convinced that even people who do not call themselves utilitarians are utilitarians at heart.[15]

The argument is less transparent than it seems to be. In the first
place, the kind of minimalism that is likely to strike people as plausible
depends on what kind of people they are. In cynical times when they are
well fed, the One Plausible Principle may seem to be "Pleasure is good."
But in violent times when they are afraid, the One Plausible Principle
may seem to be "Death is bad." In fact, this was the very principle propounded by Thomas Hobbes in 1641, in very violent times. Another
problem is that minimalism won't get you very far. Hobbes thought his
One Plausible Principle was very powerful, but he confused consensus
that death is bad with consensus that death is the *greatest* bad. Though
most people do think death is bad, most also think that there are some
things worse than death. For that reason, even if they agree that death is
to be avoided, they will not agree that death is to be avoided *above all
things*, as Hobbes would have them do.

Utilitarianism runs into similar problems. People may agree with
Wright that happiness is good, yet they may not agree with him that
happiness is the same as pleasure (most of the Western tradition has
denied it). Or they may agree with him that pleasure is good, yet they

may not agree with him that pleasure should be pursued as a *goal* (the Western tradition has maintained that pleasure is best enjoyed as a byproduct of pursuing other ends; the search for pleasure dries up the springs of pleasure). Or they may agree with him that pleasure should be pursued as a goal, yet they may not agree with him that *aggregate* pleasure should be pursued as a goal, as utilitarianism requires (if torturing one innocent soul would make everyone else much happier, then concern for the aggregate pleasure would require torturing him).

For all that, it is easy to see why naturalists find utilitarianism attractive. I asked earlier, "If material nature is all there is, how could actions have non-material properties like right and wrong?" Confronted with this question the naturalist has only two ways to proceed. He can straightforwardly deny moral properties, or he can try reducing them to non-moral properties—which is a more roundabout way to deny them. The only puzzle is why he would want to do either of these things.

The common method of reduction is to explain moral properties in terms of desire. This move has four steps.[16] *Step one* is to say that that the right is nothing but what brings about the good. This is called consequentialism. To consequentialists, a maxim like "It is wrong to do evil that good may result" means nothing, because apart from results they have no concept of evil or good. *Step two* is to say that the good is nothing but the desirable. This is the only unproblematic step in the argument. *Step three* is to say that the desirable is nothing but what we actually desire. This definition renders it impossible to make sense of perverse desires, desires we wish we had but don't, or desires we wish we didn't have but do. John Stuart Mill tied himself in knots over the problem.[17] *Step four* is to say what it is that we actually desire. According to utilitarians like Wright, this is pleasure. You may think you desire many things—love, skill, friendship, achievement, salvation—but according to utilitarians, you're wrong. They say you desire nothing except either as a part of pleasure or as a means to pleasure; hence, the only thing you ultimately desire is pleasure itself. For example, you may think you want dinner, but what you really want is the pleasure of feeling full; knowledge, but what you really want is the pleasure of feeling knowledgeable; love, but what you really want is the pleasure of feeling loved; or God, but what you really want is the pleasure of feeling—well, whatever God would make you feel. It follows that if it were possible to have the pleasures without the things, then that would be just as good. Eat, purge, and eat again.

The third and most paradoxical variety of evolutionary ethics proclaims that natural law and naturalism are not at odds after all—that they are getting at the same thing. A dash of Darwin, as it were, makes Thomas Aquinas more powerful and precise. Yes, yes, we must do away with St. Thomas's silly superstition that a God is somehow behind things and that nature is designed—but he is better off without it anyway.

This kind of evolutionary ethics has been especially popular among conservatives who think they believe in natural law theory but don't notice the sleight of hand. The most vigorous exponent of this "Darwinian" natural law is Larry Arnhart.[18] Arnhart uses the expressions "natural right" and "natural law" interchangeably. Although he borrows liberally from the other two varieties of evolutionary ethics, his approach requires more detailed attention.

*****

The structure of Arnhart's theory is easy to explain. He makes three of the four moves that utilitarians do, differing only regarding the fourth.[19]

1. He *tacitly* supposes that the right is nothing but what brings about the good, so he is a consequentialist. This critical move is not defended. The unwary reader finds himself joining in the silent assumption that the end justifies the means before he knows what is happening. What is astonishing here is that historically, the natural law tradition has been invoked *against* consequentialism in all of its forms. Yes, the tradition says that good is to be done and that evil is to be avoided, but it has also insisted that some acts are *intrinsically* good and evil aside from all consideration of their consequences. This Arnhart denies, as a consequentialist must. For him there cannot be such a thing as an intrinsically evil act—not even rape or murder. His understanding of the virtue of prudence is that there are no inviolable rules; *everything* depends on circumstances, because circumstances determine results. This utterly obliterates the distinction between the right, pursued by prudence, and the expedient, pursued by craft. Within his theory one can distinguish between socially approved expedience and socially disapproved expedience, but this is not the same thing.

2. He *explicitly* declares that the good is nothing but the desirable; in fact, he asserts and defends the claim repeatedly. Not that it helps much to do so, because this is the only step that is not problematic.

3. He *tacitly* supposes that the desirable is nothing but what we actually desire. Again there is no justification, and no discussion of cases which do not seem to fit. For example, what about a sadomasochist who strongly desires "bondage and discipline," but loathes himself for this desire and strongly desires no longer to be burdened by it? On Arnhart's

account, we would have to conclude *both* that bondage and discipline are desirable for the man, *and* that freedom from such desire is desirable for him. This seems incoherent. A more straightforward view of the matter is that the man *recognizes that what he subjectively desires is not objectively desirable.* It is for precisely this reason that he desires liberation from his burden.

Arnhart does mention one difficult case: When a person thinks he wants something, but then discovers that it wasn't what he wanted after all. Unfortunately, the case is equivocal, and Arnhart does not analyze it. Consider two instances in which I might wish to say that something wasn't what I wanted after all. Instance one: I want to be drunk. As soon as I succeed, I throw up. I tell myself "I guess that's not what I wanted after all." This is probably the sort of thing that Arnhart has in mind. Unfortunately, it isn't really true that I didn't know what I wanted. I really did want to be drunk, and I knew it—but I changed my mind. Instance two: I have a longing for "that unnamable something, desire for which pierces us like a rapier at the smell of a bonfire, the sound of wild ducks flying overhead, the title of *The Well at the World's End,* the opening lines of Kubla Khan, the morning cobwebs in late summer, or the noise of falling waves."[20] Trying to understand what it is that I want, I form one hypothesis after another: "What I *really* want is beauty," "What I *really* want is the remote and mysterious," "What I *really* want is ecstatic union with the rest of nature." Pursuing each of these things in turn, I find to my dismay that none of them actually satisfies the longing. Eventually I realize that what I long for is not to be found within the created order at all. What I am longing for is God. This case is different than the other one, because until the end, I *really don't* know what it is that I want. Unfortunately, Arnhart has no resources to analyze a case like this because he does not acknowledge the reality of God. The closest his classification comes to such longing for God is the "desire for religious understanding," which of course is not the same thing.

4. Not until the step of stating just what it is that we desire does the structure of Arnhart's theory differ significantly from that of utilitarianism. The utilitarian acknowledges only one human desire—pleasure. Arnhart acknowledges twenty, though why Darwinism is needed to discover them is not explained: The desire for a complete life, for parental care, for sexual identity, for sexual mating, for familial bonding, for friendship, for social ranking, for justice as reciprocity, for political rule, for war, for health, for beauty, for wealth, for speech, for practical habituation, for practical reasoning, for practical arts, for aesthetic pleasure, for religious understanding, and for intellectual under-

standing. No doubt it is better to recognize twenty desires than the One Big Desire of utilitarianism. In the context of Arnhart's theory, however, the list presents difficulties of its own.

The first great peculiarity is that for Arnhart the general human desires simply *are* the natural laws; there are no others. The natural law tradition has always denied this. Speaking for the mainstream of the tradition, Thomas Aquinas thought that a good summary of the natural law is found in the Decalogue, or Ten Commandments, which of course are found in divine law too.[21] The prohibition of murder, for example, is one of the "general" precepts[22] that Thomas Aquinas calls "the same for all both as to rectitude and as to knowledge," meaning that it is both right for all and known to all. General principles brook no exceptions, no matter the circumstances.[23] Arnhart denies that there are any such principles—other than the desires themselves. As he says in his discussion of prudence, "The natural *desires* of human beings constitute a universal norm for morality and politics, but there are *no universal rules* for what should be done in particular circumstances" (emphasis added).[24]

The reason that the natural *desires* constitute a universal norm for morality and politics is that for Arnhart the right is nothing but what brings about the good, the good is nothing but the desirable, and the desirable is nothing but what we actually desire; therefore, the right is what causes what we want. Together with the list of desires itself, this entails some very strange conclusions. War, for example, is one of the desires on the list; war is therefore a universal norm for morality and politics. Notice what Arnhart's theory does *not* say here. It does *not* say that war is sometimes an unfortunate necessity for securing justice, as the Just War doctrine of the natural law tradition declares. Rather it says that war is *good and right in itself*—simply because we do in fact desire war. Arnhart's actual discussion of war softens the point (there is, in fact, a great deal of softening of points in his book), but it follows inescapably from his premises.

Yet another oddity of Arnhart's list is the tension in his theory between general and exceptional desires. In the opening section of the second chapter, Arnhart affirms "I reject skeptical and solipsistic relativism, which asserts that there are no standards of ethical judgment beyond the impulses of unique individuals." Later in the chapter, in explaining the Big Twenty, he remarks "In the case of each desire, I speak of what human beings 'generally' desire, because I am speaking of general tendencies or proclivities that are true for all societies but not for all individuals in all circumstances." But although in one sense his theory is based on general desires (for he does in fact generalize about the desires), his fundamental equation between the right, the good, the desirable, and what is actually desired pulls him helplessly in the other direction. By the logic of the argument, the pursuit of what is *generally* desired is right only for the *generality* of people, those who actually experience them as desires. Should there be someone whose desires are abnormal, he must be viewed as standing outside of our morality; he has his own morality. This is necessarily the case, because what is right *for him* is what brings about the good *for him,* which is the desirable *for him,* which is what *he* actually desires.

This implication becomes strangely clear in chapter eight, which is devoted to psychopaths—those who "lack the social desires that support the moral sense in normal people." Such people, says Arnhart, are "moral strangers." Most of us would simply say that they lack the desire to do right. Because Arnhart *reduces* right to desire, however, he cannot speak this way. In his view, if desire is different for psychopaths, *then right must be different for them too.* Arnhart says they have "no moral obligation" to conform to what our "moral sense" demands. If we may use force and fear to restrain them, it is not because they are doing wrong, for given their desires they are doing right. It is merely that, given our own quite different desires, we too are doing right in restraining them.

Once this is understood, we can see that many of Arnhart's statements about his theory are misleading. Consider for example the sentence quoted a few paragraphs earlier: "I reject skeptical and solipsistic relativism, which asserts that there are no standards of ethical judgment beyond the impulses of unique individuals." It would be more accurate to say that he accepts solipsistic relativism based on the impulses of unique individuals *and* affirms standards of judgment beyond the impulses of these individuals. On the one hand, psychopaths have a morality of their own which our morality cannot touch; on the other hand, the rest of us are not psychopaths. Nor are psychopaths the only ones to get their own morality. By the logic of the case, *everyone* whose desires are significantly different than the rest of us gets his own morality. If the foundational principles of the natural law are "the same for all both as to rectitude and as to knowledge," then Arnhart's theory does not affirm the natural law but rather rejects it.

In fact, nothing in Arnhart's theory is quite as it appears. One of his most vigorously argued theses is that slavery violates natural right. He devotes all of chapter seven to the subject, warmly endorsing Lincoln's remark that "If slavery is not wrong, nothing is wrong." I have no reason to doubt Arnhart's sincerity. However, his theory cannot support his conclusion.

The reason slavery violates natural right, according to Arnhart, is that it "frustrates the desire to be free from exploitation"—put another way, the desire to enjoy justice as reciprocity (desire number eight). But if the right is nothing but what brings about the good, which is the desirable, which is what is actually desired, then the fact that the slaves and the masters desire different things is an insuperable obstacle to the conclusion that Arnhart wants to draw. He tries to get over the obstacle by emphasizing the social desires that might lead non-slaves to sympathize with the slaves' desire for justice. The difficulty, of course, is that not all non-slaves do sympathize with slaves. I believe I am right to say that members of the master class have not generally been known to do so.

The truth is that slavery represents a protracted state of war between the master class and the slave class—and Arnhart seems to forget that he has included war on his list of the twenty general human desires. Although the practice of slavery may frustrate the desire of slaves for reciprocity, it satisfies the desire of masters for war, and Arnhart's theory provides no principled basis to judge between them. As he states in another context, "When individuals or groups compete with one another, we must either find some common ground of shared interests, or we must allow for an appeal to force or fraud to settle the dispute."[25] In slavery, however, there are no shared interests; the interest of the masters is to continue ruling, and the interest of the slaves is to escape. I agree with Arnhart that slavery is against the natural law; I am glad that he reaches a different conclusion than his theory requires. But that does not change what it requires.

The quotation in the previous paragraph is not from either the chapter on war or the chapter on slavery, but from the chapter on men and women. From its context, this too is highly revealing. Arnhart criticizes Darwin for giving two conflicting accounts of "the relationship between male and female norms in the moral economy of human life":

> In one account, [Darwin] defends a moral realism that combines typically male norms such as dominance and courage and typically female norms such as nurturance and sympathy, which he presents as complementary and interdependent inclinations of the human moral constitution. In the other account, he defends a moral utopianism that subordinates the male norms to the female norms, and he expands female sympathy into a disinterested sentiment of universal humanitarianism.[26]

But Arnhart also gives two conflicting accounts. The account which he purports to defend is that typically male and typically female norms are complementary. The account which actually emerges from his theory is that these two sets of norms are substantially—though not entirely—at war. It is hard to see why else he would conclude his section on male and female complementarity with a paragraph explaining that "deep conflicts of interest between individuals or groups can create moral tragedies in which there is no universal moral principle or sentiment to resolve the conflict." This is, by the way, the same paragraph in which Arnhart offers the comment quoted above, concerning disputes that can be settled only by force and fraud. Perhaps the clearest example is the conflict between the female desire for a faithful spouse and the male desire for sexual variety, which is settled, apparently, by fraud.

To defend the idea of sexual complementarity, Arnhart argues (correctly, I think) that even though human males characteristically have a greater desire than females do for a variety of sexual partners, they are actually more satisfied by monogamous marriage than by a life of promiscuous abandon. He does *not* say, however, that males are most satisfied in *faithful* marriage, and this does not affect the conclusion that emerges from his account of male desire. The Arnhart male will want to be married, but he will also want to cheat now and then—provided that he can get away with it. In the interests of his desire for a stable relationship, he will discipline his desire for sexual variety—but not so thoroughly that he becomes faithful. Men will desire to cheat occasionally—and because Arnhart takes desire as the measure of morality, he is logically compelled to conclude that for men such cheating is right. Does he say this in so many words? No, but nothing else could follow from his premises. What of the opening to the chapter, where Arnhart says that his theory "allows us to recognize and condemn cultural practices that frustrate the natural desires of women"?[27] The statement is not wholly false; Arnhart's theory does allow us to criticize the practice of female circumcision, a subject to which he devotes a number of pages. But his discussion of female circumcision seems little more than a diversion. After all, cheating husbands also "frustrate the natural desires of women," but against the occasional furtive adultery, Arnhart has nothing to say.

The strangest implication of the Big Twenty is that in Arnhart's determined attempt to make natural law safe for atheists, he is at war with his own theory. Numbers nineteen and twenty on his list of human desires are religious and intellectual understanding—the desire to understand the world "through supernatural revelation" and the desire to understand it "through natural reason." There is no priority here; the two desires are entirely distinct and equally general. If Arnhart means what he said earlier, that "the natural desires of human beings constitute a universal norm for morality and politics," then the implication would seem to be clear: Natural law instructs us to pursue them both. Unfortunately, not only does Arnhart's discussion obscure the point, but by the time the book concludes he is saying something quite different. Here are his words.

> Moved by their desire to understand, human beings will seek the uncaused ground of all causes. This will lead some human beings to a religious understanding of God. It will lead others to an intellectual understanding of nature. Yet, in either case, the good is the desirable. And perhaps the greatest human good, which would satisfy the deepest human desire, would be to understand human nature within the natural order of the whole.

Instead of being urged to seek both kinds of understanding, suddenly we are urged to seek one or the other. They are no longer presented as either equal or distinct; natural reason is given priority over supernatural revelation, and seems to want to absorb it. This does not wash: if the right is nothing but what brings about the good, the good is nothing but the desirable, the desirable is nothing but what we desire, and we desire *both* supernatural revelation and what reason can learn on its own, then Arnhart's own theory is instructing him to lay aside his atheism and pursue supernatural revelation, but he isn't listening. As Pascal once wrote of cases like this, the heart has its reasons whereof the mind knows nothing.

From all that has been said, we may conclude that "Darwinian" natural law is entirely at odds with what has traditionally been called natural law. It differs not only in content (no precepts) and structure (consequentialist) but in basic ontology (no lawgiver and therefore no law). In these respects it affirms precisely those tendencies of thought which the natural law tradition has always sought to oppose. If any contemporary scientific movement holds promise for the furtherance of the natural law tradition, it is not the stale dogma of natural selection but the theory of Intelligent Design.

Frank J. Tipler

7. REFEREED JOURNALS

Do They Insure Quality or Enforce Orthodoxy?

I first became aware of the importance that many non-elite scientists place on "peer-reviewed" or "refereed" journals when Howard Van Till, a theistic evolutionist, said my book *The Physics of Immortality* was not worth taking seriously because the ideas it presented had never appeared in refereed journals. Actually, the ideas in that book *had* already appeared in refereed journals. The papers and the refereed journals wherein they appeared were listed at the beginning of my book. My key predictions of the top quark mass (confirmed) and the Higgs boson mass (still unknown) even appeared in the pages of *Nature,* the most prestigious refereed science journal in the world. But suppose Van Till had been correct and my ideas had never been published in referreed journals. Would he have been correct in saying that, in this case, the ideas need not be taken seriously?

To answer this question, we first need to understand what the "peer review" process is. That is, we need to understand how the process operates in theory, how it operates in practice, what it is intended to accomplish, and what it actually does accomplish in practice. Also of importance is its history. The notion that a scientific idea cannot be considered intellectually respectable until it has first appeared in a "peer" reviewed journal did not become widespread until after World War II. Copernicus's heliocentric system, Galileo's mechanics, Newton's grand synthesis—these ideas never appeared first in journal articles. They appeared first in books, reviewed prior to publication only by the authors or by the authors' friends. Even Darwin never submitted his idea of evolution driven by natural selection to a journal to be judged by "impartial" referees. Darwinism indeed first appeared in a journal, but one under the control of Darwin's friends. And Darwin's article was completely ignored. Instead, Darwin made his ideas known to his peers and to the world at large through a popular book: *On the Origin of Species*.

I shall argue that prior to the Second World War the refereeing process, even where it existed, had very little effect on the publication of novel ideas, at least in the field of physics. But in the last several decades, many outstanding scientists have complained that their best ideas—the very ideas that brought them fame—were rejected by refereed journals. Prior to the Second World War, the refereeing process worked primarily to eliminate crackpot papers; today, the refereeing process works primarily to enforce orthodoxy. I shall offer evidence that "peer" review is *not* peer review: the referee is quite often not as intellectually able as the author whose work he judges. We have pygmies standing in judgment on giants. I shall offer suggestions on ways to correct this problem, which, if continued, may seriously impede, if not stop, the advance of science.

THE PEER REVIEW PROCESS

Since the 1950s, here is how the peer review process has worked: A scholar wishing to publish a paper in a journal mails several copies of the paper to the editor of a journal. The editor does not make the decision himself about whether to publish the paper in his journal. Instead, he mails the paper to one or more scholars, whom he judges to be experts on the subject matter of the paper, asking them for advice on whether the paper is worthy of publication—their advice constituting the "peer review." Two or more experts in the same field as the author of the paper—his "peers"— are therefore to judge the worth of the paper. The editor asks the reviewers, often called the "referees," to judge the paper on such criteria as (1) validity of the claims made in the paper, (2) originality of the work (has someone already done similar work), and (3) whether the work, even if correct and original, is sufficiently "important" to be worth publishing in the journal. Generally, only if the referee or referees agree that the paper has met all three criteria will the editor accept the paper for publication in his journal. Otherwise, he returns the paper to the author, thereby rejecting it.

The peer review process was put in place after the Second World War because of the huge growth in the scientific community as well as the huge increase in pressure on scholars to publish more and more papers. Prior to the war, university professors (who have always been the main writers of scholarly papers) were mainly teachers, with teaching loads of five to six courses per semester (as opposed to the one to two course load today). Professors with this teaching load were not expected to write papers. In fact, the Austrian/English philosopher Karl Popper wrote in his autobiography that the dean of the New Zealand university where Popper taught during the Second World War said that he regarded Popper's production of articles and books a theft of time from the university!

But universities came to realize that their prestige depended not so much on the teaching skill of their professors as on the scholarly reputation of those professors. And this reputation could come only via the production of articles. So pressure began to be placed on the professors to publish. Teaching loads were reduced so that more time would be available to write papers (and perhaps do the research that would be described in the papers). Salaries began to depend on the numbers of papers published and on the grant support that well-received papers could garner. Before the war, salaries of professors of the same rank were the same (except perhaps for an age differential). Now salaries of professors in the same department of the same age and rank can differ by more than a factor of two.

As a consequence, the production of scholarly articles has increased by more than a factor of a thousand over the past fifty years. Unfortunately, the average quality of the papers has gone down. Since earlier there was no financial reward for writing a scholarly article, people wrote the papers as a labor of love. They had ideas that they wished to communicate with their peers, and they wrote the papers to communicate those ideas. Now papers are mainly written to further a career.

Einstein's experience is illustrative. He published three super breakthrough papers in 1905. One presented to the world his theory of (special) relativity. A second paper showed that light had to consist of particles that we now call photons; using this fact, he explained the emission of electrons from metals when illuminated by light. Einstein was awarded the Nobel Prize for this explanation. The third paper explained the vibration of dust particles in air by attributing the motion to molecules of air hitting the dust particles. Einstein's explanation of this "Brownian motion" allowed properties of the molecules to be calculated, and it was Einstein's explanation that finally convinced physicists that atoms actually existed. Not bad for one year! Einstein wrote these papers in his spare time, after he returned home from his paying job as a patent clerk in Bern, Switzerland.

All three papers were published in *Annalen der Physik,* one of the major physics journals in Germany. But none of the papers was sent to referees. Instead the editors—either the editor in chief, Max Planck, or the editor for theoretical physics, Wilhelm Wien—made the decision to publish. It is unlikely that whoever made the decision spent much time on whether to publish. Almost every paper submitted was published. So few people wanted to publish in *any* physics journal that editors rarely rejected submitted papers. Only papers that were clearly "crackpot" papers—papers that any professional physicist could recognize as written by someone completely unfamiliar with the elementary laws of physics—were rejected.

And if *Annalen der Physik* rejected a paper, for whatever reason, any professional German physicist had an alternative: *Zeitschrift für Physik*. This journal would publish *any* paper submitted by any member of the German Physical Society. It published quite a few worthless papers, but it also published quite a few great papers, among them Heisenberg's first paper on the Uncertainty Principle, a central idea in quantum mechanics. There was no way in which referees or editors could stop an idea from appearing in the professional journals. In illustration of this, the great Danish physicist Niels Bohr said, according to Abraham Pais, that if a physicist has an idea that seems crazy and he hesitates to publish so that someone else publishes the idea first and gets the credit, he has no one to blame but himself.[1] In other words, it never occurred to Bohr that referees or editors could stop the publication of a new idea.

PEER REVIEW TODAY

Bohr would not say that today. If one reads memoirs or biographies of physicists who made their great breakthroughs after, say, 1950, one is struck by how often one reads that "the referees rejected for publication the paper that later won me the Nobel Prize." One example is Rosalyn Yalow, who described how her Nobel-prize-winning paper was received by the journals as follows: "In 1955 we submitted the paper to *Science*. . . . The paper was held there for eight months before it was reviewed. It was finally rejected. We submitted it to the *Journal of Clinical Investigations*, which also rejected it."[2] Another example is Günter Blobel, who in a news conference given just after he was awarded the Nobel Prize in Medicine, said that the main problem one encounters in one's research is "when your grants and papers are rejected because some stupid reviewer rejected them for dogmatic adherence to old ideas." According to the *New York Times,* these comments "drew thunderous applause from the hundreds of sympathetic colleagues and younger scientists in the auditorium."[3]

In an article for *Twentieth-Century Physics*, a book commissioned by the American Physical Society (the professional organization for U.S. physicists) to describe the great achievements of twentieth-century physics, the inventor of chaos theory, Mitchell J. Feigenbaum, described the reception that his revolutionary papers on chaos theory received:

> Both papers were rejected, the first after a half-year delay. By then, in 1977, over a thousand copies of the first preprint had been shipped. This has been my full experience. Papers on established subjects are immediately accepted. Every novel paper of mine, without exception, has been rejected by the refereeing process. The reader can easily gather that I regard this entire process as a false guardian and wastefully dishonest.[4]

Earlier in the same volume, in a history of the development of optical physics, the invention of the laser by Theodore Maiman was described. The result was so important that it was announced in the *New York Times* on July 7, 1960. But the leading American physics journal, *Physical Review Letters,* rejected Maiman's paper on how to make a laser.[5]

Scientific eminence is no protection from a peer review system gone wild. John Bardeen, the only man to ever have won *two* Nobel Prizes in physics, had difficulty publishing a theory in low-temperature solid state physics (the area of one of his Prizes) that went against the established view. But rank hath its privileges. Bardeen appealed to his friend David Lazarus, who was editor in chief for the American Physical Society. Lazarus investigated and found that "the referee was totally out of line. I couldn't believe it. John really did have a hard time with [his] last few papers and it was not his fault at all. They were important papers, they did get published, but they gave him a harder time than he should have had."[6]

Stephen W. Hawking is the world's most famous physicist. According to his first wife Jane, when Hawking submitted to *Nature* what is generally regarded as his most important paper, the paper on black hole evaporation, the paper was initially rejected.[7] I have heard from colleagues who must remain nameless that when Hawking submitted to *Physical Review* what I personally regard as his most important paper, his paper showing that a most fundamental law of physics called "unitarity" would be violated in black hole evaporation, it, too, was initially rejected. (The word on the street is that the initial referee was the Institute for Advanced Study physicist Freeman Dyson.)

Today it is known that the Hawaiian Islands were formed sequentially as the Pacific plate moved over a hot spot deep inside the Earth. The theory was first developed in the paper by an eminent Princeton geophysicist, Tuzo Wilson:

> I . . . sent [my paper] to the *Journal of Geophysical Research*. They turned it down. . . . They said my paper had no mathematics in it, no new data, and that it didn't agree with the current views. Therefore, it must be no good. Apparently, whether one gets turned down or not depends largely on the reviewer. The editors, too, if they don't see it your way, or if they think it's something unusual, may turn it down. Well, this annoyed me, and instead of keeping the rejection letter, I threw it into the wastepaper basket. I sent the manuscript to the newly founded *Canadian Journal of Physics*. That was not a very obvious place to send it, but I was a Canadian physicist. I thought they would publish almost anything I wrote, so I sent it there and they published it![8]

The most important development in cloning after the original breakthrough of Dolly the Sheep was the cloning of mice. The result was once again described on the front page of the *New York Times*, where it was also mentioned that the paper was rejected for publication by the leading American science journal, *Science*.

Everyone knows today that the dinosaurs were wiped out 65 million years ago when a giant asteroid hit the Earth. *Science* did publish the article presenting this theory, but only after a fierce fight with the referees, as one of these referees later confessed. On the Nobel Prize web page one can read the autobiographies of recent laureates. Quite a few complain that they had great difficulty publishing the ideas that won them the Prize. One does not find similar statements by Nobel Prize winners earlier in the century. Why is there more resistance to new ideas today?

WHY DOES PEER REVIEW SUPPRESS NEW IDEAS TODAY?

Philip Anderson, a winner of the Nobel Prize for Physics, opines that

> in the early part of the postwar period [a scientist's] career was science-driven, motivated mostly by absorption with the great enterprise of discovery, and by genuine curiosity as to

how nature operates. By the last decade of the century far too many, especially of the young people, were seeing science as a competitive interpersonal game, in which the winner was not the one who was objectively right as [to] the nature of scientific reality, but the one who was successful at getting grants, publishing in *Physical Review Letters*, and being noticed in the news pages of *Nature*, *Science*, or *Physics Today*. . . . [A] general deterioration in quality, which came primarily from excessive specialization and careerist sociology, meant quite literally that more was worse.[9]

The interesting question is, what caused the "excessive specialization and careerist sociology" that is making it very difficult for new ideas to be published in peer review journals? There are several possibilities. One is a consequence of Anderson's observation that, paradoxically, more scientists can mean a slower rate of scientific advance. The number of physicists, for example, has increased by a factor of a thousand since the year 1900, when ten percent of all physicists in the world either won the Nobel Prize or were nominated for it. If you submitted a paper to a refereed journal in 1900, you would have a far greater chance of having a referee who was a Nobel Prize winner (or at least a nominee) than now. In fact, a simple calculation shows that one would have to submit three papers on the average to have an even chance that at least one of your papers would be "peer" reviewed by a Nobel Prize winner. Today, to have an even chance of having a Nobelist for a referee, you would have to submit several hundred papers. Thus Albert Einstein had his revolutionary 1905 papers truly peer reviewed: Max Planck and Wilhelm Wien were both later to win the Nobel Prize in physics. Today, Einstein's papers would be sent to some total nonentity at Podunk U., who, being completely incapable of understanding important new ideas, would reject the papers for publication. "Peer" review is *very* unlikely to be peer review for the Einsteins of the world. We have a scientific social system in which intellectual pygmies are standing in judgment of giants.[10]

One could argue that because the number of Nobel Prizes awarded is permanently fixed at one per year in three scientific disciplines (physics, chemistry, and medicine), the relative decrease in Nobelists does not mean a similar decrease in the number of giants to pygmies. The data contradict this proposal. The American Chemical Society made a list of the most significant advances in chemistry made over the last 100 years. There has been no change in the rate at which breakthroughs in chemistry have been made in spite of the thousand-fold increase in the number of chemists. In the 1960s, U.S. citizens were awarded about 50,000 chemical patents per year. By the 1980s, the number had dropped to 40,000. Finally, although the number of people *awarded* a Nobel Prize is fixed, the number *nominated* is unlimited. Yet the data show that the number of scientists nominated for the Prize has increased by at most a factor of three in the past century—despite the thousand-fold increase in the number of scientists.[11] Unquestionably, there has been a huge drop in the ratio of giants to pygmies over the last century.

Another possibility is that the increasing centralization of scientific research has allowed powerful but mediocre scientists to suppress any idea that would diminish their prestige. All great advances in science have by definition the effect of reducing the prestige of the "experts" in the field in which the advance is made. Laymen rarely appreciate how centralized scientific research has become in the last fifty years, but the expert's expertise is necessarily invalidated by a radical change in the underpinnings of a scientific discipline. Funding for my own area of physics, general relativity, is located in one and only one division of one and only one bureau of the federal government, the National Science Foundation. If the referees for a grant proposal submitted there happen not to like your work, your grant proposal will not be funded— period. In the first part of the twentieth century, a grant rejection, like a paper rejection, would not stop an idea from being presented or from being developed. In this earlier period, a tenured professorship came with a small amount of research funds. Since the universities of the time were not dependent on government grant money, tenure decisions were not dominated by whether a scholar up for tenure obtained a grant.

Now most American universities, even the liberal arts colleges, are desperately dependent on government grants. A typical National Science Foundation grant, for example, has an "overhead" charge, which can amount to fifty percent of the grant. This "overhead" charge goes directly to the university administration; the scientist never sees a dime of this part of his grant. If the total amount of the grant is $1,000,000, and the overhead is fifty percent, the scientist who secures the grant has $500,000 to do his research. The other $500,000 goes to the university bottom line. A university is strongly motivated to hire only those scientists who can obtain large grants. Pushing an idea that is contrary to current opinion is not a good way to obtain large grants.

I have experienced this form of discrimination first hand. When I came up for tenure at Tulane in 1983, I was already controversial. At the time I had proposed that general relativity might allow time travel, and

I had published a series of papers claiming that we might be the only intelligent life form in the visible universe. At the time, these claims were far outside the mainstream. (They are standard claims now. Kip Thorne of Cal Tech has argued for the possibility of time travel, using the same mechanism I originally proposed. The scientific community is now largely skeptical of extraterrestrial intelligence, if for no other reason than the failure of the SETI radio searches.) My views made it very difficult to get an NSF grant. One reviewer of one of my grant proposals wrote that it would be inadvisable to award me a grant because I might spend some of the time working on my "crazy" ideas on ETI. I didn't get the grant.

It began to look as if I wouldn't get tenure. I had a large number of papers published in refereed journals—including *Physical Review Letters* and *Nature*—but no government grants. For this reason, and for this reason alone (I was told later), the initial vote of the Tulane Physics Department was to deny me tenure. But I had another grant proposal under consideration by the NSF. I called Rich Isaacson, the head of the Gravitation Division of the NSF, and told him about my situation. Rich called me a few weeks later, and told me that the referee reports for my proposal were "all over the map"—some reviewers said I was the most original relativity physicist since Einstein, and others said I was an incompetent crackpot. Rich said that in such a circumstance, he could act as he saw fit. He saw fit to fund my proposal. I had grant support! I also had tenure; the physics department reversed its negative vote.

But even at the time I worried that this sequence of events boded ill for science. Rich was the head of the only government agency that supplied funds for research in relativity physics. He knew that an influential minority of physicists thought well of my work (especially John Wheeler of Princeton, who is really the father of most relativity research in the U.S.). But what if I was engaged in a long-term project that had not definitely established itself? Except for the lack of a grant, I had impressed many of my colleagues as a capable physicist. In today's science this is not enough, however. It is absolutely essential to obtain a government grant. I got the grant—and tenure—only because a single man thought well of my work. If he had not, then I would not have gotten tenure. Nor would I have gotten tenure at any other American university. I have always had a high opinion of Rich Isaacson, but no man is God. No man should have the effective power to deny or award tenure for an entire field over the entire United States. But the current grant support system has created such research czars, who are discouraged from supporting radical ideas.

The most radical ideas are those that are perceived to support religion, specifically Judaism and Christianity. When I was a student at MIT in the late 1960s, I audited a course in cosmology from the physics Nobelist Steven Weinberg. He told his class that of the theories of cosmology, he preferred the Steady State Theory because "it *least* resembled the account in Genesis" (my emphasis). In his book *The First Three Minutes,* Weinberg explains his earlier rejection of the Big Bang Theory: "[O]ur mistake is not that we take our theories too seriously, but that we do not take them seriously enough. It is always hard to realize that these numbers and equations we play with at our desks have something to do with the real world. Even worse, there often seems to be a general agreement that certain phenomena are just not fit subjects for respectable theoretical and experimental effort."[12]

I have now known Weinberg for over thirty years, and I know that he has *always* taken the equations of physics very seriously indeed. He and I are both convinced that the equations of physics are the best guide to reality, *especially* when the predictions of these equations are contrary to common sense. But as he himself points out in his book, the Big Bang Theory was an automatic consequence of standard thermodynamics, standard gravity theory, and standard nuclear physics. All of the basic physics one needs for the Big Bang Theory was well established in the 1930s, some two decades before the theory was worked out. Weinberg rejected this standard physics not because he didn't take the equations of physics seriously, but because he did not like the religious implications of the laws of physics. A recent poll of the members of the National Academy of Sciences, published in *Scientific American,* indicated that more than ninety percent are atheists. These men and women have built their entire worldview on atheism. They would be exceedingly reluctant to admit that any result of science could be valid if it even suggested that God could exist.

I discovered this the hard way when I published my book *The Physics of Immortality.* The entire book is devoted to describing what the known laws of physics predict the far future of the universe will be like. Not once in the entire book do I use anything but the known physical laws, the laws of physics that are in all the textbooks, and which agree with all experiments conducted to date. Unfortunately, in the book I gave reasons for believing that the final state of the universe—a state outside of space and time, and not material—should be identified with the Judeo-Christian God. (It would take a book to explain why.) My scientific colleagues, atheists to a man, were outraged. Even though the theory of the final state of the universe involved only known physics, my fellow physicists refused even to discuss the theory. If the known laws of physics imply that God exists, then in their opinion, this can only mean that the laws of physics have to be wrong. This past September, at a conference held at Windsor Castle, I asked the well-known cosmologist Paul Davies what he thought of my theory. He replied that he could find nothing wrong with it mathematically, but he asked what justified my assumption that the known laws of physics were correct. At the same conference, the famous physicist Freeman Dyson refused to discuss my theory—period. I would not encounter such refusals if I had not chosen to point out my theory's theological implications.

In the foreword to *The Physics of Immortality*, I included the standard acknowledgment of grant support. The government official (of Austria in this case) who provided funds to partially support my research told me that he had received enormous criticism from his fellow bureaucrats. They were outraged that a defense of Christianity was being supported by a respectable science organization. The California Skeptics Society founder, Michael Shermer, informs me that a proposal to the NSF to fund the publication of all of Isaac Newton's to-date unpublished work on theology was rejected even though the proposal was made by one of the world's leading Newton scholars. The reason given, according to Shermer, was that it would be bad for science if it became generally known that the greatest scientist of all time actually believed in God. Clearly, the scientific community is not open to any evidence or any theory that might even hint that God really exists and might actually act the in physical universe.

INTELLIGENT DESIGN

The most radical scientific theory with religious implications is Intelligent Design. It is impossible to get any member of the National Academy of Sciences to consider it seriously. The typical reaction of such scientists is to foam at the mouth when the phrase "intelligent design" is mentioned. I have recently experienced this. In the fall of 2002, I arranged for Bill Dembski to come to Tulane to debate a Darwinian on the Tulane faculty. (This faculty member was appropriately named Steve Darwin.) Bill presented only the evidence against Darwinism in the debate, while Steve's response unfortunately had quite a few ad hominem remarks. Steve has continued to be friendly to me personally. But ever since the Dembski/Darwin debate, another evolutionist on the Tulane faculty—who shall remain nameless!—glares at me every time he sees me. Before the debate he and I were friends. Now he considers me a monster of moral depravity. Yet if the religious implications of Intelligent Design are ignored, if the theory is called something besides "intelligent design," then the scientific community is quite open to intelligent design. The evolutionist Lynn Margulis, a member of the National Academy of Sciences, has made much the same criticism of modern Darwinism that Michael Behe and Bill Dembski have made. She has put her arguments in a book titled *Acquiring Genomes: A Theory of the Origins of Species,* written with her son Dorion Sagan. The book has a foreword written by Ernst Mayr, a retired professor of evolutionary biology at Harvard, who agrees with Margulis that Darwinism has the problems she discusses. This is especially significant since Mayr is not just an ordinary evolutionist. He has been called the "Dean of American Evolutionists," and he is one of the founders of the Modern Synthesis, which is the modern version of Darwinism. Mayr does not think that Margulis has resolved the problems with Darwinism, nor do I. I should mention that, to her credit, however, she cites Michael Behe's *Darwin's Black Box* in her book.

The problem that Behe, Dembski, and Margulis address is that random mutation is simply too slow and too undirected to generate the enormous change we see in the fossil record. I shall not discuss the evidence for this; the other essays in this book do an excellent job. (Or if you want a presentation by someone with impressive credentials who never uses the dreaded expression "intelligent design," read Margulis's book.) I do, however, want to make two points not raised elsewhere in this collection of essays.

The first is that "intelligent design" could have been called "Asa Gray Darwinism." Asa Gray was a nineteenth-century botanist at Harvard. He was a friend of Charles Darwin long before the publication of *On the Origin of Species by Means of Natural Selection.* He arranged for the *Origin* to be published in America. He was Darwin's greatest supporter in America, writing many articles in support of Darwin's theory of evolution. In one crucial respect he disagreed with Darwin, although not with the mechanism of natural selection. Everyone, every creationist, believes that natural selection operates in nature. The question is, and has always been, where do the superior gene complexes, the genes that are going to win the struggle for existence, come from.

Asa Gray believed that the superior mutations, the irreducible complexity in the genome, came from God. He rejected the idea that superior mutations appeared by random variation. Instead, the mutations appeared in a sequence in the genome in a way intended and actively directed by God. Once a build-up of what we would now call a gene complex was complete, this sequence would be turned on, and a new species would appear. Then, and only then, would natural selection operate.

Remarkably, Charles Darwin himself gave the strongest argument for Asa Gray Darwinism and against his own random variation version of Darwinism. Darwin pointed out in the last few pages of his second most important book, *The Variation of Animals and Plants under Domestication*, that his own version of Darwinism could not be an ultimate theory. His own version of Darwinism could only be an approximation. In actuality, at the most fundamental level, random mutations did not, and could not, occur. The reason, wrote Darwin, is simple. At the most fundamental level, the laws of physics govern everything, and the laws of physics are deterministic. Therefore, at the most fundamental level, there are no random events. The cosmic ray that causes a particular superior mutation in the genes is not a random, undetermined event but was determined by the laws of physics and the initial conditions of the universe. If we knew the ultimate laws of physics and knew the initial conditions of the universe, we could predict which mutations would occur and when they would occur. We would be able to predict the entire future course of biological history.

Charles Darwin got it exactly correct. He had a much deeper understanding of evolution than any twentieth-century evolutionist. As a physicist, I am aware that quantum mechanics, the central theory of modern physics, is even more deterministic than was the classical mechanics of which Darwin was aware. More than this, quantum mechanics is actually teleological, though physicists don't use this loaded word (we call it "unitarity" instead of "teleology"). That is, quantum mechanics says that it is completely correct to say that the universe's evolution is determined not by how it started in the Big Bang, but by the final state of the universe. Every stage of universal history, including every stage of biological and human history, is determined by the ultimate goal of the universe. And if I am correct that the universal final state is indeed God, then every stage of universal history, in particular every mutation that has ever occurred, or ever will occur in any living being, is determined by the action of God. In other words, if the laws of modern physics are correct, then Darwin has actually given the strongest argument for Asa Gray Darwinism. Charles Darwin was actually an Intelligent Design Creationist!

If my Tulane University ex-friend ever reads these words, he would want to do more than glare. He would want to strangle me for writing such a heresy! He definitely would not approve of these ideas were he to be the referee of a paper of mine wherein this argument is repeated. He would definitely reject any grant proposal I would make that contains these ideas.

SUGGESTIONS TO MAKE SCIENCE MORE OPEN TO NEW IDEAS

I shall make two recommendations that, if adopted, would make science more open to new ideas. One concerns a way of opening up the refereed journals to new ideas, and the other, a way of breaking the centralization of research funding.

The problem with the referee system for papers is that in the post–World War II period, the referees are almost never the "peers" of a scientific genius. The size of the scientific community makes true peer review impossible. Most referees are "stupid" (to use Nobelist Blobel's adjective), at least relative to the authors whose breakthrough work we would most like to see published in the leading journals. But I will grant that these "stupid" referees serve a useful purpose if the scientific community remains as large as it is today. Most papers written by most members of the scientific community are worthless. In fact, most papers are never cited by other scientists. These trash papers are written because of the "publish or perish" rule imposed by universities. A referee, even a stupid one, can at least keep out the worst of the trash papers from the journals. But we don't want to misidentify works of genius as trash, which is exactly what the typical referee in fact does.

So I propose that the leading journals in all branches of science establish a "two-tier" system. The first tier is the usual referee system. The new tier will consist of publishing a paper in the journal automatically if the paper is submitted with letters from several leading experts in the field saying, "this paper should be published." Crick and Watson followed this procedure in the case of their famous paper on the double helix structure of DNA. The paper was never sent to referees.[13] Instead the paper was submitted to *Nature* with a "publish" covering letter from Sir Lawrence Bragg, the head of the Cavendish Laboratory at Cambridge University, and also a Nobel Prize winner. Charles Darwin's first paper on evolution was published in the *Journal of the Linnean Society* upon the recommendation of several leading members of that society. In order to circumvent the referee bottleneck, a journal could list on the web the experts, and would-be authors would be advised to contact them by e-mail only. As long as the number of experts is "large"—in physics, several hundred would be sufficient—the chance of a "stupid" referee being able to stop the publication of a breakthrough paper is small. A genius could interact directly with another genius. I would think a single letter of recommendation to publish would be sufficient if the letter were from a Nobelist or an NAS member.

In all the cases mentioned above, the genius papers (as we now regard them) would have been published immediately. The chaos genius Feigenbaum, for example, mentions by name a few of his pre-publication supporters, and some of these are universally recognized as geniuses themselves. Feigenbaum had the advantage of being known to these men personally. The unknown patent office clerk has a problem. For him the physics community has the lanl database,[14] which is the modern equivalent of the early twentieth century *Zeitschrift für Physik.* Anyone can place a paper on the lanl database. There is no referee to stand in the author's way. Of course, a great deal of nonsense is placed on the lanl database, but in my own field of general relativity it seems no worse then the huge amount of nonsense that appears in the leading refereed journals, including *Physical Review Letters.* An unknown author first has to put his paper on the lanl database and then persuade a leading physicist to read it. If a leader could be persuaded to read it, and take it seriously, his recommendation would ensure that it would be published in a leading journal.

The grant-funding problem is more difficult to solve. The ideal solution would be to abolish federal support of science altogether. In the "golden years" of physics in Germany in the first thirty years of the twentieth century, the German national government provided very little support for physics, or for science of any sort. Instead, the regional German governments (the German equivalent of states in the U.S.) provided the funds for sciences through their funding of the universities. It was impossible for one small group to control thought by means of a stranglehold over a centralized funding agency. All this changed when Adolf Hitler rose to power in 1933. Hitler sought conformity of thought by centralizing all areas of intellectual endeavor in Germany. The universities were even compelled to dismiss professors whose opinions were not to the liking of the central authorities. Unfortunately, as a consequence of the Second World War and the Cold War, the United States is now enforcing a similar conformity through its own science policy.

What's needed now is the "trust-busting" philosophy of the late nineteenth century. If it was bad to have Standard Oil control ninety percent of the oil refining capacity of the U.S., it is equally bad for the federal government—or a few universities like Harvard, Princeton, MIT and Cal Tech, which disproportionately influence federal support of science—to control the production of scientific results. Monopoly is bad, both in the economy and in science.

But as I said, there are now too many special interests involved in federal science funding to abolish the system altogether. I would therefore recommend, as a second-best alternative to abolishing the system entirely, that "earmarked" funding be increased—"pork barrel" funding in the language of the monopolists. Individual senators and representatives would designate these grants to go to particular universities in their own states and districts. Such grants would bypass the centralized referee system. The individual congressmen could consult the referees they themselves regarded as "expert." While the funding decisions would indeed be based on politics, the important thing is that the politics would be coming from outside a narrow, self-selected group of "experts." If my recommendation were followed, science funding would be spread out among the states and congressional districts more or less as it was in the golden years of physics. It would be much more difficult for a small group to control the generation of new ideas in science.

My own state of Louisiana has a model program that I hope could be emulated by the other states. A decade ago, Louisiana received a billion-dollar windfall arising from a settlement with the federal government on the division of revenues from the sale of oil leases in the Gulf of Mexico. The citizens of Louisiana voted to establish an educational foundation with the money. The foundation awards grants to Louisiana scientists and only to Louisiana scientists. The foundation sometimes solicits opinions about the worth of a Louisiana scientist's work from scientists outside Louisiana, but it is not required to do so. In this way, a source of research funding not centrally controlled by the federal government has been established. If the federal government were to decrease funding to federal government labs, and use the money saved to set up foundations analogous to Louisiana's in all states, we would see an increase in scientific breakthroughs. The astronomer Martin Harwit pointed out in his book *Cosmic Discovery* that in the period 1955 to 1980, national astronomy labs absorbed seventy percent of the federal research funds in astronomy but made none of the astronomy breakthroughs of that period.[15] Shutting down the labs would not decrease the number of great scientific advances.

The federal government must not impose constraints on what is "valid" research. In particular, if a state foundation chooses to fund research in Intelligent Design, then it should be allowed to do so.

Part Three

Leaving the Darwinian Fold

Michael J. Behe

8. A Catholic Scientist Looks at Darwinism

One Day in the Lab

One slow afternoon in the late 1970s I was hanging out in my lab at the National Institutes of Health near Washington, D.C., where I worked as a postdoctoral researcher investigating aspects of DNA structure. A fellow postdoc, Joanne Nickol, and I were chewing the fat about the big questions: God, life, the universe—that sort of thing. She and I were both Roman Catholics—Joanne's brother was a priest; I'm from a family of eight children—and so had the same general attitude toward many topics, including an easy acceptance of the idea of evolution, that life unfolded over a long time under the governance of secondary causes and natural laws. Unlike some Protestant friends of mine who seemed obsessed by it, we Catholics were always cool about evolution because we knew that God could make life any way He wanted to, including indirectly. Who were we to tell Him different? The critical point was that God was the Creator of life, no matter how He went about it.

I didn't know it at the time—probably because like most people I picked up my attitudes and habits of mind indirectly through family and teachers—but my attitude pretty faithfully reflected the take the Catholic Church officially had on evolution from the beginning. To see that, consider the following excerpt from a 20,000-word article on evolution that appeared in the 1909 edition of *The Catholic Encyclopedia* (which my wife purchased at a local library's old book sale), written by two Jesuits, one of whom was a professor of biology at St. Ignatius college in Valkenburg, Holland, complete with the imprimatur of Cardinal John Farley of New York, and published "under the auspices of the Knights of Columbus Catholic Truth Committee":

A. ATTITUDE OF CATHOLICS TOWARDS THE THEORY. — One of the most important questions for every educated Catholic of to-day is: What is to be thought of the theory of evolution? Is it to be rejected as unfounded and inimical to Christianity, or is it to be accepted as an established theory altogether compatible with the principles of a Christian conception of the universe? We must carefully distinguish between the different meanings of the words *theory of evolution* in order to give a clear and correct answer to this question. We must distinguish (1) between the theory of evolution as a scientific hypothesis and as a philosophical speculation; (2) between the theory of evolution as based on theistic principles and as based on a materialistic and atheistic foundation; (3) between the theory of evolution and Darwinism; (4) between the theory of evolution as applied to the vegetable and animal kingdoms and as applied to man.[1]

In other words, Catholics, and thoughtful theists generally, should not reject evolution but should examine it and make necessary distinctions about the many different concepts that often are all bundled together under the title "theory of evolution." The principle distinctions we need to make, to re-phrase what the article states, are (1) between evolution as a scientific hypothesis reasonably supported by the data, and evolution as an assumption about the way the world must be, regardless of the availability of supporting data; (2) between evolution as an utterly random process, foreseen by no one, and evolution as the intended result of God's will; (3) between "evolution" understood simply as descent with modification, with the question of how such a process could have happened left open, and "evolution" as Darwin's specific theory, of change driven by natural selection; (4) between the theory applied to body and the theory applied to mind. We should consider the evidence, make distinctions, keep what is good and solid, and toss out the rest.

The course of my conversation with Joanne in the lab hit a little bump. Because we were taught biology well in parochial school, we both knew that the evidence for Darwinian evolution by natural selection was ultra strong. But when the topic turned to the origin of life she asked, "Well, what would you need to get the first cell?" "You'd need a membrane for sure," said I. "And metabolism." "Can't do without a genetic code," said she, "and proteins." At that point we stopped, looked at each other and, in unison, hollered "*Naaaahh!*" Then we laughed and went back to work.

From a distance of years I notice three things about my conversation with Joanne (who died about a decade ago). The first is that the notion, widely accepted among scientists, that undirected physical laws started life, struck both of us—both well-trained young scientists who would be happy to accept it—as preposterous, because of the many complicated preconditions necessary just to get things underway. Second, we apparently hadn't given it much thought before then. And third, we both just shrugged it off and went back to work. I suppose we were thinking that even if we didn't know how life started by natural processes, surely somebody must know. Or that somebody would figure it out before long. Or eventually. Or that it wasn't important. Or something.

I no longer think that way. Now I judge the topic to be quite important. Now I'm very dubious that science will figure out how life started if it restricts the scope of its investigations just to physical laws. Now I realize that it isn't just me—nobody knows how life could have started.

And now my skepticism has expanded far beyond the question of the origin of life, to the question of how life could have developed, once there were single-celled organisms, by exclusively natural processes—that is, to the question of the plausibility of Darwinian evolution. Spurred to investigate by reading *Evolution: A Theory in Crisis* by Michael Denton in the late 1980s, I discovered my blissful assumption that *somebody* must know how Darwinian evolution produced life, even if I didn't, was quite wrong. The bland assurances I got in high school, college, and graduate school, that science had a good handle on how natural selection crafted the intricate details of life, were false. Perusing the technical literature myself for detailed, meaty answers to the question of how the fantastically intricate mechanisms of the cell could develop step-by-step without guidance, as Darwinian theory said they must, yielded only sparse, hand-waving conjectures. My skepticism about Darwinism quickly led me further; I later became convinced, based on the interactive complexity of biochemical systems, that they were deliberately designed by an intelligent agent.

I will not rehearse here the arguments and examples that convince me of design, nor address the numerous objections—many spurious, some thoughtful—that have been advanced against my biochemical argument for design. The interested reader can find all those easily enough, beginning with my book *Darwin's Black Box*. Rather, in this chapter I want to develop the kind of conversation I might have with Joanne today if I could. I want to look at several aspects of evolution from a spe-cifically Catholic point of view: whether the topic is important; the free-dom a Catholic has in approaching the subject; and, finally, the obstacles that can prevent a person from judging the topic for himself.[2]

WHY IS EVOLUTION IMPORTANT?

In the year 1828 a German chemist named Friedrich Wöhler heated ammonium cyanate in his laboratory and was astonished to find that a substance called urea was formed. To most people today that result is about as interesting as reading a list of ingredients on the back of a can of processed food. Wöhler's work, however, has had far-reaching scien-tific and philosophical consequences with which we continue to wrestle. Ammonium cyanate, it turns out, is an "inorganic" chemical—one that is not derived from living material. Urea, however, is a biological waste product. Wöhler's synthesis of urea from inorganic chemicals shattered the easy distinction between life and non-life and opened up for scien-tific study all of life. For if life is made of ordinary matter, the same as rocks and gases and so on, then science can study it. And in the 170-plus years since Wöhler's experiment, science has learned a lot about life. We've discovered the structure of DNA, cracked the genetic code, learned to clone genes, and cells, and even whole organisms.

Now, here is an interesting question: Since Wöhler's work showed that the stuff of life is ordinary physical matter, and since studying the properties of matter is the job of science, why should this be the con-cern of religion? Why should the physical processes which govern the formation of life interest the Catholic Church any more than the pro-cesses which form snowflakes or mountain ranges? Well, the obvious answer is that *we* are living things, too. And we know through our faith, and through philosophical and theological reflection, that humans are not merely physical objects. Rather, in us are somehow combined both physical and spiritual elements. Therefore, both science *and* religion have a legitimate interest in the question of how life works and how it got here. Pope John Paul II made this clear in his statement to the Pontifical Academy of Sciences in October 1996: "The church's magisterium is directly concerned with the question of evolution, for it involves the con-ception of man. . . . The human individual cannot be subordinated as a pure means or a pure instrument, either to the species or to society; he has value per se. He is a person."[3]

In his statement the pope acknowledged that a theory of evolution of the human body can be a legitimate scientific conclusion. But he also noted that there is more to a theory of evolution than just a collection of facts: "Rather than *the* theory of evolution, we should speak of *several* theories of evolution. On the one hand, this plurality has to do with the different explanations advanced for the mechanism of evolution, and on the other, with the various philosophies on which it is based. Hence the existence of materialist, reductionist and spiritualist interpretations."[4]

So the pope divides a theory of evolution into two separate components: 1) the mechanism whereby life was first produced and then diversified; and 2) the philosophy that is attached to the mechanism by proponents of the theory. He clearly rejects materialistic philosophies of evolution: "Theories of evolution which, in accordance with the philosophies inspiring them, consider the spirit as emerging from the forces of living matter or as a mere epiphenomenon of this matter, are incompatible with the truth about man."[5] To see why the pope's remarks on this point are necessary, let us briefly examine some philosophical ideas that have been attached to Darwin's theory of evolution.

Charles Darwin's claim to fame, of course, is that he proposed a completely naturalistic mechanism whereby evolution might take place. Before Darwin's time the similarities between various species of living organisms had led several scientists to suggest that living things are related by descent from a common ancestor, but no one could imagine what might cause organisms to change. In retrospect, Darwin's elegant theory seemed to be simplicity itself. He observed that there is variation in all species. He reasoned that since limited food supplies could not support all organisms that are born, the ones whose chance variation gave them an edge in the struggle for life would tend to survive and reproduce, outcompeting the less favored ones. If the variation were inherited, then the characteristics of the species would change over time. Over great periods, great changes might occur. Darwin had hit upon a mechanism for evolution: random variation sifted by natural selection.

Now, the real issue for Christian theology is that one word, *random*. Many Christians have thought that evolution by natural selection was easily compatible with their faith because, in the eyes of an infinite God, there is no truly random event. What appears to us as random is nonetheless God's work of creation, planned by Him from all eternity. However, a number of people, including some prominent and influential scientists, do not share the Christian, theistic interpretation of Darwin's theory. Many of the leading voices in biology throughout this century have consistently and aggressively proclaimed that Darwin's theory leaves no room for a Creator because truly random processes, unintended by anyone, are enough to produce life. For example, in 1959 a large meeting was held at the University of Chicago to celebrate the centenary of the publication of *The Origin of Species*. One of the speakers there was Julian Huxley, the grandson of Thomas Henry Huxley, Darwin's contemporary and great defender. In his speech, Huxley proclaimed: "In the evolutionary pattern of thought there is no longer any need or room for the supernatural. . . . Man is the result of a process that did not have him in mind."[6]

Although still a distinctly minority opinion in our country, this view persists into our day. Richard Dawkins, the Oxford University professor and well-known popularizer of materialistic Darwinism, has written that "Darwin made it possible to be an intellectually fulfilled atheist."[7] In his book *Darwin's Dangerous Idea*, the philosopher Daniel Dennett compares religious believers to wild animals who may have to be caged, and says that parents should be prevented, presumably by coercion, from misinforming their children about the truth of Darwinian evolution, which is so evident to him.[8]

Well, of course, these people are professors and professors say silly things all the time; why should we pay any attention to them? Because, although usually couched in less inflammatory phrases, the materialistic interpretation of evolution is the one that dominates public discussion, and as such it is taught to many children in the nation's schools. For example, a popular high school biology textbook tells students that: "Of course, there has never been any kind of plan to [evolution] because evolution works without either plan or purpose. . . . It is important to keep this concept in mind: *Evolution is random and undirected*."[9] (Emphasis in the original.)

In 1995 the National Association of Biology Teachers adopted the following definition (since revised under pressure) of evolutionary theory: "The diversity of life on earth is the outcome of evolution: an unsupervised, impersonal, unpredictable, and natural process of temporal descent with genetic modification. . . ."[10] It is not hard to guess Whom they are trying to exclude with words like unsupervised and impersonal.

THE BOTTOM LINE

Recall that Pope John Paul II divides a theory of evolution into its mechanism and its philosophy. Now, of course, these statements I just cited are materialistic philosophy, not science. Science cannot measure plans or purposes or supervision. Nonetheless some scientists and scientific organizations try to attach highly debatable philosophical baggage to Darwin's mechanism by calling the whole package "science." Well, if materialism is philosophically inadequate, what philosophy should a Catholic scientist attach to a mechanism of evolution, or to any scientific theory?

In his recent encyclical *Fides et Ratio* the pope offers clear guidance. He begins by telling us: "Faith and reason are like two wings on which the human spirit rises to the contemplation of truth; and God has placed in the human heart a desire to know the truth—in a word, to know himself—so that, by knowing and loving God, men and women may also come to the fullness of truth about themselves."[11] Thus a Catholic scientist realizes that his faith is an integral part of his understanding of nature; faith cannot be set aside when investigating nature anymore than when studying Scripture. But as John Paul emphasizes, contrary to the caricature, faith is not constraining, it is enlightening:

> Faith intervenes not to abolish reason's autonomy nor to reduce its scope for action, but solely to bring the human being to understand that in these events it is the God of Israel who acts. Thus the world and the events of history cannot be understood in depth without professing faith in the God who is at work in them. Faith sharpens the inner eye, opening the mind to discover in the flux of events the workings of Providence.[12]

He further points out that: "It is the one and the same God who establishes and guarantees the intelligibility and reasonableness of the natural order of things upon which scientists confidently depend, and who reveals himself as the Father of our Lord Jesus Christ."[13] This, then, is the bottom line for all Catholic scientists—no matter what one hypothesizes as a mechanism of evolution or anything else in nature, one must realize that it is God who created nature and upon whom nature depends for its very existence.

Well, those are fine sentiments, but does the knowledge of faith really matter in a practical way? Looking at the same data, how different can two people's interpretations of nature be? It turns out that they can be very different indeed. To demonstrate, let's look at two people's views on what science tells us about the nature of the universe and life. The first person, Richard Dawkins, professor of the public understanding of science at Oxford University, has stated that: "The universe we observe has precisely the properties we should expect if there is at bottom no design, no purpose, no evil and no good, nothing but pointless indifference."[14]

Certainly a dreary view, but a seriously proposed view. The second point of view is that of Cardinal Joseph Ratzinger. In 1986 Cardinal Ratzinger wrote a little book entitled *In the Beginning: A Catholic Understanding of the Story of Creation and the Fall*. In the book Cardinal Ratzinger wrote:

> Let us go directly to the question of evolution and its mechanisms. Microbiology and biochemistry have brought revolutionary insights here. . . . They have brought us to the awareness that an organism and a machine have many points in common. . . . Their functioning presupposes a precisely thought-through and therefore reasonable design.[15]
>
> It is the affair of the natural sciences to explain how the tree of life in particular continues to grow and how new branches shoot out from it. This is not a matter for faith. But we must have the audacity to say that the great projects of the living creation are not the products of chance and error. . . . (They) point to a creating Reason and show us a creating Intelligence, and they do so more luminously and radiantly today than ever before. Thus we can say today with a new certitude and joyousness that the human being is indeed a divine project, which only the creating Intelligence was strong and great and audacious enough to conceive of. Human beings are not a mistake but something willed.[16]

It seems to me that one could hardly have two more divergent understandings of the universe than those of Professor Dawkins and Cardinal Ratzinger.

Now, let's notice three things about the Cardinal's statement. First, unlike Professor Dawkins, Ratzinger says that nature does appear to exhibit purpose and design. Second, to support the argument he points to *physical evidence*—the "great projects of the living creation" which "point to a creating reason"—not to philosophical, or theological, or scriptural arguments, but to tangible structures. The third point is that Ratzinger cites the science of biochemistry—the study of the molecular foundation of life—as having particular relevance to his conclusion. In the next section I will briefly explain why I think Cardinal Ratzinger has the stronger position, and why Professor Dawkins need not despair. (For a more detailed discussion, see *Darwin's Black Box*.)

Their Complex Structures

In *Fides et Ratio* Pope John Paul II writes: "Finally, I cannot fail to address a word to *scientists*, whose research offers an ever greater knowledge of the universe as a whole and of the incredibly rich array of its component parts, animate and inanimate, with their complex atomic and molecular structures."[17] Let's very briefly examine just one example of the *rich array* of the *component parts* of *animate nature, with their complex structures*, which have proved to be much more complex than anyone expected.

The bacterial flagellum[18] is quite literally an outboard motor that some bacteria use to swim. Like the machines that power motorboats, the flagellum is a rotary device, where the rotating surface pushes against the liquid medium, propelling the bacterium along. The part of the flagellum that acts as the propeller is a long whip-like structure made of a protein called flagellin. The propeller is attached to the drive shaft by hook protein that acts as a universal joint, allowing freedom of rotation for the propeller and drive shaft. The drive shaft is attached to the rotary motor, which uses a flow of acid from outside of the bacterium to the inside in order to power its turning. The drive shaft has to poke through the bacterial membrane, and several types of proteins act as bushing material to allow that to happen. Although this discussion makes the flagellum sound complicated, it really doesn't do justice to the full complexity. Thorough genetic studies have shown that about forty different proteins are required for a functional flagellum, either as parts of the flagellum itself, or as parts of the system that builds this machine in the cell. And in the absence of most of those proteins, one doesn't get a flagellum that spins half as fast as it used to, or a quarter as fast. Either no flagellum gets produced at all, or one that doesn't work.

I like to tell people of the flagellum because when they hear of it, they quickly realize that, as Cardinal Ratzinger alluded, it is a *machine*. It is not just like a machine or analogous to a machine; it is indeed a real machine. And that gives us a strong indication about where it came from.

Three Views on Origins by Catholic Academics

Now, what is a Catholic to make of the discovery of such intricate molecular machines, unimagined by any scientist in Darwin's day? How did they get here? To show the broad range of thinking available to Catholics on that question, let's examine the divergent views of three people who have published books on the subject relatively recently. First I'll discuss my own ideas; then I will just briefly touch on the writings of Brown University biologist Kenneth Miller and Georgetown University theologian John Haught.

In *Darwin's Black Box* I argued that many biochemical systems are stumbling blocks for natural selection because they are *irreducibly complex*, meaning they need several parts working together in order to function. A good illustration of an irreducibly complex system is a simple mechanical mousetrap. If the mousetrap is missing any of its pieces, it doesn't catch mice. Therefore it is irreducibly complex. It turns out that irreducibly complex systems are headaches for Darwinian theory because they are resistant to being produced in the gradual, step-by-step manner that Darwin envisioned. For example, if we wanted to evolve a mousetrap, where would we start? Could we start with just the platform and hope to catch a few mice rather inefficiently? Then add the holding bar, and improve the efficiency a bit? Then add the other pieces one at a time, steadily improving the whole apparatus? No, of course we can't do that because the mousetrap doesn't work at all until it is essentially completely assembled. Many biochemical systems, such as the bacterial flagellum, also appear to be irreducibly complex, and thus difficult to explain by Darwinian means.

I have gone on to argue that such systems are better explained as the result of design—purposeful, intentional design by an intelligent agent. Although some of my critics, noting that I am a Catholic, argue that design is a religious idea, I disagree. I think a conclusion of design is completely empirical, and can be justified solely by physical data, as well as by an understanding of how we come to a conclusion of design. To see how we detect design, consider the Far Side cartoon by Gary Larson in which a team of explorers is going through a jungle, and the lead explorer has been strung up and skewered by a hidden trap. One companion turns to another and confides, "That's why I never walk in front." Now every person who sees the cartoon immediately knows that the trap was *designed*. In fact, Larson's humor depends on you recognizing the design. It wouldn't be terribly funny if the first explorer had just fallen off a cliff or a rotted tree accidentally fell on him. No, his fate was intended. But how do you know that from looking at the cartoon? How does the audience apprehend that this trap was designed? Is it a religious conclusion? No. You can tell that the trap was designed because of the way the parts interact with great specificity to perform a function. Like the mousetrap, no one looking at the cartoon system would mistake it for an accidental arrangement of parts.

Who did the designing, when, where, and how, remain open questions that may or may not be accessible to science. But, I argue, the fact of design itself can be deduced from the structure of the systems that biochemists have elucidated in past decades. Much more can be said about design than I have space for here. For those interested in a rigorous treatment of the subject I recommend William Dembski's 1998 book, *The Design Inference*.

Although I think my arguments are nothing short of compelling, some other Catholic academics have disagreed with me and have published other views. Brown University biology professor Ken Miller describes himself as "an orthodox Catholic and an orthodox Darwinist." In his 1999 book *Finding Darwin's God* Miller defends the standard view that, despite the unexpected complexity uncovered at the molecular level, natural selection is the best explanation for life. While admitting that Darwinian explanations currently don't exist for many molecular systems, he expresses confidence that explanations will be forthcoming as science progresses. Nonetheless, in his book he argues that the universe was indeed designed, using the fine-tuning of cosmological constants as his primary evidence. He also finds scope for God's action in quantum indeterminacy and argues that miracles can occur, but that science can say nothing about them.

In *God After Darwin* Georgetown University theologian John Haught argues that Darwinian materialism cannot account for life, especially novelties such as the origin of life and mind, ordered metabolism, multicellular organisms, and so on. That, he argues, requires *information* to be added to life:

> The point I wish to emphasize here is that the use of the metaphor "information" by scientists today is a transparent indication that they now acknowledge, at least implicitly, that something more is going on in nature and its evolution than simply brute exchanges along the matter-energy continuum. Though it is not physically separate, information is logically distinguishable from mass and energy. Information is quietly resident in nature, and in spite of being non-energetic and non-massive, it powerfully patterns subordinate natural elements and routines into hierarchically distinct domains.[19]

While rejecting the phrase "intelligent design" as I and others have used it, Haught attributes to brute matter itself a sort of consciousness, a certain ability to respond to what he calls "divine enticement," and he argues that a full explanation of the unfolding of life would necessarily be theological.

The point I'm trying to drive home here by discussing my own work as well as the work of Miller and Haught, is that a very wide range of views about the *mechanism* of evolution is consistent with Catholic teaching, from the natural selection defended by Miller, to the intelligent design I have proposed, to the animated, information-suffused universe that John Haught sees. Those mechanisms are all proposed by persons who attach the same bottom-line *philosophy* to their ideas that Pope John Paul described: that "it is the God of Israel who acts" and that "it is the one and the same God who establishes and guarantees the intelligibility and reasonableness of the natural order of things upon which scientists confidently depend, and who reveals himself as the Father of our Lord Jesus Christ." Indeed, the range of possibilities that are available under a Catholic viewpoint is much wider than under a materialistic viewpoint. Materialism virtually requires something such as Darwinism to be true, and it is difficult (although not impossible) to reconcile with Haught's views or my own. Thus a Catholic is free to follow the evidence of nature wherever he or she thinks it leads, without the requirement to shoehorn all of biology into the narrow range of options permitted by materialism.

A CAUTIOUS ATTITUDE

So, the positive message here is the freedom of reason guided by faith. In the remainder of the chapter, however, I'd like to temper the upside by pointing out the need for caution in evaluating theories of evolution. My "downside" message will be the danger to reason posed by materialistic ideology. In *Fides et Ratio* Pope John Paul writes: "There are in the life of a human being many more truths which are simply believed than truths which are acquired by way of personal verification. Who, for instance, could assess critically the countless scientific findings upon which modern life is based?"[20]

Who indeed? Everyone, including scientists, relies on others for the overwhelming majority of information they receive about the way the world works. Such reliance can be a human good—an occasion for gratitude to others for knowledge about the world. But it can carry some dangers too, especially if the people upon whom we rely for straight facts mix in questionable philosophy as well. As the pope also wrote: "It is not too much to claim that the development of a good part of modern philosophy has seen it move further and further away from Christian Revelation, to the point of setting itself quite explicitly in opposition."[21] One manifestation of the antagonism of some modern philosophy to Christianity is the development of *scientism*. John Paul writes:

> Another threat to be reckoned with is *scientism*. This is the philosophical notion which refuses to admit the validity of forms of knowledge other than those of the positive sciences; and it relegates religious, theological, ethical and aesthetic knowledge to the realm of mere fantasy. . . . The undeniable triumphs of scientific research and contemporary technology have helped to propagate a scientistic outlook, which now seems boundless, given its inroads into different cultures and the radical changes it has brought.[22]

Now, a person who subscribes to scientism likely will view all of the findings of legitimate science through the lens of his worldview. But what happens if most of the people on whom we generally rely for our scientific understanding of how the world works subscribe, either consciously or unconsciously, to weaker or stronger forms of scientism? If that happened, then the presentation to the public of esoteric scientific facts about the world might commonly be tightly and implicitly intertwined with problematic philosophical interpretations. It might then be very difficult, essentially impossible, for most people to separate true science from scientistic philosophy.

There are many indications that to a large extent that has indeed happened, that descriptions of the world are heavily influenced by scientism. Now, why should that be? In his book *The Last Word* the philosopher Thomas Nagel identifies one reason for this as "the fear of religion itself":

> I speak from experience, being strongly subject to this fear myself: I want atheism to be true and am made uneasy by the fact that some of the most intelligent and well-informed people I know are religious believers. It isn't just that I don't believe in God and, naturally, hope that I'm right in my belief. It's that I hope there is no God! I don't want there to be a God; I don't want the universe to be like that. . . . [Fear of religion may be] responsible for much of the scientism and reductionism of our time.[23]

A few scientists are remarkably open about the fact that they think philosophical considerations alien to Christianity *should* guide science. Richard Lewontin wrote several years ago in the *New York Review of Books*: "Our willingness to accept scientific claims that are against common sense is the key to an understanding of the real struggle between science and the supernatural. We take the side of science *in spite of* the patent absurdity of some of its constructs, . . . *in spite of* the tolerance of the scientific community for unsubstantiated just-so stories, because we have a prior commitment, a commitment to materialism."[24]

This attitude can even sometimes be seen explicitly expressed in the primary science journals. For example, the authors of a recent review on the molecular biology of membrane traffic start off with the following paragraph.

> The greatest scientific advance of the last 1000 years was providing the evidence to prove that human beings are independent agents whose lives on earth are neither conferred nor controlled by celestial forces. Although it may be more conventional to measure scientific progress in terms of specific technological developments, nothing was more important than providing the means to release men and women from the hegemony of the supernatural.[25]

Such a statement would appear to have little to do with membrane traffic, and the fact that the editors allowed it to appear in a frontline science journal is very informative.

Let me relay a few warning signs that one has to exercise extreme caution in judging claims about what is known concerning evolution, even claims coming from apparently authoritative sources. The first warning sign is that evidence that is seen as supporting Darwinism is often accepted uncritically. As an example, for a very long time many biology textbooks contained a figure of vertebrate embryos showing that the embryos resemble each other very closely. The embryos were drawn by a man named Ernst Haeckel in the late nineteenth century. Haeckel was a great admirer of Darwin's theory. He thought that his work supported Darwinism since the early stages of embryogenesis, when the basic body plane of the organism was being laid down, would be the most difficult to change by natural selection. Later stages, thought to be less crucial, were supposed to be more pliable.

Many high school and college biology textbooks highlighted Haeckel's work because the images make a visceral impact on students, and because they illustrate a basic principle of the way evolution is thought to work. The textbook *Molecular Biology of the Cell*, authored by Bruce Alberts, who is president of the National Academy of Sciences, Nobel-laureate James Watson, and several other high-powered scientists, told us why: "[E]arly developmental stages of animals whose adult forms appear radically different are often surprisingly similar. . . . Such observations are not difficult to understand. . . . The early cells of an embryo are like cards at the bottom of a house of cards—a great deal depends on them, and even small changes in their properties are likely to result in disaster."[26]

This essentially echoes Haeckel's 100-year-old argument. But a few years ago it was discovered that Haeckel had faked the data. An English scientist by the name of Michael Richardson, suspicious of Haeckel's drawings, assembled an international team of embryologists to try to reproduce Haeckel's work. They couldn't. Elizabeth Pennisi reported their results in *Science* magazine:

> Not only did Haeckel add or omit features . . . but he also
> fudges the scale to exaggerate similarities among species, even
> when there were 10-fold differences in size. Haeckel further
> blurred differences by neglecting to name the species in most
> cases, as if one representative was accurate for an entire group
> of animals. In reality . . . even closely related embryos such as
> those of fish vary quite a bit in their appearance and develop-
> mental pathway.[27]

Nonetheless, the misleading drawings were used in biology texts for a hundred years because they were thought to support Darwinian evolution. In seventh grade in parochial school my wife's science class was shown Haeckel's drawings by their teacher, a Holy Cross brother. "Evolution is true," the good Brother told them with a flourish, "get used to it." He certainly thought he was giving his students the straight facts, and he wanted them to form their views in weighty matters based on those facts. But, unknown to him, the facts were fraudulent. He was relying on evidence provided by someone who wanted to fit all of the data into a materialistic framework.

Another example concerns the inculcating of an evolutionary worldview. Despite many difficulties, a materialistic, Darwinistic view of the unfolding of life is taught uncritically to students. For example, a biochemistry textbook by Voet & Voet contains a marvelous, full-color drawing nicely capturing the orthodox position.[28] The top third of the drawing shows a volcano, lightning, an ocean, and little rays of sunlight, to suggest how life started. The middle of the picture has a stylized drawing of a DNA molecule leading out from the origin-of-life ocean and into a bacterial cell, to show how life developed. The bottom third of the picture—no kidding—is like the Garden of Eden, depicting a number of animals that have been produced by evolution milling about. Included in the throng are a man and a woman (the woman is offering the man an apple), both especially attractive and in the buff. This undoubtedly adds to the interest for students, but the drawing is a tease. The implicit promise that the secrets of evolution will be uncovered is never consummated. Many students learn from their textbooks how to view the world through an evolutionary lens. But they are not told that they are learning scientistic philosophy, not science itself.

My final example concerns the origin of life. Modern origin of life studies can be dated to the early 1950s when Stanley Miller, then a graduate student at the University of Chicago, mixed together in a flask gases thought to have been present on the primitive earth, sparked them with an electric spark to simulate lightning, and saw that some amino acids were produced. Over the years many scientists have followed Miller's path. Nonetheless, despite considerable effort, science is currently at a loss to explain how life might have been started by random chemical processes. As the biochemist Franklin Harold stated: "The origin of life stands as the most profound mystery in biology; and we note in passing that, despite all the achievements of investigators in pre-biotic biochemistry, it remains utterly beyond our comprehension."[29]

However, in a recent publication designed to instruct science teachers how to teach about the origin and evolution of life, the National Academy of Sciences shifts the focus away from the negative experimental results to the attitude of origin of life researchers: "For those who are studying the origin of life, the question is no longer whether life could have originated by chemical processes involving nonbiological components. The question instead has become which of many pathways might have been followed to produce the first cells."[30] Evidently the prestigious Academy wants to convey to teachers and their students the attitude that thinking about the origin of life should stay strictly within the confines of "chemical processes involving nonbiological components." That attitude, however, is not demanded by the physical evidence; it arises from scientistic presuppositions.

PIUS XII'S WARNING

Over the years the church has warned people to be cautious in their judgments about evolution. In *Fides et Ratio* Pope John Paul refers back to an earlier encyclical written by Pope Pius XII: "In his Encyclical Letter *Humani Generis*, Pope Pius XII warned against mistaken interpretations linked to evolutionism, existentialism and historicism. He made it clear that these theories had not been proposed and developed by theologians, but had their origins 'outside the sheepfold of Christ'. He added, however, that errors of this kind should not simply be rejected but should be examined critically."[31]

Indeed, Pius XII was quite wary about evolution in *Humani Generis*, and he viewed it with a jaundiced eye.

> It remains for Us now to speak about those questions which, although they pertain to the positive sciences, are nevertheless more or less connected with the truths of the Christian faith. In fact, not a few insistently demand that the Catholic religion takes these sciences into account as much as possible. This certainly would be praiseworthy in the case of clearly proved facts; but caution must be used when there is rather a question of hypotheses, having some sort of scientific foundation, in which the doctrine contained in Sacred Scripture or in Tradition is involved. If such conjectural opinions are directly or indirectly opposed to the doctrine revealed by God, then the demand that they be recognized can in no way be admitted.
>
> For these reasons the Teaching Authority of the Church does not forbid that, in conformity with the present state of human sciences and sacred theology, research and discussions, on the part of men experienced in both fields, take place with regard to the doctrine of evolution, in as far as it inquires into the origin of the human body as coming from pre-existent and living matter—for the Catholic faith obliges us to hold that souls are immediately created by God. However this must be done in such a way that the reasons for both opinions, that is, those favorable and those unfavorable to evolution, be weighed and judged with the necessary seriousness, moderation and measure, and provided that all are prepared to submit to the judgment of the Church, to whom Christ has given the mission of interpreting authentically the

> Sacred Scriptures and of defending the dogmas of the faithful. Some however rashly transgress this liberty of discussion, when they act as if the origin of the human body from preexisting and living matter were already completely certain and proved by the facts which have been discovered up to now and by reasoning on those facts, and as if there were nothing in the sources of divine revelation which demands the greatest moderation and caution in this question.[32]

My closing point is that, although Pope John Paul II labeled evolution "more than a hypothesis,"[33] I think Pope Pius XII's cautious attitude is still very much warranted. Science has advanced considerably in the 50 years since Pius's encyclical, but the data we need to make definitive judgments about Darwinian evolution remain either very fragmentary or, to a skeptical mind like mine, point strongly away from the generally-accepted view. Furthermore, the interpretation of data is usually done, either explicitly or implicitly, from the vantage point of a scientistic philosophy—that material causes simply must be adequate to explain evolution—and that strongly affects the conclusions that are drawn.

Well, if the topic of evolution is fraught with pitfalls, then what is a Catholic layperson to do, who simply can't evaluate the scientific evidence himself? Although it can be very difficult, I would simply urge people to reserve judgment, to be patient, and to look toward the Church for guidance in this philosophically-charged area. As St. Augustine remarked, speaking of his embrace of the faith:

> From this time on, I gave my preference to the Catholic faith. I thought it more modest and not in the least misleading to be told by the Church to believe what could not be demonstrated—whether that was because a demonstration existed but could not be understood by all or whether the matter was not one open to rational proof—rather than from the Manichees to have a rash promise of knowledge with mockery of mere belief, and then afterwards to be ordered to believe many fabulous and absurd myths impossible to prove true.[34]

In *Fides et Ratio* Pope John Paul II explains that the Catholic faith allows a very wide latitude to reason in the area of the origin and unfolding of life, pointing out crucially that we need to realize in all things "it is the God of Israel who acts." Yet, many people do not share our faith and come at the evidence from a scientistic point of view. A mixture of scientism with ambiguous facts can easily lead to unwarranted conclusions, even by supposedly authoritative sources, which could mislead the public about the state of our knowledge of the origin and unfolding of life. Thus we would all be well-advised to imitate the cautious attitude of Pope Pius XII.

Michael John Denton

9. AN ANTI-DARWINIAN INTELLECTUAL JOURNEY
Biological Order as an Inherent Property of Matter

I was brought up in a Christian fundamentalist family and believed that man was specially created by God in the relatively recent past as described in the Book of Genesis. The church my family belonged to accepted a non-literal interpretation of the "days" in Genesis so that each day was considered to represent a long geological period. Consequently I was never a young earth fundamentalist and apart from the story of the deluge, which I saw as a local, miraculous event, I found the geological world view accepted by the scientific community easy to reconcile with my interpretation of the Bible. As with most people who accept special creationism and an ancient earth, I interpreted the biological history of life on earth as one of successive extinctions followed by Divine acts of creation to replenish the earth with new forms of life. While I was in high school, I was a vigorous advocate of a creationist interpretation of biology and argued endlessly with my biology teachers, who were all evolutionists and Darwinists.

However, even while in high school I was aware that there were many facts, particularly about the temporal and spatial distribution of life, that were a puzzle and not easy to reconcile with the special creationist position. Why, for example, should each major geographical region possess a unique set of life forms and why should the past life forms of each major continental region be related to but different from, and often seemingly more "primitive" than, their present-day inhabitants. Why, according to creationist theory, should the southern continents alone possess flightless birds and contain unique species of plants such as the southern beech? In the case of Australia, for example, why are all living and extinct mammalian species, as evidenced by the Australian fossil record, marsupials?

I was very familiar with the *Origin of Species*, which I read very carefully while at school with the goal of extracting arguments and evidence to counter Darwin's evolutionary theory. However, I found Darwin's treatment of the geographical evidence disturbing because it seemed to me that his explanations of at least some of the facts made good sense, if not actually more sense, than the creationist alternative. In the *Origin* Darwin himself issues the challenge: "Why should the species which are supposed to have been created on the Galapagos Archipelago, and no where else, bear so evidently the stamp of affinity to those created in America?"[1] And he continues: "The inhabitants of the Cape Verde Islands are related to Africa, like those of the Galapagos to Africa. Facts like these admit of no sort of explanation on the ordinary view of independent creation; whereas on the view here maintained, it is obvious that the Galapagos Islands would be likely to receive colonists from America . . . and the Cape Verde Islands from Africa."[2]

I did attempt to account for some of these spatial and temporal patterns with various *ad hoc* presumptions. Perhaps, I speculated, there might be some deep ecological reason for the curious restriction of types to certain geographical areas? Perhaps the soils of certain regions contained minerals which precluded certain types, or perhaps there were subtle climatic influences which favored one class of organism over another, and God had taken such considerations into account when creating different life forms in different regions of the globe.

When I had moments of doubt as to the veracity of the creationist world view, I was able to reinforce my creationism by contemplation of the adaptive design of living things, such as the coadaptations of insects and plants, the adaptive complexity of the eye and many other such examples of biological engineering. I found it literally inconceivable that such designs—"clever contrivances"—could be the result of "blind chance." That they could arise by a process that had no foresight but merely selected organisms on their short-term survival "value" seemed to me incredible. Like William Paley I saw organisms to be complex artifact or watch-like structures and was convinced that the adaptive design of life demanded the active involvement of God as "engineer and designer."[3]

Although I was not aware of it at the time, I subsequently came to see that my creationist conception of nature depended on a highly mechanistic view of life. The mechanistic view assumes that the only ordering principle of the organic realm is adaptation for function, and that all the complexity of living organisms is what one might call "clever contrivance"—the purposeful and adaptive arrangement of matter into contingent arrangements, as happens in a machine, to serve various biological functions. As Stephen Jay Gould points out,[4] this conception of biological order—what he calls "British Functionalism" (and what I term *mechanism* and refer to as the "superwatch" model)—has been the predominant view in the English speaking world since the seventeenth century, adhered to by both natural theologians like William Paley and their Darwinian successors after 1859.

Paley's mechanism is obvious in the following famous section from his *Natural Theology*: "Every indication of contrivance, every manifestation of design which existed in the watch exists in nature with the difference, on the side of nature, being greater and more, and that in a degree which exceeds all computation . . . yet in a multitude of cases, are not less evidently mechanical, not less evidently contrivances . . . than are the most perfect productions of human ingenuity." Darwin echoes the same mechanistic, "superwatch" model of nature in the following well-known section from his famous work on the fertilization of orchids: "If a man were to make a machine for some special purpose, but were to use old wheels, springs and pulleys, only slightly altered, the whole machine, with all its parts, might be said to be specially contrived for its present purpose. Thus throughout nature almost every part of each living being has probably served in a slightly modified condition, for diverse purposes, and has acted in the living machinery of many ancient and distinct forms."[5]

As I later came to see, not all of the order of life is adaptation or "clever contrivance" like that of a machine. However, from high school to mid-life, when I wrote *Evolution: A Theory in Crisis*,[6] I never doubted this "mechanistic," contingent view of life. Like both Paley and Darwin, the possibility that much of life's order and design might be a necessary feature of nature was *simply inconceivable*, although that is the view I now hold.

DISCOVERING EVOLUTION IN THE DISSECTION ROOM

It was during my days at medical school in Bristol in southwest England when I first began to seriously doubt the creationist worldview, although not yet the mechanistic assumption upon which it was based. As I came into direct contact with the anatomy and biology of *Homo sapiens*, it was increasingly apparent that not all the design of the human body had been created directly and specifically to serve immediate biological purposes. There were features of human anatomy which did not seem to serve any obvious adaptive purpose in present day humans—features which are paradoxical in terms of the creationist conception of the organism. I saw these anomalous features for myself in the dissecting room. A classic example was the way the recurrent laryngeal nerve, a branch of the vagus, the tenth cranial nerve, descends from the neck down into the upper thorax and winds round the aorta and then ascends up into the neck to supply the thyroid. This seems a curiously round about way to supply the thyroid—a route several centimeters longer than necessary. Why did the human body have features that seemed non-adaptive or even maladaptive?

The professor of anatomy at Bristol, Professor Yoffe, who was a world authority in hematology, was also a wonderful vertebrate comparative anatomist of the old school. He probably knew as much about the subject as any other living authority in Britain at the time. He reminded me of Richard Owen and awed me as a young undergraduate with his factual knowledge of the subject. In the dissecting room he would always tease me, in very good humor I must say, by pointing out features of human anatomy that challenged the special creationist scenario. He pointed out the diminutive muscles—some of which are not described even in leading texts of human anatomy—in the scalp and ears, which are vestigial in man but used in other mammals to move the ear and scalp. He explained how the human jaw was too small to take the full complement of "primate teeth"; hence the unique problems in humans with wisdom teeth, etc. He explained how the head of the human baby at birth is almost too large for the primate birth canal; hence the unique difficulties and indeed dangers associated with birth in human females—problems not experienced by any other primate species. He explained how the uniquely long larynx of adult humans, which is an adaptation associated with speech, leads to choking and how the fascial support of the abdominal viscera in man is typically quadrupedal and not ideally designed for an upright biped.

What Professor Yoffe was bringing me in contact with was the deep and pervasive phenomenon of homology, and with the principle that the adaptive designs of organisms are a compromise between an underlying order, what many nineteenth-century biologists looked on as the "archetype," and an overlying Paley-type of adaptive order, what Owen called in his great classic *On the Nature of Limbs* an "adaptive mask."[7] (The deep significance of this dual order, that of an underlying pattern overlain by a veneer of adaptive complexity only became apparent to me much later in my career—see below.) At medical school I could see only one rational explanation for this duality and the general facts of primate comparative anatomy that were laid out in the dissecting room: *Man must have descended with modification from a subhuman primate ancestor*—Darwin's dreaded hypothesis.

Several of my medical student colleagues who had gone up to medical school as Christian fundamentalists, on confronting in the dissecting room the facts of our primate affinity and the mysterious phenomenon of homology, were also forced to the same conclusion. However unpalatable, man must have evolved from an animal very different from the form displayed on the dissecting room table. This conclusion was for me irreversibly confirmed when one fateful day I read Richard Owen's *On the Nature of Limbs.* I was gripped by the power of Owen's arguments. I read it from cover to cover without stopping—as later I was to read Lawrence Henderson's *Fitness of the Environment.*[8]

RICHARD OWEN'S *ON THE NATURE OF LIMBS*

On the Nature of Limbs is a great classic in the history of biological thought, and as such is also perhaps the most devastating critique of special creationism ever written in the English language. Because the principle it highlights goes to the heart of the nature of biological order, it is worth considering Owen's views at length. As Owen rightly points out, biological adaptations are all, on close examination, almost without exception modifications of some pre-existing structure or "ground plan." Indeed, it was Owen who gave the term "homology" to the underlying ground plans in nature, upon which specific adaptations are built, such as the pentadactyl design of the vertebrate limb, which forms the basic pattern upon which adaptive modifications of all vertebrate limbs are based.

An obvious example of this is the foot. The foot does not give any appearance of having been specially created only for the purpose of "walking." In fact, nearly every muscle, tendon, and bone in the foot has a corresponding homologue in the hand. The foot gives every appearance of being a "modified hand." In other words, the foot, like nearly all adaptations in the organic world, gives the overwhelming *impression of being a modification of a pre-existing structure* that may well—like the hand—have existed for some quite different purpose. There is nothing "watch-like" about the foot. It provides no evidence that there was any foresight behind its design—that its parts were put together to serve the function they now serve "from the beginning."

As Owen notes, human artifacts are not as a rule modifications of pre-existing structures; and in nearly all cases their parts give every indication that they were fashioned from the beginning with the specific purpose they now serve in view. In this respect the contrast between the human foot (a biological adaptation) and the design of a jumbo jet (an artifactual adaptation) could hardly be more obvious. For Owen, the existence of deep homology in nature was incompatible with what he termed "final causation"—with the notion that adaptive design in nature is the result of the special creation of an intelligent agent.

Owen alludes to this fundamental difference—between the design of artifacts and organisms—in many places in his monograph. Contrasting the way nature has adapted the pentadactyl design to so many diverse functions—swimming, walking, burrowing, flying, etc.—with the way man has designed artifacts to serve these same purposes he comments:

> Consider the various devices that human ingenuity and perseverance have put into practice in order to obtain corresponding results. . . . Man does not fetter himself by the trammels of any common type of locomotive instrument, and increase his pains by having to adjust the parts and compensate their proportions so as to best perform the end required without deviating from the pattern previously laid down for all. There is no community of plan of structure between the boat and the balloon, between Stephenson's locomotive engine and Brunnel's tunnelling machinery: a very remote analogy if any can be traced between the instruments devised by man to travel in the air and on the sea, through the earth or along its surface. . . . Nor should we anticipate if animated in our researches by the quest for final causes in the belief that they were the sole governing principle of organization, a much greater amount of conformity in the construction of the natural instruments by means of which those different elements are traversed by different animals. The teleologist [advocate of special creation] would rather expect to find the same direct and purposeful adaptation to its office as in a machine. A deep and pregnant principle of philosophy . . . therefore is concerned in the issue of such dissections [i.e., examination and comparison of the different adaptations of the pentadactyl design in different vertebrate species].[9]

And he goes on to consider the limbs of mole, bat and man:

To skim the air and burrow in the earth would seem to require instruments as different in construction as in size and
shape; but observe how closely the skeleton of the mole's
trowel conforms in number and relative position of the parts
to that of the bat's wing! [And to the human limb!] The chief
change is this. Whatever is elongated and attenuated in the
bat is shortened and thickened in the mole. . . . The radius
and ulna are both completely developed, and enjoy all the
accessory rotatory movements as in man, but are relatively
much more powerful bones. . . . Then follows, as usual, the
double series of little carpal bones, supporting five digits
which, notwithstanding they are buried up to the claws in a
sheath of tough skin, have precisely the same number of bones
and joints as in the prehensile hand of man; only that every
bone, save the last in each digit, is as broad as it is long. The
chief deviation from the human type is by redundancy instead of deficiency and is exemplified by one or two supernumerary carpal ossicles, the most remarkable of which is sa-
bre shaped, and strengthens the digging or scraping edge of
the broad palm."[10]

In the middle of the monograph he comments on the evidence so
far reviewed:

I think it will be obvious that the principle of final adaptation fails to satisfy all the conditions of the problem. That
every bone which is present in the human arm and hand should
exist in the fin of the whale, solely because it is assumed that
they were required in such number and collocation for the
support and movement of that undivided and inflexible
paddle, squares as little with our idea of the simplest mode
of effecting the purpose. . . .[11]

And continuing he makes the telling point:

Such a final purpose is indeed readily perceived and admitted
in regard to the multiplied points of ossification of the skull
of the human foetus, and their relation to safe parturition.
But when we find the same ossification centers are established
and in similar order in the skull of the embryo kangaroo which
is born an inch in length and in that of the callow bird that

breaks the brittle egg, we feel the truth of Bacon's comparison of "final causes" to the "Vestal Virgins," and perceive
that they would be barren and unproductive of the fruits we
are laboring to attain, and would lead no clue to the comprehension of that law of conformity to which we are in quest.[12]

Finally, in summarizing his conclusions at the end of the monograph, Owen admits that his rejection of final cause explanations (special creation) might be construed by some as implying that biological
adaptations exhibit "imperfect design" or that parts of living organisms
may well have no functional significance, or, in his words, "be made in
vain."[13] He continues:

> Something also I would fain add with a view to remove or
> allay the scruples of those physiologists who admit no other
> principle to have governed the construction of living things
> than the exclusive and absolute adaptation of every part to
> its function, who may feel offended at any expression that
> seems to imply that any part or particle of a created being
> could be "made in vain."[14]

And hitting the nail right on the head he comments toward the end of
the monograph: "The fallacy of the teleologist perhaps lies in judging
of created organs by the analogy of man made machines."[15]

Owen's point can be restated: the human hand, the trowel of a
mole, and the flipper of a whale are all modifications of pre-existing
structures. None gives any indication that they were designed by an intelligent designer for the functions they currently perform. In other words,
unlike a watch their parts give no impression of being shaped by an
intelligent cause who had *their function in view from the beginning*.
They provide no evidence for an intelligent agent operating directly in
nature, to shape matter as a man shapes matter, to an adaptive end.

Owen's point has of course been echoed by all leading biologists
since, including Darwin. The same point was made by Gould in the
Panda's thumb.[16] Interestingly, the supernumerary carpal ossicle in the
hand of the mole closely corresponds to the Panda's thumb. Gould has
recently commented on the phenomenon:

> Call this, if you will, the orchid principle (though I have also
> designated it as the panda principle for my own favourite ex-
> ample, perforce unknown to Darwin, of the panda's false

thumb) to honor Darwin's argument (1862) for orchids as products of history. Their intricate adaptations to attract insects for fertilization cannot be read as wonders of optimal design, specially created for current utilities, for they represent contraptions, jury rigged from the available parts of ordinary flowers.[17]

After Darwin, the explanation of the fact that biological adaptations appear almost invariably to be modifications of pre-existing structures was explained by the fact that all biological structures are the result of descent with modification—organic evolution. But although Darwin's evolutionary explanation of why adaptations are always secondary modifications of some pre-existing structure is of enormous significance for biology in general, with regard to the argument for design, Paley's argument poses the primary and more fundamental challenge, proposing as he does the basic fact that adaptations are invariably *ad hoc* modifications of pre-existing structures, which was Owen's point. Owen's demonstration of the universality of homology, and its consequence that biological adaptations do not exhibit finality, undermined the analogy between the design of an artifact and an organism, before Darwin explained homology in terms of descent with modification.

If you accept the existence of homologous resemblance in nature and its universality, then you have in effect accepted that adaptations in nature are not the result of direct special creation, like a watch, but must have come about in some other way which has involved at least the modification of a pre-existing structure that served a pre-existing function. In effect, homology points irresistibly to some sort of cumulative process of change, and Owen himself acknowledges this in the closing paragraph of his great monograph. He talks of the "orderly succession of such organic phenomena" and how "we learn from the past history of our globe that she has advanced with slow and stately steps." This is cumulative change or, in other words, organic evolution.

Owen's point is simply this: It matters little what the mechanism of modification was. It matters little whether it was sudden or slow, whether natural selection or Lamarckian mechanisms were involved. The point is that deep homologous patterns underlie *all* adaptations throughout the organic realm, and this fact is impossible to reconcile with the idea that the specific adaptations of living things have come about by special creation. There may be indeed a grand design behind nature, as Owen himself believed, but it was clearly not executed in the way William Paley had envisaged. Its essential nature was far from clear!

THE NEED FOR A NEW SYNTHESIS

By the time I left medical school I was convinced that the standard evolutionary picture was essentially correct. I could see no other way of explaining the facts. As far as I could see, mankind and all organisms were "obviously" the modified descendants of pre-existing and different life forms. And although I still adhered to the idea that organisms were types of advanced machines and was greatly impressed by their adaptive design—though after reading Owen it was clear that the analogy was imperfect—it seemed to me that there was no evidence for believing that this "design" had come about by special creation.

The doctrine of descent with modification was based on what seemed to me irrefutable evidence. I was at the time deeply troubled by the undermining of Christian claims inherent in the evolutionary worldview. I found it increasingly difficult to see how the story of the creation and the fall of man could be reconciled with the evolutionary picture of man's emergence in Africa and his gradual migration from Africa over the past 100,000 years to all inhabitable parts of the world. Gradually my belief began to slip away. I saw my own personal journey and my growing angst to be a reflection of the grand journey that Western Civilization had taken from the sixteenth century, from a time when Christianity occupied the center and core of our civilization, to the situation today in the early twenty-first century, where it occupies a marginal and peripheral position.

After medical school, in what I think retrospectively was an attempt to recover belief, I went to Israel in 1968 and enrolled as a student at the Hebrew University in Jerusalem in the Department of Jewish studies and Biblical Archeology. I spent much of my time in Israel poring over Biblical texts and commentaries, and in endless dialogue with Christian and Jewish colleagues and students trying to find my own holy grail, a path back to belief and a way to reconcile faith and reason.

While in Israel I read parts of Augustine's *Confessions* and *City of God*. I was struck by the fact that for Augustine, one of the founders of the western Christian tradition, the need to reconcile faith with reason was a primary concern. The fact that a relatively satisfactory reconciliation between Greek rationality and Hebrew revelation was possible was a point of enormous importance for Augustine. Indeed, if there had been no possibility of a rational synthesis between faith and reason, although it is a synthesis that was never satisfactorily achieved, it is doubtful that the Christian faith would have survived as the core belief of the West for more than a thousand years. No one can read his works and not be inclined to the view that Augustine's faith was dependent on the fact that for him there was *no fundamental conflict* between reason and revelation.

What was needed if the Christian faith was to recover its central position in Western civilization was a new "synthesis." Reading Augustine reinforced my determination that a return to belief on my part would necessitate nothing less than a convincing reconciliation between faith and reason, between Genesis and science. For me, nothing less would do, and I saw this as being also true for the whole of modern mainstream society. Although my own personal faith dwindled during my stay in Israel, my intellectual interest in the relationship between religious claims and science never diminished and has remained one of the central interests in my life.

In thinking about the challenge posed by the evolutionary model to Christian belief, it seemed to me that for any new synthesis to be effective, "design" had to be reintroduced into nature without returning to special creationism. It was also clear to me that if *all the order of nature* and the *entire developmental of the tree of life* could be plausibly accounted for in terms of the unguided selection of small random changes—the Darwinian version of evolution—then in no serious sense could mankind be considered the outcome of any sort of mindful purpose. Consequently, if there was ever to be a new synthesis, the first step would have to be to show that in some way the Darwinian conception of nature was fundamentally flawed.

I was of course well aware—and had been throughout my time at medical school—that the Darwinian interpretation of evolution was not proven, that the actual mechanism that had driven the process of evolution was not understood. Even the mode, whether gradual or saltational, was controversial. In Jerusalem I read Alfred Sherwood Romer's great book, *Vertebrate Paleontology*, and other papers and books by Gaylord Simpson.[18] These works indicated to me just how incomplete the fossil record actually was. I also read papers by Crick and Woese on the origin of the genetic code, which rather than proposing a solution merely emphasized the enormous difficulty of providing a plausible Darwinian scenario, not only for the origin of the code but also for the origin of life.[19]

In short, the cause of evolution was still a great unknown. It may well have been a far more saltational process than classical Darwinism implied. Throughout this period I remained as firmly wedded as ever to a mechanical philosophy of nature—the superwatch model—and remained convinced that the adaptive complexity of life, even if it was not the result of direct special creation by God, was simply too complex to be the result of the unseeing process that Darwin had claimed. In these angstful musings while walking the streets of Jerusalem, I saw the first inklings of a long road back toward a new teleological synthesis and a new reconciliation of faith with modern science.

FROM KINGS COLLEGE TO *EVOLUTION: A THEORY IN CRISIS*

In October 1969 I commenced my research career by enrolling as a Ph.D. student in the biochemistry department at Kings College, London. My Ph.D. topic was the development of the red blood cell. Kings back then was an exciting place to be. The discovery of double helix had occurred only 16 years earlier, and everyone recalled the important contributions of Maurice Wilkins and Rosalind Franklin.

While at Kings several important developments occurred in evolutionary biology, which I saw as weakening the Darwinian position. There was the work of Kimura, a Japanese geneticist, and his neutral theory of molecular evolution.[20] Kimura's theory was a sensation at the time and was widely seen as challenging Darwinian orthodoxy, namely, that all genetic change substituted in evolution is adaptive. This work was of particular interest to researchers at Kings because in the sixties a research group led by Professor Harris, then head of the biochemistry department, and including Hopkinson (who subsequently moved to the Galton) and Spencer, with whom I worked on the differentiation of the red blood cell,[21] had been the first to discover the phenomenon of protein polymorphism, a phenomenon that posed many of the same evolutionary problems as those raised by Kimura. Another challenging development at the time was the publication of the now notorious paper by Eldredge and Gould on punctuated equilibrium, which reinforced the impression I had from my own readings of paleontology that the fossil record was far less continuous than Darwinism demanded.[22]

Another influence on my thinking while at Kings, and one that reinforced my Darwinian skepticism, was reading Noam Chomsky's *Language and Mind*.[23] I had heard Chomsky speak on one of his several visits to London in the early seventies and was very impressed by his framework and emergentist views of the human mind and human linguistic abilities. I clearly remember reading *Language and Mind* one afternoon in a coffee bar near the London School of Economics. I was fascinated. Here was one of the towering intellectuals of the twentieth century, whose views on the origin of man and language were profoundly anti-Darwinian. One felt encouraged.

By the time I left Kings late in 1974 to take up a university lecture-ship in Melbourne, Australia, I was determined to write a book criti-cally examining the Darwinian framework. Finally in the late seventies, while training in pathology in Hobart, Tasmania, I got down to the task of putting a manuscript together.

My strategy in writing *Evolution: A Theory in Crisis* was to re-strict myself to arguing *against* Darwinism rather than attempting to defend an alternative hypothesis. This was not my preferred approach. It is always better in delivering a critique to have a well-developed alter-native hypothesis in mind. However, I had at the time no alternative worldview or hypothesis with which to account for the development of life on earth. I have subsequently come to the view that the only feasible alternative to Darwinism, and the only way to introduce "design" or direction into evolution is by adopting some version of the pre-Darwin-ian conception of evolution by natural law, defended by von Baer, Rich-ard Owen and many other biologists in the early nineteenth century and popularized by Robert Chambers in his well known *Vestiges of the Natu-ral History of Creation* published in1844.[24] At the time, however, I had not the slightest idea of what an alternative explanatory evolutionary model might look like. So the strategy of restricting myself to a *critique* was not a matter of choice.

At the time I saw the foundational axiom of Darwinism to be en-capsulated in Darwin's own famous phrase in chapter six of the *Ori-gin—natura non facit saltum*. I took the view—and I still think that this is largely correct—that the Darwinian paradigm is only really credible if *all the complexity of the living world* can be achieved gradually bit by bit via continuous evolutionary pathways. As I saw it, to critique Dar-winism it was necessary therefore to undermine the presumption of the absolute continuity of nature. Thus the whole book was an attempt to show that the natural order is not the seamless continuity required by classical Darwinian gradualism. Only two chapters in *Evolution*, chap-ters thirteen and fourteen, which argue that complex adaptations are beyond the reach of chance, are not primarily focused on the question of the continuity of nature.

My biological philosophy when I wrote *Evolution* was very much the same as it had been in high school and at medical school—adapta-tional and mechanistic. I still saw organisms basically as types of com-plex machines and very much contingent assemblages of matter. My conception of types (see *Evolution* chapters five and six) was basically Cuvierian and functional rather than formalist and abstract. Although I did use triangles as representative of biological types, this was not because of any conscious formalist inclination. I saw biological types as analogous to classes of machines—automobiles, steam ships, etc. The divisions in nature were, I thought, analogous to the divisions between different categories of machine, rooted in functional necessity.

Of course I was aware, since reading Owen at medical school, of the deep homologies underlying the design of various groups of organisms (discussed in chapter seven), but I saw Owen's ideas as evidence against the special creation of life forms in their present condition rather than as support for the radical idea that some of these homologies might be afunctional, ahistoric patterns without any ultimate functional or adaptive significance. Until that time I had never fully grasped Owen's own Platonic formalist position, although in retrospect it is quite obvious on re-reading *On the Nature of Limbs*. The most important message of chapters five, six, and seven in *Evolution* was that nature *for some reason* conformed to the nineteenth-century theory of types even if the philosophical basis of typology might be "metaphysical nonsense." My commitment to the mechanistic "superwatch" model is quite evident in chapters thirteen and fourteen, which make extensive use of the analogy between organisms and machines.

Because I held to the "superwatch" model of nature, the idea that natural law might have played an important role in phylogeny or ontogeny, or the pre-Darwinian idea that a substantial proportion of biological order might be self-organizing and natural, like that of a crystal, was as alien to my thinking as it was to Paley and Darwin. The wonderful speculations of D'Arcy Thompson in *On Growth and Form* were for me just that—"wonderful speculations."[25] And it was my mechanistic bias which prevented me from appreciating the important work of Stuart Kauffman[26] and Brain Goodwin.[27]

There was only one small chink in my mechanism. While at Kings studying the development of the red cell, it became apparent to me that the mechanistic model, which was the dominant metaphor of biological order at Kings at the time, did not apply to the differentiation of the red cell. In fact, as I now see so clearly, the differentiation of the red cell is a paradigm of self-organization that is nothing like the assembly of any machine. In the case of the red blood cell, there is no evidence that its assembly occurs like that of a machine, bit by bit from below under the direction of a program. Gene expression ceases early in erythroblast differentiation. The red cell form emerges gradually from the intrinsic properties of its elemental constituents, and the extrusion of the red cell nucleus is a model of complex cyto-architectural differentiation not specified in the genes. However, although I accepted that in the case of the development of the red cell, physical law is playing a role in the shaping of organic form, I never generalized from this one example. The pre-Darwinian conception, that natural law might be an important determinant of natural order, that the basic fabric of life might be a non-adaptive pattern or that life's design might be in built into nature, was something that was still entirely alien to my way of thinking.

Henderson's *Fitness*: First Step toward a Lawful Biology

While the U.S. edition of *Evolution* was going to press, I got a note out of the blue from Professor Marcel Schützenberger, someone whom I had never met, but who I knew was one of the leading mathematicians in France and also at the time the leading anti-Darwinist in Europe. In *Evolution* I had cited one of his anti-Darwinian papers presented at a symposium held at the Wistar Institute in 1966.[28] Professor Schützenberger became a close friend and important mentor over the next decade, and every time I visited Paris I always stayed at his flat near the Bois de Boulogne. Marco, as he was affectionately known to his friends, was certainly the most impressive intellectual I have ever known—he seemed to have an encyclopedic knowledge of almost every area of interest from anthropology to medieval architecture to artificial intelligence. He seemed to be personally acquainted with a galaxy of the leading thinkers of the twentieth century. I recall telling him of my admiration of Chomsky, and of course he knew him well!

It was Schützenberger who played what was in retrospect a decisive role in my own intellectual development by recommending that I read Lawrence Henderson's *Fitness of the Environment* (subtitled *An Inquiry into the Biological Significance of the Properties of Matter* and originally published in 1913). Contemplating the evidence presented by Henderson in this great classic led me to write *Nature's Destiny*[29] and to begin to change my basic philosophy of nature from the "superwatch" adaptational model to a more naturalistic and "lawful" conception of the organic world.

No one can read Henderson's great classic and fail to be impressed. For me it opened up a whole new perspective on the living world. In *Fitness*, Henderson examines all the properties of the key building blocks of life—water, carbon dioxide, carbon compounds, basic biochemical processes like hydrolysis and oxidation. He concludes: "Hydrogen, oxygen and carbon, water and carbonic acid are not to be rivalled. The fitness of water, carbonic acid, and the three elements make up a unique ensemble of fitness for the organic mechanism. No other [set of con-

stituents] could possess such highly fit characteristics . . . to promote
. . . the organic mechanism we call life." As Henderson showed, each of
these basic compounds is maximally fit for its role. And in no case is
there any alternative. The whole ensemble can only be arranged to *one
unique end*—life as it exists on earth. The argument is elegant. The conclusion is compelling. The laws of nature are fine-tuned for life on earth.
Life must be considered an inevitable consequence of cosmic evolution.

There was one case of fitness that struck me as particularly intriguing. One of the products of metabolism that must be excreted from
the body is the end product of oxidative metabolism, carbon dioxide.
As Henderson points out: "In the course of a day a man . . . produces
some two pounds of carbon dioxide. All this must be rapidly removed
from the body. Because it is a gas, this can be easily done by breathing it
out in the lungs." And Henderson continues: "Were carbon dioxide not
gaseous, its excretion would be the greatest of physiological tasks." The
fact that carbon dioxide is a gas has another consequence. It allows the
body to rid itself of excess acid by simply exhaling it in the lungs. As
acid accumulates it is neutralized by the bicarbonate base in the blood.
The carbonic acid formed is converted to water and carbon dioxide in
the lungs, where it exits the body effortlessly.

I became aware of this brilliant adaptation while working in inten-
sive care medicine in Sydney at the Prince of Wales Hospital during the
early 1980s. This was before I had read *Fitness*. But it was only after
reading *Fitness* that I came to see that this was a case of fitness which
was in the nature of things—"in the intrinsic properties of matter" and
not the result of "cleverly contrived" arrangements of matter. It was not
the result of "clever contrivance" like the properties of a watch or artifact. It immediately occurred to me on reading Henderson that perhaps
the properties of matter had played a far more important role in evolution than I had previously imagined.

Since Henderson's day, a vast amount of new biochemical knowledge has been acquired. Many additional cases of fine-tuning have come
to light (some of these I presented in *Nature's Destiny*). But nearly all
that has been learned only reinforces his argument. For both creationists and Darwinists fitness is something imposed on nature from without, but, as Henderson shows, there is clear evidence that some adaptive
fitness is given from within. This is adaptation "for free" arising out of
the intrinsic properties of matter—a heretical notion, alien to Darwinism and creationism, that challenges the whole "superwatch" functional
conception of life.

Fitness was a turning point for me because it raised the obvious possibility that if natural law could accomplish so much—even highly sophisticated adaptations like the bicarbonate buffer—perhaps all the order and complexity of life, even perhaps specific adaptations such as the camera eye, might ultimately prove to be specified in some way by natural law. Perhaps God was far more clever than we humans can imagine!

It was Schützenberger who also first made me aware of just how much of the order of nature might be abstract afunctional pattern. On many occasions while visiting gardens in various parts of France, he would ask me to look around and tell him how much of the visible order of nature—the shape of leaves, the shape of trees, the form of flowers, etc.—I thought was adaptive? His point was of course that there was potentially a vast fabric of order in the biological realm that had never been accounted for in mechanistic functional terms, not only the shape of trees or the pattern of leaves but most cell forms, including the dazzling array of ciliate forms, most deep homologies, and the basic body plans of the major phyla.

Schützenbeger argued that even if Darwinism could account for biological adaptation—which he never accepted—it was incapable of accounting for abstract pattern that seemed to be ubiquitous in nature. Such ubiquitous patterning seemed far easier to explain in terms of generative laws such as those that gave rise to fractal patterns. When I realized later that the one thousand protein folds in microbiology represented a finite set of elegant and very beautiful afunctional abstract three-dimensional molecular patterns, I recalled Schützenberger intoning on abstract order, Goethe's travels in Italy, and the Platonic beauty of mathematics during a trip to the Loire Valley. There was more to biological order than "mere machinery."

NATURE'S DESTINY

Although the actual argument in *Fitness* was mainly restricted to showing that the laws of nature are fine-tuned to generate an environment supremely fit for life, reading it left me with the very powerful impression that the laws of nature might also be fine-tuned not only for the environment of life but also *for the existence of the actual set of life forms* for which the environment is so obviously suited. In other words, that life's constituent forms are "lawful" rather than contingent assemblages of matter. This would imply of course that life on earth is, as many nineteenth-century biologists believed, part of the changeless order of nature.

I did not abandon the mechanistic-contingent conception of life immediately on reading Henderson or on listening to Schützenberger's discourses on non-adaptive order. But *Fitness* had sowed seeds of doubt. In the wake of conversations with Schützenberger and reading *Fitness*, I could no longer dismiss the possibility of evolution by natural law—the idea that physical law may be a major determinant of organic order. I was well aware, especially after Schützenberger's lessons, that there was a great deal of biological order that might be non-adaptive and fractal, and might at least theoretically be generated in some way by natural law. I was also aware that many simple organic forms were indeed determined by natural law—the round shape of the cell and the flat shape of the cell membrane are well known examples.

But the problem I had with this lawful interpretation was that I had no idea what the laws underlying the forms of nature might be, particularly how they would generate complex organic form. Nonetheless, in the context of the extraordinary biocentricity of nature evidenced by Henderson, this possibility was something that I could no longer discount. Moreover, the possibility that biology might be a lawful and rational science was an idea I found immensely attractive. From seeing organisms entirely in terms of mechanism, as being essentially artifact-like assemblages of matter, which was my view when I wrote *Evolution*, I was increasingly open to the possibility that there might be a considerable proportion of organic order given by natural law. I was beginning to swap the "metaphor of the watch" for the pre-Darwinian "metaphor of the crystal"!

Shortly after reading Henderson, I started on the task of writing *Nature's Destiny*, which I intended to be a comprehensive and scholarly update and extension of *Fitness*. I also wanted to speculate on the possibility that the course of evolution may have been directed in some way. It took a considerable effort getting the manuscript together, and the book was not published until 1998. While I was working on it, I was continually pondering the question of how natural law might have worked as a directive agency in evolution.

Nature's Destiny represents my state of mind in transition from a mechanistic to a lawful and naturalistic conception of life. The overall thrust of the book, which is unashamedly rational and naturalistic, is that the whole pattern of life is built into nature and directed by natural law. However, my *mechanism* was still not completely put to rest. In *Nature's Destiny* (chapter twelve), I raised the possibility that evolution might have been directed via a built-in generative program in the DNA. This program would consist of facilitated routes through DNA sequence

space. Although such routes would be part of the natural order and in-
built, and hence determined by natural law, the conception of a program directing the development or evolution of life is really a mechanistic conception as it places, in conformity with the arch-mechanist August Weismann,[30] the determinants of biological order in a program
outside nature (see discussion below on the failure of the gene-centric
view of life).

In chapter fourteen of *Nature's Destiny*, I argued that evolutionary
change requires direction because of the functional integration of organisms, which is again a purely functionalist conception that can be
traced back to Cuvier. But I also considered (in chapter twelve) Kauffman
and Goodwin's purely naturalistic conceptions of evolutionary direction via "deep natural laws." Here the two basic strands of biological
thought—functionalsim and formalism—are both considered together.
In a section discussing Kauffman and Goodwin's work, I wrote: "Their
work raises the possibility that there exist additional mechanisms by
which the course of evolution might have been directed along pre-ar-
ranged paths, by mechanisms which would not have necessitated any
sort of specific directed mutations in DNA sequence space (the mecha-
nistic-functionalist view). Of course, the two different means by evolutionary direction, by a program and by direction from 'deep laws' are
not mutually exclusive."

During the six years since I finished the manuscript for *Nature's
Destiny*, my philosophy of nature has moved even further away from the
mechanistic "superwatch" model toward a lawful conception of biological form. One development influencing my thinking was the growing implausibility of the gene-centric view of nature and the other was
my own study of the role of physical law in the determination of macromolecular form.

THE GROWING IMPLAUSIBILITY OF
THE GENE-CENTRIC VIEW OF LIFE

To understand the challenge posed to the "superwatch" model by the
erosion of the gene-centric view of nature, it is necessary to recall August Weismann's seminal insight more than a century ago regarding the
need for genetic determinants to specify organic form.[31] As Weissman
saw so clearly, in order to account for the unerring transmission through
time with precise reduplication, for each generation of "*complex contingent assemblages of matter*" (superwatches), it is necessary to propose the existence of stable abstract genetic blueprints or programs in

the genes—he called them "determinants"—sequestered safely in the germ plasm, away from the ever varying and destabilizing influences of the extra-genetic environment.

Such carefully isolated determinants would theoretically be capable of reliably transmitting *contingent* order through time and specifying it reliably each generation. Thus, the modern "gene-centric" view of life was born, and with it the heroic twentieth-century effort to identify Weismann's determinants, supposed to be capable of reliably specifying in precise detail all the *contingent* order of the phenotype. Weismann was correct in this: the *contingent view of form* and indeed the entire mechanistic conception of life—the superwatch model—is critically dependent on showing that *all* or at least the *vast majority* of organic order is specified in precise detail in the genes.

Yet by the late 1980s it was becoming obvious to most genetic researchers, including myself, since my own main research interest in the '80s and '90s was human genetics, that the heroic effort to find the information specifying life's order in the genes had failed. There was no longer the slightest justification for believing that there exists anything in the genome remotely resembling a program capable of specifying in detail all the complex order of the phenotype. The emerging picture made it increasingly difficult to see genes as Weismann's "unambiguous bearers of information" or to view them as the sole source of the durability and stability of organic form. It is true that genes influence every aspect of development, but influencing something is not the same as determining it. Only a very small fraction of all known genes, such as the developmental fate switching genes, can be imputed to have any sort of directing or controlling influence on form generation. From being "isolated directors" of a one-way game of life, genes are now considered to be interactive players in a dynamic two-way dance of almost unfathomable complexity, as described by Keller in *The Century of The Gene*.[32]

As Weismann saw, the only other conceivable source of complex durable order is nature. If the genes do not contain sufficient information to specify organic forms, then only nature can supply the necessary "missing information." I was already receptive to this idea because my own research on the red blood cell at Kings implied that, at least in this case, cell differentiation arose out of the self-organizing properties of the material constituents of the cell: There was no master program in the genes. Further, all the current evidence, from the differentiation of individual cells to the development of the cognitive abilities of the human brain,[33] suggests that much biological order is lawful and self organizing and "extra-genic."

Over the past decade it has become increasingly obvious that the main role of the genes is to provide the unique material constituents that self-organize, under the direction of natural law, into the basic forms of the organic world.[34] Their role is analogous to the bricks of Aristotle's house, which are organized into the form of the house by the builders—by analogy, natural self-organization.[35] This is precisely what one might expect if organic forms are lawful natural forms that emerge spontaneously, like the spiral of the DNA helix, from the intrinsic properties of their material constituents, the four nucleotide bases.

In my view the increasingly evident failure of the gene-centric view poses a massive and growing threat to the mechanistic conception of nature and to the notion that all organic order is contingent and resides in "cleverly contrived" arrangements in the genes.

Protein and RNA Folds as Platonic Forms

After *Nature's Destiny* was published, the main focus of my research became, as it had been for many biologists of the pre-Darwinian era, a search for evidence of the lawfulness of organic form. In other words, I set my sights on "laws of form" that might determine the order of the biological world. It seemed to me that the subcellular or macromolecular level was the field of biology most likely to reveal "laws of form" if they existed. It became an obvious prediction of *Nature's Destiny* that such laws of form should exist.

In what was a very great stroke of good fortune during 1999, only three years after I had completed the manuscript of *Nature's Destiny*, it occurred to me that one set of very well-known complex macromolecular forms—the protein folds—might represent a set of lawful abstract natural forms, similar to inorganic forms such as atoms or crystals. I was very excited by the possibility. If it was true, then the folds might represent the very first identified set of lawful organic forms.

From subsequent studies carried out with my Otago University colleagues Craig Marshall and Mike Legge, both lecturers in biochemistry, it became apparent that from the 1950s, when the first three-dimensional protein structures were determined, until the early 1970s, protein folds were assumed by most biochemists to be contingent assemblages of matter put together by natural selection. But since the early 1970s, as the number of determined structures began to accumulate, it was increasingly clear that the three-dimensional structures of the folds are essentially invariant and could be classified into a number of structural types. This suggested they might be abstract natural forms.

This conjecture was eventually confirmed by the identification of a set of rules that govern the ways the various submotifs, alpha helices and beta sheets, could be combined into higher order structures. These rules predicted a set of about 1000 discrete folds. Each fold represents an energy minimum that draws the fold into its proper conformation. These laws of protein form are strictly equivalent to the rules that govern the way atoms are combined into molecules or subatomic particles are combined into atoms to generate the periodic table of elements. It was a considerable stroke of luck that we had identified the first set of important organic forms determined by a set of laws of form. I was very excited. The results were published in an invited column in *Nature*[36] and in a long follow-up paper in the *Journal of Theoretical Biology*.[37]

The folds present stunning evidence, perhaps the first clear evidence discovered in biology, that highly complex organic forms can be generated by natural law. With the folds, the impossible has become possible—the basic building blocks of nature are specified in abstract laws of form and are not simply a mechanical program in the genes. They are lawful, emergent, self-organizing forms and not contingent "cleverly contrived machines." Here is a set of forms that arise directly out of the basic properties of matter, confirming the inference I had previously drawn from reading Henderson, that life might be encoded in the basic properties of matter.

A fascinating aspect of the folds, which we first pointed out in our papers, is the way adaptations are in every case the secondary modification of a primary natural form. Thus the forms are perfect exemplars of the dualistic pre-Darwinian conception of biological order as a core of natural order, or form, concealed under Richard Owen's "adaptive mask."

Our work in this area is ongoing. There are already good grounds for interpreting other sets of macromolecular and supramolecular forms, including the RNA folds, micro-tubular forms like the aster, and various tensegrity structures, as lawful forms.[38] Moreover, the protein and RNA folds provide more than a set of complex abstract architectures—many of them provide protofunctions that are of adaptive utility to the cell, and that may be easily optimized by selection.[39]

I am now quite convinced that the discovery that the protein folds are natural forms is only the beginning of what may turn out to be a major Platonic revision of biology, and an eventual relocation of biological order away from genes and mechanism and back into nature— where it resided before the Darwinian revolution.

ORDAINED IN NATURE FROM THE BEGINNING

In this chapter I have described my own long and complex anti-Darwinian intellectual journey. I started my journey with the special creationism of my youth, when I adhered unquestioningly to the traditional, mechanistic, contingent conception of organic order, what I have referred to here as the "superwatch model" of nature. The journey has since taken me to my view today, which is that much of life's order is an intrinsic and necessary feature of nature, and largely determined by physical law.

During the course of this journey I wrote two books: *Evolution: A Theory in Crisis* and *Nature's Destiny*. *Evolution* was written while I still adhered to the superwatch model of nature. Despite this, I still believe it represents one of the most convincing critiques of the assumption that the organic world is the continuum that classical Darwinism demands. *Nature's Destiny* was written while I was already on the road to advocating a lawful biology and was increasingly skeptical of the superwatch model. I think the first part of the book presents one of the most scholarly and comprehensive reviews to date of the fine-tuning of natural law for life as it exists on earth.

Since finishing *Nature's Destiny*, it has become even more apparent to me that the superwatch model is an inadequate metaphor of nature. On the one hand, there is the challenge arising from the failure to find the determinants of biological form in the genes. On the other, we are definitely beginning to find new "laws of form" in biology at the macromolecular and subcellular levels, where physics is ever more obviously the major determinant of forms such as the protein and RNA folds. These are clearly self-organizing natural forms and as different from artifactual assemblages of matter (like a watch) as could be imagined.

My view today is that a substantial fraction of the order of life is abstract natural form, ultimately determined by the laws of nature. This is no less true for organic life than it is for inorganic forms such as atoms or crystals. Of course, I also accept that living things exhibit adaptive complexity, but I see this as a secondary order imposed upon a core order given by physics. Such a view implies ultimately that life is an intrinsic property of matter, that the course of evolution was directed by natural law, and that our own existence was ordained in nature from the beginning.

Just as the beautiful spiral of the double helix and the wonderful propensity of the molecule for self-replication both arise *naturally* without any need for *contrivance* out of their intrinsic constituents (i.e., the four nucleotide bases), I believe that many of the unique forms and properties of living systems arise like those of the double helix *naturally* from the intrinsic properties of matter. I also believe that not only the non-adaptive order but a great deal of the adaptive order of biology will ultimately prove to be—like the globin and ribosomal folds— inherent in the fabric of nature herself.

Such a view is intellectually exciting because it holds out the prospect of a final union of biology and physics, and thus of a fully rational and lawful biology. Such a biology would be as profoundly anti-Darwinian as could be imagined, as it would banish forever contingency as a major determinant of biological order. Such a biology of reason and law would be a true science and take its place alongside physics and chemistry in Plato's timeless realm of the gods. Moreover, such a view lends itself, as Henderson showed so convincingly in his *Fitness of the Environment*, to the possibility of a teleological interpretation of life and indeed of the entire natural order. I believe it is the one route that can lead to a new synthesis between faith and reason.

James Barham

10. WHY I AM NOT A DARWINIST

Darwinism means different things to different people. To most, it is probably synonymous with evolution—the idea that all living things are genealogically related, having descended from one or a few original forms. However, there were people who believed in common descent before Darwin ever lived,[1] and others afterwards who believed in it but doubted Darwin's theory of natural selection.[2] Therefore, it is incorrect to simply equate Darwinism with belief in evolution. The term "Darwinism" should properly refer to Darwin's own contribution, the idea that evolution is explained by natural selection.

Yet another important distinction should be made, one between what I shall call the *empirical* and *metaphysical* forms of Darwinism. Empirical Darwinism is the proposition that natural selection causes evolution. To be more exact, it is the idea that the formation of new species is due to random changes in individual organisms that happen to be "selected" by the environment. From time immemorial, farmers, animal breeders, and others have known that systematically culling a population can alter the statistical distribution of traits appearing within it over time. Empirical Darwinism is the idea that an analogous process, acting through the competition between organisms for limited resources, has been responsible for evolutionary change.

Even this empirical form of Darwinism is not nearly so well founded as is usually assumed. For one thing, we do not yet understand in either genetic or physiological detail how the reproductive systems of two populations of organisms that belong to the same species can change in such a way as to make successful interbreeding between them impossible. Since we cannot produce new species at will, we are in no position to state categorically that natural selection is the driving force behind evolution. For another thing, the theory of natural selection operates at such a high level of abstraction that it has relatively little empirical content.

This quality of abstraction makes Darwinism difficult to distinguish from the bald claim that evolution has occurred, which in turn makes it very hard to test. Nevertheless, as we learn more about the interaction between genomes and the organisms of which they are a part, it should be possible someday to demonstrate how speciation occurs, and so either confirm or refute Darwin's hypothesis.

The real problem with the evolution debate is not empirical Darwinism. Rather, it is a sort of theory creep in which a bold but circumscribed scientific claim becomes conflated with a much more sweeping philosophical claim. The philosophical claim is then presented as though it were a confirmed scientific fact. Metaphysical Darwinism maintains that the theory of natural selection has successfully reduced all teleological and normative phenomena to the interplay of chance and necessity, thus eliminating purpose and value from our picture of the world.[3] Metaphysical Darwinists regard belief in objective values as a primitive superstition, on a par with belief in witches and ghosts. What is worse, they perpetrate a fraud on the public by draping their profoundly speculative philosophy with the mantle of scientific authority.

Over the past two decades, metaphysical Darwinism has become entrenched as the semi-official creed of the Western educated classes. Popular writers like Richard Dawkins, Daniel Dennett, and Steven Pinker would have us believe that living matter is no different from inanimate matter, that animals work by the same mechanical principles as manmade machines, and that everything about human nature can be explained in terms of natural selection, selfish genes, viruses of the mind (memes), and ultimately matter in motion. This mechanistic image of man has now penetrated the consciousness of the broader intelligentsia to the point that Kismet, a cute robot that interacts with people in lifelike ways, is now a star of the international opera circuit,[4] while one of our best-selling novelists, Barbara Kingsolver, gushes that natural selection is "the greatest, simplest, most elegant logical construct ever to dawn across our curiosity about the workings of natural life. It is inarguable, and *it explains everything.*"[5]

For many years, I too was a Darwinist of this ilk. I would have regarded myself as a cousin to Kismet and a soul mate to Kingsolver. However, I now believe that metaphysical Darwinism is profoundly mistaken. It is mistaken about life in general, and about human nature in particular. Worst of all, the false ideas it propagates have potentially grave moral and political consequences. In this essay, I will first recount how I acquired the Darwinian faith, then explain in more detail what I now see as the main problems with metaphysical Darwinism, and how I came to lose my faith in it. Finally, I will say a few words about how we might forge an alternative to Darwinism capable of doing justice to the full range of human experience, while still regarding human beings as a part of nature.

PORTRAIT OF THE DARWINIST AS A YOUNG MAN

I lost my faith not once, but twice. The first time was when I was still quite young. I was raised in a predominantly Southern Baptist family in the 1950s. Although I was born into middle-class circumstances in Dallas, my grandparents on both sides had grown up on small, hardscrabble farms in East and North Texas, and I received an essentially rural—that is, oral—religious instruction as a child. Before I started school, my mother's mother looked after me a good deal, and I used to listen to Bible stories every afternoon snuggled in her lap. Daniel in the Lions' Den, Shadrach, Meshach, and Abednego in the Fiery Furnace, and similar stories made a deep impression on my child's imagination. Every night, I knelt beside my bed and commended my soul to the Lord, if I should die before I waked.

After I started school, I spent less time with my grandmother and more with my parents, who were less fervent in their faith. My parents were business people who worked long hours to make the most of the post-war economic boom, and gradually church attendance fell by the wayside. Although years later my mother would share her own religious doubts with me, while I was in elementary school conventional belief in God remained unchallenged in the background of my daily life, even as my religious observance all but ceased. Looking back, I can see that the secularization of my family, along with much of the rest of American culture during the 1950s and '60s, must be counted an important factor in my looming religious crisis. However, I believe there were other reasons, as well.

One of these, I think, was the emphasis placed on science education in the wake of Sputnik, which brought scientific ideas flooding into the cultural backwaters of the country. The space program, in particular, was calculated to excite the imagination of a child. I well remember carrying a transistor radio to school when I was ten to follow the flight of John Glenn. I listened to reports on the sly throughout the day, riveted by the unfolding drama. I feel sure that the romance of such experiences helped to open the door for me to the great intellectual adventure that is science.

Another factor in my loss of faith was the fact that my life was shaping up into the old story of the young social outcast who seeks refuge from his harsh provincial world in the ivory tower of learning. Nowadays, there are bully-prevention programs in the public schools, but in those days it was survival of the fittest on the playground. For timid and awkward boys like me, books provided a ladder leading to a height from which I could look down upon my tormentors, if only in my own mind. Standing on that height, I soon realized that one of the other things I was supposed to look down upon was my grandmother's simple faith in the Bible stories I had learned at her knee.

I was around twelve years old, if memory serves, when the dawning knowledge of how my own childish faith appeared in the eyes of the wider world, ripened into a full-blown crisis. I recall lying in bed one night, unable to sleep, my eyes casting fearful glances upwards into the darkness, my mind alternately imagining the torments of hell that awaited it and reproaching itself for harboring such childish fears. As I lay there, fairly writhing in anguish, I beseeched my Maker: "Please forgive me if I ever stop believing in You!"

The crisis passed quickly. Any lingering fears I had that there might be a God after all were soon put to rest when Bertrand Russell's *Why I Am Not a Christian* fell into my hands. I don't think it was so much that I found Russell's arguments persuasive—I doubt that I fully understood them—as that my courage was stiffened by his example. Here was a famous man, universally acknowledged as one of the brilliant thinkers of the age, who confidently uttered out loud thoughts that I trembled to whisper to myself.

After that, there was no turning back. Like generations of teenage apostates before me, I discovered the exhilarating irreverence of Swift, the scathing sarcasm of Voltaire, the Mark Twain they didn't teach us in school. A few years later, while studying Greek and Latin at the University of Texas, I devoured the novels of Kurt Vonnegut, Jr. All of this I supplemented with the pop-philosophical works of Carl Sagan, B. F. Skinner, Dean Woolridge, and many others. I also set about learning as much of the science that was the alleged underpinning for the materialistic worldview of these authors as was practicable for a Classics major. For the better part of twenty years—until my late thirties—I was a militant atheist, convinced that all religious belief was feeble-minded nonsense. I held religion responsible for most of the ills of mankind, and regarded reason and science as the only beacons of hope for humanity. In short, I had not so much abandoned religion as converted to a new faith. Needless to say, one of the chief gods in my pantheon was Charles Darwin.

THE MIND OF THE DARWIN BELIEVER

Darwinists hate it when their critics point out that their belief system amounts to a religious faith in its own right. In the West, of course, religion has usually involved belief in a transcendent Being—the very thing that Darwinists want most of all to deny. However, not all religions have done so, and belief in the supernatural cannot be taken as a defining characteristic of religion. Religion is many things, but if there is one characteristic that all religions have in common, surely it is faith. What is faith? This itself is a highly disputed matter, but perhaps we may define it as a strong emotional attachment to an all-encompassing worldview that outstrips the available empirical evidence. By this definition, at least, there is little doubt that metaphysical Darwinism functions as a religion for a great many people today.

It is very difficult for us to simply bracket all those questions that we cannot yet answer with scientific precision. On the contrary, such questions are an essential aspect of our humanity. We human beings are not made to be indifferent to our own place in the larger scheme of things. It is very difficult for us to simply bracket with scientific precision all those questions that we cannot yet answer. And a good thing, too, because it is precisely the drive to make sense of the world as a whole—the thirst for *consilience,* to use the term recently popularized by E. O. Wilson[6]—that is the motor of scientific progress itself. It is not wrong for Darwinists to cleave to their faith with their heart and soul; what is wrong is for them to pretend that it enjoys the exalted status of scientific knowledge.

The fundamental problem with the Darwinian philosophy is that there is no way to get value from mechanism. And yet that is exactly what metaphysical Darwinism has to do to make good on its claims, because life is normative to the core. Above all else, living things strive to go on living, which is another way of saying they value life. For an organism, whatever promotes its own life and that of its progeny is good, whatever threatens them is bad. Darwinists like to talk about "survival," but this word does not solve the problem, it merely labels it. Inanimate matter does not struggle to survive in an organized form; so appealing to survival begs the question of the normativity intrinsic to life. Furthermore, it is successful functional striving that leads to survival, not the other way around. Therefore, the explanatory logic of Darwinism is backwards. The real question is how a system capable of intelligent interaction within its environment can exist in the first place. And here, all Darwinists can do is call on chance.

According to the Darwinian creation myth, intelligent adaptations within highly complex, functionally integrated systems just happen, for no particular reason. This is the fundamental proposition that materialism in all its variants asks us to swallow. First articulated by the ancient Greek atomists, it is a bolus that has been gagging scientists and philosophers for more than two millennia. The problem was already perfectly plain to Cicero in 45 BC *(De natura deorum,* II.xxxvii):

> At this point must I not marvel that there should be anyone who can persuade himself that there are certain solid and indivisible particles of matter borne along by the force of gravity, and that the fortuitous collision of those particles produces this elaborate and beautiful world? I cannot understand why he who considers it possible for this to have occurred should not also think that, if a countless number of copies of the one-and-twenty letters of the alphabet, made of gold or what you will, were thrown on to the ground, it would be possible that they should produce the *Annals* of Ennius, all ready for the reader.[7]

The distinguished cosmologist Fred Hoyle updated Cicero's imagery in his famous analogy of a tornado passing through a junkyard and leaving a Boeing 747 in its wake,[8] but he added nothing essential. The point at issue is a matter of elementary statistical mechanics. One cannot tinker at random with a functionally integrated system and expect to achieve beneficial results. To be viable, changes must be *coordinated.* Because of combinatorial explosion, the odds against the success of truly uncoordinated changes from even one macromolecule to another would be fantastically huge, let alone uncoordinated changes in an entire cell. That is why the idea that evolution is driven by random variation of functionally uncorrelated parts is quite incredible from a physical point of view.

The real problem Darwinists face is that even in the fifteen billion odd years since the big bang, a heap of inert matter would not spontaneously organize itself into a functionally integrated system. Epic poems and Boeing 747s do not come into existence by themselves, no matter how much time is available—and neither do cells, or even proteins. Therefore, if there is no intrinsic connection between the material constitution of a system and its function, then we can say with certainty that the organization must have been imposed on the system by an external agent. On the other hand, if as naturalists we suppose that the system organized itself into a functionally integrated whole, then we must also posit some intrinsic connection between matter and function to act as a guiding principle. Either way, Darwinism has got it wrong. Invoking chance in the way that it does is tantamount to saying: "Here the laws of nature as we understand them are suspended." It is no different from invoking miracles.

Of course, Darwinists are not unaware of this problem. Their answer is to shift the ground of the debate from variation to selection. They will say it is the selection step, which is non-random, and not the variation step, that bears the real explanatory weight in their theory. They will even illustrate the point by saying that natural selection operates like a ratchet, locking in previous gains, and thus circumventing the combinatorial explosion problem. But this is a different proposition altogether from the notion that adaptations occur by chance. What Darwinists forget is that a ratchet is itself imbued with purpose. It introduces a systematic bias into a situation, by means of a particular structure that physically permits desired changes and prevents undesired ones. In the case of evolutionary change, the thing that is acting as a ratchet is precisely the functional organization that gives organisms the ability to adapt intelligently to circumstances. But if functional organization is the ratchet that natural selection depends on, then obviously we have not eliminated normativity from our account of nature at all.

None of this is to say that life is guided by a transcendent teleological principle. It is equally possible to imagine that the intelligence inherent in all life is internal to the matter of which living systems are made.[9] Nor do organisms advance unerringly toward optimal solutions. Life is intelligent, not clairvoyant. Evolution, like all learning, does indeed involve trial-and-error. However, trial-and-error is itself a profoundly teleological process.[10] Being right or wrong presupposes a standard of judging, which presupposes a judge who *cares*. A new biological trait is only a success or a failure in relation to the value that the organism of which it is a part attaches to its own life.

In summary, metaphysical Darwinism is caught on the horns of a dilemma. To carry out a genuine reduction of purpose and value to chance and necessity, evolutionary changes must occur through a truly random process. This is an absurdity from a physical point of view. On the other hand, if it is admitted that the changes that occur in organisms over geological time are functional in character, then evolution begins to make physical sense. In this case, however, reduction fails because selection theory presupposes the very teleology it is supposed to have eliminated.

*****

It is not as though the difficulties with Darwinism were a closely guarded secret. On the contrary, they are well known, and have been vigorously debated in one form or another in every generation from the publication of the *Origin of Species* until the present day.[11] This in itself shows that Darwinism does not enjoy the same secure epistemological status as other scientific theories. Why, then, are so many people who pride themselves on their skepticism so credulous when it comes to Darwinism?

Speaking for myself, it is not that I did not know of the problems, still less that I had an answer to them. It was that I did not care. Like any true believer, I saw what I wanted to see. I told myself that Darwinism's critics were ignorant of modern science. Or, that they were too stupid to understand the subtlety of the theory of natural selection. Or that they had a hidden religious agenda. Or that they were cowards. Above all, the Darwinist sees himself as a hero, someone who is brave enough to confront the terrible truth about the human condition that others cannot bear to face.

So, how did I come to lose my faith a second time? Was it, as the Darwinist will suspect, a failure of nerve? Reflecting on this question, I have come to believe that three factors have helped me arrive at my present position.

First, I think that, as an independent scholar, I had an easier time following my nose where the evidence led me. I will leave it to others to judge whether academic institutions in this country have become intolerant of dissent, but, in any case, I think the worst censorship we all face is internal—the fear of departing from the path approved by our peers. No matter how powerful the arguments against a viewpoint, it is very difficult for them to really register with us as long as we are living within a milieu in which alternatives are simply unthinkable. I no longer worked in the Academy, but I had been intellectually reared in it, and I remember well the intense discomfort I felt when it first occurred to me that the only solution to the problems with metaphysical Darwinism was to take teleology seriously. I quite sympathized with Charles Darwin when I read how he once told his friend, the naturalist Joseph Hooker, that entertaining the idea of the transmutation of species was "like confessing a murder."[12] I knew exactly what he meant! Entertaining the idea that teleology might be objectively real produced similar guilty feelings in me. Eventually, though, I became disgusted with my own pusillanimity. I did not have to worry about tenure; so what did I have to fear? If I was convinced that Darwinism was incoherent and that affirming some sort of immanent teleology was the only intelligible alternative, then why not say so in print?

Second, as one grows older, the reality principle gains the upper hand over the idealism of youth. Metaphysical Darwinism is a totalizing philosophical system—a kind of intellectual utopianism—and like any radical the Darwinist is in love with an abstraction. I stopped being a Darwinist for the same reason I eventually stopped considering myself a socialist—I came to understand that the world is what it is, and that reality cannot be merely wished away. For human beings, the world of purpose and value is the warp and woof of our existence. Not only is reason subordinate to the passions, as Hume noted, but human reason is itself but one manifestation of the intelligence of life—the power of living systems to adjust means to ends in the light of circumstances. Thus, with age, I gradually came to see that those who strive for consilience cannot deny teleology and normativity without pulling the rug out from under themselves, for in so doing they deny the existence of the very biological principles underpinning their denial itself. I began to understand the truth of Alfred North Whitehead's observation that "Scientists animated by the purpose of proving that they are purposeless constitute an interesting subject for study."[13]

I had always been immersed in the humanities, but somehow I had managed to keep the part of my mind that was drawn to the exploration and expression of human feeling separate from the part that was preoccupied with rational understanding. The only way to be a consistent Darwinist was to discount all the experiences that as a humanist I held most dear. Joy and suffering, good and evil, beauty and ugliness, nobility and baseness of spirit—all of this the Darwinist dismisses as a veil of illusion. As the eminent philosopher of science Bas van Fraassen recently remarked, "There is . . . not a great distance between the philosophical materialist and the philistine."[14] Since I could not bring myself to be a consistent philistine, I settled for incoherence. If asked, I would have said that I believed there are objective values, that some things are better than others, and that the higher human values have nothing whatever to do with the struggle for survival or reproductive success. And yet, as a Darwinist, I was committed to the notion that all of human nature can be reduced to the blind operation of natural selection on the selfish genes. Eventually, I realized the absurdity of regarding the human world as ontologically inferior to the world of quarks and atoms. It occurred to me that if neither of these realms of existence can be ignored, then seeking consilience means finding a way to accommodate them both. I then saw that this meant breaking with the materialistic worldview I had held all of my adult life. And, finally, I came to understand that a person who is stirred, say, by listening to the music of Mozart, or reading the stories of Chekhov, or viewing the films of Satyajit Ray—and who reflects on such works of art and what they tell us about what it means to be a human being—that person has already ceased to be a Darwinist.

However, even with the twin advantages of independence and age, I doubt that I would have ever had the courage to reject Darwinism outright were it not for a third and decisive factor—the good fortune of stumbling one day upon an alternative. A stronger character than mine might have been content to say, "Well, I know that purpose and value are real, even if I don't know how this can be so," but I required something positive to believe in. Then one day, while browsing in the stacks, I stumbled upon a thick volume entitled *Self-Organizing Systems*,[15] which contained a pioneering collection of essays aimed at applying insights gathered from the science of nonlinear dynamics to various problems in biology and psychology. Fascinated by what I found in this book, I plunged into the literature and soon discovered a wealth of empirical research and theoretical speculation completely new to me. I knew that no one was citing this body of work in the philosophical journals, but I immediately sensed in it a great potential to effect the consilience that Darwinism promised but could not deliver. With this discovery, my life's work was launched, and my second loss of faith was complete.

THE STRUGGLE FOR SURVIVAL AND THE GENTLE LAW

Darwinists would have us believe that their philosophy is the only naturalistic game in town. Furthermore, they are convinced that if there is no transcendental ground of value, then value must be an illusion. In their minds, this means that the human moral impulse, for example, must be reducible to the random shuffling of the selfish genes. Thanks to the theory of kin selection, they think they have a scientific formula for altruism: "I will lay down my life for two brothers or eight cousins."[16] This was no doubt first spoken in jest, but these cynical Darwinian witticisms have a nasty way of catching on. It has gotten to the point now where one cannot pick up a newspaper without seeing Darwin trotted out and put through his paces. For example, in the wake of the destruction of the space shuttle *Columbia*, in an article in the *Science Times* reflecting on the fact that we are moved more by the deaths of individuals than by statistics, we were assured that "emotions, developed to enhance the species' survival, keeping early humans one step in front of hungry lions, sometimes mislead in the modern world."[17] Such silliness would be amusing, were it not symptomatic of a deeply troubling trend in our culture.

How can kin selection explain the moral sense that sometimes prompts us to stand in opposition to our own kinsmen? Do Darwinists really imagine that their theory can shed light, for example, on the White Rose, the clandestine organization created in Munich in 1942 by a handful of university students to distribute pamphlets protesting the crimes of their own tribe, actions that ultimately cost most of them their lives?[18] How can natural selection—which Barbara Kingsolver assures us explains everything—explain the courage of the many Serbs who took up arms to *defend* Sarajevo? How can it account for the dawning awareness in my own conscience, and that of many other white Southerners in the 1960s, that the American apartheid system was evil? The Darwinian view of life is so crude, so thoughtless, so utterly false to all that is noblest in human beings, that truly one does not know whether to laugh or cry.

There is no question that we are animals. Just as our bodies are subject to the law of gravity, so too are our lives subject to the struggle for survival. But just as life transcends inanimate matter, so too do human beings transcend the other animals. After all, we can bend gravity to our will by using our intelligence to build flying machines. In the same way, we can also bend our animal nature to our will by using our moral sense to strive for the good. Our innate desire to oppose the harsh law of the struggle for survival constitutes what the great Austrian novelist Adalbert Stifter called the *gentle law* of human nature:

> We want to try to observe the gentle law that guides the human race. There are forces that aim for the survival of the individual. They take and use everything necessary to its survival and development. They secure the endurance of the one and thus of all. But if someone unreservedly seizes upon everything that his being needs, when he destroys the conditions of the existence of someone else, then something higher grows angry in us; we help the weak and the oppressed; we restore the state of affairs in which one person can survive beside the other and walk his human path; and when we have done that, we feel satisfied, we feel ourselves higher and more ardent than we feel as individuals, we feel ourselves as all humanity. Thus there are forces that work toward the survival of mankind as a whole that may not be checked by individual forces, indeed, that, on the contrary, must check the

individual forces themselves. It is the law of these forces, the
law that wants everyone to be respected, honored, and
unthreatened beside the other, that he may walk his higher
human path, may earn the love and admiration of his fellow
men, that he may be protected as a precious object, as every
person is a precious object for all other persons. This law
obtains everywhere, wherever people live beside people. . . .
As in nature the general laws work silently and incessantly
and the conspicuous is only an individual expression of these
laws, so the moral law works silently, animating the soul,
through the endless communion of men with men, and the
miracles of the moment when deeds occur are only small to-
kens of this general force. Thus this law is the sustaining law
of mankind as the law of nature is the sustaining law of the
world.[19]

What is the source of the gentle law? How can we understand the
place of value in nature, if not through the theory of natural selection?
At present, it is very hard to say; but there are a few observations we can
make by triangulating between the relevant scientific disciplines and our
everyday, commonsense experience of the world.

It is an empirical fact that living matter behaves very differently
from nonliving matter. Broken bones heal, broken stones don't. The
question is: What is the physical basis of this difference? A little reflection shows that it must lie in the specific nature of living matter. Why?
Because robots, computers, and all other cybernetically organized systems designed by us cannot *instantiate* this self-preserving property of
living matter, however well they may *simulate* certain aspects of it. Why
not? Because the function or goal state of a manmade system lies entirely outside of the system itself, in the mind of the human designer.

For example, Kismet's function is to interact with a human inter-
locutor in a lifelike fashion. Its creators have achieved this result by im-
posing a set of boundary conditions upon the matter of which Kismet is
made; the bits and pieces that comprise Kismet have no tendency to
seek this goal state on their own. The success or failure of Kismet's performance is invisible to Kismet itself—it exists entirely in the eye of the
beholder. This will remain true of all future robots made of inorganic
parts, no matter how sophisticated they become. That is because the
second law of thermodynamics will ensure that the configuration of a
robot's parts that gives rise to a humanly desired goal state will continuously degrade; at the same time, there is nothing intrinsic to the robot

that is striving to oppose that degradation and preserve the goal state. Adding more feedback loops is futile. It can improve performance from the human point of view, but it cannot cause an ontological shift from an external to an internal criterion of what counts as a good performance. No matter how cleverly contrived, robots will always remain simulacra of living things; they will never live. To be alive is to value one's own continued existence as a functionally organized system. As noted before, it is to *care*. And, like Rhett Butler, robots just don't give a damn.

What is it about living matter that makes it care about its own self-preservation? That is the real question at the heart of the mystery of life. Again, it must be admitted that at present we simply do not know. However, two bodies of physical theory have been developed over the past half-century or so that I believe show promise of supplying us with an answer someday. One of these is nonlinear dynamics, and the other is condensed-matter physics. The former studies the universal aspects of coherent behavior in macroscopic systems, apart from the details of microstructure, while the latter studies the underlying microscopic forces that give rise to macroscopic coherence in matter. As yet, neither has been systematically applied to biology, but that is now beginning to change.[20] The ultimate goal is to understand the physical basis of the purposive dynamics of life—how the means-end coordination of all the myriad processes in cells has arisen out of the intrinsic causal powers of the living state of matter. It is too soon to say whether this enterprise will be successful, but the very existence of these disciplines at least allows us to envisage what a scientific account of value might look like.

Above all, such an account would be emergentist rather than reductionist. Just as water is qualitatively different from molecular hydrogen or oxygen, so too are the giant molecules of life qualitatively distinct from the monomer units of which they are composed. This principle of emergence, encapsulated by the Nobel Prize winning theorist Philip W. Anderson in the slogan "more is different," is well established in low-temperature physics, even if it is considered heresy by the high priests of high-temperature physics.[21] This means that our goal should not be to reduce higher levels to lower ones but rather to *integrate* all the levels of reality by means of a dynamical principle of cosmic evolution. As Anderson has explained:

> The actual universe is the consequence of layer upon layer of
> emergence, and the concepts and laws necessary to under-
> stand it are as complicated, subtle and, in some cases, as uni-

versal as anything the particle folks are likely to come up with. This also makes it possible to believe that the structure of science is not the simple hierarchical tree that the reductionists envision, but a multiply connected web, each strand supporting the others. Science, apparently, like everything else, has become qualitatively different as it has grown.[22]

I submit that the integration of emergent levels along the lines suggested by Philip Anderson, and not E. O. Wilson's Darwinian pan-reductionism, is the only sensible way to pursue consilience. Value is a fact of life, and we cannot achieve the understanding we seek by sticking our heads in the sand and denying its existence. We can only do so by searching for the natural ground of normativity in living matter.

From an emergentist perspective, we can at last begin to get a glimpse of the true nature of the gentle law. Yes, everything that lives struggles to survive. But this only means that function, not selection, is the bedrock upon which life is built. As soon as we see this, then many things fall into place. If intelligent striving is an objective property of living matter, then it is not so surprising that out of the primordial value of survival there might have emerged an infinity of other values. Once we escape the conceptual straitjacket of the selection principle and adopt a functional perspective grounded in dynamics, the air of paradox surrounding symbiosis, cooperation, curiosity, play, and myriad other higher cognitive functions begins to dissipate.

As for the gentle law, it is of course built upon general mammalian and primate forms of sociality. However, with the emergence of language came the ability not only to feel spontaneous affection for members of one's own family and tribe but also to assume in one's imagination an infinity of perspectives different from one's own. This ability, in turn, has created sympathy in us for all other human beings, no matter how different from us they are, if only we reflect in our imagination upon what their experience must be like. Piggybacking on the intrinsic value of life, language and culture have conjured into existence the distinctively human values we call the good, the true, and the beautiful.

The gentle law within us is itself a law of nature. It is the law of *our* nature—of *human* nature. It governs human conduct as surely as gravity governs the planets in their orbits. It is a law that prompts us to lay down our lives, not just for two brothers or eight cousins, but for perfect strangers and, if need be, for our very ideals.

Where the Stakes Are Highest

Darwinists want to be hardheaded, to avoid anything smacking of mysticism, but in the end they wind up being superficial. This is inevitable, because their chief conceptual tool, natural selection, is too blunt an instrument for the task at hand.

By refusing to ask what makes cells distinctive as physical systems, reductionists continue to tread the old path of behaviorism. It is ironic that over the past several decades, during the time of the apotheosis of Darwin and the ascendancy of molecular biology, the neurosciences have finally shaken off the behaviorist mindset. Indeed, we are now in the midst of a renaissance of scientific interest in our mental life.[23] It is time for biologists to pluck up their courage and take this step as well. To do this, they must join forces with physicists in probing the physical basis of the teleological and normative properties of living matter.

The transition from metaphysical Darwinism to immanent teleology is likely to have far-reaching repercussions. As philosopher of biology Lenny Moss has noted, "To unearth the enigma of the apparent purposiveness in living nature carries with it large stakes—it is to open the door to fundamentally different conceptions of the organism."[24] Such a shift is apparent, for example, in the new notion of "dynamical diseases," which has already begun to have some practical payoffs, particularly in cardiology, while other medical benefits—in neurology, oncology, gerontology, and elsewhere—will likely accrue in the future.[25]

However, it is in the philosophical and cultural spheres where the stakes are highest. As Whitehead noted, "The status of life in nature . . . is the central meeting point of all the strains of systematic thought, humanistic, naturalistic, philosophic."[26] If our conception of our own nature and our place in the universe matters in the way we conduct our lives—and I believe it does—then the struggle against metaphysical Darwinism matters, and matters deeply, in more ways than we can yet fathom.

Given its colossal philosophical pretensions compared with its modest scientific achievements, the theory of natural selection may one day come to be seen as a blunder of historic proportions, on a par with crystalline spheres, phlogiston, and the ether. Metaphysical Darwinism simply does not live up to its billing. It claims to explain everything about life, but in fact explains almost nothing—certainly nothing about the nature of purpose and value, and how they fit into the natural order. That is why I am not a Darwinist.[27]

PART FOUR
Auditing the Books

11. Why Evolution Fails the Test of Science

Fifty years ago, a young graduate student performed a seminal experiment that became a popular icon in evolutionary studies. Stanley Miller, working in the laboratory of Nobel laureate Harold Urey at the University of Chicago, sent electrical charges through a mixture of lifeless organic ingredients and produced amino acids. The electrical charges and organic brew were thought to represent the conditions on the early earth, and the amino acids were seen as providing the first steps toward the formation of life.

Miller's experiment was not the first to investigate how life originated, but it was an important turning point. "Life in a test tube," proclaimed the newspaper headlines. The results bolstered the evolutionary vision that natural mechanisms could have created life. A century earlier Charles Darwin had speculated that life may have begun in a warm little pond with protein compounds ready to undergo more complex changes. Proteins are made of amino acids, and now Miller had shown that amino acids could form spontaneously.

In later years, variations of the Miller-Urey experiment showed that just about every one of life's twenty amino acids could form spontaneously. But while origin-of-life researchers found these results encouraging, they soon encountered difficulties. Amino acids are, headlines notwithstanding, a long way from life itself. Yes, amino acids could form spontaneously, but how could they assemble to form simple proteins? How could those proteins meaningfully interact? How could genetic information be created and passed on? At what point did natural selection become important? And so forth. In short, how could evolutionists bridge the gap between amino acids and the first living cell?

These are the types of questions origin-of-life researchers need to answer. They are not easy questions, for as the second half of the twentieth century revealed, the gap between amino acids and what is envisioned as the first living cell is enormous. Though an animal consists of an astronomical number of cells, its complexity consists in the quality and mutual arrangement of those cells, not in their sheer quantity. Biological complexity is not the result of a multitude of simple building blocks but of the inherent complexity of those building blocks at the cellular level and, for multicellular organisms, the patterns in which those building blocks are arranged. Thus even the simplest unicellular organisms are phenomenally complex.

How, then, could life have arisen from a warm little pond with nothing more than amino acids floating about? This post–Miller-Urey problem remains as elusive as ever. What's more, even the Miller-Urey experiment and its variants can be questioned. For example, do they really represent early earth conditions? And could they produce anything but highly dilute solutions, too weak to support further chemical activity? All these questions reveal problems, but there is a still deeper problem with origin-of-life research.

We can discuss the various problems in origin-of-life research. We can debate whether or not this or that mechanism is improbable. What is abundantly clear, however, is that the research is speculative and that there is no compelling solution to the problem. Researchers have many ideas, but this is because there is no compelling answer. Indeed, for many the idea that the most complex thing we know of, life itself, spontaneously arose from inorganic material is simply far-fetched. Where, then, do origin-of-life researchers gain their confidence?

What I find intriguing is not the various unresolved problems with origin-of-life research, but rather the utter confidence of origin-of-life researchers about where the solution to life's origin lies. For example, the prestigious National Academy of Sciences recently wrote:

> For those who are studying the origin of life, the question is no longer whether life could have originated by chemical processes involving nonbiological components. The question instead has become which of many pathways might have been followed to produce the first cells.[1]

Or again, evolutionist Carl Zimmer writes that scientists "have found compelling evidence that life could have evolved into a DNA-based microbe in a series of steps."[2] Such sentiments are simply inaccurate to the point of being misleading. Origin-of-life research is in no position to make such claims.

This unrealistic assessment is the deeper problem with origin-of-life research. Nor is it limited to origin-of-life research. Evolution in general is consistently promoted as a scientific fact. From textbooks to popular works ever since the nineteenth century and up through the present, the message has been the same: We are to believe that evolution is so well documented, so well understood, and so well proven that it should be considered on a par with facts such as gravity. The details of evolution may not all be completely understood, but any question as to whether it actually occurred, say evolutionists, has long since been decisively answered in the affirmative.

As with the origin-of-life problem, there is a tremendous disparity between the scientific evidence and the claims of evolutionists. This problem is deeper than merely misunderstanding the science. We shall examine the science in the next section and see that evolution does not qualify as a scientific fact, much less as even a good scientific theory. But in the final section we shall examine the deeper problem: Why do evolutionists believe their theory is a fact?

I am not surprised that there are those who advocate evolution. The general idea that the world arose via purely natural means without any intelligent input has been around long before Darwin. One can find writings of the ancient Greeks that read as though they come from one of today's evolution textbooks. What I find far more intriguing is the high confidence of evolutionists. It is, from a scientific perspective, unjustified. But evolutionists do not restrict themselves to scientific reasoning. As we shall see in the final section, there are powerful non-scientific arguments for evolution, and these are why evolutionists call their theory a fact.

THE SCIENTIFIC REASONING AGAINST EVOLUTION

There is, as evolutionists like to say, a mountain of evidence for Charles Darwin's theory. But quantity does not always make for quality. For the most part, this evidence falls into three categories: comparative anatomy, small-scale change, and the fossil record. We will survey each category and see the same pattern in each case: only when used selectively or superficially does the evidence support evolution. When carefully considered, the evidence is ambiguous and even argues against evolution.

Comparative Anatomy

Everyone knows that the different species share a great many similarities. Humans and chimpanzees, coyotes and wolves, moose and deer, and the fir and pine trees are all examples of different species that are highly similar. Since evolution is supposed to have modified existing species rather than to have created brand new ones, we would expect many similarities. Hence, the simple fact that species share so many similarities is evidence for evolution.

Furthermore, the species fall into what the great naturalist Linnaeus described a century before Darwin as a series of nested hierarchies. That is, while similar species fall into clusters, those clusters also tend to cluster, and those sets of clusters tend to cluster, and so forth. As Darwin put it, the groupings of species "seem clustered round points, and these round other points, and so on in almost endless cycles."[3] Today, evolutionists argue this is precisely what one would expect if the species evolved from each other via common descent.

In addition, many of these similarities seem to be the product of a blind, unguided process inasmuch as some similarities between species have no apparent function or are similar for no apparent reason. For example, whales have a small set of bones that appear to be the distant relative of the pelvis of earlier tetrapods. The whale is a mammal and is thought to have evolved from a four-legged carnivore. The hind limbs, evolutionists say, were lost in the whale's evolutionary process and therefore the pelvis would have played a less important role. Evolution explains perfectly why we see in whales the vestige of an earlier tetrapod's pelvis.

Just as revealing are those cases where a structure is fully functional yet is curiously similar throughout a range of species. The pentadactyl pattern is a favorite example. Found at the end of the limb structure of frogs, birds, humans, whales and bats, to name a few, the same five-bone pattern is employed for such diverse tasks as grasping, flying, digging, and walking. Anyone who has studied biology knows that there are usually at least a few different designs that will do the job. Branches may be pre-stressed in compression on their underside for structural support, or they may be pre-stressed in tension on their upperside. Hearts may have two, three, or four chambers. There are dozens of different eye designs. Necessary designs are hard to find, and nature consistently finds different ways of doing the same task.

Why, then, is the pentadactyl pattern so prevalent? Is this not the sign of an unguided force constrained by the contingencies of history?

The pentadactyl pattern worked and it was available—that is what counts in evolution. In biology, contingency dominates necessity. As a result, we find uncanny similarities produced by the evolutionary process. Sure, there probably was a better design in some instances, but it wasn't necessary. Natural selection didn't weed out the pentadactyl pattern just because it wasn't always optimal.

Arguments such as these were advanced by Darwin and continue to be used by today's evolutionists. In addition, we now have biochemical evidences that evolutionists see as adding yet more corroboration. From the early blood serum tests to today's genome data, we find that biochemical comparisons, in general, mimic morphological comparisons. Given evolution, this is exactly what we would expect from tracking inherited genetic changes: DNA mutations alter the biochemistry as well as the morphology; as species evolve over time they distance themselves at both molecular and morphological levels.

In fact, contingency seems to overshadow necessity at the molecular level as well. For example, hemoglobin carries oxygen throughout the body. It is a protein and as such consists of a sequence of amino acids. But there is no single sequence of amino acids that defines hemoglobin. Instead, there is a multitude of sequences that will work. Nonetheless, in similar species, such as the human and chimpanzee, we find very similar hemoglobin proteins; and in more distant species we find greater differences in the respective hemoglobins. In general, molecular comparisons are consistent with the morphological comparisons. The chances of such a strong correspondence are miniscule if the species were unrelated (i.e., if they didn't share a common ancestor).[4]

These are examples of arguments for evolution based on evidence from comparative anatomy. This evidence is regarded as a critical pillar of evolutionary theory. In fact, Darwin felt that this evidence alone was sufficient to advance his theory.[5] But though these arguments sound impressive, they are superficial. There are subtleties, alternative explanations, and even enormous problems that are ignored. Unfortunately, evolutionists do not give an even-handed account of the situation. The point is not that evolution is disproven, but that evolution is not a good explanation for the facts in hand.

First, there are many striking similarities shared by distant species. In these cases, the similarities could not have been the result of common descent, but instead must have evolved independently. The marsupial-placental convergence is a popular example. Over millions of years and in different corners of the earth, the marsupial and placental lineages, supposedly evolving from a mouse-like species, produced a host of similar designs. Everything from saber-toothed carnivores and wolves to fly-ing squirrels and anteaters were produced independently. Nature is full of lesser-known examples. From salamanders to cacti we find striking similarities that must have arisen independently. If biology is ruled by contingency rather than necessity, then why do we find duplicated de-signs? When similarities are found among allied species they are cited as powerful evidence for evolution. When similarities are found among dis-tant species, they are noted as cases of convergent evolution. Evolution can explain either case, but the explanations presuppose evolution. This is not powerful evidence for the theory.

Even the similarities claimed by evolutionists are often ambigu-ous, for they do not share the same developmental pattern. For example, two closely related species of frog, *Rana fusca* and *Rana esculents*, have eye lenses that are similar but they form very differently in embryologi-cal development. Did these two similar species evolve their eye lenses independently? There are many such similarities that develop differently or arise from different genes, and they seriously challenge the claim that they could have arisen through common descent. As Sir Gavin de Beer asked in 1964: "What mechanism can it be that results in the production of . . . the same 'patterns,' in spite of their not being controlled by the same genes? I asked this question in 1938, and it has not been answered."[6]

Regarding the so-called vestigial organs, the rule-of-thumb is that sooner or later a function will be found. About a hundred years ago Robert Wiedersheim listed 86 organs in the human body that he sup-posed to be useless leftovers of evolution. Today, we have found func-tions for virtually all of them. And what about those whale bones that are thought to be vestigial? It may well be that they support the whale's reproductive organs.

Molecular comparisons, in spite of what evolutionists report, are equally ambiguous. It is not surprising that molecular comparisons are generally consistent with morphological comparisons. After all, molecu-lar and morphological features are all part of the same organism. Only the extreme view, that there is no necessity in biology and that contin-gency is utterly dominant, would so divorce molecules from morphol-ogy. Yes, nature does reveal different solutions to similar design prob-lems, but this does not mean that designs are random. If two automo-biles are similar in appearance and function, are we surprised when their gears are also similar? Of course not.

In fact, the claim that molecular comparisons constitute powerful evidence for evolution essentially amounts to circular reasoning. Con-tingency is *assumed* to dominate, and so the similarities must have no functional explanation; therefore evolution is the only alternative. But the amino acid sequences of proteins, for example, have many functional implications. These include quaternary interactions, free-energy tuning, transport interactions, mRNA destabilization, positioning interactions, and amino acid storage and transport. It is logical to conclude that differences between species are found at all levels simply because all levels contribute to function in one way or another.

When evolutionists argue that all these similarities prove that species are related, they are again telling only half the story. True, the comparisons tell us that species are not randomly designed. The different design features are not randomly determined, but so what? Who would have thought such thing in the first place? Yes, when random design is the null hypothesis, evolution looks good. But this is a false dichotomy.

Imagine a physicist arguing for a faulty theory of gravity because, after all, his theory at least compares well with random motion. The use of random design as the null hypothesis hides a multitude of problems, including that of similar designs where differences are expected and vice versa. For example, non-coding regions of DNA in the mouse and human genomes have been found to be practically identical.[7] Or again, mitochondrial protein comparisons place chickens next to fish. It is, as one researcher put it, "clearly the wrong answer."[8] Examples such as these are abundant. From bats to microbes, the comparisons are in clear violation of expectations. Yet they appear as minor anomalies when compared to random design.

Evolutionists claim the Linnaean hierarchy is a crucial test that their theory has passed. But from the placental and marsupials to molecular comparisons, nature is full of deviations from that pattern. If the theory predicts the Linnaean hierarchy, then do the many deviations disprove the theory? Not according to evolutionists. Instead, they employ a battery of ad hoc explanatory devices, from convergent evolution and non-gradualistic evolutionary change to massive horizontal gene transfer and computational adjustments. But if evolution can explain the many deviations from the Linnaean hierarchy so well, it can hardly claim the general hierarchical pattern of the species as a crucial test.

What if there were yet even more deviations? At what point would evolution be unable to explain them? Evolutionists can define no such point because they allow their theory to explain such a wide variety of outcomes. In fact, it is not even clear that evolution really does predict the Linnaean hierarchy. The problem is that the Linnaean hierarchy is a striking pattern that is not easily produced by any hypothetical evolutionary process. That is, even if we grant that evolution could produce large-scale change, that change would, on the one hand, have to create tremendous biological variation and yet, on the other hand, have to create not so much variation that evolutionary relationships would be lost through saturation effects. Because evolution's purported process of creating large-scale change remains undefined, we don't have the necessary details to seriously verify the claim that it predicts the Linnaean hierarchy.

Comparative anatomy gives us a rich and diverse set of information. It is a fascinating aspect of biology, but it is subtle and complex. There are few hard-and-fast rules, and the information is hardly amenable to simple generalizations. Unfortunately, evolutionists consistently give a one-sided interpretation of the facts, portraying their theory as the only explanation.

SMALL-SCALE EVOLUTION

It is no secret that evolutionary adaptation is constantly occurring. From animal husbandry to horticulture, breeders are creating new varieties and species. Insects evolve in response to pesticides and microbes evolve in response to antibiotics. Also, in the wild, species evolve in response to changing conditions. There are several well-documented cases, such as the variations in the beaks of finches, caused by drought on the Galapagos Islands. Biologists studied the birds in detail from the 1970s to the 1990s. They found a four percent increase in the average beak size of one species after the drought of 1977.

What is less well known is the remarkable evolutionary change that has been observed in bacteria. When subjected to conditions harsh enough to stress a population, bacteria have been observed to undergo significant evolutionary change, including that of creating new proteins and metabolic pathways.

These evidences for evolution are not circumstantial. They can be observed and experiments can be repeated. We know that new species can be created and, according to evolutionists, the only extra ingredient required for large-scale evolution is time. As Carl Zimmer put it, "If you accept microevolution, you get macroevolution for free."[9] This is how evolutionists present the evidence of small-scale evolution. For them, it makes a compelling case for evolution in general. Thus for Isaac Asimov, the example of coloration change in peppered moths proved evolution.[10]

But this is not the whole story. Evolution appears to have its limits, especially in multicellular organisms. Small-scale evolution is a fact, but there is no reason to think it is unbounded. In fact, the evidence indicates that small-scale evolution does not extrapolate to the large-scale change that Darwinism requires. The point is not that such an extrapolation has been disproven but rather that it has little basis in fact. The beaks of the Galapagos finches, for example, returned to normal when the rains returned to the Galapagos Islands.

Evolutionists need to show that large amounts of change are feasible. Bacteria to fish to amphibia to reptiles to mammals is a tremendous amount of change compared to small-scale evolution; and the organism must be viable and fit at every point along the way. What actually has been demonstrated are many examples of change that lead to reduced fitness, or sterility, and some examples of change that represent a tiny fraction of the required change. The question of whether viable large-scale evolutionary pathways exist remains unanswered.

In fact, if one looks into the research journals, one finds that evolutionists are unsure whether small-scale evolution could possibly account for the needed large-scale change. As one evolutionist put it, the large-scale patterns of life reveal "a richness to evolution unexplained by microevolution."[11] Likewise, leading paleontologists agree that "the observed fossil pattern is invariably not compatible with a gradualistic evolutionary process."[12] The fossil record does not reveal a pattern of accumulated small-scale change. Furthermore, it is not clear from genetics how small-scale change is supposed to contribute to large-scale change. As evolutionist Ernst Mayr admits:

> When we look at what happens to the genotype during evolutionary change, particularly relating to such extreme phenomena as highly rapid evolution and complete stasis, we must admit that we do not fully understand them. The reason for this is that evolution is not a matter of changes in single genes; evolution consists of the change of entire genotypes.[13]

From genetics to paleontology and other disciplines, the message is that evolution's necessary large-scale change does not appear to be a simple case of small-scale change extrapolated over time. Why is the fact of small-scale evolution such powerful and compelling evidence for evolution, if the extrapolation from small-scale to large-scale evolution is an open question? The inference is drawn because evolutionists are not presenting an even-handed assessment of the evidence.

As for the adaptations we observe in bacteria, they are, to be sure, remarkable. But do they constitute compelling evidence for large-scale evolution? Again, there is more to the story. In fact, the adaptations we observe are produced by a machine that is set up to produce such changes. Rather than mutations aimlessly exploring new designs, we are witnessing the actions of a complex and robust machine.

For example, when bacteria in a population are subjected to harsh conditions, they tend to increase their mutation rate. It is as though a signal has been sent saying, "It's time to adapt." In addition, a small fraction of the population increases the mutation rates still more. These hypermutators ensure that an even greater variety of adaptive changes are explored. Such hypermutation may be essential to the survival of the bacteria population in some cases. The mutations themselves do not appear randomly throughout the genome but are concentrated in certain areas that can produce helpful changes. In other words, pathways of adaptation are, to a certain extent, already laid out.

Likewise, our knowledge of pesticide resistance in insects suggests a similar scenario. One study of the common fruit fly found that pesticide resistance arises from a gene that has been present all along. The gene serves to break down the pesticide. Before the stress of the pesticide, the gene used to be less active. But now, given the pesticide, the gene is more active in resistant flies. The gene's increased activity results from a special signal inserted into the gene to lift production constraints. It therefore appears that pesticide resistance is conferred merely by flipping a switch on the genetic production line rather than by creating a new factory.

These findings are remarkable, but they hardly suggest evolution. Instead of single mutations leading to a new functionality one step at a time, we are now called to believe that evolution produced marvelous machines by which more complicated changes can occur. Genomes must have evolved the capacity to respond to predictable environmental challenges with predictable changes. Mutational rates are sped up when needed and concentrated in those locations where needed. Fortunately, multiple mutations can occur in a single step.

In this way evolution has produced a machine that can evolve. Evolution, originally conceived as Darwin's general principle, has created evolution, now conceived as a biological function. This is sometimes called the evolution of evolvability. But the evolution of evolvability hardly accounts for evolution in the first place, for it has no explanation of how evolution produced the machines capable of facilitating evolution or how they could be endowed with such clever design capabilities.

THE FOSSIL RECORD

The fossils show that evolution is a fact. George Simpson said it in 1951, and evolutionists have been repeating it ever since. Along with the evidence of comparative anatomy and small-scale evolution, the fossil record is also said to prove evolution. Perhaps the most outstanding example of this evidence is the sequence of fossils that is transitional between synapsid reptiles and mammals. The jaw transition is a key anatomical change that is particularly well documented. The reptilian jaw contains several bones while the mammalian jaw consists of a single bone. Paleontologists have reconstructed what Stephen Jay Gould called a "lovely sequence of intermediates,"[14] where the reptilian jaw bones move aft and become the mammalian middle ear. *Cynognathus*, estimated to date from the early Triassic, at least 240 million years ago, is a key specimen in the sequence. It sports two jaw joints, one corresponding to the old reptilian articulation and one to the new mammalian connection.

Other fossil sequences that reveal large-scale change include the horse and whale histories. The horse evolutionary sequence was first reconstructed by the ardent Darwinist Thomas Huxley in 1870. Huxley introduced his reconstruction to the Geological Society in London as evidence intended to stand up to rigorous criticism. But within a few years he was persuaded by American paleontologists that his reconstruction was mistakenly based on a series of migrations and did not represent a true evolutionary lineage. The American reconstruction prevailed for much of the twentieth century.

The whale is a mammal whose entire existence is in the ocean. The history of evolution usually proceeds from the ocean to land, but one terrestrial creature is thought to have reversed the trend on the pathway to the whale. Along this pathway evolutionists have identified a sequence of fossil specimens. There is *Pakicetus* from the early-mid Eocene, 52 million years ago. It was not a deep diver, did not have the whale's famous blowhole, and may have been amphibious. Dramatic improvements to the whale sequence reconstruction came with two fossil specimens discovered in the early 1990s. *Ambulocetus natans*, estimated to be from the early-mid Eocene, 50 million years ago, was something like the sea lion. Its nearly complete fossil looks to be a walking and swimming whale, though because the pelvis was not found it is not known how the legs attached to the rest of the skeleton.[15] *Rodhocetus*, estimated to be from the mid-Eocene, 46 million years ago, had smaller hind legs, although it was likely it could still move awkwardly on land. After these came *Basilosaurus isis*, estimated to be from the late Eocene, 42 million years ago, with yet smaller legs. It is thought to be related to modern whales but not directly ancestral. The sequence is finally completed with a series of "archeocete whales," which showed an increase in size and which eventually lost the hind legs.

It is evidences such as these that give evolutionists their confidence. Evolution, they say, must be a fact. But how exactly does the proof proceed? A critical premise, it seems, is that similar species must be related via common descent. If we find similar designs from the same time period, then they must share an evolutionary relationship. But in fact, this premise cannot be true, for there are many cases of similar species that evolutionists do not believe serve as such strong proof. In the supposed reptile-mammal sequence and others, there are many similar fossil species that nonetheless do not fall into the reconstructed evolutionary sequence. It is, as one evolutionist put it, "notoriously difficult to decipher true ancestral-descendant relationships"[16] amongst the boxes of fossil finds. Or as Douglas Futuyma put it: "The gradual transition from therapsid reptiles to mammals is so abundantly documented by scores of species in every stage of transition that it is impossible to tell which therapsid species were the actual ancestors of modern mammals."[17]

In other words, similar fossils need not be considered to be within the same lineage. This has prompted evolutionists to switch from the evolutionary tree metaphor to the evolutionary bush. Thus according to evolutionists, many similar species are radiating out to form a bush-like pattern. All of this follows if evolution is assumed to be true, but what if evolution is not presupposed? Why should we believe that the fossil record mandates evolution, as evolutionists claim it does? In fact, each fossil species is, as paleontologist Henry Gee put it, "an infinitesimal dot, lost in a fathomless sea of time, whose relationship with other fossils and organisms living in the present day is obscure."[18]

With evolution we must believe that across the reptile-mammal transition, organisms evolved so rapidly that they appear fully formed and diverse in the fossil record, that there are large gaps between the reptiles and mammals, and that convergent evolution must have occurred many times. So too, the horse sequence turned out to be more problematic than evolutionists thought. It turned out that the species that were supposed to align in an evolutionary lineage actually persist unchanged and co-exist in the fossil record. As Niles Eldredge admitted:

> There have been an awful lot of stories, some more imaginative than others, about what the nature of that history [of life] really is. The most famous example, still on exhibit down-

stairs, is the exhibit on horse evolution prepared perhaps fifty years ago. That has been presented as the literal truth in text-book after textbook. Now I think that that is lamentable, particularly when the people who propose those kinds of stories may themselves be aware of the speculative nature of some of that stuff.[19]

Overly simplified, optimistic versions of whale evolution are also too often given, for instance Carl Zimmer's account in his book *Evolution*. A diagram illustrates an evolutionary progression starting with a four-legged carnivore and ending with an ancient whale. In the text Zimmer gives more details about the actual fossil data but, as they say, a picture is worth a thousand words. The diagram conveys a simplified and carefully tailored version of the true fossil data. A diagram illustrating all the relevant fossils would be far less suggestive of evolution.[20]

Another way to see that the fossil record does not suggest evolution is by recognizing that the vast majority of fossils reveal nothing of the sort. New species appear fully formed, as though planted there, and they remain unchanged for eons. As paleontologist Robert Carroll explains, the fossil record "emphasizes how wrong Darwin was in extrapolating the pattern of long-term evolution from that observed within populations and species."

Carroll identifies five specific problems for evolutionists. For example, how did major new structures evolve, and why do the multitude of species that we find almost invariably cluster together, rather than forming a continuous spectrum of intermediates? "Paleontologists," explains Carroll, "in particular have found it difficult to accept that the slow, continuous, and progressive changes postulated by Darwin can adequately explain the major reorganizations that have occurred between dominant groups of plants and animals."[21]

These are a few of the reasons why the fossil data do not prove evolution as Darwinists claim they do. In this section we have seen that the positive scientific evidences, taken as whole and carefully considered, do not point to evolution. In fact, they raise serious problems with the theory. I have discussed these facts with a great many evolutionists and almost inevitably the response is that these evidential problems do not disprove the theory. That is, of course, correct. In fact, disproving evolution would be difficult given its great flexibility. It can incorporate a wide variety of evidences. But what we need are reasons why we should accept evolution, not rationalizations of why we should not reject it. There are all sorts of ideas we cannot disprove, but this does not make them good science. Good scientific theories have strong evidences. Certainly, a scientific fact would be expected to have compelling arguments behind it. What are the compelling arguments for evolution? As we shall see in the next section, evolution does have compelling arguments, but they are not scientific.

THE RELIGIOUS REASONING FOR EVOLUTION

The scientific evidence that evolutionists cite to support their theory is not strong and at points even argues against the theory. In addition, there is the fundamental problem that evolution has no good explanation for how the many complexities of life arose. Biology is full of examples of phenomenally complex designs, from the molecular level up to interactions between species. These are the evidences against evolution that are too often ignored when evolutionists claim the theory is proven or well established. Sometimes, without any warrant, evolutionists will even invoke these complexities as evidence *for* evolution.

Consider the universal genetic code. The genetic code is sometimes referred to as the DNA code because it is used to interpret the information stored in the cell's DNA. There are a few minor variations in the code, but otherwise the same code is found in all species, from bacteria to whales to oak trees.

The DNA code is routinely used as strong evidence for evolution, but why? Everyone knows that one cannot use a code without having a method for encoding and decoding the information that is being transmitted. And, of course, the sender and receiver must be using the same code for the system to work. Volumes have been written on the cellular machinery that is involved in nature's scheme for using the DNA code, and we still don't understand all the details. It is phenomenally complex and is not easily explained as a product of Darwin's evolutionary process.

Furthermore, evolution does not predict there to be a universal DNA code. A number of explanations of the code's supposed evolution are currently under consideration. In one way or another, the code is supposed to have evolved from simpler codes; but if the code could have evolved over time, then it is easily conceivable that it could have evolved into several different codes. In other words, evolutionary theory could explain the existence of multiple codes in nature. As such, evolution does not require there to be a single DNA code.

The universal genetic code doesn't seem like a good candidate to serve as strong evidence for evolution. Evolution has trouble explaining how the code and its attendant machinery came about, and evolution does not require there to be a single code. How then does the universal genetic code support evolution so strongly? The answer is that evolutionists believe that if the species had been created independently, they would not share the same code.[22]

This is remarkable. The universal genetic code is claimed to be, as one professor tells his undergraduate students, the "best evidence that all life shares a common ancestor,"[23] and yet evolution neither predicts nor requires the code to be universal, nor can evolution tell us how the code evolved. How could this possibly be judged to be compelling evidence for common descent? The underlying, and often unspoken, assumption is metaphysical: The universal genetic code is powerful evidence not because evolution must have worked this way but rather because creation must *not* have worked this way.

The idea that the world must have arisen on its own because God would not have created it this way can be traced back to antiquity. It was an idea also prevalent in western Europe in the centuries leading up to Darwin. There were, in fact, several different traditions that, in different ways, emphasized secondary causes (i.e., naturalistic mechanisms) as the primary or sole means of the world's creation.

For example, English deism in the seventeenth and eighteenth centuries argued against the understanding that God had acted in history in order to bring people to a saving faith. The deistic view was that special revelation, miracles, Providence, and so forth would be unavailable to those not present when they occurred. In order for all people to have access to faith-producing evidence, that evidence must have been present in creation from the beginning. Therefore God's actions in history should be limited to His initial acts of creation. Not only should secondary causes suffice to explain all of subsequent history, but those causes should bring about a rather pleasant creation. If our faith is to be strengthened by what we find in creation, then that creation ought to be harmonious.

The increased burden on creation was particularly emphasized in natural theology, where creation was used as evidence of God. If God made the world, then it should be perfect. From such notables as John Ray and William Paley, to a number of less well known naturalists, creation was consistently expected to fulfill our expectations and sensibilities of perfection. Hence the natural theologians interpreted everything in nature idealistically. The eighteenth century naturalist Griffith Hughes supplied us with a typical example when he wrote that nature's creatures were "without defect, without superfluity, exactly fitted and enabled to answer the various purposes of their Creator, to minister to the delight and service of man, and to contribute to the beauty and harmony of the universal system."[24]

Natural theology was a sunny version of Christianity. Where the apostle James told Christians to "count it all joy when you fall into various trials,"[25] Paley insisted that God "wills and wishes for the happiness of His creatures." But if God would only have created an ideal world and yet, in fact, the world wasn't ideal, then God must not have created it. David Hume and later Charles Darwin would point to the misery and evil in the world as proof that natural theology had it all wrong. They did not disagree with natural theology's view of God; they merely reconciled that view with the realities of the world.

In fact, natural theology would not be as opposed to the evolutionary perspective as one might assume. Creation via secondary causes, according to Paley, was merely evidence of an even greater God. Hence Darwin's theory could, and does to this day, service the pious as well as the religious skeptics.

This divine sanction for naturalistic explanations of the world should be no great surprise, for Paley was drawing on a well-established tradition. A century earlier it had been promoted by the Anglican nonconformist Thomas Burnet. Burnet was in communication with Isaac Newton and wrote a popular seventeenth century book on geology. Burnet cast Newton's formulation of classical physics into a creation-by-secondary-causes cosmogony—a story he declared to be more befitting of the Creator: "We think him a better Artist that makes a Clock that strikes regularly at every hour from the Springs and Wheels which he puts in the work, than he that hath so made his Clock that he must put his finger to it every hour to make it strike."[26] Direct divine intervention was increasingly frowned upon. Darwin's grandfather Erasmus vividly captured this sentiment:

> The world itself might have been generated, rather than created; that is, it might have been gradually produced from very small beginnings, increasing by the activity of its inherent principles, rather than by a sudden evolution of the whole by the Almighty fiat. What a magnificent idea of the infinite power of the great architect! The Cause of Causes! Parent of Parents! Ens Entium! For if we may compare infinities, it would seem to require a greater infinity of power to cause the causes of effects, than to cause the effects themselves.[27]

Another strong driving force behind the high view of secondary causes was the problem of evil. If God is all good and all powerful, then why is there evil? In the seventeenth century, the Cambridge Platonists were concerned with the problems of natural evil. Evil, however, may be too strong a word as the concern was more often with the question of dysteleology, or the apparent lack of design in the world. As Ralph Cudworth put it, nature was full of "errors and bungles" that were better explained as the result of a universe developing gradually in the absence of divine guidance. The Cambridge Platonists distanced God from creation with the notion of a "plastic nature," where God's spiritual deputy directed the natural processes. Replace errors and bungles with quandaries such as the pentadactyl pattern and extinctions, and replace plastic nature with natural selection, and two centuries later you have Darwinism.

After the Cambridge Platonists, thinkers such as Gottfried Leibniz and Nehemiah Grew expounded on their theodicies, or solutions to the problem of evil. Both took secondary causes to the extreme. Leibniz envisioned a system where secondary causes extended even into the realm of ethics, for morality was built into the laws of creation. The Scriptures explain that God renders to each according to one's work. For Leibniz this was the result of nature's mechanism where "sins carry their punishment with them by the order of nature and by virtue of the mechanical structure of things itself; and that in the same way noble actions will attract their rewards by ways which are mechanical as far as bodies are concerned, although this cannot and should not always happen immediately."[28] Grew believed that the miracle stories of the Bible are true, but that they were the result of an intricate interplay of natural forces. Yes, they were miracles, but by virtue of God's design and timing rather than His direct intervention.

By Darwin's time the dismissal of the supernatural's action within history and the emphasis on secondary causes were pervasive. For example, Scottish social reformer George Combe argued that the idea of a continually interfering God was flawed. Combe argued that God governs through unchangeable laws and not supernatural interventions. Likewise, the Lord Chancellor of England Henry Peter Brougham found that miracles proved nothing but the exercise of miraculous power and left the Creator's trustworthiness in question.

These sentiments were typical. From scientists and clergy to writers and politicians, the Victorians were distancing God from this gritty world. For a variety of reasons, God, it was thought, was better viewed as working exclusively through secondary causes. Hence thinkers were formulating natural laws, whether they worked well or not, to explain just about everything, from sociology to geology. The idea of divine intervention as agent in creation was rapidly approaching extinction among intellectuals; so Charles Darwin's theory of evolution fit like the missing piece of a puzzle into the mid-nineteenth century European worldview.

When Darwin proposed his theory, a number of the evidences and arguments he presented were hardly compelling. He argued, for example, that the fossils failed to reveal evolution because the fossil record was incomplete; that the failure of breeders to produce anything beyond small-scale change was caused by their artificial selection; and that the failure of his theory to explain complexity was not a problem because critics could not *prove* natural mechanisms to be incapable of producing complexity. None of these arguments was particularly powerful, but Darwin did bring powerful metaphysical arguments to bear. Over and over, his arguments drew their persuasiveness from the religious sentiment of the day.

If species had been created, Darwin argued, then "no explanation would have been possible" for the Linnaean classification. Why should species cross so easily if they were created separately? And if fauna and flora have been created for their environments by a wise Creator, then how is it that plants that are introduced into new regions may be successful though they have little in common with the indigenous flora? Indeed, what seemed to be specialized fauna or flora sometimes flourished in foreign environments. Why were the inhabitants of similar but separate environments, such as cave dwelling creatures on different continents, often so vastly different? Then there were the ill-adapted species, such as the land animals with webbed feet and the marine life with non-webbed feet. There were also insects that spent hours underwater yet differed little from their terrestrial cousins. Why was the water ouzel, a member of the thrush family, so active under water, and why were woodpeckers found in treeless pampas?

Nature seemed to lack precision and economy in design and was often, according to Darwin, "inexplicable on the theory of creation." The underlying religious reasoning was obvious and often unstated. Darwin and evolutionists who came after him had idealistic expectations of creation. Not surprisingly, these expectations were consistent with those of earlier thinkers: From the deists to the natural theologians, God was supposed to satisfy our sensibilities by creating a pleasant, orderly, and harmonious world. It is interesting and important to understand the history of thought leading up to Darwinism. For our purposes, however, identifying the underlying religious assumptions is less important than simply understanding that there *are* underlying religious assumptions. Stephen Jay Gould accurately summarized the role of religion in evolution:

> Odd arrangements and funny solutions are the proof of evolution—paths that a sensible God would never tread but that a natural process, constrained by history, follows perforce. No one understood this better than Darwin. Ernst Mayr has shown how Darwin, in defending evolution, consistently turned to organic parts and geographic distributions that make the least sense.[29]

Today we have far more evidence than in Darwin's day, but the situation has not changed. Evolutionists like to say there is a convergence of evidence and the weight of all this evidence taken together makes evolution the unavoidable conclusion. The convergence, however, lies not with the evidence but rather in its religious interpretation. I discovered this when I surveyed the evolution literature and assembled all the evidence and the arguments used to promote evolution. The arguments for evolution inevitably and consistently rely on an underlying conception of God.[30]

Though evolutionary thinking has gone through many changes since 1859, Darwin gave it a trajectory that is still considered cogent. Darwin canonized a new way of looking at biology. After Darwin, evolutionists would hypothesize that a strictly naturalistic mechanism could account for all of biological evolution. Moreover, the evidence for this mechanism would henceforth be assessed on religious grounds, based on presuppositions about the nature of God and what this God would and would not do. Thus even something as challenging to evolution as the DNA code could be converted into powerful evidence for the theory. And because evolution is by definition restricted to naturalistic mechanisms, its religious underpinnings are occluded and it appears to be merely another scientific theory.

In fact, evolution is not a scientific theory but rather a religious belief about God and nature, held so strongly that it is called a fact. The weaknesses of the positive evidence cited in support of evolution, and the powerful negative evidence against evolution, matter little when the opposing theory—divine creation—has been ruled out from the start. This is why evolutionists can speak of their theory as a fact; indeed, it explains why the factual status of the theory is so important to evolutionists. The arguments for evolution refute divine creation. If God did not create the species, then they must have arisen naturally. As such, evolution *must be* a fact, in one form or another, even though it fails to explain much of what we observe in biology. Hence evolutionists speak of the *fact of evolution* and the *theory of evolution*. Evolution is regarded as a fact because they know the species must have arisen naturalistically. But evolution is also a theory because we have nothing more than speculation as to how this possibly could have occurred. The naturalistic mechanism, whatever form it may take, is the theory of evolution. The religious doctrine of how to interpret the evidence brings about the fact of evolution.

It would be far more accurate to view Darwinian evolution as a religious theory that has penetrated natural science rather than as a scientific theory that impinges on our religious understandings. In purporting to keep science free from religion, evolution foists religion on science and thereby subverts the very integrity of science. Instead of fostering science, it constitutes the greatest threat modern science has ever faced. Evolutionists have consistently promoted their theory as an objective conclusion based on a purely scientific analysis of the data. This is simply inaccurate. Evolution is an unlikely story fueled by theological presuppositions and religious sentiment, not scientific reasoning.

Roland F. Hirsch

12. Darwinian Evolutionary Theory and the Life Sciences in the Twenty-First Century[*]

Evolutionary theory has had a major impact on the development of biology since the appearance of *On the Origin of Species* in 1859.[1] During the century following publication of that book, experiments and field observations led to successive refinements of the Darwinian theory of evolution, and it was confidently proclaimed as the foundation of biology in the Darwin centennial year of 1959.

Such confidence is not warranted today. New technologies developed in the past four decades have revealed to us the chemistry underlying biological processes. These technologies have revealed that life is far more complicated than was imagined in 1959, and that much of its complexity cannot easily be addressed by existing evolutionary theory. Indeed, some of the major discoveries in the life sciences presented in this article were hardly anticipated by evolutionary theory, but instead came out of advances in experimental technologies. The physicist Freeman Dyson put it this way in his book of essays, *Imagined Worlds*:

> There are two kinds of scientific revolutions, those driven by new tools and those driven by new concepts. . . . The effect of a concept-driven revolution is to explain old things in new ways. The effect of a tool-driven revolution is to discover new things that have to be explained. In almost every branch of science, and especially in biology and astronomy, there has been a preponderance of tool-driven revolutions. We have been more successful in discovering new things than in explaining old ones.[2]

* This essay represents the views of the author and does not reflect an official position of any unit of the U.S. Department of Energy or imply an endorsement of these views by the agency.

This essay is a personal account of how the author's assessment of evolutionary theory has been changed by advances in biology. During the past fifteen years my involvement in analytical chemistry, genome sequencing technologies and structural biology has brought home to me the great impact on the way we understand life of new technologies in these fields.[3] Much has been revealed about the nature of the genome; the complicated networks that regulate expression of genes; the chemical transformations that expressed proteins undergo after synthesis in the cell; the structure of proteins in three dimensions; and how proteins and other biological molecules form the complex machines that carry out most of the functions of a cell. Much has also been learned about how cells interact, especially about how microbes interact in communities. We will discuss several recent, technology-driven advances in the life sciences that have convinced the author that the standard evolutionary theory is inadequate, and that evolution should no longer hold the place once claimed for it as the foundation of the life sciences.

What Genome Sequences Tell about Evolution

The genome of an organism consists of one or more segments of deoxyribonucleic acid (DNA). DNA consists of two long, complementary strands, each of which is composed of a backbone onto which are bound the four bases that comprise the "alphabet" of the genetic code: adenine, cytosine, guanine, and thymine. The sequence in which these bases are organized determines both the composition of proteins that carry out the functions of the organism, and whether or not a particular protein will be expressed or not at any given time. Advances in analytical chemistry, automation, bioinformatics, and other fields during the last two decades changed the process of obtaining the sequence of bases in a genome, from one that was slow and expensive to one that is rapid and inexpensive.[4] As a result, base sequences for many complete genomes have been determined, more than 100 as of this writing.[5]

These complete genome sequences have revealed several complexities that Darwinian evolutionary theory did not anticipate. Four of these will be discussed here: the major role played by transfer of genes from one species to another, as opposed to inheritance from ancestors; the fact that bacterial species do not evolve solely in a random fashion, but show a bias toward deletion of genetic material; the discovery that much of the portions of the genome that do not code for proteins is not "junk DNA" but in fact has a critical function; and the observation that expression of genes is controlled by regulatory circuits that are as complicated and as precisely arranged as the most sophisticated engineering diagrams.

The established Darwinian concept of inheritance is in a vertical direction, that is, from the older generation to the younger generation, extending down in time from a single ultimate ancestor cell. As time proceeds, branchings repeatedly occur that represent the formation of new species. This is commonly represented symbolically by a diagram that looks like a tree. The National Academy of Sciences booklet *Teaching about Evolution and the Nature of Science* (published in 1998) shows a diagram of a tree of descent and states: "The ability to analyze individual biological molecules has added great detail to biologists' understanding of the tree of life. For example, molecular analyses indicate that all living things fall into three domains—the Bacteria, Archaea, and Eucarya—related by descent from a common ancestor."[6]

Yet just a year after this book was published it was clear that this was not so; the availability of complete genome sequences for two dozen microbial species led to a surprising discovery, one that previous information had only hinted at.[7] The genome sequences revealed that for at least two microbial domains (bacteria and archaea), much of the inheritance is in a horizontal direction. Significant portions of the genome of a particular species came not from its ancestors but arrived at various times from the species that were its neighbors through what is termed "horizontal gene transfer" (hgt, sometimes also called "lateral gene transfer" or lgt). The relationships among species could no longer be arranged in a tree of descent, for the genome of a species was only partially inherited from an ancestor species. Each gene in the DNA of a particular species that arose through hgt would trace a different ancestry, as it could have come from a different neighboring species, in a different generation of the species being studied.

Thus there is no single "tree of life" but rather a "web" or "net" of interconnections that are both vertical and horizontal. As stated by W. F. Doolittle, "If, however, different genes give different trees, and there is no fair way to suppress this disagreement, then a species (or phylum) can 'belong' to many genera (or kingdoms) at the same time: There really can be no universal phylogenetic tree of organisms based on such a reduction to genes."[8] It also seems likely that—contrary to the assertion in the National Academy of Sciences document cited above—there was no "common ancestor cell"; rather it is now thought more likely that there was a pool of cells that changed communally over a long period of time.[9]

Indeed, so much transfer has occurred across the three domains of life that they must be defined not on the basis of ancestry but on the basis of functional properties. If the focus was on evolutionary ancestry of species during the twentieth century, clearly the focus will be on function—how the component parts of a cell or organism work—rather than ancestry during the twenty-first century. The construction of evolutionary trees does continue, as it enables identification of logical functional groupings of species. However, the goal no longer is construction of a single unique tree of life, but rather development of statistical best fits to genome data. In some cases individual genes are used to construct the trees, in order to identify organisms that share a particular property coded for by that gene, regardless of whether they share any other common properties. In other cases, an average "whole-genome tree" will be constructed to give an estimate of overall similarities among, and differences between, species. Even the choice of which type of tree to use is the subject of considerable controversy in phylogenomics, the study of family relationships among species.[10]

A particularly significant example of horizontal gene transfer involves the photosynthetic microorganisms. Photosynthetic bacteria are found in five quite different phyla. The Darwinian inheritance model would predict that either the five phyla diverged from a common ancestor or that the photosynthetic function evolved independently five times. A study of the genomes of a representative from each phylum reveals that neither of these predictions is correct: the genomic comparisons show that significant numbers of genes relevant to photosynthetic function must have been transferred horizontally among the species studied.[11]

Horizontal gene transfer (hgt) was already identified in bacteria and archaea by 1990. It was thought for the following decade that hgt was not a significant factor for the more complex eukaryotes. Recent studies of complete genome sequences, however, have identified substantial hgt in many of the branches of the eukaryotic domain. Examples include hgt involving the protists (unicellular eukaryotes), such as the parasite *Giardia Lamblia*,[12] flowering plants,[13] algae,[14] fungi,[15] and nematodes, the most abundant of all metazoans, including the worm *Caenorhabditis elegans*, as well as many plant and animal parasites.[16] The latter group is especially significant for it involved relatively complex, multicellular organisms, and because some of the transferred genes are critical to the functioning of the recipient species.

Thus horizontal gene transfer must be considered a significant source of genetic variation in all three domains of life. The purely vertical pattern of inheritance axiomatic to Darwin's theory of evolution, from his own writings down to the present, clearly is inadequate to explain the observed complexities of the origin of genes.

The second discovery that throws doubt upon the Darwinian evolutionary paradigm also comes out of the increasing availability of complete bacterial genome sequences. While horizontal gene transfers would increase the size—the number of base pairs, called bp—of a genome, bacterial genomes turn out to be remarkably small. The genome size for the bacteria and archaea ranges from about 500,000 bp (e.g., 580,000 for *Mycoplasma genitalium)* to under 10 million bp (e.g., about 7 million bp for *Mesorhizobium loti*). Yet through many generations of a species, numerous instances of hgt can be documented, as well as cases of gene duplication. Why, then, are the genomes uniformly small in these two domains of life? A persuasive answer is that there is a bias toward deletion of genetic material in bacteria, that is, that portions of the DNA tend to fall away when the bacterium reproduces: "The obvious answer is that lineages must undergo the inactivation and loss of genes, and the elimination of the corresponding DNA that made up the genes. This could result if the mutational process driving the structural evolution of chromosomes is biased towards DNA loss."[17] Thus the standard Darwinian mechanism of random mutation and natural selection is inconsistent with the observed fact of a non-random bias toward deletion of DNA.

The third unexpected discovery deals with regions of a genome that do not carry the code for a protein. When the project to sequence the complete human genome began, it was already realized that most of the genome did not code for a protein. As little as 2 percent, and probably even less, of the human genome of some 3 billion base pairs was thought to be in the actual genes. The rest was thought to be largely "junk DNA," that is, stretches of DNA that had no function. The theoretical evolutionary basis for the idea of "junk DNA" was that, if a segment of DNA was not part of a gene that carried the code for a protein, then there was no mechanism for natural selection to act on this segment. The segment would be hidden from the action of natural selection because it would not be expressed in any form that affected the functional properties and hence the survival of the organism. Instead, the segment would be affected by periodic random mutations that would scramble any code that originally might have been carried by the segment.

Today the experimental evidence suggests that much, though probably not all, of the non-coding regions of the genome have critical roles in the development and function of an individual. Completion of the human and mouse genome sequences in particular has resulted in useful insights into the function of non-coding DNA.[18] There appear to be fewer genes in the human genome than the more than 100,000 that many specialists thought were present before the completion of the human genome project. Most current estimates range from 30,000 to 60,000 genes, with a few going higher. The small number of genes suggests that the non-coding regions must have key roles to play, including even repetitive portions of the DNA.[19] As the authors of a recent review point out, "From genomic analysis it is evident, however, that with increase of an organism's complexity, the protein-coding contribution of its genome decreases. . . ."[20] Clearly the non-coding regions must have crucial roles in accounting for this complexity.

This leads to the fourth point. It is clear that the mechanism by which expression of many of these genes is controlled is much more complicated than was previously believed. It is not simply a matter that the code carried by a gene is decoded to make a messenger RNA (mRNA) to enable the synthesis of a protein. Instead, a group of genes encodes a set of regulatory factors, a set that controls the transcription of the gene that is to be decoded for synthesis of a protein by the cell—translation of the genome code into a polypeptide. In many cases, the expression of several genes is controlled by a single set of regulatory genes, since a cellular function may depend on a number of different proteins being produced at the same time. The set of genes, and associated regulatory factor(s) in the genome required for a particular cellular function, forms an operon. The components in an operon act in a precisely timed fashion so that the entire process is best visualized as a circuit diagram that resembles closely the diagrams used in the design of processes in chemical engineering, or the design of circuits in electrical engineering or electronics. Even the language is similar: "oscillators," "feedback loops," etc.

There indeed is considerable interest in using engineering principles to understand gene networks and to design new ones. The authors of a recent review of the topic note that interest in mathematical modeling of gene regulatory networks appeared already in the 1970s and state: "[R]ecent experimental advances have reignited interest in the development of circuit analysis techniques for describing complex gene networks."[21]

While gene regulation applies to expression of practically all genes at all times, the regulation of gene expression during development is of especial interest. The genome of an animal is fixed at conception, yet expression of the genome changes constantly from stage to stage of development both before and after birth. The genomic code that regulates these changes works both by encoding factors that regulate transcription of the genes for structural and functional proteins, and by encoding the regulatory network that controls expression of these factors. The diagrams of these gene regulatory networks visualize the high level of interconnection and interdependence of the individual genes and regulatory factors for each component of development.[22]

The study of the regulation of gene expression has led to an appreciation that variation in gene sequence does not explain all variation in function among members of a species. Modifications of the genome that do not affect the gene sequence are one form of *epigenetic* phenomena. Such changes are responsible for cells in a particular organ of a multicellular organism showing the appropriate characteristics of that organ, even though the cells carry the complete genome and not just the components required for becoming the organ's specialized cells. It is also possible that the development of cancer and other diseases depends on epigenetic modifications in the DNA of cells rather than on mutations in the base sequence itself.[23] There is speculation as well that Lamarck's concept of the inheritance of acquired traits may be valid in some cases.[24]

The study of gene expression has been greatly aided by new developments in technologies such as mass spectrometry and gene microarrays. The study of protein composition in a cell using these high resolution techniques has been called *proteomics*.[25] Mass spectrometry now allows identification of large numbers of proteins in a cell grown under particular conditions. It then also allows comparison of the amounts of each protein, relative to the amounts in the same species grown under different conditions.[26] The effects of stress on expression of a large number of proteins can thus be assessed, and the changes in gene expression with time can be determined, in order to obtain insight into the complexities of the process that are not revealed by the genome itself. Gene microarrays make it possible to follow expression patterns across an organism, determining which genes are induced and which are repressed at various points in the life cycle of a cell.[27]

To sum up this section, Darwinian evolutionary theory failed, in this author's view, to anticipate several key discoveries about genetics, inheritance, and gene expression and development. In each case, evolutionary theory should have guided researchers to make these discoveries, but in fact the opposite seems true: changes were made in evolutionary theory after the fact, in order to account, for example, for the significance of horizontal gene transfer or to explain the complexities of regulation of gene expression.

What Proteins Tell about Evolution

We have seen that the relationship between the genome and the function of an organism is more complex than can be accounted for by the traditional Darwinian-oriented concept of:

one gene →one protein →one function.

But we have only looked at the first part of this sequence; there is more to consider. Additional complexities come into play after translation of the genetic code into a protein molecule, complexities that again seem beyond the reach of evolutionary theory. In this section I will discuss how an expressed protein is chemically transformed into the actual molecule that participates in cell functioning, how it folds into the shape required for exhibiting its characteristic activity, and how the transformed, folded protein then must become part of a multi-protein complex that is actually responsible for the function in which that protein participates.

Proteins are not ready to perform their function as they are synthesized in the cellular protein factory called the ribosome—about which more shortly. Each protein must undergo a series of changes in shape and composition before it can "do" anything. It is likely that a majority of proteins in most cells are involved in chemical reactions that change the covalent structure of the protein molecule into its active form, reactions such as methylation, acetylation, phosphorylation, deamidation, oxidation and dozens of others. An interesting example of this is a study of modifications of proteins in lens tissues of eyes, a study that seeks to understand the changes that are responsible for the formation of cataracts. The authors note that 90 percent of the protein in the lens is in one family of proteins, the crystallins, and that these proteins are long-lived and thus subject to post-translational modification during aging and cataract formation. The cataract studied was congenital, so a linkage to the genome of the patient exists, even though the linkage is likely to be complex given the large number of modifications discovered.[28]

The protein molecule must fold into the shape in which it is active. Folding is a complicated process that requires some steps to occur on the picosecond time scale, while others may take milliseconds to seconds.[29] Portions of the process are often mediated by chaperone or co-factor[30] proteins that are required to guide folding into the proper shape or to prevent misfolding.

The folded shape of a protein is determined by several factors, among them internal covalent bonds (such as disulfide bridges between cysteine units in the chains), hydrogen bonds, and hydrophilic and hydrophobic interactions with the solvent surrounding the protein molecule. Two proteins with very different amino acid sequences can fold into a closely similar shape and have a similar function. The three-dimensional design of the resulting protein is thus more important than the sequence in explaining function. There is much interest in classifying folds of proteins to better understand function and to identify the likely function of newly discovered proteins.[31] The shape is also affected by interaction of the protein with the other molecules, large and small, that participate with it in carrying out a particular activity in a cell.

This folding process is possible only because it is guided. A process of folding in which the protein chain bends entirely in random ways could not achieve the functional fold of that protein in any useful period of time. Several models have been developed to describe the folding process.[32] "Misfolding" of proteins also is of considerable interest, as it may be a significant factor in the onset of a variety of diseases, such as Alzheimer's syndrome. Proteins that can pass from one molecule to another through changes in folding conformation, from the normal conformation (without involvement of the genome), include the prions, protein molecules implicated in a number of diseases.[33]

Most cellular functions are carried out by highly organized protein machines that are assembled with what amounts to engineering precision. This was not realized until relatively recently, in part because experimental technologies were inadequate to detect the structure of the machines, but also—in the author's view—because the Darwinian concept of evolution by random mutation and natural selection encouraged—in fact practically required—treating each protein—gene product—as a distinct unit in the functioning of an organism. Otherwise, how could a function requiring multiple proteins in a cellular machine ever arise through the required random mutations that developed, one protein molecule at a time and in a stepwise manner; mutations that provided no intermediate product with any function that would allow Darwinian natural selection to work?

Thus the traditional view of protein function was that a protein catalyzes the reaction of a substrate to form product(s). Other proteins would be involved in preceding or following steps in a metabolic cycle but not in a complex with the protein in question. There is no doubt that much progress was made in enzyme biochemistry using this concept. However, proteins usually do not carry out functions in isolation, and the development of electron microscopy, macromolecular crystallography, mass spectrometry and other technologies from the 1950s, enabled visualization of the complex protein machines that actually are responsible for most of the properties of a cell.

Recognition of the true complexity of cellular processes has led to a major change in the vocabulary used to describe cells. Words such as "machine", "factory" and "motor" are in routine use,[34] and a cellular function is best explained in terms of design of the machine(s) responsible for the function. As biologist and president of the National Academy of Sciences Bruce Alberts explained it:

> We have always underestimated cells. Undoubtedly we still do today. But at least we are no longer as naive as we were when I was a graduate student in the 1960s. Then, most of us viewed cells as containing a giant set of second-order reactions: molecules A and B were thought to diffuse freely, randomly colliding with each other to produce molecule AB— and likewise for the many other molecules that interact with each other inside a cell. . . .
>
> But, as it turns out, we can walk and we can talk because the chemistry that makes life possible is much more elaborate and sophisticated than anything we students had ever considered. Proteins make up most of the dry mass of a cell. But instead of a cell dominated by randomly colliding individual protein molecules, we now know that nearly every major process in a cell is carried out by assemblies of ten or more protein molecules. And, as it carries out its biological functions, each of these protein assemblies interacts with several other large complexes of proteins. Indeed, the entire cell can be viewed as a factory that contains an elaborate network of interlocking assembly lines, each of which is composed of a set of large protein machines.[35]

Thus, the traditional concept of function, of a protein acting rather randomly and in relative isolation from the other proteins in the cell, the concept influenced by evolutionary theory, has given way to the view that a protein's function can only be defined through its interactions with other proteins and smaller molecules in cellular machines.

Many of these machines are extraordinarily complex, including those responsible for the essential core functioning of a cell. The ribosome, which is responsible for the synthesis of nearly all cellular proteins, itself is comprised of two distinct subunits that contain in all some fifty-five proteins and three ribosomal RNAs in the simplest (bacterial) form, and about seventy-five proteins and four ribosomal RNAs in the eukaryotic form. Considering the ribosome as the equivalent of an assembly line in a factory makes sense when one describes what it does: binds the messenger RNA (mRNA) that contains the code for the protein to be built; binds a transfer RNA (tRNA) that holds the first amino acid in the protein chain, based on the first three nucleotides of the mRNA (the codon, or "triplet" code specifying which amino acid to select); binds another tRNA carrying the second amino acid in the chain; forms the peptide bond between the two amino acids in the proper order; moves the peptide chain forward so that the next amino acid can be added; finally, recognizes the stop codon on the mRNA that indicates that all the necessary amino acids have been added, and releases the completed protein. All this is done with extremely high accuracy.

Imaging the structure of ribosomes has been an extraordinary challenge. At present, remarkably good pictures of the three-dimensional structure of a bacterial ribosome have been produced through a combination of technologies, such as neutron scattering, electron microscopy, and x-ray diffraction.[36] This structural information shows how tightly interlocked the components of the machine are. No simpler machine is known or even imagined that could carry out all of the steps in protein synthesis with such accuracy and speed. Yet no living cell can exist without the means to rapidly and continually synthesize hundreds of proteins over and over again with high fidelity to the code in its DNA. Even the formation of the ribosome itself requires a large number of synchronized steps and more than 100 proteins and 100 small RNA segments.[37] Clearly the traditional idea that organisms evolve from simple to complex does not apply to the protein synthesis machinery.

Much of the functioning of a cell is carried out by similar machines, even if few have as many components as the ribosome. RNA polymerase II, which synthesizes messenger RNA in eukaryotes, is another critical machine. It is a complex of twelve proteins that holds the DNA strand to be transcribed and puts together the mRNA that will guide the ribosome in producing a protein. The mass of the complex is more than 500,000 daltons, involving more than 3,500 amino acid residues. The structure of RNA polymerase II from yeast has been solved in an elegant series of experiments. The references describing these experiments should be read, if only to see how the complex is put together from its components by the cellular machinery, with a precision exceeding that of the most complicated devices designed and engineered by humans.[38]

Another important category of protein complexes, and one that also has implications for evolutionary theory, comprises the molecular chaperones. These are complexes that contain several proteins and perform a number of cellular functions, such as assisting in the folding of proteins[39] and controlling the binding of hormones to hormone receptors.[40] The first group of chaperones prevents the misfolding or aggregation of a protein as it folds after transcription, and appears to be required for the proper folding of many proteins. Failure of the system of chaperones to properly guide folding of a protein is implicated in neurodegenerative diseases such as Alzheimer's and Parkinson's.[41] The second group of chaperones helps stabilize the receptor in a shape that allows access by the appropriate hormone and, following binding of the hormone to the receptor, helps start transcription of the segment of DNA that is controlled by the hormone.

Another category of chaperones helps control the movement of metal ions in cells. Many of the metals (e.g., copper, iron, zinc) are incorporated in key biochemical constituents of cells. Each cell contains a significant number of ions of these metals, yet it appears that all of the atoms of the metals are tightly bound to regulatory and chaperone proteins.[42] Breakdown of the metal control system allows abnormal binding of a metal ion to any of a large number of proteins where it normally might not attach, shutting down the function of those proteins and potentially leading to disease. Malfunctions of copper metabolism, for example, are implicated in familial amyotrophic lateral sclerosis and may be involved in several other diseases.[43]

In this section I have discussed two levels of complexity of cellular chemistry that extend beyond the control of the gene that codes for a protein: post-translational chemical modification, and folding of proteins into their active form, including the requirement that most proteins be incorporated into large, multi-protein complexes in order to participate in a cellular function. Both of these phenomena were known in 1959, but the extensiveness of each was unexpected. Certainly, evolutionary theory did not alert biologists to the significance of these modifications or to the protein machines, given the one-gene/one-protein outlook that random mutation and natural selection strongly encouraged. Can Darwinian evolution really be as fundamental to biology as is claimed by its proponents, if it gave no guidance to scientists about the extraordinary complexity and high degree of organization of cellular chemistry that new experimental tools were to discover?

WHAT MICROBES AND MICROBIAL
COMMUNITIES TELL ABOUT EVOLUTION

The impact of the discovery of horizontal gene transfer on the Darwinian picture of evolution has already been discussed. There are some important cases of gene transfer into and within the eukaryotic domain,[44] but as far as we know these are rather isolated and infrequent. On the other hand, many of the species in the archaeal and bacterial domains that have been characterized have been affected by this phenomenon.

But there are several other aspects of the biology of microbes that have been discovered since 1959 that also seem to the author to be inconsistent with Darwinian evolutionary theory as it is commonly understood. As with the genome and protein discoveries already discussed, these surprising properties of microbes are the result of levels of complexity greater than can be explained by evolutionary theory.

The Darwinian evolutionary theories are based on the assumption of continual competition among species and among individuals of a given species. Darwin himself stated that his reading of the theory of Malthus, who argued that a population will increase to the limit of available resources, was the critical step in formulating his own theory of natural selection. Successive generations of biologists refined the theory in various ways but retained the principle of competition as the basis for natural selection. Even the "selfish gene" hypothesis of Dawkins is based on the idea that reproduction is the measure of (competitive) fitness of an organism.

Yet research in microbiology over the past three decades has shown that this often is not so. Microbes of many different species do not under normal conditions compete with each other. Instead, they form stable communities in which each individual has a role and is dependent on other individuals of the same species and of other species in the community. Microbes studied in pure cell cultures, the traditional method of microbiology, therefore behave differently from microbes in real environments. This discovery has had great practical implications, for example, in understanding human health and treating diseases, and in describing contaminated environments and discovering how to clean up the contaminants.

One common form of microbial community is called a biofilm—a population of cells growing on a surface and enclosed in a porous polymer matrix. Microbes are commonly found as part of a biofilm, whether on the surface of a soil particle, the root of a plant, on a tool or container, or inside a higher organism such as a human.[45] As stated in a review of the implications of biofilms for clinical medicine, "We now understand that biofilms are universal. . . . Using tools such as the scanning electron microscope and, more recently, the confocal laser scanning microscope, biofilm researchers now understand that biofilms are not unstructured, homogeneous deposits of cells and accumulated slime, but complex communities of surface-associated cells enclosed in a polymer matrix containing open water channels."[46]

Biofilms are thought to play an important role in many human infections. Biofilms formed by pathogenic bacteria also may be responsible for some of the antibiotic resistance that is observed in bacteria. The common explanation for development of resistance is that a portion of the population of the pathogenic organism is a mutant form that is not affected by the antibiotic. Individuals of normal form of the pathogen are killed by the antibiotic, leaving the resistant, mutant form behind to proliferate. However, cells that are not antibiotic-resistant mutants also can and do survive and reproduce to recreate the original population size. If these *persistent* cells are treated again with the same antibiotic they are killed by it as were the normal cells in the original treatment, demonstrating that they are not an antibiotic-resistant mutant. This mechanism of resistance is not an evolutionary one. Persistence appears common in bacteria that form biofilms and needs to be taken into account in handling difficult-to-treat infections.[47]

Microbial communities, whether or not they are fixed in biofilms on surfaces, show a great deal of cooperation. Communication among members of these communities is an active field for research. Chemical signals are released by bacteria and influence the behavior of the entire community. Quorum sensing is an important type of signaling that induces a specific behavior in the community when the numbers of a particular species is sufficiently high—hence the name for this function.[48] The behavior is induced by the concentration of a signaling compound (the autoinducer) exceeding a specified level. At that point transcription of previously inactive genes occurs as it is induced by the autoinducing compound. Several of these compounds may be released within a community of microbes, controlling a number of different functions of the members of the community. Quorum sensing is a widespread phenomenon and appears to play a critical role in regulating a variety of human bacterial infections, such as those that cause the complications of cystic fibrosis.[49]

Thus the behavior of a group of bacteria has a level of complexity beyond that of the individual members. Where more than one species is present, the growth and functioning of the community is therefore controlled at a higher level than the functioning of the individual species. The behavior of the species in a community is thus not reducible to the sum of the behaviors of the species isolated in pure cultures. As a review article about the formation of biofilms by human oral bacteria states, "A successful search for genes critical for mixed-species community organization will be accomplished only when it is conducted with mixed-species communities."[50]

The communal behavior of microbes has another important consequence. It means that the simplest microbes—those with the smallest genomes—cannot survive in the absence of other species that contribute needed nutrients or remove waste products. There is much interest in determining the smallest genome that an organism can have and still be viable. But this means viability only in a suitable microbial community. It is important to remember this as we look at the question of the simplest microbial genome.

The question of the smallest microbial genome is interesting also because it determines the complexity that would have been required for the very first living cells on the Earth. Under the *abiogenesis* hypothesis, life arose from non-living chemicals on the early earth. The requirement for this prebiotic chemistry is that it must have been able to generate all of the components of the simplest living cell. Much thought has gone into attempting to understand possible mechanisms for the generation of these chemical species on the early Earth.[51] While it is estimated that the earth is about 4.5 billion years old, the first few hundred million years were inhospitable to life—indeed inhospitable to accumulation of any but the simplest organic chemicals because of repeated sterilizations caused by the impact of huge objects striking the earth. Some evidence points to the first appearance of life within as little as a hundred million years after the end of the last massive impacts, and most experts agree that the complexity of that first living cell was achieved within at most three hundred million years, with no more than the basic inorganic chemicals. Thus, it is important for evaluating abiogenesis theories to have an idea of what the end result required.

The smallest genomes yet found in a living organism, excluding viruses, include those of *Nanoarchaeum equitans*, which has about 500,000 base pairs (bp) in its genome;[52] *Buchnera* species, some of which have genomes as small as 450,000 bp;[53] and *Mycoplasma genitalium*, which has a genome of about 580,000 bp.[54] These species are quite dependent on the host species in which they are found, being symbiotic or parasitic. Thus, they cannot serve to define the minimum genome size for the very first organism that appeared according to the abiogenesis theory. However, they do provide an idea of the magnitude of the challenge. Earlier we saw the bias toward minimization of the size of a bacterial genome. There is very little in the genomes of these organisms that is not critical to their functioning, and probably no fewer than about 300 of their genes in each case are a necessary minimum.

Not only must the 300 or so genes be present in the genome, they must code for proteins that are properly matched to their functions as part of the large cellular machines, such as the ribosome, which are required even in these simplest of organisms. The expression control system must be able to produce the proteins when they are needed, and in the amounts that are needed, in the presence of the reagents needed to transform the proteins into active forms, and under conditions favoring proper folding of each protein.

It is controversial whether "evolution" of the first living organism on earth is a necessary part of the theory of evolution. However, the improbability of this having occurred through the required chance variations in chemistry is so great that it argues against any purely naturalistic history of life on earth. To the author of this essay, the doubts about the mechanism for life getting started on earth motivate him to question other naturalistic theories about the early history of life on earth. They should not be easily accepted when they are based on so many premises that are based on minimal actual evidence.

In this section I have explained how microbial species do not tend to compete to out-reproduce one another but tend instead to cooperate in stable communities which are more complex that the sum of the properties of the individual species. They engage in intercellular signaling that controls many aspects of the behavior of each species in a community. Even the simplest known microbes are exceedingly complicated, requiring a set of several hundred genes of just the right kinds to function. This complexity was not known to Darwin, who lived at a time when microbes were just beginning to be characterized, and indeed little of it was known at the time I consider the peak of Darwinian influence on biology in the 1950s and 1960s. It requires many twists and turns in evolutionary theory to accommodate these complexities, few of which were anticipated by such theories. Indeed, the more that is learned about microbes, the clearer it becomes that while evolutionary theory plays a role in understanding life, it is a much smaller role than its proponents would have the world believe.

A HIGHLY SUPERFLUOUS IDEA

I have no doubt that these and other technology-driven advances in the life sciences present a serious challenge to the validity of the main principles of Darwinian evolutionary theory. Much of what was taught forty years ago has had to be unlearned or has become irrelevant; much of what today's experiments and field research reveal about life cannot be explained by the evolutionary theory of the past.[55] Life as revealed by new technologies is more complicated than the Darwinian viewpoint anticipated. Thus evolutionary theory, which was considered to be a key foundation of biology in 1959, today has a more peripheral role. Adam S. Wilkins, the editor of the review journal *BioEssays*, put it this way in introducing an issue of his journal devoted to evolution in December 2000:

> The subject of evolution occupies a special, and paradoxical, place within biology as a whole. While the great majority of biologists would probably agree with Theodosius Dobzhansky's dictum that "nothing in biology makes sense except in light of evolution," most can conduct their work quite happily without particular reference to evolutionary ideas. "Evolution" would appear to be the indispensable unifying idea and, at the same time, a highly superfluous one.[56]

Perhaps the reader will recognize from the preceding examples that assuming all one needs to know about an organism is contained in its genome is an unsatisfactory way to study biology. The much-anticipated completion of sequencing the human genome—and of many other genomes—has only revealed that life is more complex than the previously dominant gene-oriented evolutionary theory led scientists to believe. Biologists are now increasingly turning to a systems approach to studying biology, using, for example, the concepts of engineering and design.[57] There is good reason to believe that this trend will continue as the twenty-first century progresses. In the view of this author, modern science makes it possible to be a scientifically informed doubter of Darwinian theories of evolution.

Christopher Michael Langan

13. CHEATING THE MILLENNIUM:

The Mounting Explanatory Debts of Scientific Naturalism

INTRODUCTION: THESIS + ANTITHESIS = SYNTHESIS

In agreeing to write this essay, I have promised to explain why I find
Darwinism unconvincing. In order to keep this promise, I am compelled
to acknowledge the apparently paradoxical fact that I find it convincing
as well. I find it convincing because it is in certain respects correct, and
in fact tautologically so in the logical sense; I find it unconvincing because it is based on a weak and superficial understanding of causality
and is therefore incomplete. Explaining why this is so will require a rather
deep investigation of the nature of causality. It will also require not only
that a direction of progress be indicated, but that a new synthesis embracing the seemingly antithetical notions of teleology and natural selection be outlined. But first, some essential background.

It would be hard to imagine philosophical issues bearing more
strongly on the human condition than the nature of life and the meaning of human existence, and it would be hard to imagine a scientific
issue bearing more strongly on the nature and meaning of life than biological origins. Our view of evolutionary biology, whatever it happens
to be at any particular juncture, tells us much of what we believe about
who and what we are and why we are here, unavoidably affecting how
we view (and ultimately treat) ourselves and each other. Unfortunately,
the prevailing theory of biological origins seems to be telling us that at
least one of these questions, *why are we here?,* is meaningless[1] . . . or at
least this is the message that many of us, whether or not we are directly
aware of it, seem to have received. As a result, the brightest hope of the
new millennium, that we would see the dawn of a New Enlightenment
in which the Meaning of it All would at last be revealed, already seems

to have gone the way of an extravagant campaign promise at an inauguration ceremony.

The field of evolutionary biology is currently dominated by *neo-Darwinism*, a troubled marriage of convenience between post-Mendelian genetics and *natural selection*, a concept propounded by the naturalist Charles Darwin in his influential treatise *On the Origin of Species*.[2] It has often been noted that the field and the theory appear to be inseparable; in many respects, it seems that evolutionary biology and Darwinism originated and have evolved together, leading some to conclude that the field properly contains nothing that is not already accommodated by the theory.

Proponents of this view frequently assert that the limitations of the theory are just the general limitations imposed on all scientific theories by standard scientific methodology, and that to exceed them is thus to transgress the boundaries of science. Others have noted that this seems to assume a prior justification of scientific methodology that does not in fact exist. To say merely that scientific methodology works for certain purposes does not imply that it is optimal, particularly when it is evidently useless for others. In any case, the putative falsifiability of neo-Darwinism distinguishes it from any definition of *science* according to which the truth or falsity of such theories can be scientifically determined.[3] Nevertheless, neo-Darwinism continues to claim exclusive dominion over the "science" of evolutionary biology.

Until the latter part of the eighteenth century, the story was quite different. People tended to regard the matter of biological origins in a religious light. The universe was widely considered to have been freely and purposively designed and created by God as described in the Book of Genesis, and divine purpose was thought to be immanent in nature and open to observation and study. This doctrine, called *teleology*, drew rational support from traditional theological "arguments from design" holding that nature could only have been designed and created by a supreme intelligence. But teleology began to wane with the rise of British empiricism, and by the time Darwin published his theory in 1859, the winds of change were howling his anthem. Since then, the decline of teleology has accelerated to a point at which every supposedly universal law of nature is confidently presented as "irrefutable evidence" that natural events unfold independently of intent, and that purpose, divine or otherwise, is irrelevant to natural causation.

The concept of teleology remains alive nonetheless, having recently been granted a scientific reprieve in the form of *Intelligent Design theory*. "ID theory" holds that the complexity of biological systems implies the involvement of empirically detectable intelligent causes in nature. Although the roots of ID theory can be traced back to theological arguments from design, it is explicitly scientific rather than theological in character, and has thus been presented on the same basis as any other scientific hypothesis awaiting scientific confirmation.[4]

Rather than confining itself to theological or teleological causation, ID theory technically allows for any kind of intelligent designer—a human being, an artificial intelligence, even sentient aliens. This reflects the idea that intelligence is a generic quality, one that leaves a signature that can be identified by techniques already heavily employed in such fields as cryptography, anthropology, forensics and computer science. It remains only to note that while explaining the inherent complexity of a material designer would launch an explanatory regress ending only with some sort of Prime Mover, thus coming down to something very much like teleology after all, ID theory has thus far committed itself only to design inference. That is, it currently proposes only to explain complex biological phenomena in terms of design, not to explain the designer itself.[5] With regard to deeper levels of explanation, the field remains open.

Because neo-Darwinism is held forth as a "synthesis" of Darwinian natural selection and post-Mendelian genetics, it is sometimes referred to as the "Modern Synthesis." However, it appears to fall somewhat short of this title, for not only is its basic approach to evolutionary biology no longer especially modern, but it actively resists meaningful extension despite the existence of cogent and far more popular alternatives, including theistic evolution[6] and ID theory.[7] Many of its most influential proponents have dismissed ID theory virtually on sight, declaring themselves without need of justification or remedial dialectic despite the many points raised against them. Such a blanket dismissal is not something that the proponents of a "modern synthesis" would ordinarily have the privilege of doing. A synthesis is ordinarily expected to accommodate all sides of the controversy about a subject, not just the side favored by the synthesist.[8]

Given the dissonance of the neo-Darwinist and teleological viewpoints, it is hardly surprising that many modern authors and scientists regard the neo-Darwinian and teleological theories of biological evolution as mutually irreconcilable, dwelling on their differences and ignoring their commonalities. Each side of the debate seems intent on pointing out the real or imagined deficiencies of the other while resting its case on its own real or imagined virtues. This paper will take a road less traveled, treating the opposition of these views as a problem of reconciliation, and seeking a consistent, comprehensive framework in which to combine their strengths, decide their differences, and unite them in synergy. To the extent that both theories can be interpreted in such a framework, any apparent points of contradiction would be separated by context, and irreconcilable differences thereby avoided.

The ideal reconciliatory framework would be self-contained but comprehensive, meaning that both theories could be truthfully interpreted within it to the maximum possible extent, and consistent, meaning that irreconcilable differences between the theories could not survive the interpretation process. It would also reveal any biconditionality between the two theories; were they in any way to imply each other, this would be made explicit. For example, were a logical extension of neo-Darwinism to somehow yield ID-related concepts such as teleological agency and teleological causation, these would be seen to emerge from neo-Darwinist premises; conversely, were ID-theoretic concepts to yield ingredients of neo-Darwinism, this too would be explicated. In any case, the result would wear the title of "synthesis" far more credibly than neo-Darwinism alone.

TWO THEORIES OF BIOLOGICAL CAUSALITY

In order to talk about origins and evolution, one must talk about causality, and because causality is a function of the system called "nature," one must talk about nature. Theories of biological origins and evolution, such as neo-Darwinism and ID theory, are both theories of causality restricted to the context of biological origins and evolution; and because causality is a function of nature, each points toward an underlying theory of nature incorporating an appropriate treatment of causality.

That is, biological origins and evolution, being for scientific purposes instances of causation or the outcomes of causal processes, require definitions, theories and models of nature and causality. But these definitions, theories, and models involve deeper and more complex criteria than are evident through casual observation. Even to experts in science and philosophy, it is not entirely obvious how to meet all of these criteria. This is why causality remains a controversial subject.

A *cause* is something that brings about an effect or result, and *causality* is the quality or agency relating cause and effect. Because there are different requirements for bringing about an event or situation, there are different kinds of causation. In common usage, a "cause" may be an event which causes another event, the reason or rationale for an event, an agent or the motive thereof, the means by which an event transpires, supporting conditions for an event, or in fact anything satisfying any logical or physical requirement of a resultant effect. Because causal relationships necessarily exist in a causal medium that provides a basic, generic connection between cause and effect, the study of causation has typically focused on the medium and its connectivity . . . i.e., on the "fabric of nature."

The kinds of causation that are required in order to explain natural changes or events were enumerated by Aristotle in the fourth century BC. He posed four questions involving four types of causes: (1) What is changed to make the entity (of what is it composed)? (2) What makes the entity change, and how? (3) What is the shape or pattern assumed by the entity as it changes? (4) What is the goal toward which the change of the entity is directed? Aristotle defined the answers to these questions as, respectively, the *material cause*, the *efficient cause*, the *formal cause*, and the *final cause*. With its explicit allowance for formal and final causation, Aristotle's classification ultimately implied the existence of a purposive, pattern-generating Prime Mover, and thus laid the groundwork for a teleological explanation of nature that went all but unchallenged for well over a millennium.

But when the Age of Reason (circa 1650–1800) had finished taking its toll on traditional Scholastic doctrines based on Aristotelian insight, only material and efficient causes retained a place in scientific reasoning; and in the hands of philosophers like Hume and Kant, even these modes of causation were laid open to doubt. Hume claimed that causal relationships are nothing more than subjective expectations that certain sequences of events observed in the past will continue to be observed in the future,[9] while Kant went on to assert that causality is a category of cognition and perception according to which the mind organizes its experience of basically unknowable objects.[10] Nevertheless, contemporary science retains its concern for material and efficient causes while letting formal and final causes languish in a state of near-total neglect.[11]

Distilled to a single sentence, the prevailing scientific view of nature and causality is roughly this: "Nature is associated with a space, generalizable to a spacetime manifold, permeated by fields under the causal influence of which objects move and interact in space and time according to logico-arithmetical laws of nature." Despite its simplicity, this is a versatile causal framework with the power to express much of our scientific knowledge. But the questions to which it leads are as obvious as they are unanswered. For example, where do these laws reside? Of what are they composed? How and why did they originate? What are their properties? How do they function, and how are they sustained?[12]

In addition to generating questions about natural laws in general, the prevailing oversimplification of causality contains further gaps which have done as much to impede our understanding of nature as to further it.[13] The associated problems are numerous, and they lead to yet another set of questions. For example, is causality formally and dynamically contained, uncontained or self-contained? What is its source, on what does it function, and what additional structure does it predicate of that on which it functions? What is its substance—is it mental, physical, or both? How does it break down, and if it is stratified, then what are its levels? These questions lead in turn to further questions, and until all of these questions are answered at least in principle, no theory of biological causality stands on *terra firma*.

But before attempting to answer these questions, let us have a look at the models of causality on which neo-Darwinism and ID theory are currently based.

CAUSALITY ACCORDING TO INTELLIGENT DESIGN THEORY

Teleological causation is "top-down" causation in which the design and design imperative reside at the top, and the individual actualization events that realize the design reside at the bottom. The model universe required for teleological causality must therefore incorporate (1) a source and means of design, i.e. a designer or designing agency; (2) a design stage in which designs are generated and/or selected; (3) an actualization stage in which designs become physically real from the viewpoints of physical observers; and (4) a means or mechanism for passing from the design stage to the actualization stage. If this type of model universe permits observers to empirically detect interesting instantiations of teleology, so much the better.

Particular teleological model universes that have been proposed include celestial hierarchies and heavenly bureaucracies with God at the top giving the orders, angels of various ranks serving on intermediate levels as messengers and functionaries, humans lower still, and other forms of life at the bottom; the Aristotelian universe, incorporating formal and final causation and embodying the *telos* of a Prime Mover; teleologically "front-loaded" mechanistic universes in which causation resembles clockwork that has been set in autonomous motion by a purposive, mechanically talented designer; and the panentheistic universe explicated by (among others) Alfred North Whitehead, in which the teleological will of the designer is immanent in nature because, in some sense, nature is properly contained *within* the designer.[14] Although each has its strengths, these and other well-known teleological models are, as formulated, inadequate to support various logical implications of requirements one through four.

The model universe of ID theory, which can be regarded as a generalization of traditional teleological design theory with respect to causal agency, has essentially the same requirements. However, it also contains certain novel ingredients, including a focus on intelligence, an emphasis on mathematical and information-theoretic concepts, and two novel ingredients called *irreducible complexity* and *specified complexity*.

Irreducible complexity, which is intended to describe biological systems and subsystems unlikely to have been produced by gradual (piece-by-piece) evolution, is by definition a property of any integrated functional system from which the removal of any one or more core components critically impairs its original function.[15] Although proposed examples have drawn fire—examples including the bacterial flagellum, the human eye, the blood clotting cascade, and even the conventional spring-loaded mousetrap—the concept has a valid basis with roots in logic, graph theory, and other branches of mathematics and engineering.

Specified complexity, which is intended as a more general description of the products of intelligent causation, is by definition a property of anything that exhibits a recognizable pattern which has a very low probability of occurring by chance. Whereas irreducible complexity is based on the sheer improbability of complex, functionally coherent systems, specified complexity adds an *intelligence* (rational pattern generation and recognition) criterion that lets functional complexity be generalized to a pattern-based form of complexity better suited to probabilistic and information-theoretic analysis.[16]

Specified complexity amounts to a relationship between three attributes: *contingency, complexity,* and *specification*. Contingency corresponds to freedom and variety (as when there are many distinct possibilities that may be selectively actualized), complexity corresponds to improbability, and specification corresponds to the existence of a meaningful pattern which, in conjunction with the other two attributes in sufficient measure, indicates an application of intelligence. Wherever all three of these attributes are coinstantiated, specified complexity is present.

Contingency is associated with *specificational* and *replicational* probabilistic resources. Specificational resources consist of a set or class of distinct pre-specified target events, while replicational resources consist of chances for at least one of the specified target events to occur. The chance of occurrence of an instance of specified complexity is the chance that these two kinds of resource will intersect in light of total contingency.

For example, the total contingency of a four-digit lottery consists of the set of all possible drawings over unlimited trials and is associated with the numbers from 0000 to 9999, the specificational resources consist of a subset of distinct pre-specified four-digit winning numbers to be replicated (matched or predicted), and the replicational resources consist of the tickets purchased. The chance that the lottery will have at least one winner equals the probability of intersection of the set of winning numbers and the set of tickets, given that there are ten thousand distinctly numbered tickets that might have been purchased.

More topically, the total contingency of a particular evolutionary context consists of all possible lines of evolution that might occur therein, whether productive or leading to a dead end; the specificational resources consist of instances of specified complexity or "intelligent design"; and the replicational resources consist of all possible lines of evolution which can occur within some set of practical constraints imposed on the context, such as time or space constraints tending to limit replication. The chance that an instance of specified complexity will evolve equals the probability of intersection of the set of instances and the set of constrained lines of evolution, given the multiplicity of all of the possible lines of evolution that could occur. Where this probability is extremely low, some form of intelligent design is indicated.

Specified complexity is a powerful idea that yields insight crucial to the meaning and satisfaction of requirements one through four. First, probability estimates for instances of specified complexity are so low as to require that specificational and replicational resources be linked in such a way that such events can actually occur, in effect raising their probability. It must therefore be determined whether the satisfaction of this requirement is consistent with the premise that low probabilities can actually be calculated for instances of specified complexity; if so, how and why can this be reliably accomplished? Next, it must be shown that the actual linkage between specificational and replicational resources is such as to imply intelligence and design.

Up to its current level of detail and coherence, the model universe of ID theory does not necessarily conflict with that of neo-Darwinism with respect to causality, but rather contains it, requiring only that causality be interpreted in light of this containment.

CAUSALITY ACCORDING TO NEO-DARWINISM

Neo-Darwinism is the application of Darwinian natural selection to modern (post-Mendelian) genetics, which indifferently assumes that genetic mutations occur because of "random" DNA copying errors. This short but revealing description contains a certain amount of useful information. First, it reveals that causality is being at least partially reduced to some (ontic or epistemic) form of randomness. Even more revealingly, the phrase *natural selection* explicitly implies that nature is selective. Indeed, the term *natural* alone is instructive, for it reflects a naturalistic viewpoint according to which existence is ascribed exclusively to the natural world, i.e. "nature."

In practice, most scientists consider *nature* to consist of that which is physical, observable, and amenable to empirical investigation as prescribed by the scientific method, in their adherence to which they see themselves as following a naturalistic agenda. This is in keeping with *scientific naturalism,* a worldview of which neo-Darwinism is considered representative. Scientific naturalism ascribes existence strictly to the physical or natural world consisting of space, time, matter, and energy. Two strains of naturalism are sometimes distinguished, *philosophical* and *methodological.* While philosophical naturalism claims ontological force, methodological naturalism is epistemological in flavor, merely asserting that nature *might as well* equal the physical world for scientific purposes. But in either case, scientific naturalism effectively confines the scientific study of nature to the physical. So, inasmuch as neo-Darwinism is exemplary of scientific naturalism, it is physical or materialistic in character.[17]

In the picture of causality embraced by scientific naturalism, processes are either *random* or *deterministic.* In deterministic processes, objects are affected by laws and forces external to them, while in random processes, determinacy is either absent or unknown. A process can be "random" because of ignorance, statistics, or presumed acausality—that is, because epistemological or observational limitations prevent identification of its hidden causal factors, because its causal outcomes are unpredictably but symmetrically distributed in the large, or because it is presumed to be nondeterministic. The first two of these possibilities involve some amount of causal determinacy, while the third is exclusively (but unverifiably) acausal. So a neo-Darwinist either takes a deterministic view of causality or sees it in terms of the dichotomy between determinism and nondeterminism, in either case relying heavily on the theory of probability.

In fact, given that natural selection is based on the essentially trivial observation that nature imposes constraints on survival and reproduction,[18] neo-Darwinism boils down to little more than probability theory, genetics, and a very simple abstract, but nominally physical, model of biological causality based on "survival and reproduction of the fittest" and *common descent,* according to which diverse species arise from common ancestors by random reproductive mutation and natural selection. Thus, when neo-Darwinians claim to have generated a prediction, it is generally not a deep secret of nature unearthed by means of advanced theoretical manipulation, but merely the result of applying what amounts to a principle of indifference[19] to some question about mutation, adaptation, selection, or reproduction, obtained by running the numbers and tracking the implications through the simplistic neo-Darwinian model universe. If there were no such "theory" as neo-Darwinism, the same conclusion might have been reached with a straightforward combination of biology, genetics, chemistry, physics, a statistics calculator, and a bit of common sense. This is why neo-Darwinism is so astonishingly able to absorb new effects and mechanisms the minute they come out of the core sciences.

Something else that neo-Darwinism seems to do with astonishing ease is absorb what appear on their faces to be contradictions. For example, many people, some might say a large majority, find it to some degree incredible that what amounts to a principle of indifference can be seriously offered as a causal explanation for the amazing complexity of the biological world, or for that matter any other part of the world. The fact that a principle of indifference is essentially devoid of information implies that neo-Darwinism yields not a causal explanation of biological complexity, but merely an open-ended simulation in which every bit of complexity delivered as output must have been present as input, appearances to the contrary notwithstanding. This implies that neo-Darwinism *per se*, as distinguished from the core sciences from which it routinely borrows, adds precisely nothing to our knowledge of biological complexity or its source.

In order to deal with this seemingly inescapable problem, the proponents of neo-Darwinism have eagerly adopted the two hottest slogans in the theory of complex systems, *self-organization* and *emergence*. Self-organization is a spontaneous, extrinsically unguided process by which a system develops an organized structure, while emergence refers to those global properties (functions, processes) of composite hierarchical systems that cannot be reduced to the properties of their component subsystems—the properties in which they are more than the sums of their parts. But the fact that these terms have been superficially defined does not imply that they have been adequately explained. Actually, they remain as much of a mystery in complexity theory as they are in biology, and can do nothing for neo-Darwinism but spin the pointer toward another hapless and equally helpless field of inquiry.

Because scientific naturalism denies that existence of any kind is possessed by anything of a supernatural or metaphysical character, including an intelligent cosmic designer, the definitions, theories, and models of nature and causality on which it implicitly relies must be "physical," at least in name. However, as we have already noted and will shortly explain in detail, what currently passes for an understanding of causality in the physical sciences leaves much to be desired. In particular, since the kind of causality treated in the physical sciences is ontologically and functionally dependent on the origin and evolution of the cosmos, scientific naturalists trying to answer questions about causality are obliged to consider *all* stages of causation and generation all the way back to the cosmic origin, constantly testing their answers to see if they continue to make sense when reformulated in more fundamental terms.

Unfortunately, this obligation is not being met. One reason is the reluctance of those who most need an understanding of causality to admit the extent of their ignorance. Another is the seeming intractability of certain problems associated with the causality concept itself.

A DEEPER LOOK AT CAUSALITY: THE CONNECTIVITY PROBLEM

Because causal relationships would seem to exist in a causal medium that provides some sort of basic connection between cause and effect, the study of causation has typically focused on the medium and its connectivity, that is, on the "fabric of nature." How does this fabric permit different objects to interact, given that to *interact* is to *intersect* in the same events governed by the same laws, and thus to possess a degree of sameness? How can multiple objects each simultaneously exhibit two opposite properties, sameness and difference, with respect to each other?

Equivalently, on what underlying form of connectivity is causality defined? When one asserts that one event "causes" another, what more general connection does this imply between the events? If there is no more general connection than the causal connection itself, then causality is underivable from any logically prior condition; it is something that happens *ex nihilo*, the sudden synthesis of a connection out of nothing. It would then be just as Hume maintained: causal relationships would be mere accidental correlations of subjectively associated events, as inexplicable in their regularity as in their sensibility.

But it can't be quite that simple. In fact, Hume's characterization of causality as mere random correlation presupposes the existence of a correlating agent who recognizes and unifies causal correlations through experience, and the abstractive, experiential coherence or *consciousness* of this correlation-inducing agent constitutes a prior connective medium. So in this case, explaining causality requires that the subjective medium of experience, complete with its correlative "laws of causality," be related to the objective world of real events.

Unfortunately, Hume's thesis includes a denial that any such objective world exists. In Hume's view, experience is all there is. And although Kant subsequently registered his qualified disagreement, asserting that there is indeed an objective outside world, he pronounced it unknowable, relegating causality to the status of a category of perception.[20] This, of course, perpetuated the idea of causal subjectivity by continuing to presuppose the existence of an *a priori* subjective medium.

How can the nature of subjective causality be understood? As Kant observed, perception and cognition are mutually necessary; concepts without percepts are empty, and percepts without concepts are blind.[21] It must therefore be asked to what extent perceptual reality might be an outward projection of cognitive processes, and natural processes the mirror images of mental processes.

This leads to another problem, that of *mind-matter dualism*.

THE DUALISM PROBLEM

The Kantian distinction between phenomenal and noumenal reality, respectively defined as those parts of reality[22] which are dependent on and independent of perception, mirrors a prior philosophical viewpoint known as *Cartesian (mind-matter) dualism*. Associated with René Descartes, the polymath mercenary who laid the groundwork for analytic geometry by helping to develop the concept of coordinate spaces, this is a form of *substance dualism* which asserts that reality consists of two immiscible "substances," mind and matter. Cartesian dualism characterizes a certain influential approach to the *problem of mental causation*: how does the mind influence the physical body?

Cartesian dualism leads to a problem associated with the connectivity problem we have just discussed: if reality consists of two different "substances," then what connects these substances in one unified "reality"? What is the medium which sustains their respective existences and the putative difference relationship between them? One possible (wrong) answer is that their relationship is merely abstract, and therefore irrelevant to material reality and devoid of material influence; another is that like the physical epiphenomenon of mind itself, it is essentially physical. But these positions, which are seen in association with a slew of related philosophical doctrines including *physicalism, materialism, naturalism, objectivism, epiphenomenalism* and *eliminativism,* merely beg the question that Cartesian dualism was intended to answer, namely, the problem of mental causation.

Conveniently, modern logic affords a new level of analytical precision with respect to the Cartesian and Kantian dichotomies. Specifically, the branch of logic called *model theory* distinguishes *theories* from their *universes,* and considers the intervening semantic and interpretative mappings. Calling a theory an *object language* and its universe of discourse an *object universe,* it combines them in a *metaobject domain* consisting of the correspondences among their respective components and systems of components, and calls the theory or language in which this metaobject domain is analyzed a *metalanguage.* In like manner, the relationship between the metalanguage and the metaobject domain can be analyzed in a higher-level metalanguage, and so on. Because this situation can be recursively extended, level by level and metalanguage by metalanguage, in such a way that languages and their universes are conflated to an arbitrary degree, reality can with unlimited precision be characterized as a "metalinguistic metaobject."

In this setting, the philosophical dichotomies in question take on a distinctly mathematical hue. Because theories are abstract, subjectively-formed mental constructs,[23] the mental, subjective side of reality can now be associated with the object language and metalanguage(s), while the physical, objective side of reality can be associated with the object universe and metauniverse(s), i.e. the metaobject domain(s). It takes very little effort to see that the mental/subjective and physical/objective sides of reality are now combined in the metaobjects, and that Cartesian and Kantian "substance dualism" have now been transformed to "property dualism"[24] or *dual-aspect monism.* That is, we are now talking, in mathematically precise terms, about a "universal substance" of which mind and matter, the abstract and the concrete, the cognitive-perceptual and the physical, are mere properties or aspects.

Translating this into the scientific status quo is not difficult. Science regards causality as "objective," taking its cues from observation while ignoring certain philosophical problems involving the nature of objectivity. But science also depends on theoretical reasoning, and this involves abstract analogues of causality to which science is equally indebted. To the extent that scientific theories accurately describe the universe, they are *isomorphic* to the universe; in order that nature be amenable to meaningful theorization, science must therefore assume that the basic cognitive ingredients of theories, and for that matter the perceptual ingredients of observations, mirror the corresponding ingredients of nature up to some minimal but assured level of isomorphism. Consistent theories of science thus require that physical and abstract causation be brought into basic correspondence as mandated by this necessity.

Abstract analogues of physical causation are already well-understood. Logically, causality is analogous to *implication*, an active or passive relationship between antecedents and consequents; theoretically, it is analogous to the application of rules of inference to expressions formulated within a theory; linguistically, it amounts to substitution or production according to the rules of a generative grammar; and mathematically, it amounts to the application of a rule, mapping, function, operation or transformation. In every case, the analogue is some form of recursive[25] or iterative morphism to which a nonlogical interpretation may be attached.[26] The object is therefore to understand physical reality in terms of such operations defined in terms of an appropriate form of dual-aspect monism.

This leads directly to the *structure problem*.

THE STRUCTURE PROBLEM

A description or explanation of causality can only be formulated with respect to a particular "model universe" in which space, time and matter are defined and related to each other in such a way as to support the description. Their relationship must account for the laws of nature and their role in natural processes. A little reflection should reveal that both neo-Darwinism and ID theory, as well as all other scientific theories, are currently deficient in this regard. At best, scientists have a very limited idea where the laws of nature reside, how they came to be, and how they work; and because of the limitations of their empirical methodology,[27] they have no means of clarification.

We have already encountered Aristotle's four modes of causation: *material, efficient, formal* and *final*. These follow no special prescription, but are merely generic answers to questions about certain features of Aristotle's mental representation of nature, that is, his model universe. There are as many additional modes of causation as there are meaningful questions regarding the structure and dynamics of a given model universe. For example, in addition to Aristotle's questions *of what*, *who and how*, *what* and *why*, we could also ask *where* (positional causation), *when* (order or timing of causation), *by virtue of what* (facilitative causation), and so forth. Thus, we could say that something happened *because* it was positioned in a medium containing its material cause and supporting its efficient cause, *because* the time was right or certain prerequisites were in place, *because* certain conditions were present or certain tools were available, et cetera.

On what kinds of model universe can a causality function be defined? Among the mathematical structures which science has long favored are *coordinate spaces* and *differentiable manifolds*. In differentiable coordinate spaces, laws of physics formulated as algebraic or differential equations may conveniently define smooth geometric curves which faithfully represent, for example, the trajectories of physical objects in motion. A model universe based on these constructs supports certain causal relationships to an impressive level of accuracy. However, it fails with respect to others, particularly those involving discrete or nonlocal[28] changes or requiring high levels of coherence. In particular, it is incapable of modeling certain generative processes, including any generative process that might have led to its own existence; and beyond a certain point, its "continuity" attribute has eluded a completely satisfactory explanation.[29]

These and other difficulties have prompted some theorists to suggest model universes based on other kinds of mathematical structure. These include a new class of models to which the concepts of *information* and *computation* are essential. Called "discrete models," they depict reality in terms of bits, quanta, quantum events, computational operations and other discrete, recursively-related units. Whereas continuum models are based on the notion of a *continuum*, a unified extensible whole that can be subdivided so that any two distinct points are separated by an infinite number of intermediate points, discrete models reflect the fact that it is impossible to describe or define a change or separation in any way that does not involve a sudden finite jump in some parameter. Discrete models reflect the rising investment of the physical sciences in a quantum-theoretic view of reality, and the increasing dependence of science on computer simulation as an experimental tool.[30]

Discrete models have the advantage that they can more easily incorporate modern cybernetic concepts, including information, computation, and feedback, which conduce to an understanding of reality as an integrated control and communication system. In the context of such models, informational and computational reductionism is now pursued with a degree of enthusiasm formerly reserved for attempts to reduce the universe to matter and energy. However, certain difficulties persist. Discrete models remain dualistic, and they still cannot explain their own origins and existences. Nonlocality is still a problem for them, as are the spacetime deformations posited by General Relativity and so easily formulated in continuum models. Because they allow the existence of discrete gaps between events, they tend to lack adequate connectivity. And in the shadow of these deficiencies, they can illuminate the interrelationship of space, time and object no more successfully than their continuum counterparts.

The unregenerate dualism of most discrete models demands particular attention. As we reasoned above, solving the problem of dualism requires that the mental and physical aspects of reality be brought into coincidence. Insofar as information and computation are essentially formal and abstract, reducing the material aspects of nature to information and computation should bring the concrete and the abstract, the material and the mental, into perfect coincidence. But because most discrete models treat information and computation as objective entities, tacitly incorporating the assumption that bits and computations are on the same ontological footing as particles and collisions, their mental dimension is overlooked. Since making no explicit provision for mind amounts to leaving it out of the mix, mind and matter remain separate, and the problem of dualism remains unsolved.

Is there another alternative? The model-theoretic perspective, which simultaneously juxtaposes and conflates subjective languages and their objective universes, suggests that reality embodies an ontic-nomothetic medium with abstract and physical aspects that are respectively related as syntax is related to language. For example, because scientific observation and theorization must be consistent, and logic is the backbone of consistency, the syntax of every scientific theory must incorporate logic. In the case of a geometric theory of physical reality, like classical mechanics or relativity theory, this amounts—by model-theoretic implication—to the requirement that logic and geometry literally coincide. But where geometry is a property of "physical" spacetime, so then is logic; and if logic resides in spacetime, then so must logical grammar. This leads to the requirement that physical dynamics be explicitly fused with the formal grammar of logic and logic-based theories, ultimately including the entire abstract apparatus of causality.

Obviously, conventional continuum and discrete models of reality fail to meet this requirement. As far as they and most of those who embrace them are concerned, the physical world is simply not answerable to any theory whatsoever, even logic. According to the standard empirical doctrine of science, we may observe reality but never impose our preconceptions upon it, and this means that theory—even a theory as necessary to cognition and perception as logic—is always the beggar and never the master at the scientific table. The reason for this situation is clear: scientists need a means of guarding against the human tendency to confuse their own inner subjective worlds, replete with fantasy, desire, and prejudice, with the factual external world conventionally studied by science.

But there is a very clear difference between logic on one hand, and fantasy and prejudice on the other. While science never needs the latter, it *always* needs the former. By excluding logic from nature, mainstream science has nothing to gain and everything to lose; in not attributing its own most basic requirements to its subject matter, it is cheating itself in a crucial way. Whether or not a theory turns out to be valid which fails to predicate of its universe the wherewithal of its own validity, it can be neither more nor less valid because of its false and subtly pretentious humility. On the other hand, failing to attribute these requirements to its universe when its universe in fact exhibits them, and when its universe would in fact be unintelligible without them, can ultimately cost it every bit of truth that it might otherwise have had, particularly if its methodology is inadequate to identify the problem and mandate a remedy.

Because they fail to provide definitive answers for questions about causality, conventional continuum and discrete models of reality devolve to acausality or infinite causal regression. No matter what causal explanations they seem to offer, one of two things is implied: (1) a cause prior to that which is cited in the explanation, or (2) random, spontaneous, acausal emergence from the void, with no explanation supposedly required. Given the seeming absence of alternatives to determinism or randomness, or to extrinsic[31] and null causation, how are meaningful causal explanations to be completed?

THE CONTAINMENT PROBLEM

A certain philosophically controversial hypothesis about causality presently rules the scientific world by fiat. It asserts that physical reality is closed under causal regression: "no physical event has a cause outside the physical domain."[32] That is, if a physical event has a cause, then it has a *physical* cause. Obviously, the meaning of this principle is strongly dependent on the definition of *physical*, which is not as cut and dried as one might suppose.[33] It also contradicts the conventional assumption that causality is an abstraction, at best indirectly observable through its effects on matter, which functions independently of any specific item of material content. How, then, does this principle manage to maintain its hold on science? The answer: false parsimony and explanatory debt. Concisely, *false parsimony* is when a theory achieves deceptive simplicity in its native context by sweeping its unpaid *explanatory debts* or explanatory deficiencies into unkempt piles located in or between other areas of science.

It is an ill-kept secret that the scientific community, far from being one big happy family of smoothly connected neighborhoods, consists of isolated, highly-specialized enclaves that often tend toward mutual ignorance and xenophobia. Under these circumstances, it is only natural to expect that when caught between an observational rock and a theoretical hard place, some of those sheltered within these enclaves will take advantage of the situation and "pass the explanatory buck," neither knowing nor caring when or where it comes to rest as long as the maneuver takes some of the heat off them and frees them to conduct business as usual. While the explanatory buck-passing is almost never productive, it can be conveniently hidden in the deep, dark cracks and crevices between disciplines. As a result, many pressing explanatory obligations have been successfully exiled to interdisciplinary limbo, an intellectual dead zone from which they cannot threaten the dominance of the physical causal closure thesis.

However, the ploy does not always work. Because of the longstanding scientific trend toward physical reductionism, the buck often gets passed to physics, and because physics is widely considered more fundamental than any other scientific discipline, it has a hard time deferring explanatory debts mailed directly to its address. Some of the explanatory debts for which physics is holding the bag are labeled "causality," and some of these bags were sent to the physics department from the evolutionary biology department. These debt-filled bags were sent because the evolutionary biology department lacked the explanatory resources to pay them for itself. Unfortunately, physics can't pay them either.

The reason that physics cannot pay explanatory debts generated by various causal hypotheses is that it does not itself possess an adequate understanding of causality. This is evident from the fact that in physics, events are assumed to be either *deterministic* or *nondeterministic* in origin. Given an object, event, set or process, it is usually assumed to have come about in one of just two possible ways: either it was brought about by something prior and external to it, or it sprang forth spontaneously as if by some subtle form of magic. The prevalence of this dichotomy, *determinacy versus randomness*, amounts to an unspoken scientific axiom asserting that everything in the universe, up to and including the universe itself, is ultimately either a function of external causes, or no function of anything whatsoever. In the former case, there is a known or unknown explanation, albeit external; in the latter case, there is no explanation at all. In neither case can the universe be regarded as causally self-contained.

To a person unused to questioning this dichotomy, there may seem to be no middle ground. It may indeed appear that where events are not actively and connectively produced according to laws of nature, there is nothing to connect them; thus their distribution can only be random, patternless, and meaningless. But there is another possibility after all: *self-determinacy*. Self-determinacy involves a higher-order generative process that yields not only the physical states of entities, but the entities themselves, the abstract laws that govern them, and the entire system which contains and coherently relates them. Self-determinism is the causal dynamic of any system that generates its own components and properties independently of prior laws or external structures. Because self-determinacy involves nothing of a preexisting or external nature, it is the only type of causal relationship suitable for a causally self-contained system.

In a self-deterministic system, causal regression leads to a completely intrinsic, self-generative process. In any system that is *not* ultimately self-deterministic, including any system that is either random or deterministic in the standard extrinsic sense, causal regression terminates at null causality or does not terminate. In either of the latter two cases, science can fully explain nothing; in the absence of a final cause, even material and efficient causes are subject to causal regression toward ever more general and fundamental substances and processes, or if random in origin, toward primitive acausality. Insofar as explanation is largely what science is all about, science would seem to have no choice but to treat the universe as a self-deterministic, causally self-contained system.[34]

Thus, questions about evolution become questions about the self-generation of causally self-contained, self-emergent systems. In particular, they become questions about *how* and *why* such a system self-generates.

THE UTILITY (SELECTION) PROBLEM

As we have just noted, deterministic causality transforms the states of
preexisting objects according to preexisting laws associated with an external medium. Where this involves or produces feedback, the feedback
is of the conventional cybernetic variety; it transports information
through the medium from one location to another and then back again,
with transformations at each end of the loop. But where objects, laws
and media do not yet exist, this kind of feedback is not yet possible.
Accordingly, causality must be reformulated so that it can not only transform the states of natural systems, but account for self-deterministic
relationships between states and laws of nature. In short, *causality* must
become *metacausality*.[35]

Self-determination involves a generalized, atemporal[36] kind of feedback between physical states and the abstract laws that govern them.
Ordinary cybernetic feedback consists of information passed back and
forth among controllers and regulated entities through a preexisting
conductive or transmissive medium according to ambient sensory and
actuative protocols; one may think of the internet, with its closed informational loops and preexisting material processing nodes and communication channels, as a ready example. Self-generative feedback, however, must be ontological and *telic* rather than strictly physical in character.[37] That is, it must be defined in such a way as to "metatemporally"
bring the formal structure of cybernetics and its physical content into
joint existence from a primitive, undifferentiated ontological groundstate.
To pursue our example, the internet, beginning as a timeless self-potential, would have to self-actualize, in the process generating time and causality.

But what is this ontological groundstate, and what is a "self-potential"? For that matter, what are the means and goals of cosmic self-
actualization? The ontological groundstate may be somewhat simplisti-
cally characterized as a complete abeyance of binding ontological constraint, a sea of pure telic potential or "unbound telesis." Self-potential
can then be seen as a telic relationship of two lower kinds of potential:
potential *states*, which are the possible sets of definitive properties possessed by an entity along with their possible values, and potential *laws*
(nomological syntax) according to which states are defined, recognized
and transformed.[38] Thus, the ontological groundstate can for most purposes be equated with all possible state-syntax relationships or "self-
potentials." The means of self-actualization is then a telic, metacausal
mode of recursion through which telic potentials are refined into spe-

cific state-syntax configurations. The particulars of this process depend on the specific model universe—and in light of dual-aspect monism, the *real self-modeling* universe—in which the telic potential is actualized.

And now we come to what might be seen as the pivotal question: what is the *goal* of self-actualization? Conveniently enough, this question contains its own answer: self-actualization, a generic analogue of Aristotelian final causation and thus of teleology, is *its own* inevitable outcome and thus its own goal.[39] Whatever its specific details may be, they are actualized by the universe alone, and this means that they are mere special instances of cosmic self-actualization. Although the word "goal" has subjective connotations—for example, some definitions stipulate that a goal must be the object of an instinctual drive or other subjective impulse—we could easily adopt a reductive or functionalist approach to such terms, taking them to reduce or refer to objective features of reality. Similarly, if the term "goal" implies some measure of design or pre-formulation, then we could easily observe that "natural selection" does so as well, for nature has already largely determined what "designs" it will accept for survival and thereby render fit.

Given that the self-containment of nature implies causal closure, which in turn implies self-determinate self-actualization, how is the latter to be achieved? Obviously, nature must select some possible form in which to self-actualize. Since a self-contained, causally closed universe does not have the luxury of external guidance, it needs to generate an *intrinsic* self-selection criterion in order to do this. Since *utility* is the name already given to the attribute which is maximized by any rational choice function, and since a totally self-actualizing system has the privilege of defining its own standard of rationality,[40] we may as well speak of this self-selection criterion in terms of global or generic self-utility. That is, the self-actualizing universe must generate and retrieve information on the intrinsic utility content of various possible forms that it might take.

The utility concept bears more inspection than it ordinarily gets. Utility often entails a subject-object distinction; for example, the utility of an apple in a pantry is biologically and psychologically generated by a more or less conscious subject of whom its existence is ostensibly independent. It therefore makes little sense to speak of its "intrinsic utility." While it might be asserted that an apple or some other relatively non-conscious material object is "good for its own sake" and thus in possession of intrinsic utility, attributing self-interest to something implies that it is a subject as well as an object, and thus that it is capable of subjective self-recognition.[41] To the extent that the universe is at once an *object* of selection and a self-selective *subject* capable of some degree of self-recognition, it supports intrinsic utility (as does any coherent state-syntax relationship). An apple, on the other hand, does not seem at first glance to meet this criterion.

But a closer look again turns out to be warranted. Since an apple is a part of the universe and therefore embodies its intrinsic self-utility, and since the various causes of the apple (material, efficient and so on) can be traced back along their causal chains to the intrinsic causation and self-utility of the universe, the apple has a certain amount of intrinsic utility after all. This is confirmed when we consider that its taste and nutritional value, wherein reside its utility for the person who eats it, further its genetic utility by encouraging its widespread cultivation and dissemination. In fact, this line of reasoning can be extended beyond the biological realm to the world of inert objects, for in a sense they too are naturally selected for existence. Potentials that obey the laws of nature are permitted to exist in nature and are thereby rendered "fit," while potentials that do not are excluded.[42] So it seems that in principle, natural selection determines the survival of not just actualities but potentials, and in either case it does so according to an intrinsic utility criterion ultimately based on global self-utility.

It is important to be clear on the relationship between utility and causality. Utility is simply a generic selection criterion essential to the only cosmologically acceptable form of causality, namely self-determinism. The subjective gratification associated with positive utility in the biological and psychological realms is ultimately beside the point. No longer need natural processes be explained under suspicion of anthropomorphism; causal explanations need no longer implicitly refer to instinctive drives and subjective motivations. Instead, they can refer directly to a generic objective "drive," namely intrinsic causality, the "drive" of the universe to maximize an intrinsic self-selection criterion over various relational strata within the bounds of its internal constraints.[43] Teleology and scientific naturalism are equally satisfied; the global self-selection imperative to which causality necessarily devolves is a generic property of nature to which subjective drives and motivations necessarily "reduce," for it distributes by embedment over the intrinsic utility of every natural system.

Intrinsic utility and natural selection relate to each other as both reason and outcome. When an evolutionary biologist extols the elegance or effectiveness of a given biological "design" with respect to a given function, as in "the wings of a bird are beautifully *designed* for flight," he is really talking about intrinsic utility, with which biological fitness is thus entirely synonymous. Survival and its requisites have intrinsic utility for that which survives, be it an organism or a species; that which survives derives utility from its environment *in order to* survive and *as a result of* its survival. It follows that neo-Darwinism, a theory of biological causation whose proponents have tried to restrict it to determinism and randomness, is properly a theory of intrinsic utility and thus of self-determinism. Athough neo-Darwinists claim that the kind of utility driving natural selection is non-teleological and unique to the particular independent systems being naturally selected, this claim is logically insupportable. Causality ultimately boils down to the tautological fact that on all possible scales, nature is both *that which selects* and *that which is selected.* This means that natural selection is ultimately based on the intrinsic utility of nature at large.

But in light of causal self-containment, teleology is *also* based on the intrinsic utility of nature at large. Why, then, do so many supporters of teleology and neo-Darwinism seem to think them mutually exclusive?

The Stratification Problem

It is frequently taken for granted that neo-Darwinism and ID theory are mutually incompatible, and that if one is true, then the other must be false. But while this assessment may be accurate with regard to certain inessential propositions attached to the core theories like pork-barrel riders on congressional bills,[44] it is not so obvious with regard to the core theories themselves. In fact, these theories are dealing with different levels of causality.

The scientific method says that experiments must be replicable, and this means that the same laws must govern the same kinds of events under the same conditions throughout nature. Where possible, the laws of nature are scientifically formulated in such a way that they distribute over space and time, the same laws applying under similar conditions at all times and places. Science also requires that the laws of nature be formulated in such a way that the next state of an object depends only on its present state, including all of the forces impinging on it at the present moment, with no memory of prior states required. It is little wonder that science enforces these two conditions with extreme prejudice wherever possible, for in principle they guarantee its ability to predict the future of any physical system from a mere knowledge of its current state and the globally distributed laws of nature.[45]

Science imposes yet further constraints on causality. One, the empirical discernability criterion of the scientific method,[46] guarantees the recognizability of physical states by insisting that they be formulated in terms of *observables,* first-order properties[47] that can be unambiguously measured in conjunction with physical objects. Another, which we have already encountered, is the locality principle, which says that there can be no "nonlocal" jumps from one point in a physical manifold to another non-adjacent point.[48] This adds an adjacency or continuity constraint to the Laplacian ideal; the laws of nature must not only be formulated in such a way that the next state of an object depends only on its present state, but in such a way that successive states are "near" each other, i.e., so that smaller amounts of time and energy correspond to smaller displacements under any given set of laws. To the extent that it holds, this proportionality of cause and effect permits the laws of causality to be consistently applied on the macroscopic and microscopic scales.

Of all the preconceived restrictions and unnecessary demands imposed on causality by science, the least questioned is the requirement that the relationship between physical states and laws of nature be one-way, with states depending on laws but not vice versa. Science regards the laws of nature as immutable; states exist and transform at their beck and call, and the directional dependency relationship between laws and states is considered to be something that has existed for all time. When the laws of nature dictate that an event should happen, it happens; on the other hand, any event chancing to occur without the guidance of natural laws is uncaused and totally "random." This leads to the determinacy-versus-randomness dichotomy already discussed in connection with the containment and utility problems.

Because of these criteria, what science calls a "law of nature" is typically an autonomous relationship of first-order properties of physical objects, and likewise for the laws of state transformation that govern causation. There can be little doubt that science has succeeded in identifying a useful set of such laws. Whether or not they suffice for a full description of nature and causality (and they do not), they are an important part of the total picture; wherever possible, they should indeed be tracked down and exploited to their full descriptive and prescriptive potential. But at least one caveat is in order: they should be regarded as explaining *only that which they can be empirically and/or rationally shown to explain.* As with any other scientific assertion, they must be kept pure of any metaphysical prejudice tending to artificially inflate their scope or explanatory weight.

It is thus a matter of no small concern that in pursuing its policy of causal simplification, the scientific mainstream seems to have smuggled into its baggage compartment a certain piece of contraband which appears, despite its extreme resistance to rational or empirical justification, to be masquerading as a tacit "meta-law of nature." It states that every higher-order relationship of objects and events in nature, regardless of complexity or level of dynamic integration, *must* be strictly determined by globally distributed laws of nature acting independently on each of its individual components. Along with the other items on the neo-Laplacian wish-list of causal conveniences to which the scientific mainstream insists that nature be held, this criterion betrays a marked preference for a "bottom-up" approach to causation, suggesting that it be called the *bottom-up thesis*.[49]

The bottom-up thesis merely underscores something that we already know about the scientific mainstream: it wants with all of its might to believe that in principle, the whole destiny of the natural world and everything in it can be exhaustively predicted and explained on the basis of (1) a Laplacian snapshot of its current details, and (2) a few distributed laws of nature from which to exhaustively develop the implications. So irresistable is this desire that some of those caught in its grip are willing to make a pair of extraordinary claims. The first is that science has completely explained some of nature's most complex systems in terms of microscopic random events *simply by generically classifying the microscopic events that might possibly have been involved in their realization*. The second is that observed distributions of such events, which they again call "random," prove that no system in nature, regardless of its complexity, has ever come into being from the top down.

The genotype-to-phenotype mapping is a case in point. Many neo-Darwinists seem to have inferred that what happens near the endpoints of this mapping—the seemingly random mutation of genotypes and the brutal, deterministic competition among phenotypes—offers more insight regarding nature and causality than does the delicate, exquisitely complex ontogenic symphony performed by the mapping itself. In response to the observation that the theoretical emphasis has been lopsided, one hears that *of course* neo-Darwinists acknowledge the involvement of intermediate processes in the emergence of biological complexity from strings of DNA. For are not genes translated into proteins, which fold into functional forms and interact with other molecules to alter the patterns and timing of gene expression, which can lead to cytodifferentiation, pattern formation, morphogenesis and so on, and is this whole self-organizational process not highly sensitive to developmental interactions with the environment?

Unfortunately, where the acknowledged processes and interactions are still assumed to be micro-causal and deterministic, the acknowledgement is meaningless. In fact, the higher-order structure and processing of complex biological systems has only been shoveled into an unkempt pile sexily labeled "emergent phenomena" and bulldozed across the interdisciplinary divide into complex systems theory. Thus begins a ramose paper trail supposedly leading to the final owners of the explanatory debt, but instead looping, dead-ending, or petering out in interdisciplinary limbo. The explanatory buck is thereby passed into oblivion, and the bottom-up thesis rolls like righteous thunder over any voice daring to question it.

In fact, the top-down and bottom-up approaches to causality are not as antithetical as they might seem. In the bottom-up view of causality, states evolve according to laws of nature in a temporal direction preferred by the second law of thermodynamics, which holds true under the assumption that physical states are governed by laws of nature independent of state (and particularly of complex patterns among states). But this assumption can hold only up to a point, for while the prevailing model universe supports only a bottom-up form of causation in which complex patterns among states are strictly determined by invariant functions of the states of individual objects, the situation is dramatically reversed with respect to cosmology. Because cosmological causal regression terminates with an ancestral cosmic singularity representing the whole of nature while excluding all details regarding its localized internal states, standard cosmology ultimately supports *only* a top-down approach. The natural affinity of the cosmos for top-down causation— the fact that it is *itself* an instance of top-down causation—effectively relegates bottom-up causation to secondary status, ruling out the bottom-up thesis and thus making room for a new model universe supporting and reconciling both approaches.

It turns out that in a certain kind of model universe, the top-down and bottom-up approaches are to some degree mutually transparent.[50] Two necessary features of such a model universe are (1) sufficient causal freedom to yield probabilistic resources in useful amounts, and (2) structural support for metacausal access to those resources. As it happens, a well-known ingredient of nature, *quantum uncertainty*, provides the required sort of causal freedom. But while nature exhibits quantum uncertainty in abundance and can thus generate probabilistic resources at a certain respectable rate, the prevailing model universe supports neither metacausal relationships nor sufficient access to these resources. In fact, it fails to adequately support even quantum mechanics itself.

The new model universe must remedy these shortcomings. But how?

SYNTHESIS: SOME ESSENTIAL FEATURES OF A
UNIFYING MODEL OF NATURE AND CAUSALITY

Classical mechanics, inarguably one of the most successful theories in history, is often cited as a model of theoretical progress in the sciences. When certain problems arose that could not be solved within its conceptual framework, it was extended to create a *metatheory* in which it exists as a "limiting case." In fact, this was done three times in fairly rapid succession. The first extension created the Special Theory of Relativity, in which classical mechanics holds as a low-to-medium velocity limit. The second created the General Theory of Relativity, in the curved spacetime manifold of which the flat Minkowskian manifold of Special Relativity holds as an inertial, non-gravitational limit. And the third created quantum mechanics, in which observable reality exists as a "decoherence limit."[51] Indeed, whenever a theory is extended by adjoining to it one or more new concepts, this creates a metatheory expressing the relationship between the adjoint concept(s) and the original theory.

The model universe of neo-Darwinism is a special-purpose refinement of the continuous coordinate spaces of classical mechanics, and its causal limitations are shared with most other scientific theories. This is because most sciences, not including certain branches of physics and engineering, have been unable to absorb and utilize the relativistic and quantum extensions of the classical model, each of which shares many of the same difficulties with causality. It follows that another extension is required, and since neo-Darwinism, minus its inessential philosophical baggage, holds true within a limited causal domain, it must hold in this extension as a limiting case. In other words, *causality* must become the objective, invariant limit of *metacausality.*

Such an extension has already been described,[52] and it embodies solutions for all of the problems discussed in this paper. Concisely, it embeds physical reality in an extended logico-algebraic structure, a *Self-Configuring Self-Processing Language* or SCSPL. SCSPL incorporates a pregeometric[53] *conspansive manifold* in which the classical spacetime manifold is embedded as a limiting configuration. SCSPL brings formal and physical causality into seamless conjunction by generically equating the laws of nature with SCSPL syntax, and then contracting the semantic, model-theoretic correspondence between syntax and state (or laws and observables)[54] so that they coincide in *syntactic operators*, or physical quanta of self-transducing information. Through properties called *hology* (syntactic self-similarity) and *triality* (space-time-object conflation), total systemic self-containment is achieved. In particular, the system is self-deterministically closed under causation.

SCSPL evolves by *telic recursion*, a higher-order process[55] of which causality is the physical limit (as required). In standard causality, physical states evolve according to laws of nature; in telic recursion, syntax-state relationships evolve by maximization of intrinsic utility. The temporal phase of telic recursion is *conspansion*, a dual-aspect process co-ordinating formal/telic and physical modes of evolution. By virtue of *conspansive duality*, SCSPL simultaneously evolves like a (metacausal, telic-recursive) generative grammar and a physical dynamical system, at once implementing top-down metacausation and bottom-up causation. Conspansion involves an alternation between *self-replication* and *self-selection*, thus constituting a generalization of Darwinian evolution in which specificational and replicational probabilistic resources are rationally linked. In this way, neo-Darwinist and design-theoretic (bottom-up and top-down) modes of causality become recognizable as complementary aspects of a single comprehensive evolutionary process.

From a formal standpoint, SCSPL has several unique and interesting features. Being based on logic,[56] it identifies itself with the logical syntax of its perceptual universe on grounds of logical-perceptual isomorphism. This eliminates the conventional model-theoretic distinctions among theory, universe, and theory-universe correspondence, contracting the problematic mapping between abstract and concrete reality on the syntactic (nomological) level. This brings the physical world into coincidence with its logical counterpart, effecting dual-aspect monism and putting logical attributes on the same explanatory footing as physical attributes. SCSPL thus adjoins logic to nature, injecting[57] nature with the abstract logical infrastructure of perception and theorization and endowing physical reality with the remedial conceptual apparatus demanded by the problems, paradoxes, and explanatory deficiencies straining its classical descriptions. At the same time, it adjoins nature to logic in the form of perceptual categories and necessary high-level theoretical properties including closure, comprehensiveness, consistency, and teleo-nomological coherence, thus opening logical routes to physical insight.

SCSPL offers yet further advantages. In defining nature to include logic and cognition, it relates physics and mathematics on a basic level, thus merging the rational foundations of mathematics with the perceptual foundations of physics and letting each provide crucial support for the other. By affording an integrated conceptual framework for prior conflicting extensions of classical reality, it sets the stage for their ultimate reconciliation. And its cross-interpretation of the cognitive and physical aspects of nature renders the universe *self-explaining* and *self-modeling*, thus effecting self-containment on the theoretic and model-theoretic levels. That is, SCSPL self-containment effects not just causal and generative closure, but closure under the inverse operations of explanation and interpretation, thus permitting nature to physically model and teleo-nomologically justify its own self-configurative determinations. In SCSPL, natural laws and physical states are seen as expressions of the intrinsic utility *of* nature *by* and *for* nature.

The reflexive self-processing and (telic) self-configuration functions of SCSPL imply that nature possesses generalized functional analogues of human self-awareness and volition, and thus a generalized capacity for utilitarian self-design. The self-design and self-modeling capacity of nature suggests that the universe is a kind of stratified "self-simulation" in which the physical and logico-telic aspects of reality can be regarded as respectively "simulated" and "simulative" in a generalized quantum-computational sense. This makes SCSPL relevant to self-organization, emergence, and other complexity-theoretic phenomena that are increasingly attractive to the proponents of neo-Darwinism and other causally-challenged theories. At the same time, the fact that SCSPL evolution is both nomologically coherent and subject to a rational intrinsic utility criterion implies that the universe possesses properties equivalent to generalized intelligence, suggesting the possibility of an integrated SCSPL approach to the problems of consciousness and evolution.

The overall theory which logically extends the concepts of nature and causality to SCSPL and telic recursion, thereby merging the perceptual manifold with its cognitive and telic infrastructure, is known as the *Cognitive-Theoretic Model of the Universe* or CTMU; its approach to biological origins and evolution is called *Teleologic Evolution*.[58] Based on the concept of telic-recursive metacausation, a generative process in which SCSPL syntax and state are dynamically linked, Teleologic Evolution is a dynamic interplay of replication and selection through which the universe creates itself and the life it contains. Teleologic Evolution is a stratified process which occurs on levels respectively associated with the evolution of the cosmos and the evolution of life, thus permitting organic evolution to mirror that of the universe in which it occurs. It improves on traditional approaches to teleology by extending the concept of *nature* in a way that eliminates any need for "supernatural" intervention, and it improves on neo-Darwinism by addressing nature and its causal dynamics to the fullest possible extent.

Because of their implicit reliance on different models of causality, teleology and evolution were once considered mutually exclusory. While teleology appears to require a looping kind of causality consistent with the idea that ends are immanent in nature (even in beginnings), evolution seems to require that mutation and natural selection exhibit some combination of nondeterminacy and linear determinacy. In contrast, the phrase *Teleologic Evolution* reflects their complementarity within a coherent self-configurative ensemble that identifies nature with its own utilitarian self-actualization imperative. In the associated metacausal extension of physical reality, the two central processes of evolution, replication and selection, are seen to occur on at least two mutually-facilitative levels respectively associated with the evolution of the universe and that of organic life.[59] Meanwhile, the intrinsic utility criterion of cosmic self-selection implies that nature, as rationally defined in the CTMU, possesses a generalized form of intelligence by which all levels of evolution are driven and directed, equating selection with specification and metacausally relating it to replication.[60] Reality is united with its generative principle by the rational linkage between the domain and codomain of the teleological, meta-Darwinian level of natural selection.

Where nature consists of all that is logically relevant to perception, and logic consists of the rules of thought and therefore comprises an essential theory of cognition, the CTMU couples mind and nature in a way suggestive of Ouroboros divided and reunited—two intimately entwined constrictors, estranged centuries ago by mind-body dualism but now locked in a renewed embrace, each swallowing the other's entailments. Perhaps this reunion will deter the militant torch-bearers of scientific naturalism from further reneging on their explanatory debts and fleecing mankind of its millennial hopes and dreams after all. And if so, then perhaps we can snuff the rapidly dwindling fuse of our insidious ontological identity crisis while these hopes and dreams still have a fighting chance of realization, and the intrinsic utility of our species remains salvageable.

David Berlinski

14. The Deniable Darwin

The Fossil Record Is Incomplete, the Reasoning Flawed: Is the Theory of Evolution Fit to Survive?

Charles Darwin presented *On the Origin of Species* to a disbelieving world in 1859—three years after Clerk Maxwell had published "On Faraday's Lines of Force," the first of his papers on the electromagnetic field. Maxwell's theory has by a process of absorption become part of quantum field theory, and so a part of the great canonical structure created by mathematical physics. By contrast, the final triumph of Darwinian theory, although vividly imagined by biologists, remains, along with world peace and Esperanto, on the eschatological horizon of contemporary thought.

"It is just a matter of *time*," one biologist wrote recently, reposing his faith in a receding hereafter, "before this fruitful concept comes to be accepted by the public as wholeheartedly as it has accepted the spherical earth and the sun-centered solar system." Time, however, is what evolutionary biologists have long had, and if general acceptance has not come by now, it is hard to know when it ever will.

In its most familiar, textbook form, Darwin's theory subordinates itself to a haunting and fantastic image, one in which life on earth is represented as a tree. So graphic has this image become that some biologists have persuaded themselves they can *see* the flowering tree standing on a dusty plain, the mammalian twig obliterating itself by anastomosis into a reptilian branch and so backward to the amphibia and then the fish, the sturdy chordate line—our line, *cosa nostra*—moving by slithering stages into the still more primitive trunk of life and so downward to the single irresistible cell that from within its folded chromosomes foretold the living future.

This is nonsense, of course. That densely reticulated tree, with its lavish foliage, is an intellectual construct, one expressing the *hypothesis* of descent with modification. Evolution is a process, one stretching over four billion years. It has not been observed. The past has gone to where the past inevitably goes. The future has not arrived. The present reveals only the detritus of time and chance: the fossil record, and the comparative anatomy, physiology, and biochemistry of different organisms and creatures. Like every other scientific theory, the theory of evolution lies at the end of an inferential trail.

The facts in favor of evolution are often held to be incontrovertible; prominent biologists shake their heads at the obduracy of those who would dispute them. Those facts, however, have been rather less forthcoming than evolutionary biologists might have hoped. If life progressed by an accumulation of small changes, as they say it has, the fossil record should reflect its flow, the dead stacked up in barely separated strata. But for well over 150 years, the dead have been remarkably diffident about confirming Darwin's theory. Their bones lie suspended in the sands of time—theromorphs and therapsids and things that must have gibbered and then squeaked; but there are gaps in the graveyard, places where there should be intermediate forms but where there is nothing whatsoever instead.[1]

Before the Cambrian era, a brief 600 million years ago, very little is inscribed in the fossil record; but then, signaled by what I imagine as a spectral puff of smoke and a deafening *ta-da!*, an astonishing number of novel biological structures come into creation, and they come into creation at once.

Thereafter, the major transitional sequences are incomplete. Important inferences begin auspiciously, but then trail off, the ancestral connection between *Eusthenopteron* and *Ichthyostega*, for example— the great hinge between the fish and the amphibia—turning on the interpretation of small grooves within *Eusthenopteron's* intercalary bones. Most species enter the evolutionary order fully formed and then depart unchanged. Where there should be evolution, there is *stasis* instead— the term is used by the paleontologists Stephen Jay Gould and Niles Eldredge in developing their theory of "punctuated equilibria"—with the fire alarms of change going off suddenly during a long night in which nothing happens.

The fundamental core of Darwinian doctrine, the philosopher Daniel Dennett has buoyantly affirmed, "is no longer in dispute among scientists." Such is the party line, useful on those occasions when biologists must present a single face to their public. But it was to the dead that Darwin pointed for confirmation of his theory; the fact that pale-ontology does not entirely support his doctrine has been a secret of long standing among paleontologists. "The known fossil record," Steven Stanley observes, "fails to document a single example of phyletic evolu-tion accomplishing a major morphologic transition and hence offers no evidence that the gradualistic model can be valid."

Small wonder, then, that when the spotlight of publicity is dimmed, evolutionary biologists evince a feral streak, Stephen Jay Gould, Niles Eldredge, Richard Dawkins, and John Maynard Smith abusing one an-other roundly like wrestlers grappling in the dark.

Pause for the Logician

Swimming in the soundless sea, the shark has survived for millions of years, sleek as a knife blade and twice as dull. *The shark is an organism wonderfully adapted to its environment.* Pause. And then the bright brittle voice of logical folly intrudes: *after all, it has survived for millions of years.*

This exchange should be deeply embarrassing to evolutionary bi-ologists. And yet, time and again, biologists do explain the survival of an organism by reference to its fitness and the fitness of an organism by reference to its survival, the friction between concepts kindling nothing more illuminating than the observation that some creatures have been around for a very long time. "Those individuals that have the most off-spring," writes Ernst Mayr, the distinguished zoologist, "are by defini-tion . . . the fittest ones." And in *Evolution and the Myth of Creation-ism*, Tim Berra states that "[f]itness in the Darwinian sense means re-productive fitness—leaving at least enough offspring to spread or sus-tain the species in nature."

This is not a parody of evolutionary thinking; it *is* evolutionary thinking. *Que sera, sera.*

Evolutionary thought is suffused in general with an unwholesome glow. "The belief that an organ so perfect as the eye," Darwin wrote, "could have been formed by natural selection is enough to stagger any-one." It is. The problem is obvious. "What good," Stephen Jay Gould asked dramatically, "is 5 percent of an eye?" He termed this question "excellent."

The question, retorted the Oxford professor Richard Dawkins, the most prominent representative of ultra-Darwinians, "is not excellent at all": "Vision that is 5 percent as good as yours or mine is very much worth having in comparison with no vision at all. And 6 percent is better than 5, 7 percent better than 6, and so on up the gradual, continuous series."

But Dawkins, replied Phillip Johnson in turn, had carelessly assumed that 5 percent *of* an eye would see 5 percent as well *as* an eye, and that is an assumption for which there is little evidence. (A professor of law at the University of California at Berkeley, Johnson has a gift for appealing to the evidence when his opponents invoke theory, and vice versa.)

Having been conducted for more than a century, exchanges of this sort may continue for centuries more; but the debate is an exercise in irrelevance. What is at work in sight is a visual *system*, one that involves not only the anatomical structures of the eye and forebrain, but the remarkably detailed and poorly understood algorithms required to make these structures work. "When we examine the visual mechanism closely," Karen K. de Valois remarked recently in *Science*, "although we understand much about its component parts, we fail to fathom the ways in which they fit together to produce the whole of our complex visual perception."

These facts suggest a chastening reformulation of Gould's "excellent" question, one adapted to reality: *could a system we do not completely understand be constructed by means of a process we cannot completely specify?*

The intellectually responsible answer to *this* question is that we do not know—we have no way of knowing. But that is not the answer evolutionary theorists accept. According to Daniel Dennett (in *Darwin's Dangerous Idea*), Dawkins is "almost certainly right" to uphold the incremental view, because "Darwinism is basically on the right track." In this, he echoes the philosopher Kim Sterelny, who is also persuaded that "something like Dawkins's stories *have got to be right*" (emphasis added). After all, he asserts, "natural selection is the only possible explanation of complex adaptation."

Dawkins himself has maintained that those who do not believe a complex biological structure may be constructed in small steps are expressing merely their own sense of "personal incredulity." But in countering their animadversions, he appeals to his own ability to believe almost anything. Commenting on the (very plausible) claim that spiders could not have acquired their web-spinning behavior by a Darwinian mechanism, Dawkins writes: "It is not impossible at all. That is what I firmly believe and I have some experience of spiders and their webs." It is painful to see this advanced as an argument.

UNFLAGGING SUCCESS

Darwin conceived of evolution in terms of *small* variations among organisms, variations which by a process of accretion allow one species to change continuously into another. This suggests a view in which living creatures are spread out smoothly over the great manifold of biological possibilities, like colors merging imperceptibly in a color chart.

Life, however, is absolutely nothing like this. Wherever one looks there is singularity, quirkiness, oddness, defiant individuality, and just plain weirdness. The male redback spider (*Latrodectus hasselti*), for example, is often consumed during copulation. Such is sexual cannibalism—the result, biologists have long assumed, of "predatory females overcoming the defenses of weaker males." But it now appears that among *Latrodectus hasselti*, the male is complicit in his own consumption. Having achieved intromission, this schnook performs a characteristic somersault, placing his abdomen directly over his partner's mouth. Such is sexual suicide—awfulness taken to a higher power.[2]

It might seem that sexual suicide confers no advantage on the spider, the male passing from ecstasy to extinction in the course of one and the same act. But spiders willing to pay for love are apparently favored by female spiders (no surprise, there); and female spiders with whom they mate, entomologists claim, are less likely to mate again. The male spider perishes; his preposterous line persists.

This explanation resolves one question only at the cost of inviting another: why such bizarre behavior? In no other *Latrodectus* species does the male perform that obliging somersault, offering his partner the oblation of his life as well as his love. Are there general principles that specify sexual suicide among this species, but that forbid sexual suicide elsewhere? If so, what are they?

Once asked, such questions tend to multiply like party guests. If evolutionary theory cannot answer them, what, then, is its use? Why is the pitcher plant carnivorous, but not the thorn bush, and why does the Pacific salmon require fresh water to spawn, but not the Chilean sea bass? Why has the British thrush learned to hammer snails upon rocks, but not the British blackbird, which often starves to death in the midst of plenty? Why did the firefly discover bioluminescence, but not the wasp or the warrior ant; why do the bees do their dance, but not the spider or the flies; and why are women, but not cats, born without the sleek tails that would make them even more alluring than they already are?

Why? Yes, *why*? The question, simple, clear, intellectually respectable, was put to the Nobel laureate George Wald. "Various organisms try various things," he finally answered, his words functioning as a verbal shrug, "they keep what works and discard the rest."

But suppose the manifold of life were to be given a good solid yank, so that the Chilean sea bass but not the Pacific salmon required fresh water to spawn, or that ants but not fireflies flickered enticingly at twilight, or that women but not cats were born with lush tails. What then? An inversion of life's fundamental facts would, I suspect, present evolutionary biologists with few difficulties. *Various organisms try various things.* This idea is adapted to any contingency whatsoever, an interesting example of a Darwinian mechanism in the development of Darwinian thought itself.

A comparison with geology is instructive. No geological theory makes it possible to specify precisely a particular mountain's shape; but the underlying process of upthrust and crumbling is well understood, and geologists can specify something like a mountain's *generic* shape. This provides geological theory with a firm connection to reality. A mountain arranging itself in the shape of the letter "A" is not a physically possible object; it is excluded by geological theory.

The theory of evolution, by contrast, is incapable of ruling *anything* out of court. That job must be done by nature. But a theory that can confront any contingency with unflagging success cannot be falsified. Its control of the facts is an illusion.

SHEER DUMB LUCK

"Chance alone," the Nobel Prize-winning chemist Jacques Monod once wrote, "is at the source of every innovation, of all creation in the biosphere. Pure chance, absolutely free but blind, is at the very root of the stupendous edifice of creation."

The sentiment expressed by these words has come to vex evolutionary biologists. "This belief," Richard Dawkins writes, "that Darwinian evolution is 'random,' is not merely false. It is the exact opposite of the truth." But Monod is right and Dawkins wrong. Chance lies at the beating heart of evolutionary theory, just as it lies at the beating heart of thermodynamics.

It is the second law of thermodynamics that holds dominion over the temporal organization of the universe, and what the law has to say we find verified by ordinary experience at every turn. Things fall apart. Energy, like talent, tends to squander itself. Liquids go from hot to lukewarm. And so does love. Disorder and despair overwhelm the human enterprise, filling our rooms and our lives with clutter. Decay is unyielding. Things go from bad to worse. And overall, they go *only* from bad to worse.

These grim certainties the second law abbreviates in the solemn and awful declaration that the entropy of the universe is tending toward a maximum. The final state in which entropy is maximized is simply more *likely* than any other state. The disintegration of my face reflects nothing more compelling than the odds. Sheer dumb luck.

But if things fall apart, they also come together. *Life* appears to offer at least a temporary rebuke to the second law of thermodynamics. Although biologists are unanimous in arguing that evolution has no goal, fixed from the first, it remains true nonetheless that living creatures have organized themselves into ever more elaborate and flexible structures. If their complexity is increasing, the entropy that surrounds them is decreasing. Whatever the universe-as-a-whole may be doing—time fusing incomprehensibly with space, the great stars exploding indignantly—*biologically* things have gone from bad to better, the show organized, or so it would seem, as a counterexample to the prevailing winds of fate.

How so? The question has historically been the pivot on which the assumption of religious belief has turned. How so? "God said: 'Let the waters swarm with swarms of living creatures, and let fowl fly above the earth in the open firmament of heaven.'" That is how so. And who on the basis of experience would be inclined to disagree? The structures of life are complex, and complex structures get made in this, the purely human world, only by a process of deliberate design. An act of intelligence is required to bring even a thimble into being; why should the artifacts of life be different?

Darwin's theory of evolution rejects this counsel of experience and intuition. Instead, the theory forges, at least in spirit, a perverse connection with the second law itself, arguing that precisely the same force that explains one turn of the cosmic wheel explains another: sheer dumb luck.

If the universe is for reasons of sheer dumb luck committed ultimately to a state of cosmic listlessness, it is *also* by sheer dumb luck that life first emerged on earth, the chemicals in the pre-biotic seas or soup illuminated and then invigorated by a fateful flash of lightning. It is again by sheer dumb luck that the first self-reproducing systems were created. The dense and ropy chains of RNA—*they* were created by sheer dumb luck, and sheer dumb luck drove the primitive chemicals of life to form a living cell. It is sheer dumb luck that alters the genetic message so that, from infernal nonsense, meaning for a moment emerges; and sheer dumb luck again that endows life with its *opportunities*, the space of possibilities over which natural selection plays, sheer dumb luck creating the mammalian eye and the marsupial pouch, sheer dumb luck again endowing the elephant's sensitive nose with nerves and the orchid's translucent petal with blush.

Amazing. *Sheer dumb luck.*

LIFE, COMPLEX LIFE

Physicists are persuaded that things are in the end simple; biologists that they are not. A good deal depends on where one looks. Wherever the biologist looks, there is complexity beyond complexity, the entanglement of things ramifying downward from the organism to the cell. In a superbly elaborated figure, the Australian biologist Michael Denton compares a single cell to an immense automated factory, one the size of a large city:

> On the surface of the cell we would see millions of openings, like the portholes of a vast space ship, opening and closing to allow a continual stream of materials to flow in and out. If we were to enter one of these openings we would find ourselves in a world of supreme technology and bewildering complexity. We would see endless highly organized corridors and conduits branching in every direction away from the perimeter of the cell, some leading to the central memory bank in the nucleus and others to assembly plants and processing units. The nucleus itself would be a vast spherical chamber more than a kilometer in diameter, resembling a geodesic dome inside of which we would see, all neatly stacked together in ordered arrays, the miles of coiled chains of the DNA molecule. . . . We would notice that the simplest of the functional components of the cell, the protein molecules, were, astonishingly, complex pieces of molecular machinery. . . . Yet the life of the cell depends on the integrated activities of thousands, certainly tens, and probably hundreds of thousands of different protein molecules.

And whatever the complexity of the cell, it is insignificant in comparison with the mammalian nervous system; and beyond that, far impossibly ahead, there is the human mind, an instrument like no other in the biological world, conscious, flexible, penetrating, inscrutable, and profound.

It is here that the door of doubt begins to swing. *Chance* and *complexity* are countervailing forces; they work at cross-purposes. This circumstance the English theologian William Paley (1743–1805) made the gravamen of his well-known argument from design:

> Nor would any man in his senses think the existence of the watch, with its various machinery, accounted for, by being told that it was one out of possible combinations of material forms; that whatever he had found in the place where he found the watch, must have contained some internal configuration or other, and that this configuration might be the structure now exhibited, viz., of the works of a watch, as well as a different structure.

It is worth remarking, it is simply a *fact,* that this courtly and old-fashioned argument is entirely compelling. We *never* attribute the existence of a complex artifact to chance. And for obvious reasons: complex objects are useful islands, isolated amid an archipelago of useless possibilities. Of the thousands of ways in which a watch might be assembled from its constituents, only one is liable to work. It is unreasonable to attribute the existence of a watch to chance, if only because it is *unlikely.* An artifact is the overflow in matter of the mental motions of intention, deliberate design, planning, and coordination. The inferential spool runs backward, and it runs irresistibly from a complex object to the contrived, the artificial, circumstances that brought it into being.

Paley allowed the conclusion of his argument to drift from man-made to biological artifacts, a human eye or kidney falling under the same classification as a watch. "Every indication of contrivance," he wrote, "every manifestation of design, exists in the works of nature; with the difference, on the side of nature, of being greater or more, and that in a degree which exceeds all computation."

In this drifting, Darwinists see dangerous signs of a non sequitur. There *is* a tight connection, they acknowledge, between what a watch is and how it is made; but the connection unravels at the human eye—or any other organ, disposition, body plan, or strategy—if only because another and a simpler explanation is available. Among living creatures, say Darwinists, *the design persists even as the designer disappears.*

"Paley's argument," Dawkins writes, "is made with passionate sincerity and is informed by the best biological scholarship of his day, but it is wrong, gloriously and utterly wrong."

The enormous confidence this quotation expresses must be juxtaposed against the weight of intuition it displaces. It is true that intuition is often wrong—quantum theory is intuition's graveyard. But quantum theory is remote from experience; our intuitions in biology lie closer to the bone. We are ourselves such stuff as genes are made on, and while this does not establish that our assessments of time and chance must be correct, it does suggest that they may be pertinent.

THE BOOK OF LIFE

The discovery of DNA by James D. Watson and Francis Crick in 1952 revealed that a living creature is an organization of matter orchestrated by a genetic text. Within the bacterial cell, for example, the book of life is written in a distinctive language. The book is read aloud, its message specifying the construction of the cell's constituents, and then the book is copied, passed faithfully into the future.

This striking metaphor introduces a troubling instability, a kind of tremor, into biological thought. With the discovery of the genetic code, every living creature comes to divide itself into alien realms: the alphabetic and the organismic. The realms are conceptually distinct, responding to entirely different imperatives and constraints. An alphabet, on the one hand, belongs to the class of finite combinatorial objects, things that are discrete and that fit together in highly circumscribed ways. An organism, on the other hand, traces a continuous figure in space and in time. How, then, are these realms coordinated?

I ask the question because in similar systems, coordination is crucial. When I use the English language, the rules of grammar act as a constraint on the changes that I might make to the letters or sounds I employ. This is something we take for granted, an ordinary miracle in which I pass from one sentence to the next, almost as if crossing an abyss by means of a series of well-placed stepping stones.

In living creatures, things evidently proceed otherwise. There is *no* obvious coordination between alphabet and organism; the two objects are governed by different conceptual regimes, and that apparently is the end of it. Under the pressures of competition, the orchid *Orphrys apifera* undergoes a statistically adapted drift, some incidental feature in its design becoming over time ever more refined, until, consumed with longing, a misguided bee amorously mounts the orchid's very petals, convinced that he has seen shimmering there a female's fragile genitalia. As this is taking place, the marvelous mimetic design maturing slowly, the orchid's underlying alphabetic system undergoes a series of *random* perturbations, letters in its genetic alphabet winking off or winking on in a way utterly independent of the grand convergent progression toward perfection taking place out there where the action is.

We do not understand, we cannot re-create, a system of this sort. However it may operate in life, randomness in language is the enemy of order, a way of annihilating meaning. And not only in language, but in any language-*like* system—computer programs, for example. The alien influence of randomness in such systems was first noted by the distinguished French mathematician M. P. Schützenberger, who also marked the significance of this circumstance for evolutionary theory. "If we try to simulate such a situation," he wrote, "by making changes randomly . . . on computer programs, we find that we have no chance . . . even to see what the modified program would compute; it just jams.[3]

PLANETS OF POSSIBILITY

This is not yet an argument, only an expression of intellectual unease; but the unease tends to build as analogies are amplified. The general issue is one of size and space, and the way in which something small may be found amidst something very big.

Linguists in the 1950s, most notably Noam Chomsky and George Miller, asked dramatically how many grammatical English sentences could be constructed with 100 letters. Approximately ten to the twenty-fifth power, they answered. This is a very large number. But a sentence is one thing; a sequence, another. A sentence obeys the laws of English grammar; a sequence is lawless and comprises any concatenation of those 100 letters. If there are roughly ten to the twenty-fifth power sentences at hand, the number of sequences 100 letters in length is, by way of contrast, twenty-six to the 100th power. This is an inconceivably greater number. The space of possibilities has blown up, the explosive process being one of *combinatorial inflation.*

Now, the vast majority of sequences drawn on a finite alphabet fail to make a statement: they consist of letters arranged to no point or purpose. It is the contrast between sentences and sequences that carries the full, critical weight of memory and intuition. Organized as a writhing ball, the sequences resemble a planet-sized object, one as large as pale Pluto. Landing almost anywhere on that planet, linguists see nothing but nonsense. Meaning resides with the *grammatical* sequences, but they, those *sentences*, occupy an area no larger than a dime.

How on earth could the sentences be *discovered by chance* amid such an infernal and hyperborean immensity of gibberish? They cannot be discovered by chance, and, of course, chance plays no role in their discovery. The linguist or the native English-speaker moves around the place or planet with a perfectly secure sense of where he should go, and what he is apt to see.

The eerie and unexpected presence of an alphabet in every living creature might suggest the possibility of a similar argument in biology. It is DNA, of course, that acts as life's primordial text, the code itself organized in nucleic triplets, like messages in Morse code. Each triplet is matched to a particular chemical object, an amino acid. There are twenty such acids in all. They correspond to letters in an alphabet. As the code is read somewhere in life's hidden housing, the linear order of the nucleic acids induces a corresponding linear order in the amino acids. The biological finger writes, and what the cell reads is an ordered presentation of such amino acids—a protein.

Like the nucleic acids, proteins are alphabetic objects, composed of discrete constituents. On average, proteins are roughly 250 amino acid residues in length, so a given protein may be imagined as a long biochemical word, one of many.

The aspects of an analogy are now in place. What is needed is a relevant contrast, something comparable to sentences and sequences in language. Of course nothing completely comparable is at hand: there are *no* sentences in molecular biology. Nonetheless, there is this fact, helpfully recounted by Richard Dawkins: "The actual animals that have ever lived on earth are a tiny subset of the theoretical animals that *could* exist." It follows that over the course of four billion years, life has expressed itself by means of a particular stock of proteins, a certain set of life-like words.

A combinatorial count is now possible. The MIT physicist Murray Eden, to whom I owe this argument, estimates the number of the viable proteins at ten to the fiftieth power. Within this set is the raw material of everything that has ever lived: the flowering plants and the alien insects and the seagoing turtles and the sad shambling dinosaurs, the great evolutionary successes and the great evolutionary failures as well. These creatures are, quite literally, composed of the proteins that over the course of time have performed some useful function, with "usefulness" now standing for the sense of sentencehood in linguistics.

As in the case of language, what has once lived occupies some corner in the space of a larger array of possibilities, the actual residing in the shadow of the possible. The space of all *possible* proteins of a fixed length (250 residues, recall) is computed by multiplying twenty by itself 250 times (twenty to the 250th power). It is idle to carry out the calculation. The number is larger by far than seconds in the history of the world since the Big Bang or grains of sand on the shores of every sounding sea. Another planet now looms in the night sky, Pluto-sized or bigger, a conceptual companion to the planet containing every sequence composed by endlessly arranging the twenty-six English letters into sequences 100 letters in length. This planetary *Doppelgänger* is the planet of all possible proteins of fixed length, the planet, in a certain sense, of every *conceivable* form of carbon-based life.

And there the two planets lie, spinning on their soundless axes. The contrast between sentences and sequences on Pluto reappears on Pluto's double as the contrast between useful protein forms and all the rest; and it reappears in terms of the same dramatic difference in numbers, the enormous (twenty to the 250th power) overawing the merely big (ten to the fiftieth power), the contrast between the two being quite literally a contrast between an immense and swollen planet and a dime's worth of area. That dime-sized corner, which on Pluto contains the English sentences, on Pluto's double contains the living creatures; and there the biologist may be seen tramping, the warm puddle of wet life achingly distinct amid the planet's snow and stray proteins. It is here that living creatures, whatever their ultimate fate, breathed and moaned and carried on, life evidently having discovered the small quiet corner of the space of possibilities in which things *work*.

It would seem that evolution, Murray Eden writes in artfully ambiguous language, "was directed toward the incredibly small proportion of useful protein forms . . . ," the word "directed" conveying, at least to me, the sobering image of a stage-managed search, with evolution bypassing the awful immensity of all that frozen space because in some sense evolution *knew* where it was going.

And yet, from the perspective of Darwinian theory, it is chance that plays the crucial—that plays the *only*—role in generating the proteins. Wandering the surface of a planet, evolution wanders blindly, having forgotten where it has been, unsure of where it is going.

The Artificer of Design

Random mutations are the great creative demiurge of evolution, throwing up possibilities and bathing life in the bright light of chance. Each living creature is not only what it is but what it might be. What, then, acts to make the possible palpable?

The theory of evolution is a materialistic theory. Various deities need not apply. Any form of mind is out. Yet a force is needed, something adequate to the manifest complexity of the biological world, and something that in the largest arena of all might substitute for the acts of design, anticipation, and memory that are obvious features of such day-to-day activities as fashioning a sentence or a sonnet.

This need is met in evolutionary theory by natural selection, the filter but not the source of change. "It may be said," Darwin wrote, "that natural selection is daily and hourly scrutinizing, throughout the world, every variation, even the slightest; rejecting that which is bad, preserving and adding up all that is good: silently and insensibly working, whenever and wherever opportunity offers, as the improvement of each organic being in relation to its organic and inorganic conditions of life." Natural selection emerges from these reflections as a strange force-like concept. It is strange because it is unconnected to any notion of force in physics, and it is force-*like* because natural selection *does* something, it has an effect and so functions as a kind of cause.[4]

Creatures, habits, organ systems, body plans, organs, and tissues are *shaped* by natural selection. Population geneticists write of selection forces, selection pressures, and coefficients of natural selection; biologists say that natural selection sculpts, shapes, coordinates, transforms, directs, controls, changes, and transfigures living creatures. It is natural selection, Richard Dawkins believes, that is the artificer of design, a cunning force that mocks human ingenuity even as it mimics it: "Charles Darwin showed how it is possible for blind physical forces to mimic the effects of conscious design, and, by operating as a cumulative filter of chance variations, to lead eventually to organized and adaptive complexity, to mosquitoes and mammoths, to humans and therefore, indirectly, to books and computers."

In affirming what Darwin showed, these words suggest that Darwin *demonstrated* the power of natural selection in some formal sense, settling the issue once and for all. But that is simply not true. When Darwin wrote, the mechanism of evolution that he proposed had only life itself to commend it. But to refer to the power of natural selection by appealing to the course of evolution is a little like confirming a story in the *New York Times* by reading it twice. The theory of evolution is, after all, a *general* theory of change; if natural selection can sift the debris of chance to fashion an elephant's trunk, should it not be able to work elsewhere—amid computer programs and algorithms, words and sentences? Skeptics require a demonstration of natural selection's cunning, one that does not involve the very phenomenon it is meant to explain.

No sooner said than done. An extensive literature is now devoted to what is optimistically called artificial life. These are schemes in which a variety of programs generate amusing computer objects and, by a process said to be similar to evolution, show that they are capable of growth and decay and even a phosphorescent simulacrum of death. An algorithm called "Face Prints," for example, has been designed to enable crime victims to identify their attackers. The algorithm runs through hundreds of facial combinations (long hair, short hair, big nose, wide chin, moles, warts, wens, wrinkles) until the indignant victim spots the resemblance between the long-haired, big-nosed, wide-chinned portrait of the perpetrator and the perpetrator himself.

It is the presence of the *human* victim in this scenario that should give pause. What is *he* doing there, complaining loudly amid those otherwise blind forces? A mechanism that requires a discerning human agent cannot be Darwinian. The Darwinian mechanism neither anticipates nor remembers. It gives no directions and makes no choices. What is unacceptable in evolutionary theory, what is strictly forbidden, is the appearance of a force with the power to survey time, a force that conserves a point or a property because it will be useful. Such a force is no longer Darwinian. How would a blind force know such a thing? And by what means could future usefulness be transmitted to the present?

If life is, as evolutionary biologists so often say, a matter merely of blind thrusting and throbbing, any definition of natural selection must plainly meet what I have elsewhere called a rule against *deferred success.*[5] It is a rule that cannot be violated with impunity; if evolutionary theory is to retain its intellectual integrity, it cannot be violated at all. But the rule is widely violated, the violations so frequent as to amount to a formal fallacy.

ADVENT OF THE HEAD MONKEY

It is Richard Dawkins's grand intention in *The Blind Watchmaker* to demonstrate, as one reviewer enthusiastically remarked, "how natural selection allows biologists to dispense with such notions as purpose and design." This he does by exhibiting a process in which the random exploration of certain possibilities, a *blind* stab here, another there, is followed by the filtering effects of natural selection, some of those stabs saved, others discarded. But could a process so conceived—a *Darwinian* process—discover a simple English sentence: a target, say, chosen from Shakespeare? The question is by no means academic. If natural selection cannot discern a simple English sentence, what chance is there that it might have discovered the mammalian eye or the system by which glucose is regulated by the liver?

A thought experiment in *The Blind Watchmaker* provides an illustration. Randomness in the experiment is conveyed by the metaphor of the monkeys, perennial favorites in the theory of probability. There they sit, simian hands curved over the keyboards of a thousand typewriters, their long agile fingers striking keys at random. It is an image of some poignancy, those otherwise intelligent apes banging away at a machine they cannot fathom; and what makes the poignancy pointed is the fact that the system of rewards by which the apes have been induced to strike the typewriter's keys is from the first rigged against them.

The probability that a monkey will strike a given letter is one in twenty-six. The typewriter has twenty-six keys: the monkey, one working finger. But a letter is not a word. Should Dawkins demand that the monkey get two English letters right, the odds against success rise with terrible inexorability from one in twenty-six to one in 676. The Shakespearean target chosen by Dawkins—"Methinks it is like a weasel"—is a six-word sentence containing twenty-eight English letters (including the spaces). It occupies an isolated point in a space of 10,000 million, million, million, million, million, million possibilities. This is a very large number; combinatorial inflation is at work. And these are very long odds. And a six-word sentence consisting of twenty-eight English letters is a very short, very simple English sentence.

Such are the fatal facts. The problem confronting the monkeys is, of course, a double one: they must, to be sure, find the right letters, but they cannot *lose* the right letters once they have found them. A random search in a space of this size is an exercise in irrelevance. This is something the monkeys appear to know.

What more, then, is expected; what more required? *Cumulative* selection, Dawkins argues—the answer offered as well by Stephen Jay Gould, Manfred Eigen, and Daniel Dennett. The experiment now proceeds in stages. The monkeys type randomly. After a time, they are allowed to survey what they have typed in order to choose the result "which *however slightly* most resembles the target phrase." It is a computer that in Dawkins's experiment performs the crucial assessments, but I prefer to imagine its role assigned to a scrutinizing monkey—the Head Monkey of the experiment. The process under way is one in which stray successes are spotted and then saved. This process is iterated and iterated again. Variations close to the target are conserved *because* they are close to the target, the Head Monkey equably surveying the scene until, with the appearance of a miracle in progress, randomly derived sentences do begin to converge on the target sentence itself.

The contrast between schemes and scenarios is striking. Acting on their own, the monkeys are adrift in fathomless possibilities, any accidental success—a pair of English-like letters—lost at once, those successes seeming like faint untraceable lights flickering over a wine-dark sea. The advent of the Head Monkey changes things entirely. Successes are *conserved* and then conserved again. The light that formerly flickered uncertainly now stays lit, a beacon burning steadily, a point of illumination. By the light of that light, other lights are lit, until the isolated successes converge, bringing order out of nothingness.

The entire exercise is, however, an achievement in self-deception. A *target* phrase? Iterations that *most resemble* the target? A Head Monkey that *measures* the distance between failure and success? If things are sightless, how is the target represented, and how is the distance between randomly generated phrases and the targets assessed? And by whom? And the Head Monkey? What of him? The mechanism of deliberate design, purged by Darwinian theory on the level of the organism, has reappeared in the description of natural selection itself, a vivid example of what Freud meant by the return of the repressed.

This is a point that Dawkins accepts without quite acknowledging, rather like a man adroitly separating his doctor's diagnosis from his own disease.[6] Nature presents life with no targets. Life shambles forward, surging here, shuffling there, the small advantages accumulating *on their own* until something novel appears on the broad evolutionary screen—an arch or an eye, an intricate pattern of behavior, the complexity characteristic of life. May we, then, see this process at work, by seeing it simulated? "Unfortunately," Dawkins writes, "I think it may be beyond my powers as a programmer to set up such a counterfeit world."[7]

This is the authentic voice of contemporary Darwinian theory. What may be illustrated by the theory does not involve a Darwinian mechanism; what involves a Darwinian mechanism cannot be illustrated by the theory.

DARWIN WITHOUT DARWINISM

Biologists often affirm that as members of the scientific community they positively welcome criticism. Nonsense. Like everyone else, biologists loathe criticism and arrange their lives so as to avoid it. Criticism has nonetheless seeped into their souls, the process of doubt a curiously Darwinian one in which individual biologists entertain minor reservations about their theory without ever recognizing the degree to which these doubts mount up to a substantial deficit. Creationism, so often the target of their indignation, is the least of their worries.

For many years, biologists have succeeded in keeping skepticism on the circumference of evolutionary thought, where paleontologists, taxonomists, and philosophers linger. But the burning fringe of criticism is now contracting, coming ever closer to the heart of Darwin's doctrine. In a paper of historic importance, Stephen Jay Gould and Richard Lewontin expressed their dissatisfaction with what they termed "just-so" stories in biology.[8]

It is by means of a just-so story, for example, that the pop biologist Elaine Morgan explains the presence in human beings of an aquatic diving reflex. An obscure primate ancestral to man, Morgan argues, was actually aquatic, having returned to the sea like the dolphin. Some time later, that primate, having tired of the water, clambered back to land, his aquatic adaptations intact. Just so.

If stories of this sort are intellectually inadequate—preposterous, in fact—some biologists are prepared to argue that they are unnecessary as well, another matter entirely. "How seriously," H. Allen Orr asked in a superb if savage review of Dennett's *Darwin's Dangerous Idea,* "should we take these endless adaptive explanations of features whose alleged Design may be illusory? Isn't there a difference between those cases where we recognize Design *before* we understand its precise significance and those cases where we try to make Design manifest *by* concocting a story? And isn't it especially worrisome that we can make up arbitrary traits faster than adaptive stories, and adaptive stories faster than experimental tests?"

The camel's lowly hump and the elephant's nose—these, Orr suggests, may well be adaptive and so designed by natural selection. But beyond the old familiar cases, life may not be designed at all, the weight of evolution borne by neutral mutations, with genes undergoing a slow but pointless drifting in time's soft currents.

Like Orr, many biologists see an acknowledgment of their doubts as a cagey, a *calculated,* concession; but cagey or not, it is a concession devastating to the larger project of Darwinian biology. Unable to say *what* evolution has accomplished, biologists now find themselves unable to say *whether* evolution has accomplished it. This leaves evolutionary theory in the doubly damned position of having compromised the concepts needed to make sense of life—complexity, adaptation, design—while simultaneously conceding that the theory does little to explain them.

No doubt, the theory of evolution will continue to play the singular role in the life of our secular culture that it has always played. The theory is unique among scientific instruments in being cherished not for what it contains, but for what it lacks. There are in Darwin's scheme no biotic laws, no *Bauplan* as in German natural philosophy, no special creation, no *élan vital*, no divine guidance or transcendental forces. The theory functions simply as a description of matter in one of its modes, and living creatures are said to be something that the gods of law indifferently sanction and allow.

"Darwin," Richard Dawkins has remarked with evident gratitude, "made it possible to be an intellectually fulfilled atheist." This is an exaggeration, of course, but one containing a portion of the truth. That Darwin's theory of evolution and biblical accounts of creation play similar roles in the human economy of belief is an irony appreciated by altogether too few biologists.

POSTSCRIPT: ON THE DERIVATION
OF *ULYSSES* FROM *DON QUIXOTE*

I imagine this story being told to me by Jorge Luis Borges one evening in a Buenos Aires café.

His voice dry and infinitely ironic, the aging, nearly blind literary master observes that "the *Ulysses*," mistakenly attributed to the Irishman James Joyce, is in fact derived from "the *Quixote*."

I raise my eyebrows.

Borges pauses to sip discreetly at the bitter coffee our waiter has placed in front of him, guiding his hands to the saucer.

"The details of the remarkable series of events in question may be found at the University of Leiden," he says. "They were conveyed to me by the Freemason Alejandro Ferri in Montevideo."

Borges wipes his thin lips with a linen handkerchief that he has withdrawn from his breast pocket.

"As you know," he continues, "the original handwritten text of the *Quixote* was given to an order of French Cistercians in the autumn of 1576."

I hold up my hand to signify to our waiter that no further service is needed.

"Curiously enough, for none of the brothers could read Spanish, the Order was charged by the Papal Nuncio, Hoyo dos Monterrey (a man of great refinement and implacable will), with the responsibility for copying the *Quixote*, the printing press having then gained no currency in the wilderness of what is now known as the department of Auvergne. Unable to speak or read Spanish, a language they not unreasonably detested, the brothers copied the *Quixote* over and over again, re-creating the text but, of course, compromising it as well, and so inadvertently discovering the true nature of authorship. Thus they created Fernando Lor's *Los Hombres d'Estado* in 1585 by means of a singular series of copying errors, and then in 1654 Juan Luis Samorza's remarkable epistolary novel *Por Favor* by the same means; and then in 1685, the errors having accumulated sufficiently to change Spanish into French, Molière's *Le Bourgeois Gentilhomme;* their copying continuous and indefatigable, the work handed down from generation to generation as a sacred but secret trust, so that in time the brothers of the monastery, known only to members of the Bourbon house and, rumor has it, the Englishman and psychic Conan Doyle, copied into creation Stendhal's *The Red and the Black* and Flaubert's *Madame Bovary;* and then as a result of a particularly significant series of errors, in which French changed into Russian, Tolstoy's *The Death of Ivan Ilyich* and *Anna Karenina.* Late in the last decade of the 19th century there suddenly emerged, in English, Oscar Wilde's *The Importance of Being Earnest,* and then the brothers, their numbers reduced by an infectious disease of mysterious origin, finally copied the *Ulysses* into creation in 1902, the manuscript lying neglected for almost thirteen years and then mysteriously making its way to Paris in 1915, just months before the British attack on the Somme, a circumstance whose significance remains to be determined."

I sit there, amazed at what Borges has recounted. "Is it your understanding, then," I ask, "that *every* novel in the West was created in this way?"

"Of course," replies Borges imperturbably. Then he adds: "Although every novel is derived directly from another novel, there is really only one novel, the *Quixote.*"

LETTERS: DAVID BERLINSKI AND CRITICS

EDITOR'S COMMENT: *When "The Deniable Darwin" appeared in the June 1996 issue of* Commentary, *it provoked an enormous response. Over thirty letters pro and con appeared in the September 1996 issue of* Commentary. *These letters, together with Berlinski's replies, totaled three times the length of Berlinski's original essay. I am including here some of the key letters critical of Berlinski's essay along with Berlinski's replies. All the letters that appear here are reprinted in their entirety and by permission of the original letter writers (occasional ellipses in the text represent* Commentary's *own editing of these letters). I've also summarized the letters by Randy Wadkins and Robert Shapiro (neither could be contacted for permission).*

David Berlinski opens the discussion:

Some readers seem to have been persuaded that in criticizing the Darwinian theory of evolution, I intended to uphold a doctrine of creationism. This is a mistake, supported by nothing that I have written.

Confronted with a complex human artifact like a watch, William Paley inquired into the source of its complexity. Insofar as such a complex object is unlikely, Paley reasoned, its existence can be explained only in terms of a human act, one in which material objects (gears, springs, levers) are deliberately arranged in a particular configuration. The same pattern of observation and inference, Paley went on to argue, indicates that complex biological structures are likewise the products of a deliberate act of design, the designer in such cases being the Christian deity.

Darwinian theorists accept the first of Paley's inferences, but reject the second. Biological artifacts are complex, they say, but not designed. Their existence may be explained in terms of random variation and natural selection. I dispute this claim, without endorsing Paley's theological inference. It is not necessary to choose between doctrines. The rational alternative to Darwin's theory is intelligent uncertainty.

H. Allen Orr:

Having thoroughly enjoyed David Berlinski's recent book, *A Tour of the Calculus,* I am not eager to squabble publicly with him. But I am afraid I must. In his article, "The Deniable Darwin" [June], Mr. Berlinski discusses an essay of mine in which I criticize an extremist style of evolutionary thinking called "adaptationism." He concludes: "Like Orr, many biologists see an acknowledgment of their doubts as a cagey, a *calculated*, concession; but cagey or not, it is a concession devastating to the larger project of Darwinian biology."

I admit I briefly enjoyed the suggestion that my essay is so clever that it manages to undermine Darwinism. But, alas, Mr. Berlinski is exaggerating just a tad. The claim that my criticism of adaptationism, or, . . . for that matter, any other biologist's criticism of any other "ism," has pulled the rug out from under Darwin is just wrong.

But Mr. Berlinski has his own, fairly novel, criticisms of Darwinism. A couple of these are very clever and, to a nonbiologist, surely seductive. I am writing, therefore, to explain why I think these criticisms are wrong.

But first a few facts. Near the beginning of his essay, Mr. Berlinski states: "Evolution is a process, one stretching over four billion years. It has not been observed." While it is true that no biologist attended the last four billion years of evolution, the claim that evolution has not been observed is simply wrong. Examples are a dime a dozen. When antibiotics were first introduced, most bacteria were susceptible. Antibiotics were handed out like candy and anyone who had read a page of Darwin could have predicted the result: now, many bacteria are resistant. And Mr. Berlinski surely knows what happened when we threw DDT at insects: they evolved insecticide resistance. On a grander scale, botanists have documented the recent evolution of new species and some species have even been recreated from their ancestors in the lab. Though hardly packing the drama of reptiles metamorphosing into mammals (but what do you expect in 100 years of observation?), these are all iron-clad—and witnessed—examples of evolution.

But on to Mr. Berlinski's more novel criticisms of Darwinism. He has two worries. First, can random changes in an "alphabetic" system (like DNA) fuel evolution? And second, if evolution is fueled by such changes, how does it know "where to go"?

Mr. Berlinski's first question is more sophisticated than it might seem. He is not just rehashing the tired argument that Darwinism depends on random mutations and that such changes cannot build something as fancy as an eye. He knows that Darwinism is not just "random mutations" but "random mutations *plus* natural selection," which is a different beast altogether. His worry is more subtle. It is this: DNA is "alphabetic," a discrete language of A's, T's, G's, and C's that somehow encodes all the designs we find in organisms. But how can random perturbations in such a language yield usable material for evolution? In every other language we know of, Mr. Berlinski writes, "randomness . . . is the enemy of order." Random changes in English yield gibberish. Random changes in computer programs are even worse: we cannot even ask what a "modified program would compute; it just jams." And so, he argues, look what Darwinism really asks of us: it demands we believe that selection uses random changes in DNA, when—by analogy with any other formal language—such changes should yield mere gibberish, hopelessly "jamming" organisms.

Mr. Berlinski's objection is one of those beautiful theories that gets killed by an ugly fact. The fact is: whether or not random DNA changes *should* invariably jam organisms, they do not. While lethal mutations— changes which so derail an organism that it dies—are common, so are mutations of such benign and subtle effect that heroic chemical measures are required just to find them. The existence of subtle, functional, *usable* mutations in DNA is a simple fact that no amount of analogizing with computer programs can make go away. That random changes in computer programs—but not DNA—invariably jam things does not show that there is something wrong with Darwinism but that there is something wrong with the analogy.

What about Mr. Berlinski's second criticism? Even if random mutation could provide usable material for evolution, how does evolution know where to go? Mr. Berlinski retells the story of the proverbial monkeys who—banging away at their typewriters—try to create a phrase from Shakespeare. In Mr. Berlinski's version, a "Head Monkey" preserves any stray letter that matches the target phrase. For the evolutionist who usually tells the story, the point is that it does not take long for this cumulative sifting process to yield the desired phrase: mutation (typing) plus selection (save the matches) works. But Mr. Berlinski is not sold: "A *target* phrase? Iterations that *most* resemble the target? A Head Monkey that *measures* the distance between success and failure? If things are sightless, how is the target represented?" The Designer, allegedly tossed out of a job by Darwinism, has apparently reappeared as the guy who erects the target and measures the distance between here and there.

Mr. Berlinski certainly shows that the monkey analogy is imperfect. But that is true of any analogy . . . and the monkey analogy captures an important part of Darwinism. It shows that, by saving favorable random changes, evolution can gradually build fancy structures. One need not wait for all the "parts" to appear miraculously at once.

But the analogy completely flubs another part of Darwinism: evolution does not, of course, work toward any "target." So how, then, does evolution know where to go? The answer is the most radical and beautiful part of Darwinism: it does not. The only thing that "guides" evolution is sheer, cold demographics. If a worm with a patch of light-sensitive tissue leaves a few more kids than a worm that cannot tell if the lights are on, that is where evolution will go. And, later, if a worm with light-sensitive tissue and a rough lens escapes a few more predators, that is where evolution will go. Despite all the loose talk (much of it, admittedly, from evolutionary biologists), evolution knows nothing of "design" and "targets." . . .

In the end, I am afraid that Mr. Berlinski's criticisms do not fare any better than those of other anti-evolutionists. I will be the first to admit, though, that Mr. Berlinski is not a traditional anti-evolutionist. I know him well enough to know that he, unlike them, is neither anti-scientific nor doctrinaire. His criticisms—like those from any good scientist—are, I think, both sincere *and* tentative.

Berlinski replies to H. Allen Orr:

In maintaining that evolution is a process that has not been observed, H. Allen Orr writes, I appear to have overlooked examples of evolution like the speckled moth, which undergoes mimetic changes in wing coloration as the result of environmental pollution, or the development of antibiotic resistance in bacteria. Mr. Orr is correct that there are such examples; I scruple only at the conclusions he draws from them. Changes in wing color and the development of drug resistance are intraspecies events. The speckled moth, after all, does not develop antlers or acquire webbed feet, and bacteria remain bacteria, even when drug-resistant. The most ardent creationists now accept micro-evolution as genuinely Darwinian events. They had better: such are the facts. But the grand evolutionary progressions, such as the transformation of a fish into a man, are examples of *macro*-evolution. They remain out of reach, accessible only at the end of an inferential trail.

In calling attention to "species [that] have even been recreated from their ancestors in the lab," Mr. Orr is, no doubt, referring to the recent work of L. H. Rieseberg and his co-workers ("Role of Gene Interaction in Hybrid Speciation: Evidence from Ancient and Experimental Hybrids," *Science* 272, 1996). The example is pertinent to my critique. Rieseberg and his co-authors reproduced under artificial conditions the genetic changes that have historically led from *H. annus* and *H. petiolaris* to *H. anomalus.* The plants in question are sunflowers. What is remarkable is the extent to which this experiment contravenes Darwinian doctrine. Given the crucial role played by random events in evolutionary theory, many biologists have drawn the conclusion that the tape of life, if rewound, would produce "a different array of evolutionary end products" (Stephen Jay Gould, *Wonderful Life*). The number of crossing schemes notwithstanding, the tape in this experiment ran to precisely the same genetic end product each time it was played.

Mr. Orr contends that in my discussion of the role played by randomness in formal systems, I appear to be upholding an analogy at the expense of the facts. Random events, he writes, *do* occur in molecular biological systems; so much the worse, then, for my analogy. But the interpretation of molecular biological facts in formal terms is hardly a matter of analogy. It is molecular biologists themselves who have found unavoidable the language of codes and codons, information, algorithms, organization, complexity, entropy, and the like. There is little by way of analogy in all this. DNA is not *like* a code; it *is* a code. It follows, then, that circumstances known to degrade meaning or information in formal systems should be the source of alarm in the context of theoretical biology.

No one denies that random events take place within molecular biological systems. The relevant question is how. In a formal context, the matter is not a mystery. Codes may be designed to remain robust in the face of background noise; what is required is redundancy, and the genetic code is, in point of fact, highly redundant. In communication systems, redundancy appears as a matter of design. It does not arise spontaneously. In the case of the genetic code, according to one commentator, "strong selection pressures" created the requisite redundancy. But this is to dispel one mystery by promoting another, as the familiar Darwinian circle again makes its appearance, the tail of one concept lodged firmly in the mouth of another. I will return to this point in a number of other responses, but let me repeat what I stressed in my essay, that I am not advancing an argument on this issue, only expressing intellectual unease.

In inserting a Head Monkey into Richard Dawkins's thought experiment, my aim was to show how the mechanism of design, purged on one level of Darwinian analysis, makes a stealthy reappearance at another. Mr. Orr is unpersuaded. "The monkey analogy," he believes, "shows that by saving favorable random changes, evolution can gradually build fancy structures." Such indeed is the perennial hope of Darwinian theorists, but Mr. Orr has, I believe, underestimated the force of my criticism. Favorable changes are one thing; changes that *will* be favorable, another. If the mechanism of Darwinian evolution is restricted to changes that are favorable at the time they are selected, I see no reason to suppose that it could produce any fancy structures whatsoever. If the mechanism is permitted to incorporate changes that are neutral at the time of selection, but that will be favorable some time in the future, I see no reason to consider the process Darwinian.

This is hardly a matter of semantics. A system conserving certain features in view of their future usefulness has access to information denied a Darwinian system; it functions by means of alien concepts. But this is precisely how Dawkins's experiment proceeds. My estimable Head Monkey conserves certain alphabetic changes because he *knows* where the experiment is going. This is forbidden knowledge; the Darwinian mechanism is blind, a point often stressed by Darwinian theorists themselves (see George C. Williams, *Natural Selection*, 1992). I develop this in more detail in responding to Randy M. Wadkins.

In his final argument, Mr. Orr repeats what is certainly the current orthodoxy, namely, that evolution has no targets and so like the rest of us is not going anywhere at all: "The only thing that 'guides' evolution is sheer, cold demographics." Although this is not a point I discuss in my essay, I remain unconvinced. There are certainly long-term trajectories visible in the progression of life. The development of neurological complexity is the obvious example.

Richard Dawkins:

David Berlinski's article reminds me of the tactics employed by a certain creationist with whom I once shared a platform in Oxford. The great evolutionist John Maynard Smith was also on the bill, and he spoke after this creationist. Maynard Smith was, of course, easily able to destroy the creationist's case, and in his good-natured way he soon had the audience roaring with appreciative laughter at its expense. The creationist had his own peculiar way of dealing with this. He sprang to his feet, palms facing the audience in a gesture eloquent of magnanimous reproof. "No, no!" he cried reproachfully, "Don't laugh. Let Maynard Smith have his say. It's only fair!" This desperate pretense that the audience was laughing at Maynard Smith, when in fact it was laughing *with* Maynard Smith at the creationist himself, reminds me of Mr. Berlinski's pretending to misunderstand Jacques Monod and me to the extent of thinking we disagree with each other over the issue of chance.

As for the identity of the creationist who tried to pull this little stunt on Maynard Smith, it was none other than David Berlinski. The audience, by the way, saw through his tactic instantly and treated it with hoots of derision.

Berlinski replies to Richard Dawkins:

Richard Dawkins has succumbed to the endearing weakness of revising the history of an unpleasant encounter in one's own favor. I have done as much myself. But a public charge calls for a public response. In 1992, Mr. Dawkins, John Maynard Smith, and I did share a podium at Oxford University. His hands trembling with indignation, Mr. Dawkins proposed to attack organized religion; I proposed to attack Richard Dawkins; and John Maynard Smith, seeing that it was required, proposed to defend Mr. Dawkins from my attack. The intellectual drubbing that Mr. Dawkins imagines I received, I recall in distinctly different terms. But why argue over the past? I have a videotape of our encounter, which I would be happy to make publicly available. If he wishes to debate again, Mr. Dawkins need only set the time and the place. [*Editor's note: the videotape in question is available through Discovery Institute's Center for Science and Culture, www.discovery.org.*]

In remarks that have by now become well known, Jacques Monod observed with some sorrow that under Darwin's theory, it is chance that plays the crucial role in the emergence and evolution of life. Mr. Dawkins proposes to deny this. His views and those of Monod are in conflict, a point clear to anyone able to read the English language. Mr. Dawkins's continuing insistence that two contradictory propositions are mutually consistent is evidence of an alarming logical deficiency.

In fact, Mr. Dawkins has simply misunderstood the fundamental character of the theory to which he has committed his passionate defense. Darwin's theory *is* both random *and* deterministic. True enough. Mutations occur randomly, but once they have occurred, natural selection acts deterministically to cull the successes and discard the failures. By and large, true again. Nonetheless, Darwin's theory is *essentially* stochastic, a term which in statistics refers to a process involving a random sequence of observations.

Let me call a random mutation together with its deterministic consequences an evolutionary *episode*. The proto-tiger develops claws; he lives to mate successfully. Such is a single evolutionary episode. According to Darwin's theory, evolutionary episodes are independent. A snapshot of any given episode does not suffice to determine the character of future episodes. And for obvious reasons: future events are contingent on further random events. It follows that the episodes must themselves be represented by what probability theorists (and everyone else) call a random variable. And processes represented by a random variable are by definition stochastic. These facts are understood by anyone in possession of the requisite technical concepts. For all his flaws as a philosopher, Monod was quite clear about the character of Darwin's theory.

On one important matter, Mr. Dawkins's letter requires a word of reproof. At our debate, I was asked by a member of the audience whether I held to any creationist beliefs or doctrines. I replied unequivocally that I did not. My views of Darwinism, I said, were negative, but rational. On the videotape, as I utter these forthright words, Richard Dawkins may be seen sitting placidly on the podium, staring somberly into space.

Daniel C. Dennett:

I love it: another hilarious demonstration that you can publish bull---t at will—just so long as you say what an editorial board wants to hear in a style it favors. First there was Alan Sokal's delicious unmasking of the editors of *Social Text*, who fell for his fashionably anti-scientific "proof" that according to quantum physics, the world is a social construction. Now David Berlinski has done the same to the editors of *Commentary*, who fell just as hard for his parody of "scientific" creationism. They must really be oppressed by evolutionary theory to publish such inspired silliness without running it by a biologist or two for soundness. Two such similar pranks in a single month make one wonder if this is just the tip of the *Zeitgeist*. What next? A hoax extolling the educational virtues of machine guns for tots in the *American Rifleman*?

I love the rich comic patina of smug miseducation Mr. Berlinski exudes: Latin names for species mixed with elementary falsehoods in about equal measure, the subtle misuse of "*Doppelgänger*," the "unwitting" creation of a new term, "combinatorial inflation," and the deft touch of "betraying" his cluelessness by referring to Kim Sterelny as "she." [*Editor's note: I corrected this in Berlinski's article, changing "she" to "he"; Sterelny is a male philosopher of biology.*]

The hints are subtle but conclusive. No serious opponent of evolutionary theory would trot out the ill-considered remarks of the mathematician M. P. Schützenberger—a line of discredited criticism quietly abandoned by others years ago—without so much as a hint about their standing. How could the heroic misunderstanding of Jacques Monod that enables our author to pit Monod against Richard Dawkins be anything but disingenuous? Could any actual professor of mathematics and philosophy "in American and French universities" misrepresent the import of the second law of thermodynamics with such poetic fervor, such blithe overconfidence?

Whoever this David Berlinski is, he is clever enough to fool *Com-

mentary, and I wouldn't even be surprised if some evolutionists take him seriously enough to rebut him in detail. Even better, some earnest creationists may clasp him to their bosom. That is, one presumes, his larger joke. The only reason I am exposing it now (killjoy that I am) is to make it clear that so far as I know, we evolutionists did not put him up to it. We feel no need to burden our critics with such *agents provocateurs*, but they are welcome to him if they want him.

Postscript (2003): My prediction was amply borne out: a handful of biologists humorlessly took on the thankless task, in their short letters to *Commentary*, of trying to expose the many errors and confusions in Berlinski's article, complaining as they labored that there were just too many to deal with in short compass. And as this present volume attests, the creationists (or "Intelligent Design theorists") still don't get the joke. Bravo Berlinski, you've made fools of quite a roster!

Berlinski replies to Daniel C. Dennett:

Daniel C. Dennett is under the curious impression that the best rejoinder to criticism is a robust display of personal vulgarity. Nothing in his letter merits a response.

Still, one general point deserves attention. Both Daniel Dennett and Richard Dawkins have fashioned their reputations as defenders of a Darwinian orthodoxy. Their letters convey the impression of men who expect never to encounter criticism and are unprepared to deal with it. This strikes me as a deeply unhealthy state of affairs. Ordinary men and women are suspicious of Darwin's theory; Dennett and Dawkins hardly go far here in persuading them that their intellectual anxieties are in any way misplaced.

Arthur M. Shapiro:

. . . When I debate anti-evolutionists, I always warn the audience that a critic can raise more issues in a given amount of time than a defender can answer. The defender is thus vulnerable to the claim that he has failed to address this or that criticism. In replying to David Berlinski's eloquent but deeply flawed article, let me stress that I am not concerned with a point-by-point refutation. I am much more interested in his uses of rhetoric to create unjustified impressions in the mind of the reader. . . .

Most biologists I know are driven by curiosity, not ideology. We recognize that it is pointless to deny that a real world exists, and dangerous to place perfect faith in our own objectivity in interpreting it. That is why science has institutionalized skepticism in the process of criticism and competition. . . . We are indeed human in becoming enamored of or trapped in our own ideas, but we are surrounded by hungry rivals who work to keep us honest.

That is just as true in evolutionary biology as in other sciences. So how can Mr. Berlinski get away with accusing us of hushing up our disagreements in order to present a united front against our cultural foes? There is no more contentious, pugnacious, querulous bunch of professionals on earth than evolutionary biologists, . . . and intergenerational and ideological conflicts within academia keep the pot boiling in a very public way. In the process, anti-evolutionists are provided with a mountain of very quotable quotes, usually presented to the public out of context. If we were so concerned with papering over our differences, why would we debate them before the public? . . .

I was at the Wistar Institute in 1966 when Murray Eden and M. P. Schützenberger presented their arguments, cited approvingly by Mr. Berlinski. If he had read the proceedings of that meeting, he would know that it was organized at the instance of the biologists, who wanted the opportunity to hear and discuss the criticisms of their mathematical colleagues. He would also know that some of the objections he cites now were actually dealt with effectively from the floor. Instead, he disingenuously implies that those arguments still bear as much force now as they did then—that they somehow have been swept under the rug or ignored by biologists.

Mr. Berlinski ignores the fact that mathematics has been the indispensable handmaiden of evolutionary biology for over seventy years. Does he really think nothing interesting has happened in evolutionary biology for thirty years, or that anything interesting that has happened has merely weakened the Darwinian paradigm? Perhaps. After all, with the avalanche of technical, semipopular, and popular books on paleobiology published in recent years, Mr. Berlinski sends his readers off to consult Alfred S. Romer's classic treatise on vertebrate paleontology, also published in 1966, and showing its age badly.

In another display of disingenuousness, Mr. Berlinski wants evolutionary biologists to explain from first principles why one species of widow spider commits sexual suicide while another does not. He knows perfectly well that the chain of causes is too long, with too many opportunities for historical contingency to operate, for anyone with less than the omniscience of the deity to do that. But just as physics rules out mountains shaped like inverted cones, so, too, does Darwinism rule out certain things. For example, it rules out any organism displaying a structure or behavior that enhances the fitness of some other species while reducing its own: the cartoonist Al Capp's altruistic "Shmoos" were a Darwinian impossibility. That is precisely why "altruism" was such a hot topic among evolutionists in the 1960s and '70s, when numerous biologists tried and failed to demonstrate its existence in nonhuman species.

One final point, which, while seemingly a trivial matter of semantics, illuminates the deepest problem of Mr. Berlinski's essay: our ability to reconstruct the history of life (phylogeny) depends upon the "tree of life" not only *not* being "densely reticulated," but *not reticulated at all*. "Reticulated" means net-like; branches diverge, then anastomose. But in phylogeny, branches, once separate, stay separate. It is this fact that enables us to reconstruct phylogeny through the method of nested, shared resemblances, now usually called "cladistics." That method fails if branches really do anastomose—either through hybridization, which is rare in many groups but frequent in others, or through a more arcane process such as the vectoring of genetic information across taxonomic lines by viruses.

If the tree of life were very reticulate, formal phylogenetic reconstruction would be impossible, and we truly would have a problem—not with the Darwinian paradigm *per se*, but with our ability to know whether it was true or false.

Mr. Berlinski could write a good essay about a living, breathing issue like that—were he not so preoccupied with rehashing the debates of thirty years ago. . . .

Berlinski replies to Arthur M. Shapiro:

Contrary to what Arthur M. Shapiro asserts I do not doubt that evolutionary biologists are contentious; I said as much in my essay. What I deplored was their tendency to conceal their differences from the public. This is another matter entirely.

Evolutionary biologists have a habit of ignoring the most pertinent criticisms of their theory until they can decently call them out-of-date. My references to papers by M. P. Schützenberger and Murray Eden not surprisingly prompt Mr. Shapiro to the conclusion that my arguments are anachronistic. In fact, Schützenberger and Eden enter my essay unobtrusively in largely a stage-setting role—Schützenberger to call attention to a conceptual problem at the very heart of evolutionary theory and Eden to offer, for the first time, a quantitative assessment of the space within which evolutionary searches must be undertaken. Their papers are historically important, the points they make no longer controversial.

Does Mr. Shapiro doubt that randomness introduces an alien and discordant note into the dynamics by which very complex objects change? Or that combinatorial inflation blows up the space of possible proteins? These themes have been pursued in countless papers, monographs, and books. Thus, Hubert Yockey, arguing that the discovery by chance of a single molecule of iso-1-cytochrome c requires a miracle, continues the line initiated by Schützenberger and Eden (Hubert Yockey, *Information Theory and Molecular Biology*, 1992. But see also Gregory J. Chaitin, "Toward a Mathematical Definition of 'Life,'" in *The Maximum Entropy Formalism*, eds. R. D. Levine and M. Tribus, 1979; Francis Crick, *Life Itself, Its Origin and Nature*, 1981; Max Delbruck, *Mind from Matter?*, 1986; Robert Shapiro, *Origins: A Skeptic's Guide to the Creation of Life on Earth*, 1986). The language of choice has changed—a fragile consensus is emerging that Kolmogorov complexity is a natural measure of biological complexity or specificity—but the problems remain the same. (I discuss Kolmogorov complexity in an earlier essay, "The Soul of Man under Physics," *Commentary*, January 1996.) The space of possible objects is entirely too large to be successfully searched by random means, a theme pursued yet again in Michael Denton's *Evolution: A Theory in Crisis* (1986).

I agree that much has happened in biology over the past 30 years—who could doubt it? Developments taking place within molecular genetics, molecular biology, and biochemistry *do* seem to me to be profoundly at odds with the Darwinian paradigm, and those within paleontology flamboyantly so. I mentioned some points of conflict in my essay; I refer to others here.

Consider, for example, the question of how an undifferentiated cell manages the task of specialization, becoming over the course of time a neuron, or a muscle cell, or any other particular and peculiar biological object. The requisite information is contained, of course, within the cell's genetic apparatus; the problem is one of specificity. What regulates the expression of some parts of that apparatus, while simultaneously suppressing the expression of other parts? One suggestion of long standing is that regulatory mechanisms are switched on and off by means of biochemical signals sent from neighboring cells.

It is this suggestion that experiments conducted by Chiou-Hwa Yuh and Eric Davidson seem to support (C.-H. Yuh and E. H. Davidson,

"Modular *cis*-regulatory Organization of Endo 16, a Gut-specific Gene of the Sea Urchin Embryo," *Development* 122, 1996). A gene in the sea urchin *Strongylocentrotus purpuratus* contains over 30 binding sites for more than 13 regulatory factors. These regulatory factors turn parts of the genetic apparatus on and off. They are sensitive to signals from adjacent cells, and, what is more, they are clustered in discrete modules; different module combinations lead to different patterns of cellular development.

The system that results is one of extraordinary combinatorial intricacy and complexity. What of randomness in all this? We have no idea how the general mechanism for cell-specific transcription came into existence; to argue otherwise would be sheer dogmatism. But one might have thought that a system of such delicacy, once it came into existence, would be unusually sensitive to random perturbations. Not so. The regulatory apparatus seems designed to incorporate mutations. Certain sites within each module function as key switches, turning the module on or off; mutations have a specific, but highly discrete effect. Modules are largely independent, functioning as more or less complete sets of instructions, like blocks of code. As one commentator puts it, the transposition of cis-regulatory modules from one gene to the next "may be a convenient way for nature to develop novel patterns of development" (Wade Roush, *Science* 272, 1996).

As is so often the case in molecular genetics, the description of a specific biological system reveals a pattern at odds with the one demanded by Darwinian theory. Differentiation is a highly sophisticated, enormously complex, and stable process, one in which the system is protected from noise by its very design. Mutations play a role in developmental change, but not a driving role. Rather, the facts suggest a system in which there are a finite number of combinatorial possibilities, with mutations serving to initiate certain carefully stage-managed sequences. The possibilities for module combination are fixed from the first; random changes serve simply to throw the various switches.

Examples of this sort could be multiplied at length; as our knowledge increases, the crude Darwinian scheme seems progressively remote from the evidence. How, for example, to account for the astonishing fact that from the point of view of the informational macromolecules, human beings and chimpanzees are virtually identical, their sequences in alignment to 99 percent (M. C. King and A. C. Wilson, "Evolution at Two Levels in Humans and Chimpanzees," *Science* 188, 1975)? The remaining slight difference evidently has controlled the development of a bipedal gait, with the profound neurological changes that this requires;

the fully formed hand; the formation of the organs of speech and articulation; and, of course, the elaboration of the human mind, an organ unlike anything else found in the animal kingdom. Nothing in this suggests even remotely a continuous accretion of small changes. The evolutionary promotion of our ancestors seems to have been under the control of powerful *regulatory* genes, instructional blocks capable of coordinating a wide variety of novel functions. We simply have no idea how any of this works.

Still, the real infirmities of Darwin's theory are conceptual and not empirical. By the standards of the serious sciences, Darwin's theory of evolution remains little more than a collection of anecdotal remarks. Criticism is often a matter of clarification. Thus, making a point unrelated to the evidence, I argued that Darwinian theory is logically troubled. When I maintain that both Messrs. Dennett and Dawkins introduce by means of the backdoor the element of design they have ostentatiously booted from the front, my criticisms are again intended to show that the theory is deficient if only because it fails to meet its *own* standards for success.

The redback spider gives Mr. Shapiro pause; my request that its dining habits be deduced from first principles—from any principles at all—strikes him as disingenuous. "The chain of causes," he remarks, "is simply too long to be mastered by anyone other than an omniscient deity." I do not for a moment doubt that that is so, but precisely this circumstance prompts the request for scientific theory in the first place. The chain of causes is *everywhere* too long to be explored and then mastered; it is the purpose of a theory to abbreviate and compress the data. Imagine a biologist who, on the grounds that the chain of causes is too long, failed to explain the fact that while men develop arms, geese develop wings!

The fact that the redback spider commits sexual suicide is interesting; one wishes to know why it is so. In this, and in countless similar cases, evolutionary theory simply has no explanation. What good is it, then?

Finally, I am astonished that Mr. Shapiro should think to object to Romer's *Vertebrate Paleontology* as a reference. The subject at hand is not particle physics; the main lines of vertebrate development have been clear for more than a century. My aim in suggesting Romer was to point the reader toward his stratigraphic charts: these plot vertebrate groups against time, the very many dotted lines between groups indicating purely hypothetical phylogenetic relationships.

Paul R. Gross:

Berlinski No. 1 ["The Soul of Man Under Physics," January] was amusing: especially his silly similes, such as Jupiter's moons in the guise of testicles. Most of the science was OK, although marred by glosses that were themselves errors. . . .

Berlinski No. 2 is much more presumptuous and more seriously wrong. How could *Commentary* not have let *some* biologist or other read it? I do not have the space to deal with all his unsupported or dead-wrong assertions, so I will just make a few counterassertions which perhaps will reduce the encouragement Mr. Berlinski has given creationists and other consumers of anti-science who might be among *Commentary's* readers.

The claim that intermediate fossil forms are absent is simply false. It is the oldest canard in the creationist handbook. Picking and choosing from among a few of the more florid statements of Stephen Jay Gould and Niles Eldredge does not reveal to the innocent reader . . . why these two are and have always been convinced of the essential truth of organic evolution as Darwin first described it and of natural selection as at least one mechanism of it.

The "fitness" argument is dealt with, seriously, in every introductory course in biology, including the ones I have taught. Mr. Berlinski's fixation on it was out of date a very long time ago.

"What good is 5 percent of an eye?" is a stupid question if asked in the context in which Mr. Berlinski places it. Moreover, there is new and astonishing evidence of the genetic, hence selective, mechanism underlying the embryology of *all* eyes—insects, mice, humans.

Mr. Berlinski grossly misrepresents Jacques Monod's argument, as he does the way in which "chance" is used and understood in modern biology. It is possible he really does not know, but I am not sure; maybe he is a postmodernist at heart.

"*Bauplan*," like a few other fancy words, is comically misused.

I could go on and on, . . . but for a small fee I would be glad to support all these assertions with citations of solid science from the *current* literature of molecular and evolutionary biology. A bit of that literature Mr. Berlinski may have mined; but if so, he has done it the same way that "Intelligent Design theorists" mine it: to extract a few sentences here and there for the comfort of creationists. This second Berlinski opus amounts to a charge that biologists are in a conspiracy to hide from outsiders the bankruptcy of the central principle of biology. . . .

As I did once before, I deplore *Commentary*'s giving such comfort to Luddites.

Berlinski replies to Paul R. Gross:

Paul R. Gross is anxious lest in criticizing Darwinian theory I give comfort to creationists. It is a common concern among biologists, but one, I must confess, to which I am indifferent. I do not believe biologists should be in the business of protecting the rest of us from intellectual danger.

I did not say in my essay that the fossil record contains no intermediate forms; that is a silly claim. What I did say was that there are gaps in the fossil graveyard, places where there should be intermediate forms but where there is nothing whatsoever instead. No paleontologist writing in English (R. Carroll, *Vertebrate Paleontology and Evolution*, 1988), French (J. Chaline, "*Modalites, rythmes, mecanismes de l'evolution biologique: gradualisme phyletique ou equilibres ponctues?*," reprinted in *Editions du* CNRS, 1983), or German (V. Fahlbusch, "*Makroevolution, Punktualismus,*" in *Palaontologie 57*, 1983), denies that this is so. It is simply a fact. Darwin's theory and the fossil record are in conflict. There may be excellent reasons for the conflict; it may in time be exposed as an artifact. But nothing is to be gained by suggesting that what is a fact in plain sight is nothing of the sort.

I do not doubt that Stephen Jay Gould and Niles Eldredge are convinced of the "essential truth of organic evolution"; or that they believe natural selection to be "at least one mechanism of it." The difficulty with this observation is that it is compromised by its qualifications. At any given moment, if the phases of the moon happened to be right, I might align myself with Mr. Gross's essential truth of organic evolution; as for natural selection, nothing at all remains at issue if it is demoted from its central position in Darwin's theory. The idea that evolution proceeds by means of many different forces is both unanswerable and uninteresting. To his credit, this is something Richard Dawkins recognizes.

It may well be true that my concerns for the logical niceties of Darwinian theory are out of date, as Mr. Gross suggests. So much the worse for evolutionary biology. To those of us on the outside, Darwin's theory will continue to seem seriously infected by conceptual circularity. (In *Concepts and Methods in Evolutionary Biology*, the philosopher Robert Brandon begins by at least recognizing the problem.)

The pattern of self-deception that I mocked in my essay is on display in any number of publications. In the first chapter of *The Causes of Molecular Evolution* (1991), John H. Gillespie is concerned to determine why a certain kinetic parameter (the Michaelis constant, K_m) reaches intermediate values in a certain class of fish, the ectotherms. "If natural selection is responsible for the evolution of K_m," Gillespie writes, "we should be able to understand why it would be maladaptive to exhibit values that are much less or much greater than the intermediate value." In fact, the two biochemical explanations Gillespie considers are flatly in conflict. They cannot both be true, although both may be false. To Gillespie, though, it hardly matters. ". . . [A]t this point in our discussion," he writes, "it is important merely to accept that there are plausible reasons for K_m to be evolutionarily adjusted to intermediate values. This forms the theoretical basis of our acceptance of the conservation of K_m in ectotherms as *evidence* for the action of natural selection in response to different thermal environments" (emphasis added). If the discussion has proceeded beyond the observation that K_m reaches intermediate values in ectotherms, the fact is not discernible by me.

On the matter of the eye, Mr. Gross has misunderstood me. I did not propose to champion Stephen Jay Gould's question, "What good is 5 percent of an eye?" Instead, I argued that the question is hopelessly premature. Without knowing *how* the visual system works, we cannot determine *whether* it is accessible to a Darwinian mechanism. This seems to me an incontrovertible point, if also one that in my experience evolutionary biologists indignantly deny.

Let me offer an analogy. Starting from one and adding by twos, I cannot hope to reach the number eighteen. So far, so good. Starting from one and adding by two's, can I hope to reach the number *n*, where *n* is some number or other? Who knows? The question is underdetermined. Starting from *some* principle of addition or other, could I expect to reach *some* number or other? The question is now doubly underdetermined, functioning as a single equation in two unknowns. So, too, the question of whether a Darwinian mechanism with unspecified properties could reach a mammalian visual system whose properties are not yet completely understood. It is only credulous philosophers who imagine that a Darwinian mechanism is universally competent.

I am in agreement with Mr. Gross when he refers to "new and astonishing evidence" about the origin of the eye. Herewith the facts. Halder, Callaerts, and Gehring's research group in Switzerland discovered that the *ey* gene in *Drosophila* is virtually identical to the genes controlling the development of the eye in mice and men. The doctrine of convergent evolution, long a Darwinian staple, may now be observed receding into the darkness. The same group's more recent paper, "In-

duction of Ectopic Eyes by Targeted Expression of the Eyeless Gene in
Drosophila" (*Science* 167, 1988) is among the most remarkable in the
history of biology, demonstrating as it does that the *ey* gene is related
closely to the equivalent *ey* gene in Sea squirts (Ascidians), Cephalo-
pods, and Nemerteans. This strongly suggests (the inference is almost
irresistible) that *ey* function is universal (universal!) among multicellular organisms, the basic design of the eye having been their common
property for over a half-billion years. The *ey* gene clearly is a master
control mechanism, one capable of giving general instructions to very
different organisms.

No one in possession of these facts can imagine that they *support*
the Darwinian theory. How could the mechanism of random variation
and natural selection have produced an instrument capable of *anticipat-
ing* the course of morphological development and controlling its expression in widely different organisms?

I deny that I have in any way misrepresented Jacques Monod's arguments; his words are clear and unequivocal, in English and in the original French. If the word "chance" has an idiosyncratic use among evolutionary biologists, the secret has been closely kept. As far as I can determine, evolutionary theorists make use of the same technical concepts as
the rest of the mathematical community, a point evident in any current
text—*Mathematical Evolutionary Theory*, ed. R. Feldman (1989), for
example.

The notion of a *bauplan (der Bauplan, die Bauplänne)*, or body
plan, has had some currency in the English-speaking world; Stephen Jay
Gould and Richard Lewontin use the term and so does J. W. Valentine.
But it is in general dismissed as a concept by Darwinians—George C.
Williams, for example. The idea of a body plan gained currency in the
work of the great turn-of-the-century embryologists (Driesch, Child,
Boveri, Spemann), and before that in the writings of pre-Darwinian
French biologists (Saint-Hilaire, Cuvier, Serres). I cannot imagine why
Mr. Gross thinks it a term I have misused. (For reasons that are obscure
to me, both he and Daniel Dennett carelessly assume that they are in a
position to instruct me on a point of usage in German, my first language.)

I do not for a moment suppose, nor have I ever written, that biologists are in *conspiracy* "to hide from outsiders the bankruptcy of the
central principle of biology." For one thing, the theory of evolution is
hardly the central principle of contemporary biology. That description
must surely be reserved for the thesis that all of life is to be understood
in terms of the "coordinative interaction of large and small molecules"

(James Watson, *The Molecular Biology of the Gene*). Rather, the theory of evolution functions as biology's reigning ideology. And no conspiracy is required to explain the attachment of biologists to a doctrine they find sustaining; all that is required is Freud's reminder that those in the grip of an illusion never recognize their affliction.

Eugenie C. Scott:

. . . The content of David Berlinski's article does not differ from more traditional creation-science material, though his tone is more genteel and his writing a lot more literate. . . . But true to the creation-science genre, his approach consists of constructing strawmen, then knocking them down with misinterpreted, faulty, or nonexistent data as well as carefully selected quotations from evolutionary scientists. . . .

For example, the "intermediate/ transitional-fossil" strawman is a staple of anti-evolutionist rhetoric. . . . Because their theology says God created all living things as separate "kinds," creationists assert that there can be no transitional fossils, and no descent with modification. As a result, they persist in their inability to recognize mosaic specimens. Show them a fossil like the part bird/part dinosaur *Archaeopteryx*, and they will claim that because it has feathers, it is "100-percent bird," regardless of the fact that specimens which lack clear feather imprints are indistinguishable from small, toothed, clawed, bipedal dinosaurs. Show them a hominid fossil with a small brain, teeth similar in some respects to those of an ape and in others to those of a human, and a pelvis requiring bipedal locomotion, and they will see "just an ape." . . .

Readers can write me at NCSE for a bibliography of articles and books that refute the Cambrian-explosion argument, refute the impossibility of amino acids coming together to form a protein, explain the difference between chance and evolution, discuss why William Paley's argument from design has been supplanted in science by arguments based on natural causes. . . .

One can be a believer and accept evolution. Articles like Mr. Berlinski's confuse rather than elucidate issues. Mostly, however, they perpetrate bad science in a society that needs more science literacy, not ignorance.

Berlinski replies to Eugenie C. Scott:

I am happy to salute *Archaeopteryx*, recognizing the little monster as half-bird and half-reptile (or anything Eugenie C. Scott wishes).

Strawmen? As long as I am at it, let me knock down a few more. There is no "Cambrian-explosion argument"; there is the fact that an explosion of biological forms took place in the Cambrian era. Far from being impossible, amino acids come together to form proteins all the time; no one has provided a plausible account of the *origin* of the informational macromolecules. And there is no need to explain the difference between evolution and chance to any native speaker of English: the words mean different things.

Randy M. Wadkins:

EDITOR'S COMMENT: *Randy Wadkins could not be reached for permission to have his letter reprinted here. Let me therefore summarize it. Wadkins begins by charging Berlinski with "misstatements" that "make virtually everything he says on the matter of evolution . . . suspect." He then points out that there are fossils of bacteria and stromatolites that predate the Cambrian explosion, claiming that this fact supports evolution. Next he points to transitional fossils in the evolution of horses as further undermining Berlinski's critique of Darwinism. Next Wadkins examines continuity and randomness in evolution, claiming that Berlinski misunderstands their proper roles. Finally, Wadkins defends Dawkins's use of computer simulations to support evolution, citing Keen and Spain's* Computer Simulation in Biology *as making up for Dawkins's deficiencies as a computer programmer.*

Berlinski replies to Randy M. Wadkins:

What Randy M. Wadkins affirms about the pre-Cambrian era is true enough (but see E. H. Davidson, K. Peterson, and R. Cameron, "Origin of Bilaterian Body Plans: Evolution of Developmental Regulatory Mechanism" *Science* 270, 1995, for a real sense of the inadequacy of our grasp of fundamental facts concerning the Cambrian explosion). I only wonder why he imagines that his observations are in conflict with anything I have written.

In the same spirit, Mr. Wadkins calls me to task for failing to cite "the specific cases where transitional fossil forms are found in abundance." The fossil record does contain many intermediate forms; a recent publication on the Internet (Kathleen Hunt, *Transitional Vertebrate Fossils*, FAQ [Frequently Asked Questions], jespah@u.washington.edu) lists more than 250. But Mr. Wadkins has misunderstood the nature of the argument. My concern was to state the obvious: the fossil record contains gaps, places where the continuity assumptions of Darwinian theory break down. That there are places where the gaps are filled is interesting, but irrelevant. It is the gaps that are crucial.

Classical physics suggests that the spectral distribution of intensity in black-body radiation should be a continuous function of temperature. Experiments conducted at the end of the 19th century indicated otherwise. Continuity is an essential aspect of classical mechanics, impossible to discard without discarding the entire theory. Since the anomaly of black-body radiation could not be understood within classical mechanics, physicists sensitive to the evidence were persuaded to attach their allegiance to the new quantum theory.

The classical Darwinian theory of random variation and natural selection requires a continuous distribution of animal forms, one that must be reflected in the fossil record. The assumption of continuity is a crucial aspect of Darwinian theory; it cannot be carelessly discarded. This again is something that Richard Dawkins has rightly emphasized. The fossil record does not appear to support the assumption of evolutionary continuity, or anything much like it. Why is it that evolutionary biology is immune to evidence of the sort that falsified classical physics?

It is upon the horse that Mr. Wadkins pins his best hopes: its evolution, he suggests, comprises an unassailable sequence, one bright bursting beast after the other. To a certain extent, however, the neat evolutionary progression from *Eohippus* to *Equus* is an artifact of selection. The original groupings of species are far thicker (or bushier, to use the term of choice) than first thought, so that the sequence depends on a judicious selection of horse-like organisms at each stage of development. It is rather as if one were to explain the emergence of the word *cat* by selecting the "c" from cattle, the "a" from abattoir and the "t" from tattle. Although almost 50 years old, G. G. Simpson's discussion in *The Major Features of Evolution* still repays study; for the modern point of view there is B. J. MacFadden, "Horses, the Fossil Record, and Evolution: A Current Perspective" (*Evolutionary Biology* 22, 1988).

But setting these reservations aside, what follows if the *Equus* sequence is accepted as a Darwinian progression? Very little. There are no more than three or four evolutionary sequences that, under the best of circumstances, suggest a complete progression of forms. By contrast, there are thousands upon thousands of species whose significant morphological features are not explained by complete or even highly suggestive sequences. Are the existing evolutionary sequences representative, or anomalous? In view of the striking discontinuities in the fossil record, I urge that they are anomalous; it would be interesting to know why Mr. Wadkins demurs.

When I observed that Richard Dawkins was unable to write a computer program that simulated his linguistic thought experiment, I did not mean that the task at hand was difficult. It is impossible. Mr. Wadkins commends the discussion in Keen and Spain's *Computer Simulation in Biology* as a counterexample; it is no such thing. What Keen and Spain have done is transcribe Dawkins's blunder into the computer language Basic. Here are the steps they undertake. A target sentence is selected— BASIC BIOLOGICAL MODELING IS FUN. The computer is given a randomly derived set of letters. The letters are scrambled. At each iteration, the computer (or the programmer) compares the randomly derived sequence with the target phrase. If the arrays—sequences on the one hand, target phrase on the other—do not match, the experiment continues; if they do, it stops.

There is nothing in this that is not also in Dawkins, the fog spreading from one book to the next. The experiment that Keen and Spain conduct is successful inasmuch as the computer reaches its target; but unsuccessful as a defense of Darwinian evolution. In looking to its target and comparing distances, the computer is appealing to information a biological system could not possess.

This point seems to be less straightforward than I imagined, so let me spell out the mistake. Starting from a random string, suppose the computer generates the sequence BNDIT DISNE SOT SODISWN TOSWXMSPW SSO. Comparing the sequence with its target, it proposes to conserve the initial "B." But why? The string is gibberish. Plainly, the conservation of vagrant successes has been undertaken with the computer's eye fixed firmly on its future target, intermediates selected not for what they are (gibberish, after all), but for what they *will* be (an English sentence). This is a violation of the rule against deferred success. Without the rule, there is nothing remotely like Darwinian evolution. What the computer has in fact done is to match randomly selected items to a template, thus inevitably reintroducing the element of deliberate design that was banished from the Darwinian world.

Robert Shapiro:

EDITOR'S COMMENT: *Robert Shapiro could not be reached for permission to have his letter reprinted here. Let me therefore summarize it. Shapiro begins by commending Berlinski for "capturing the complexity of living things" and for calling to account "those biologists who exchange skepticism for dogma and proclaim that our current level of understanding is enough to provide a full account of the origin and development of life." But then Shapiro calls Berlinski to account for having a hidden agenda of promoting Intelligent Design. Shapiro, who rejects Intelligent Design as not a scientific option, views a "polarized two-way choice" between Darwinism and Intelligent Design as a false dilemma. "Fortunately, there is a third alternative," writes Shapiro. For this third alternative, Shapiro looks to the ideas about self-organization of Stuart Kauffman, citing with approval Kauffman's* At Home in the Universe *(1995).*

Berlinski replies to Robert Shapiro:

Robert Shapiro has modestly withheld from readers the fact that he is the author of a penetrating work on pre-biotic evolution, which I have already cited: *Origins: A Skeptic's Guide to the Creation of Life on Earth.* As I might have hoped, Mr. Shapiro is with me for nine-tenths of my argument. He jumps ship at the thought that our options may have narrowed to a choice between Darwin and what he calls Intelligent Design. But, contrary to what Mr. Shapiro supposes, I entertain no supernatural explanations for the complexity of living systems. The thing is a mystery, and if there is never to be a naturalistic explanation, I shall forever be content to keep on calling it a mystery. The two of us might have gone on together to the end.

A skeptic about so much, Mr. Shapiro now feels compelled to commend theories of self-organization and complexity as solutions to the problems that vex us. For me, the papers, books, and monographs coming from the Santa Fe Institute, with which Stuart Kauffman is prominently identified, convey something familiar. I once spent a good deal of time demolishing the set of fashionable mathematical theories collected under the generic term of systems analysis (*On Systems Analysis: An Essay on the Limitations of Some Mathematical Methods in the Social, Political, and Biological Sciences*, MIT Press, 1976). Reading Kauffman's *The Origins of Order* (1993), I was flooded with memories. Had I time, I would go after Santa Fe with gusto; but soon the night comes, Dr.

Johnson reminds us, wherein no man can work. I find nothing of value in various theories of self-organization; the very idea is to my mind incoherent; but I leave it to others to make the case.

Notes

Introduction: The Myths of Darwinism
William A. Dembski

1. Richard Dawkins, Book Review of *Blueprints: Solving the Mystery of Evolution*, by Maitland A. Edey and Donald C. Johanson, *New York Times* (April 9, 1987, section 7): 34.
2. Richard Dawkins, "Ignorance is No Crime," *Free Inquiry* 21, no. 3 (2001), available online at www.secularhumanism.org/library/fi/dawkins_21_3.html.
3. Barbara Kingsolver, *Small Wonder* (New York: HarperCollins, 2002), 96, emphasis added.
4. Daniel C. Dennett, *Darwin's Dangerous Idea: Evolution and the Meaning of Life* (New York: Simon & Schuster, 1995), 519.
5. John Stuart Mill, *On Liberty* (1859; reprinted Indianapolis: Hackett, 1978), 50.
6. Charles Darwin, *On the Origin of Species,* facsimile 1st ed. (1859; reprinted Cambridge, Mass.: Harvard University Press, 1964), 2.
7. See "Santorum Amendment" (encyclopedia entry), *Wikipedia,* available online at http://en.wikipedia.org/wiki/Santorum_Amendment.
8. Paul Gross, Letter to Editor, *Commentary* (March 2003), 9.
9. Dennett, *Darwin's Dangerous Idea,* 21.
10. Quoted from interview with Judith Hooper, "A New Germ Theory," *Atlantic Monthly* (February 1999), available online at www.theatlantic.com/issues/99feb/germs.htm.
11. David Berlinski, "A Scientific Scandal? David Berlinski and Critics," *Commentary* (July 2003), available online at www.discovery.org/scripts/viewDB/index.php?program=CRSC&command=view&id=1509.

12. Richard Dawkins, "The Future Looks Bright," *Guardian* (June 21, 2003), available online at http://books.guardian.co.uk/review/story/ 0,12084,981412,00.html. See also Daniel Dennett, "The Bright Stuff," *New York Times* (July 12, 2003), available online at www.the-brights.net/ dennett_nyt.htm, which makes the same point.

13. See James Shapiro, "In the Details . . . What?" *National Review* (September 16, 1996): 62–65, as well as Franklin Harold, *The Way of the Cell: Molecules, Organisms and the Order of Life* (Oxford: Oxford University Press, 2001), 205. Shapiro writes, "There are no detailed Darwinian accounts for the evolution of any fundamental biochemical or cellular system, only a variety of wishful speculations. It is remarkable that Darwinism is accepted as a satisfactory explanation for such a vast subject—evolution—with so little rigorous examination of how well its basic theses work in illuminating specific instances of biological adaptation or diversity." In virtually identical language, and without citing Shapiro, Franklin Harold writes, "We must concede that there are presently no detailed Darwinian accounts of the evolution of any biochemical or cellular system, only a variety of wishful speculations."

14. David Ray Griffin, *Religion and Scientific Naturalism: Overcoming the Conflicts* (Albany, N.Y.: State University of New York Press, 2000), 287, n. 23.

15. Andrea Bottaro, Letter to WNYE, available online at www.ncseweb.org/ resources/articles/2730_bottaro39s_letter_to_wnye_7_8_2003.asp.

16. See www.millerandlevine.com/km/evol.

17. This article is available online at www.arn.org/docs/behe/ mb_evolutionaryliterature.htm.

18. Richard E. Lenski, Charles Ofria, Robert T. Pennock, and Christoph Adami, "The Evolutionary Origin of Complex Features," *Nature* 423 (May 8, 2003): 139–44.

19. The Nobel press release is available at www.nobel.se/physics/laureates/ 1972/press.html.

20. David Berlinski, "Darwinism Versus Intelligent Design: David Berlinski and Critics," *Commentary* (March 2003): 23.

21. Richard Feynman, *"Surely You're Joking, Mr. Feynman!"* (New York: Norton, 1985), 342–43.

22. See, for instance, Teresa Watanabe, "Enlisting Science to Find Fingerprints of a Creator," *Los Angeles Times* (March 25, 2001), available online at www.arn.org/docs/news/fingerprints032501.htm. See also Nancy Pearcey, "Creation Mythology: Defenders of Darwinism Resort to Suppressing Data and Teaching Outright Falsehoods," *World* (June 24, 2000), available online at www.arn.org/docs/pearcey/np_world-

creationmythology62400.htm. Pearcey reports: "In 1998 a new superin-
tendent ordered Mr. DeHart to cease and desist from teaching students
about intelligent design; he could, however, still talk about problems in
Neo-Darwinism. Then this May, the administration imposed even more
draconian restrictions. Mr. DeHart wanted to alert students to recent
reversals in key evidence for Neo-Darwinism, and sought approval to
distribute articles from mainstream scientific journals to correct old,
outdated information in the textbooks. Astonishingly, the principal said
no. In short, the ACLU's intimidation tactics have been so successful that
Mr. DeHart is being compelled to teach a caricature of the scientific
method."

23. See the sidebar titled "Afraid of the Truth?" in Citizen Magazine (April
    1999), available online at http://family.org/cforum/citizenmag/features/
    a0005469.cfm. The sidebar mentions, "A Michigan school district is
    under fire for purchasing books that question the theory of evolution. On
    Feb. 8, the Melvindale-Northern Allen Park School Board approved 19
    books for libraries used by senior and junior high students. Among the
    books are . . . Phillip Johnson's *Darwin on Trial,* Michael Behe's *Darwin's
    Black Box,* and *Of Pandas and People* by Percival Davis and Dean
    Kenyon. The district's decision angered the National Center for Science
    Education (NCSE), which supports Darwinian evolutionary theory.
    NCSE has issued an Internet alert asking "supporters of good science
    education" to denounce the district board in letters to the *Detroit News.*"

24. Richard Halvorson, "Questioning the Orthodoxy: Intelligent Design
    Theory Is Breaking the Scientific Monopoly of Darwinism," *Harvard
    Political Review* (May 14, 2002), available online at www.hpronline.org/
    news/2002/05/14/United States/Questioning.The.Orthodoxy-
    251835.shtml.

25. Frank Tipler's article appears on the International Society for Complex-
    ity, Information, and Design's website: www.iscid.org/papers/
    Tipler_PeerReview_070103.pdf.

1. The Check Is in the Mail
Robert C. Koons

1. Etienne Gilson, *The Christian Philosophy of Saint Augustine* (New York:
   Random House, 1960), 206–08.

2. John Manley Robinson, *An Introduction to Early Greek Philosophy*
   (Boston: Houghton Mifflin, 1968), 166–68.

3. David Hume, *Dialogues concerning Natural Religion* (London: Penguin,
   1990), 92–95.

4. "Biology is the study of complicated things that give the appearance of having been designed for a purpose." Richard Dawkins, *The Blind Watchmaker: Why the Evidence of Evolution Reveals a Universe without Design* (New York: Norton, 1986), 1.

5. Cicero, *On the Nature of the Gods*, translated by C. D. Yonge (London: George Bell & Sons, 1907), 78–79.

6. Thomas Reid, *Essays on the Intellectual Powers of Man*, edited by A. D. Woozley (London: Macmillan, 1941), 385–86.

7. Richard Dawkins, *Climbing Mount Improbable* (New York: Norton, 1996), 161-68.

8. D. E. Nilsson and S. Pelger, "A pessimistic estimate of the time required for an eye to evolve." *Proceedings of the Royal Society of London*, B 256 (1994): 53–58.

9. Richard M. Weaver, *Visions of Order: The Cultural Crisis of Our Time* (Baton Rouge, La.: Louisiana State University Press, 1964), 138.

10. Ibid.

11. Ibid., 139.

12. Charles Darwin, *The Origin of Species*, 6th edition (New York: New York University Press, 1988), 154.

13. Phillip E. Johnson, *Darwin on Trial* (Downers Grove, Ill.: InterVarsity, 1990), 43.

14. Weaver, *Visions of Order*, 139.

15. There are unanswered objections to the possibility of a naturalized epistemology: Alvin Plantinga, *Warrant and Proper Function* (New York: Oxford University Press, 1993), 216–37; *Naturalism Defeated? Essays on Plantinga's Evolutionary Argument against Naturalism*, edited by James Beilby (Ithaca, N.Y.: Cornell University Press, 2002); Michael Rea, *World without Design: The Ontological Consequences of Naturalism* (Oxford: Clarendon Press, 2002); and Robert C. Koons, *Realism Regained: An Exact Theory of Causation, Teleology and the Mind* (New York: Oxford University Press, 2000). There are, in addition, serious metaphysical problems concerning the possibility of mental causation and the explanation of consciousness: *Objections to Physicalism*, edited by Howard Robinson (Oxford: Clarendon Press, 1993); *Naturalism: A Critical Analysis*, edited by William Lane Craig and J. P. Moreland (London: Routledge, 2001); *Physicalism and Its Discontents*, edited by Carl Gillett and Barry Loewer (Cambridge: Cambridge University Press, 2001); and David J. Chalmers, *The Conscious Mind: In Search of a Fundamental Theory* (New York: Oxford University Press, 1996).

16. Robert C. Koons, "Science and Theism: Concord, not Conflict," in *The Rationality of Theism*, edited by Paul Copan and Paul Moser (London:

Routledge, 2003); Robert C. Koons, *Realism Regained*, 220–32; Robert C. Koons, "The Incompatibility of Naturalism and Scientific Realism" in *Naturalism: A Critical Analysis*, edited by Craig and Moreland (2001), 49–63.

17. Quoted by Hugh Kearney, *Science and Change, 1500–1700* (New York: McGraw-Hill, 1971), 86–87.

18. See F. J. Ayala, "The Autonomy of Biology as a Natural Science," in *Biology, History and Natural Philosophy*, ed. A. D. Breck and W. Yourgau (New York: Plenum Press, 1974), 7; and E. W. Sinnott, *Cell and Psyche: The Biology of Purpose* (New York: Harper & Row, 1961), 46.

19. Wolfgang Yourgrau and Stanley Mandelstam, *Variational Principles in Dynamics and Quantum Theory* (New York: Dover, 1979), 19–23, 164–67; Cornelius Lanczos, *The Variational Principles of Mechanics*, 4th edition (New York: Dover, 1986), 345–46; Robert Bruce Lindsay and Henry Morgenau. *Foundations of Physics* (New York: Dover, 1957), 133–36; Jim Hall, "Least Action Hero." *Lingua Franca* 9 (October 1999): 68.

20. Max Planck, "The Principle of Least Action." *A Survey of Physical Theory*, trans. by R. Jones and D. H. Williams (New York: Dover, 1960), 69–81; "Science and Faith," in *Scientific Autobiography and Other Papers*, trans. by W. H. Johnson (New York: Norton, 1936), 119–26.

21. H. Allen Orr, review of William A. Dembski's *No Free Lunch: Why Specified Complexity Cannot be Purchased without Intelligence* (New York: Rowman & Littlefield, 2001) in the *Boston Review* (summer 2002).

22. See Michael Ruse on the reality of ethics as a natural illusion, foisted upon us by natural selection, in *Taking Darwin Seriously* (Oxford: Blackwell, 1986), 216, 277.

23. Ludwig Wittgenstein, *On Certainty*, trans. by G. E. M. Anscombe and Denis Paul (New York: Harper & Row, 1969), 18.

24. Michael Denton, *Nature's Destiny: How the Laws of Biology Reveal Purpose in the Universe* (New York: Free Press, 1998).

25. Weaver, *Visions of Order*, 140.

26. Daniel C. Dennett, *Darwin's Dangerous Idea: Evolution and the Meanings of Life* (New York: Simon & Schuster, 1995), 63.

27. Ibid., 516–17, 519–20.

28. Larry Arnhart, Michael J. Behe, and William A. Dembski. "Conservatives, Darwin, and Design: An Exchange," *First Things* 107 (2000): 23–31.

29. John O. McGinnis, "The Origins of Conservatism," *National Review* (Dec. 22, 1997).

30. E. O. Wilson, *On Human Nature* (Cambridge, Mass.: Harvard University Press, 1978), 119–20, 133, 167, 208–09.

31. I am referring to Daniel C. Dennett, who has written, besides *Darwin's*

Dangerous Ideas, a series of books attempting to show that human agency is nothing more than a useful fiction (the "intentional stance"): yet another illusion foisted upon us by a nature indifferent to everything but our reproductive fecundity. See Dennett's *Brainstorms: Philosophical Essays on Mind and Psychology* (Montgomery, Vt.: Bradford Books, 1978), *The Intentional Stance* (Cambridge, Mass.: MIT Press, 1989), and *Consciousness Explained* (Boston: Little, Brown, 1991).

32. Peter R. Grant, *Ecology and Evolution of Darwin's Finches* (Princeton, N.J.: Princeton University Press, 1986).

4. DARWIN MEETS THE BERENSTAIN BEARS
Nancy R. Pearcey

1. Personal interview with John Calvert. Calvert has made similar statements in several contexts, many of which are available at www.intelligentdesignnetwork.org. The controversy in Ohio began when the state board of education instituted new standards requiring students to learn that "[s]cientific knowledge is limited to natural explanations for natural phenomena." See Grade 10, "Scientific Ways of Knowing (The Nature of Scientific Inquiry) #4." *Ohio's Academic Content Standards for Science* (Spring 2002 Review Draft).

2. This paper adapts and expands material from my forthcoming book, *Total Truth: Liberating Christianity from Its Cultural Captivity* (Wheaton, Ill.: Crossway Books).

3. Richard Dawkins, *The Blind Watchmaker* (New York: Norton, 1986), 287, emphasis added.

4. S. C. Todd, correspondence to *Nature* 410, 6752 (Sept. 30, 1999): 423, emphasis added.

5. Tom Bethell, "Against Sociobiology," *First Things* 109 (January 2001): 18–24.

6. Francis A. Schaeffer, *A Christian Manifesto*, Complete Works of Francis Schaeffer (Wheaton, Ill.: Crossway Books, 1982 [1981]), vol. 5, 423.

7. Richard Dawkins, *The Selfish Gene* (New York: Oxford University Press, 1976); Robert Wright, *The Moral Animal: Evolutionary Psychology in Everyday Life* (New York: Vintage, 1994); Leonard D. Katz, ed., *Evolutionary Origins of Morality* (New York: Norton, 1998); E. O. Wilson and Michael Ruse, "The Evolution of Ethics," in *Religion and the Natural Sciences: The Range of Engagement*, ed. J. E. Hutchingson (Orlando, Fla.: Harcourt and Brace, 1991).

8. Scott Atran, *In Gods We Trust: The Evolutionary Landscape of Religion* (New York: Oxford University Press, 2002), and Pascal Boyer, *Religion*

Explained: The Evolutionary Origins of Religious Thought (New York: Basic, 2001).

9. Paul H. Rubin, *Darwinian Politics: The Evolutionary Origin of Freedom* (New Brunswick, N.J.: Rutgers University Press, 2002). Arthur E. Gandolfi, Anna S. Gandolfi, and David P. Barash, *Economics as an Evolutionary Science: From Utility to Fitness* (New Brunswick, N.J.: Transaction, 2002). Dean Keith Simonton, *Origins of Genius: Darwinian Perspectives on Creativity* (New York: Oxford University Press, 1999). Wenda Trevathan, James J. McKenna, and Euclid O. Smith, eds., *Evolutionary Medicine* (New York: Oxford University Press, 1999); Randolph M. Nesse and George C. Williams, *Why We Get Sick: The New Science of Darwinian Medicine* (New York: Vintage, 1996).

10. Nigel Nicholson, *Executive Instinct: Managing the Human Animal in the Information Age* (New York: Crown, 2000). Kingsley Browne, *Divided Labours: An Evolutionary View of Women at Work* (New Haven, Conn.: Yale University Press, 1999). Martin Daly and Margo Wilson, *The Truth about Cinderella: A Darwinian View of Parental Love* (New Haven, Conn.: Yale University Press, 1999).

11. David M. Buss, *Evolution of Desire: Strategies of Human Mating* (New York: Basic, 1995); Malcolm Potts and Roger Short, *Ever Since Adam and Eve: The Evolution of Human Sexuality* (New York: Cambridge University Press, 1999); David M. Buss, *The Dangerous Passion: Why Jealousy Is as Necessary as Love and Sex* (New York: Free Press, 2000).

12. The phrase has been echoed by other critics of evolutionary psychology as well. See Hilary Rose and Steven Rose, eds., *Alas, Poor Darwin: Arguments Against Evolutionary Psychology*, (London: Jonathan Cape, 2000).

13. H. Allen Orr, "Dennett's Strange Idea: Natural Selection: Science of Everything, Universal Acid, Cure for the Common Cold . . . ," in the *Boston Review* (summer 1996), at http://bostonreview.mit.edu/br21.3/Orr.html.

14. Randy Thornhill and Craig Palmer, *The Natural History of Rape: Biological Bases of Sexual Coercion* (Cambridge, Mass.: MIT Press, 2000).

15. Jerry Coyne and Andew Berry, "Rape as an Adaption," *Nature* 404 (March, 9, 2000): 121–22.

16. Tom Bethell, "Against Sociobiology," *First Things* 109 (January 2001): 18–24.

17. Steven Pinker, *The Blank Slate: The Modern Denial of Human Nature* (Viking, 2002).

18. Steven Pinker, "Why They Kill Their Newborns," *New York Times* (November 1997).

19. H. Allen Orr, "Darwinian Storytelling," review of Steven Pinker's *The Blank Slate, New York Review of Books*, February 27, 2003. Orr describes Pinker's *New York Times* piece as "a nearly data-free account that comes perilously close to parody."

20. Cited in Ben Wiker, "Darwin and the Descent of Morality," *First Things* 117 (November 2001): 10–13. Darwin's *Descent of Man* is available online at www.literature.org/authors/darwin-charles/the-descent-of-man/chapter-04.html.

21. Peter Singer, "Heavy Petting," a review of *Dearest Pet: On Bestiality*, by Midas Dekkers (2001), on Nerve.com at www.nerve.com/Opinions/Singer/heavyPetting/main.asp.

22. For a discussion of the role that evolution played in Kinsey's thought, see Nancy Pearcey, "Creating the 'New Man': The Hidden Agenda in Sex Education," *Bible-Science Newsletter* (May 1990): 9–11. For a later treatment, see my chapter on the subject in *How Now Shall We Live?* coauthored by Charles Colson, with Harold Fickett (Wheaton, Ill.: Tyndale, 1999), chapter 25, "Salvation Through Sex?"

23. Stan and Jan Berenstain, *The Bears' Nature Guide* (New York: Random House, 1975).

24. For a fuller discussion, see Nancy Pearcey, "Canonizing the Cosmos: Carl Sagan's Naturalistic Religion," *Bible-Science Newsletter* (July 1986). See also Norman Geisler, *Cosmos: Carl Sagan's Religion for the Scientific Mind* (Dallas: Quest, 1983). For a later discussion, see my chapter on the subject in *How Now Shall We Live?* chapter 6, "Shattering the Grid."

25. Mark Ridley, "'Darwin's Blind Spot': Biotech Merger," *New York Times* (March 23, 2003), review of *Darwin's Blind Spot: Evolution Beyond Natural Selection*, by Frank Ryan.

26. Daniel Dennett, *Freedom Evolves* (New York: Viking, 2003).

27. John Gray, review of *Freedom Evolves* by Daniel Dennett, the *Independent* online, February 8, 2003, at http://enjoyment.independent.co.uk/books/reviews/story.jsp?story=376373.

28. John Gray, "Exposing the myth of secularism," *Australian Financial Review* (Jan 3, 2003), at http://afr.com/review/2003/01/03/FFX9CQAJFAD.html.

29. Daniel Dennett, *Darwin's Dangerous Idea* (New York: Simon and Schuster, 1995), 63.

30. Mary Midgely, "Why Memes?" in *Alas, Poor Darwin; Arguments against Evolutionary Psychology*, eds. Hilary Rose and Steven Rose (London: Jonathan Cape, 2000), 72.

31. For discussions of memes, see Dennett's *Freedom Evolves,* as well as Susan Blackmore's *The Meme Machine* (Oxford: Oxford University Press, 1999).

32. Richard Dawkins, "Viruses of the Mind," in *Free Inquiry* 13, no. 3 (summer 1993).

33. Mary Midgely, "Fate by Fluke," a review of *Freedom Evolves* by Daniel C. Dennett, the *Guardian* (March 1, 2003).

34. Ernst Mayr, book review of "Evolution and God," *Nature* 248 (March 22, 1974): 285.

35. Neal Gillespie, *Charles Darwin and the Problem of Creation* (Chicago: University of Chicago Press, 1979). See also Nancy Pearcey, "You Guys Lost," in *Mere Creation,* ed. William A. Dembski (Downers Grove, Ill.: InterVarsity), 73–92.

36. Edward A. Purcell Jr., *The Crisis of Democratic Theory: Scientific Naturalism and the Problem of Value* (Lexington, Ky.: University Press of Kentucky, 1973), 8, 21.

37. Morton White, *Science and Sentiment in America: Philosophical Thought from Jonathan Edwards to John Dewey* (New York: Oxford University Press, 1972), 175. Dewey held that mathematics was a process of strictly empirical investigation, "a product of long historic growth," of successes and failures. White, 281–82.

38. John Dewey, "The Influence of Darwin on Philosophy," in *The Influence of Darwin on Philosophy and Other Essays in Contemporary Thought* (New York: Henry Holt and Company, 1910), 9.

39. Cited in Paul F. Boller Jr., *American Thought in Transition: The Impact of Evolutionary Naturalism, 1865–1900* (Chicago: Rand McNally, 1969), 142.

40. See James Ward Smith, "Religion and Science in American Philosophy," in *The Shaping of American Religion,* ed. James Ward Smith and A. Leland Jamison (Princeton, N.J.: Princeton University Press, 1961), 427, 441.

41. James's religious views are discussed by Paul Conkin in *Puritans and Pragmatists: Eight Eminent American Thinkers* (New York: Dodd, Mead, & Co., 1968), especially 339–40.

42. Philip P. Wiener, *Evolution and the Founders of Pragmatism* (New York: Harper and Row, 1965), chapter 4.

43. Hartshorne said that the two thinkers who influenced him most were Peirce and Alfred North Whitehead, a British philosopher who was a close associate of the pragmatists and who taught a philosophy known as Process Thought.

44. See Boller, Chapter 6, "William James and the Open Universe," especially

134–38. An intense debate is being carried out today over whether Open Theism is derivative from Process Theology, with some theologians denying it, while others acknowledge the influence of Peirce and Whitehead.

45. For a detailed treatment of Holmes and legal pragmatism, including its continuing impact today, see Nancy R. Pearcey, "Darwin's New Bulldogs," *Regent University Law Review*, vol. 13, No. 2 (2000–01): 483–511. A shorter and adapted version appeared as "Why Judges Make Law: The Roots and Remedies of Judicial Imperialism," *Human Events* (December 1, 2000), available at http://arn.org/pearcey/nphome.htm.

46. See Alexander W. Alschuler, *Law Without Values: The Life, Work, and Legacy of Justice Holmes* (Chicago: University of Chicago Press, 2000), 58.

47. Oliver Wendell Holmes, "Law in Science and Science in Law," in *The Essential Holmes* (Chicago: University of Chicago Press, 1996), 191.

48. Cited in James Kloppenberg, *Uncertain Victory: Social Democracy and Progressivism in European and American Thought, 1879–1920* (Oxford: Oxford University Press, 1986), 84.

49. See Nancy Pearcey, "The Evolving Child: John Dewey's Impact on Modern Education," Part 1 and 2, *Bible-Science Newsletter* (January and February 1991); and Nancy Pearcey, "What Is Evolution Doing to Education?" *Bible-Science Newsletter* (January 1986). For a later treatment, see my chapter on education in *How Now Shall We Live?* chapter 34, "Still at Risk."

50. Cited in James Davison Hunter, *The Death of Character: Moral Education without Good or Evil* (New York: Basic, 2000), 61.

51. Thomas Lickona, *Educating for Character* (New York: Bantam Books, 1992), 237.

52. Catherine Fosnot, "Constructivism: A Psychological Theory of Learning," in Catherine Fosnot, ed., *Constructivism: Theory, Perspectives, and Practice* (New York: Teachers College Press, 1996), 8–33, emphasis added.

53. J. F. Osborne, "Beyond Constructivism," *Science Education* 80 (1996): 63.

54. Cited in Allen Quist, *FedEd: The Federal Curriculum and How It's Enforced* (St. Paul, Minn.: Maple River Education Coalition, 2002), 118.

55. Ernst von Glasersfeld, "A Constructivist Approach to Teaching," in *Constructivism in Education*, ed. L. P. Steffe and J. Gale (Hillsdale, N.J.: Lawrence Erlbaum Associates, Publishers, 1995), 3–15, at http://platon.ee.duth.gr/~soeist7t/Lessons/lesson7.htm.

56. George S. Counts, *Dare the Schools Build a New Social Order?* (New York: John Day Pamphlets, 1932), No. 11. For a good description of

reconstructionism, see George R. Knight, *Issues and Alternatives in Educational Philosophy*, 3rd edition (Berrien Springs, Mich.: Andrews University Press, 1982).

57. Frederic T. Sommers, "A Campus Forum on Multiculturalism," *New York Times* (December 9, 1990).

58. Richard Rorty, *Contingency, Irony, and Solidarity* (Cambridge: Cambridge University Press, 1989), Chapter One, passim.

59. Richard Rorty, "Trotsky and the Wild Orchids," in *Wild Orchids and Trotsky: Message from American Universities*, ed. Mark Edmundson (New York: Viking, 1993), 38.

60. Richard Rorty, "Untruth and Consequences," *New Republic* (July 31, 1995): 27.

61. Francis Darwin, ed., *Life and Letters of Charles Darwin*, vol 1 (New York: D. Appleton and Co., 1898), 285. For several additional quotations from Darwin on this topic, see Nancy Pearcey, "The Influence of Evolution on Philosophy and Ethics," *Science at the Crossroads* (Richfield, Minn.: Onesimus Publishing, 1985), 166–71.

62. Alvin Plantinga, *Warrant and Proper Function* (New York: Oxford University Press, 1993), 218.

63. Stephen Jay Gould, *Rocks of Ages: Science & Religion in the Fullness of Life* (New York: Ballantine, 1999), 4.

64. Allan Bloom is author of the bestseller *The Closing of the American Mind*. This quotation is from *The Republic of Plato*, Translated with Notes and an Interpretative Essay by Allan Bloom (New York: Basic, 1968), x.

65. Phillip Johnson, *The Wedge of Truth: Splitting the Foundations of Naturalism* (Downers Grove, Ill.: InterVarsity, 2000), 115.

66. Johnson, *The Wedge of Truth*, 148.

67. Victor Greto, "Delaware a leader in teaching evolution," *The News Journal*, Wilmington, Delaware (February 25, 2003).

68. Backgrounder for the PBS program "Evolution," titled "Emi & Nathan: Personal Testimonies," at www.pbs.org/wgbh/evolution/library/08/1/l_081_07.html.

5. Teaching the Flaws in Neo-Darwinism
Edward Sisson

1. This essay reflects my personal opinions and is not written on behalf of any client. I write here in my personal capacity only, not as counsel to any person or organization, nor on behalf of any firm or any of its clients.

2. Thomas Kuhn, *The Structure of Scientific Revolutions*, 3rd ed. (Chicago: University of Chicago Press, 1996).

3. Naomi Oreskes, *The Rejection of Continental Drift: Theory and Method in American Earth Science* (New York: Oxford University Press, 1999) (hereinafter *Rejection of Continental Drift*); Naomi Oreskes, *Plate Tectonics, An Insider's History of the Modern Theory of the Earth: Seventeen Original Essays by the Scientists Who Made Earth History* (Boulder, Colo.: Westview, 2001) (hereinafter *Plate Tectonics*), 3–13

4. Oreskes, *Rejection of Continental Drift*, 180–81.

5. Ibid., 207.

6. Oreskes, *Plate Tectonics*, 12.

7. Oreskes, *Rejection of Continental Drift*, 208–19 and notes 112–44 at pages 350–51; Oreskes, *Plate Tectonics*, 12.

8. Oreskes, *Plate Tectonics*, 12.

9. Stephen Jay Gould, "The Validation of Continental Drift," reprinted in Stephen Jay Gould, *Ever Since Darwin: Reflections In Natural History* (New York: Norton, 1979), 160; excerpted for a University of Washington geophysics class in spring, 2002 (located on the internet at www.geophys.washington.edu/People/Faculty/kcc/gphys202/ continental_drift.htm).

10. Science writer William Corliss also discusses the discrediting of the land-bridge theory, although he focuses not on Schuchert and Willis but on earlier scientists such as Melchior Neymayr, Edward Suess, and John Gregory. Although Corliss shines his spotlight on a different cast of characters than does Oreskes, the story he tells is the same. See William Corliss, the chapter "Up and Down Land Bridges," in *Mysteries Beneath the Sea* (New York: Thomas Y. Crowell, 1970), 61-72.

11. Douglas J. Futuyma, *Evolutionary Biology*, 3rd ed. (Sunderland, Mass.: Sinauer Assoc., 1998), 15; Gerald Audesirk, Teresa Audesirk, & Bruce Byers, *Life on Earth*, 2nd ed. (Upper Saddle River, N.J: Prentice Hall, 2000), 8–9, 12, 235.

12. Jacques Roger, trans. by Sarah Lucille Bonnefoi, *Buffon: A Life in Natural History* (Ithaca, N.Y.: Cornell University Press, 1997) (hereinafter *Buffon*), 316, 321–23, 329–31. See also the website of Prof. Jonathan Marks, University of North Carolina, where he has posted excerpts of his 1997 article on Buffon in *The History of Physical Anthropology*, at www.uncc.edu/jmarks/Buffon/Biology.html and /Crypto.html.

13. Michael Denton, *Evolution: A Theory in Crisis*, (Bethesda, Md.: Adler & Adler, 1985), 157–98.

14. I must offer one caveat: having not seen the other contributions to this volume at the time I write, I cannot be certain that every argument I find

persuasive has been included. Moreover, I have developed some additional arguments that I have not found presented elsewhere, which I would have included here but for space limitations.

15. Alternatively, which amounts to the same thing, the gene might have been present in all individuals, but is now "switched on" or "switched off" in a different proportion of the population.

16. Roger, *Buffon*, 316, 322, 413–14. It should be apparent from my several citations of Buffon that I do not believe that his work can be rejected with the facile comment that it predated Darwin's insights. Rather, I cite Buffon as an example of state-of-the-art science *prior* to the point that Darwin and his proponents sidetracked and hijacked the debate in order to serve the sociological goal of promoting the scientific establishment and demoting the religious establishment. I believe that for the science of the origins of the diversity of life to get back on track, it should give renewed respect to the state of science before the great Darwinian diversion, building on that science in a productive and rigorous fashion that is divorced from the sociological project that unintelligent evolution serves.

17. *Science* 134 (Sept. 1, 1961): 596–602.

18. Bernard Barber, *Social Studies of Science* (New Brunswick, N.J.: Transaction, 1990), 80, 97–113.

19. Sir Fred Hoyle, *Mathematics of Evolution* (Memphis, Tenn.: Acorn, 1999), 104.

20. Ibid., 106.

21. Gould, "The Validation of Continental Drift," *supra* note 9.

22. Kuhn, *Structure of Scientific Revolutions*, 150–53, 157–59.

23. "Priorities in Scientific Discovery," *American Sociological Review* 22 (1957): 635–59, reprinted in *The Sociology of Science* (Westport, Conn.: Greenwood, 1962), 454.

24. Daniel Dennett, *Darwin's Dangerous Idea: Evolution and the Meanings of Life* (New York: Touchstone Books, 1995), 63, 82, 144–45, 521.

25. *The Scopes Trial* (Birmingham, Ala.: Gryphon Editions Notable Trials Library, 1990), facsimile reprint of *The World's Most Famous Court Trial* (Cincinnati: National Book Company, 1925) (hereinafter "*The Scopes Trial*").

26. George Hunter, *A Civic Biology* (New York: American Book Company, 1914).

27. George Hunter, *Laboratory Problems in Civic Biology* (New York: American Book Company, 1916).

28. *The Scopes Trial*, 229–80 (statements of Drs. Metcalf, Nelson, Lipman,

Judd, and Newman read in court; statements of Drs. Cole and Curtis also submitted in writing).

29. Ibid., 206, 220–21, 223. The prosecution's trial tactics—arguing that the truth of the theory was irrelevant—explain in part the failure of evolution to undergo cross-examination in the Scopes Trial. The judge initially kept the scientists from testifying, which meant that the prosecution lost one opportunity to cross-examine them. Later when the judge allowed the scientists' written testimony to be read in open court, the prosecution sought to cross-examine, but Darrow successfully persuaded the judge to deny the prosecution any chance to challenge that testimony.

30. Ibid., 284, 88.

31. Ibid., 306–07.

32. Hoyle, *Mathematics of Evolution*, 106.

33. *The Scopes Trial*, 299.

34. Hunter, *A Civic Biology*, 261–64; Hunter, *Laboratory Problems in Civic Biology*, 182–84.

35. Hunter, *A Civic Biology*, 196, 262–63.

36. Hunter, *Laboratory Problems in Civic Biology*, 182.

6. ACCEPT NO IMITATIONS
J. Budziszewski

1. The idea of a divine authority behind the natural law is often misunderstood. Some people imagine that if God had ordained that we rape instead of marry, murder instead of cherish, hate Him instead of love him, then such things would be right. The absurdity of this idea is considered an objection to God's authority. What the objection overlooks is that a being capable of commanding such things would not be God. God is neither constrained by nor indifferent to the good; he *is* the good, the uncreated good in which created goods are grounded.

2. For discussion, see J. Budziszewski, *What We Can't Not Know* (Dallas: Spence Publishing, 2003), chaps. 4–5.

3. William B. Provine, "Scientists, Face it! Science and Religion Are Incompatible," *The Scientist* (5 September 1988): 10–11. See also William Provine, "Evolution and the Foundation of Ethics," *MBL Science* 3:1 (1988): 25–29. The article is conveniently reprinted in Steven L. Goldman, *Science, Technology, and Social Progress* (Bethlehem, Pa.: Lehigh University Press, 1989).

4. Richard Dawkins, *River Out of Eden* (New York: HarperCollins, 1995), 132–33.

5. Edward O. Wilson, *On Human Nature* (Cambridge, Mass.: Harvard University Press, 1978), 176.

6. Michael Ruse and E. O. Wilson, "The Evolution of Ethics." *New Scientist* 108:1478 (17 October 1985), 51–52.

7. Robert Wright, *The Moral Animal: The New Science of Evolutionary Psychology* (New York: Random House, 1994), 212.

8. Richard Dawkins, *The Selfish Gene* (Oxford: Oxford University Press, 1989), preface, 3.

9. Edward O. Wilson, "What is nature worth? There's a powerful economic argument for preserving our living natural environment." *San Francisco Chronicle* (May 5, 2002). Wilson's book *The Future of Life* was published by Alfred Knopf (New York: 2002).

10. It seems likely that imagination is not a property of matter either, but we may leave this question for another time.

11. There is a danger of circularity: Unless they had already developed the tendency to mutual aid, why *would* they have lived in family groups?

12. William D. Hamilton, "The Evolution of Altruistic Behavior," *American Naturalist* 97 (1963): 354–56, and "The Genetical Evolution of Social Behavior," *Journal of Theoretical Biology* 7 (1964): 1–52.

13. Wright, *The Moral Animal*, 313–14.

14. Ibid., 211–12.

15. Ibid., 332–33.

16. For a more detailed discussion of the significance of these four steps for utilitarianism, see J. Budziszewski, *Written on the Heart: The Case for Natural Law* (Downers Grove, Ill.: InterVarsity, 1997), chaps. 10–12.

17. See his essay *Utilitarianism*.

18. Larry Arnhart, *Darwinian Natural Right: The Biological Ethics of Human Nature* (Albany, N.Y.: State University of New York Press, 1998). See also Larry Arnhart, Michael J. Behe, and William A. Dembski, "Conservatives, Darwin & Design: An Exchange," *First Things* 107 (November 2000): 23–31; and Larry Arnhart, "Evolution and Ethics: E. O. Wilson Has More in Common With Thomas Aquinas Than He Realizes," *Books & Culture* 5:6 (November/December 1999): 36.

19. John Hare pursues a similar line of reasoning in his paper "Evolutionary Naturalism and the Reduction of the Ethical Demand," presented at "The Nature of Nature: An Interdisciplinary Conference on the Role of Naturalism in Science," Baylor University, April, 2000. Because Hare's purpose in writing is somewhat different than mine, he does not comment on the confusion between naturalism and Natural Law, nor does he draw out the parallel between Arnhart's theory and utilitarianism. However, he vigorously criticizes Arnhart for what he calls the "double

identity" of equating the good with the desirable and the desirable with what in fact is desired (my steps two and three), and our arguments coincide at several points.

20. C. S. Lewis, *The Pilgrim's Regress*, preface to 3rd ed., xii. Lewis's analysis of the experience is illuminating.

21. Thomas Aquinas, *Summa Theologica* I-II, Q. 100.

22. Not all exceptionless precepts are "first" principles. The prohibition of murder, for example, is not a first principle because it rests on the still more basic precept that we must never gratuitously harm our neighbors; nevertheless it binds without exception.

23. *Summa Theologica* I-II, Q. 94, Art. 4.

24. Arnhart, 1978, chap. 2.

25. Ibid., chap. 6, section on "The Moral Complementarity of Male and Female Norms."

26. Ibid.

27. Ibid., introductory section.

7. REFEREED JOURNALS
Frank J. Tipler

1. Abraham Pais, *The Genius of Science* (New York: Oxford University Press, 2000), 307.

2. Quoted from Walter Shropshire Jr., ed., *The Joys of Research* (Washington: Smithsonian Institution Press, 1981), 109.

3. *New York Times*, October 12, 1999, p. A29.

4. Mitchell J. Feigenbaum, in Laurie M. Brown, Abraham Pais, and Brian Pippard, eds., *Twentieth Century Physics* (New York: American Institute of Physics Press, 1995), 1850.

5. Ibid., 1426.

6. Quoted in Lillian Hoddeson, *True Genius: The Life and Science of John Bardeen* (Washington: Joseph Henry Press, 2002), 300.

7. Jane Hawking, *Music to Move the Stars: A Life with Stephen Hawking* (Philadelphia: Trans-Atlantic Publications, 1999), 239.

8. Tuzo Wilson, quoted in *The Joys of Research*, 130.

9. Philip Anderson, in *Twentieth Century Physics*, 2029.

10. See Paula E. Stephan and Sharon G. Levin, *Striking the Mother Lode in Science* (New York: Oxford University Press, 1992), chapter 7, for a detailed discussion of the Pygmy Effect.

11. Robert Root-Bernstein, *Discovering* (Boston: Harvard University Press, 1989), 39–40.

12. Steven Weinberg, *The First Three Minutes* (New York: Basic, 1977), chapter 6.
13. *New York Times*, February 25, 2003, D4.
14. The database can be found at http://xxx.lanl.gov.
15. Martin Harwit, *Cosmic Discovery* (New York: Basic, 1981), 260–61.

8. A Catholic Scientist Looks at Darwinism
Michael J. Behe

1. E. Wasman & H. Muckermann, "Evolution," in *The Catholic Encyclopedia,* vol. 5, (New York: The Encyclopedia Press, Inc., 1909), 654.
2. The rest of this chapter is adapted from a talk I gave at Catholic University in Washington, D.C., on October 16, 2000, in a series of talks exploring the implications of Pope John Paul II's encyclical *Fides et Ratio.*
3. Pope John Paul II, Message to the Pontifical Academy of Sciences. *L'Osservatore Romano*, Oct. 30, 1996. Reprinted in *Quarterly Review of Biology* 1997, *72*, 381–83.
4. Ibid.
5. Ibid.
6. Quoted in Phillip E. Johnson, *Darwin on Trial* (Washington: Regnery Gateway, 1991),150–51.
7. Richard Dawkins, *The Blind Watchmaker* (London: Norton, 1986), 6.
8. Daniel Dennett, *Darwin's Dangerous Idea* (New York: Simon & Schuster, 1995), 515–16.
9. K. R. Miller and J. Levine, *Biology* (Englewood Cliffs, N.J.: Prentice Hall, 1995), 658.
10. National Association of Biology Teachers.1995. "Statement on the Teaching of Evolution," quoted in C. Raymo, "The hand on the controls is survival," *Boston Globe*, April 20, 1998, C2.
11. Pope John Paul II, Encyclical Letter, *Fides et Ratio* of the Supreme Pontiff John Paul II to the Bishops of the Catholic Church on the Relationship Between Faith and Reason (Boston: Pauline Books and Media, 1998), 7.
12. Ibid., 29.
13. Ibid., 47–48.
14. Richard Dawkins, quoted in Gregg Easterbrook, "Science and God: a Warming Trend?" *Science* 277 (1997): 890–93.
15. Joseph Ratzinger, *In the Beginning: A Catholic Understanding of the Story of Creation and the Fall* (Grand Rapids, Mich.: Eerdmans,1986), 54.
16. Ibid., 55–57.
17. Pope John Paul II, 1998, 129.

18. R. M. Macnab, "The Bacterial Flagellum: Reversible Rotary Propellor and Type III Export Apparatus." *J. Bacteriol* 181 (1999): 7149–53.

19. John F. Haught, *God After Darwin: a Theology of Evolution* (Boulder, Colo.: Westview, 2000), 70.

20. Pope John Paul II, 1998, 43.

21. Pope John Paul II, 1998, 61–62.

22. Pope John Paul II, 1998, 109–10.

23. Thomas Nagel, *The Last Word* (New York: Oxford University Press, 1997), 130.

24. Richard Lewontin, "Billions and Billions of Demons," *New York Review of Books* (January 9, 1997): 28.

25. I. Mellman & G. Warren, "The Road Taken: Past and Future Foundations of Membrane Traffic," *Cell* 100 (2000): 99–112.

26. Bruce Alberts et al, *Molecular Biology of the Cell* (New York: Garland Pub., 1994), 33.

27. E. Pennisi, "Haeckel's Embryos: Fraud Rediscovered," *Science* 277 (1997): 1435.

28. Donald Voet & Judith G. Voet, *Biochemistry*, 2nd ed. (New York: John Wiley & Sons, 1995), 19.

29. F. M. Harold, "From Morphogenes to Morphogenesis," *Microbiology* 141 (1995): 2765–78.

30. National Academy of Sciences. *Science and Creationism: a View From the National Academy of Sciences* (Washington: National Academy Press, 1999), 6.

31. Pope John Paul II, 1998, 71–72.

32. Pope Pius XII. *Humani Generis*, Encyclical Letter of Pope Pius XII; (Washington: National Catholic Welfare Conference,1950).

33. Pope John Paul II, 1996.

34. Quoted in Pope John Paul II, 1998, 54.

9. AN ANTI-DARWINIAN INTELLECTUAL JOURNEY
Michael John Denton

1. Charles Darwin, *The Origin of Species*, 6th ed. (London: Murray, 1972), 332.

2. Ibid., 333.

3. William Paley, *Natural Theology* (London: R. Faulder, 1892).

4. Stephen Jay Gould, *The Structure of Evolutionary Theory* (Cambridge, Mass: Harvard University Press, 2002).

5. Charles Darwin, *On the Various Contrivances by Which British and*

Foreign Orchids Are Fertilized by Insects (London: Murray, 1862), 283–84.

6. Michael J. Denton, *Evolution: A Theory in Crisis* (London: Burnett Books, 1984).

7. Richard Owen, *On the Nature of Limbs* (London: John Van Voorst, 1849), 41.

8. Lawrence J. Henderson, *The Fitness of the Environment* (New York: Macmillan, 1913).

9. Owen, op cit., 9.

10. Ibid., 12

11. Ibid., 39.

12. Ibid., 40.

13. Ibid., 84.

14. Ibid., 84.

15. Ibid., 85.

16. Stephen Jay Gould, *The Panda's Thumb.* (New York: Norton, 1980).

17. Gould, *The Structure of Evolutionary Theory.*

18. Alfred Sherwood Romer, *Vertebrate Paleontology,* 3rd ed. (Chicago: University of Chicago Press, 1966). Gaylord G. Simpson, *The Major Features of Evolution.* (New York: Columbia University Press, 1953). Gaylord G. Simpson, "The History of Life," in *The Evolution of Life,* edited by Sol Tax (Chicago: University of Chicago Press, 1960).

19. F. H. C. Crick, "The Origin of the Genetic Code," *Journal of Molecular Biology* 38 (1968): 367–79. C. Woese, "The Origin of the Genetic Code," *Proceedings of the National Academy of Sciences U.S.* 54 (1965): 1546–52.

20. Motoo Kimura, *The Neutral Theory of Molecular Evolution* (Cambridge: Cambridge University Press, 1983).

21. Michael J. Denton, N. Spencer, and H. R. V. Arnstein, "Biochemical and Enzymic Changes during Red Cell Differentiation: The Significance of the Final Cell Division," *Biochemical Journal* 146 (1975): 205–11.

22. N. Eldredge and S. J. Gould, "Punctuated Equilibrium: An Alternative to Phyletic Gradualism." In *Models in Paleontology,* edited by T. J. M. Schopf (San Francisco: Freeman, 1973), 82–115.

23. Noam Chomsky, *Language and Mind* (New York: Harcourt Brace Jovanovich, 1972).

24. E. S. Russell, *Form and Function* (London: J. S. Murray, 1916). Robert Chambers, *Vestiges of the Natural History of Creation* (London: John Churchill, 1844).

25. D'Arcy W. Thompson, *On Growth and Form* (Cambridge: Cambridge University Press, 1917).

26. Stuart Kauffman, *The Origins of Order* (New York: Oxford University Press, 1993).

27. Brian Goodwin, *How the Leopard Changed Its Spots* (London: Weidenfeld and Nicolson, 1994).

28. P. S. Moorehead and M. M. Kaplan, *Mathematical Challenges to the Darwinian Interpretation of Evolution* (Wistar Institute Symposium Monograph, 1967).

29. Michael J. Denton, *Nature's Destiny* (New York: Free Press, 1998).

30. August Weismann, *The Evolution Theory* (London: Edward Arnold, 1904).

31. Ibid.

32. Evelyn Fox Keller, *The Century of the Gene* (Cambridge, Mass.: Harvard University Press, 2000).

33. Annette Karmiloff-Smith, *Beyond Modularity: A Developmental Perspective on Cognitive Science* (Cambridge, Mass.: MIT Press, 1992).

34. H. F. Nijhout, "Metaphors and the Role of Genes in Development," *Bioessays* 12 (1990): 441–46. See also Thompson op. cit. and Kauffman, op. cit.

35. Aristotle. *Parts of Animals*, trans. by A. L. Peck (London: Heinemann, 1937).

36. M. J. Denton and J. C. Marshall, "The Laws of Form Revisited," *Nature* 410 (2001): 411.

37. M. J. Denton, J. C. Marshall, and M. Legge, "The Protein Folds as Platonic Forms: New Support for the Pre-Darwinian Conception of Evolution by Natural Law," *Journal of Theoretical Biology* 219 (2002): 325–42.

38. M. J. Denton, P. K. Dearden, and S. J. Sowerby, "A New Pre-Darwinian World of Abstract Forms: Physical Law, Not Natural Selection as the Major Determinant of Organic Form at the Sub-Cellular Level," submitted to *Biosystems* (2003).

39. S. J. Sowerby and M. J. Denton, "The Use of Self-Organizing Natural Forms Like the Protein and RNA Folds Which Provide *Emergent Complexity for Free* May Be a Necessary Feature of any Self-Replicating System." Manuscript in preparation (2003).

10. Why I Am Not a Darwinist
James Barham

1. Robert J. Richards, *The Meaning of Evolution: The Morphological Construction and Ideological Reconstruction of Darwin's Theory* (Chicago: University of Chicago Press, 1992).

2. Peter J. Bowler, *The Non-Darwinian Revolution: Reinterpreting a Historical Myth* (Baltimore: Johns Hopkins University Press, 1988).

3. It is doubtful whether Charles Darwin himself was anything resembling a metaphysical Darwinist: see John F. Cornell, "Newton of the Grassblade? Darwin and the Problem of Organic Teleology," *Isis* 77 (1986): 405–21; and James G. Lennox, "Darwin *Was* a Teleologist," *Biology and Philosophy* 8 (1993): 409–21.

4. In *Three Tales*, by Steve Reich and Beryl Korot. On Kismet, see Cynthia L. Breazeal, *Designing Sociable Robots* (Cambridge, MA: Bradford Books/MIT Press, 2002). For the extravagant claim that such robots deserve to be regarded by us as persons, see Anne Foerst, "Artificial Sociability: From Embodied AI toward New Understandings of Personhood," *Technology in Society* 21 (1999): 373–86.

5. Barbara Kingsolver, *Small Wonder* (New York: HarperCollins, 2002), 96 (my emphasis).

6. Edward O. Wilson, *Consilience: The Unity of Knowledge* (New York: Knopf, 1998).

7. Cicero, *De natura deorum* and *Academica*, translated by H. Rackham (Cambridge, Mass.: Harvard University Press, 1933), 213.

8. Fred Hoyle, *The Intelligent Universe* (New York: Holt, Rinehart and Winston, 1983), 19.

9. Franklin M. Harold, *The Way of the Cell: Molecules, Organisms, and the Order of Life* (New York: Oxford University Press, 2001); Frank T. Vertosick, *The Genius Within: Discovering the Intelligence of Every Living Thing* (New York: Harcourt, 2002).

10. There is now increasing empirical evidence that at least some genetic mutations are functionally regulated: see Lynn Helena Caporale, ed., *Molecular Strategies in Biological Evolution* (New York: New York Academy of Sciences, 1999).

11. Robert G. B. Reid, *Evolutionary Theory: The Unfinished Synthesis* (Ithaca, N.Y.: Cornell University Press, 1985).

12. Cited in Adrian Desmond and James Moore, *Darwin: The Life of a Tormented Evolutionist* (New York: Warner Books, 1991), 314.

13. Alfred North Whitehead, *The Function of Reason* (Boston: Beacon Press, 1958), 16. (Originally published by Princeton University Press in 1929.)

14. Bas C. van Fraassen, Response to John Haldane's "Thomism and the Future of Catholic Philosophy," *New Blackfriars* 80 (1999): 177–81; 179.

15. F. Eugene Yates, ed., *Self-Organizing Systems: The Emergence of Order* (New York: Plenum, 1987).

16. Attributed to J. B. S. Haldane; cited in Stephen Jay Gould, *Ever Since Darwin* (New York: Norton, 1977), 262.

17. Erica Goode, "Some Deaths Resonate, Others Pass Unnoticed," *New York Times* (February 4, 2003): D1 & D4; D4.

18. Inge Scholl, *The White Rose: Munich, 1942–1943,* 2nd ed., translated by Arthur R. Schultz (Hanover, N.H.: Wesleyan University Press, 1983). (Originally published as *Die Weisse Rose* in 1952.)

19. Adalbert Stifter, "Preface to *Many-colored Stones,*" translated by Jeffrey L. Sammons, in Jeffrey L. Sammons, ed., *German Novellas of Realism,* vol. 1 (New York: Continuum, 1989), 1–6; 3–5. (Originally published as "Vorrede" to the novella collection *Bunte Steine* in 1853.)

20. See, for example, Mae-Wan Ho, *The Rainbow and the Worm: The Physics of Organisms,* 2nd ed. (Singapore: World Scientific, 1998); Charles J. Lumsden, Wendy A. Brandts, and Lynn E. H. Trainor, eds., *Physical Theory in Biology: Foundations and Explorations* (Singapore: World Scientific, 1997); Gerald H. Pollack, *Cells, Gels, and the Engines of Life: A New, Unifying Approach to Cell Function* (Seattle: Ebner & Sons, 2001); and Jan Walleczek, ed., *Self-Organized Biological Dynamics and Nonlinear Control: Toward Understanding Complexity, Chaos and Emergent Function in Living Systems* (Cambridge: Cambridge University Press, 2000). For a programmatic statement of the scientific aims of such approaches, see Robert B. Laughlin, David Pines, Joerg Schmalian, Branko P. Stojkoví, and Peter Wolynes, "The Middle Way," *Proceedings of the National Academy of Sciences, USA* 97 (2000): 32–37. For the philosophical implications, as well as further references to the scientific literature, see my "Biofunctional Realism and the Problem of Teleology," *Evolution and Cognition* 6 (2000): 2–34; and "Theses on Darwin," *Rivista di Biologia/Biology Forum* 95 (2002): 115–47.

21. Philip W. Anderson, "More Is Different," *Science* 177 (1972): 393–96; reprinted in Philip W. Anderson, *A Career in Theoretical Physics* (Singapore: World Scientific, 1994), 1–4. See, also, Robert B. Laughlin and David Pines, "The Theory of Everything," *Proceedings of the National Academy of Sciences, USA* 97 (2000): 28–31; and Silvan S. Schweber, "The Metaphysics of Science at the End of a Heroic Age," in Robert S. Cohen, Michael Horne, and John Stachel, eds., *Experimental Metaphysics* (Dordrecht, Holland: Kluwer Academic, 1997), 171–98.

22. Philip W. Anderson, "More Is Different—One More Time," in N. Phuan Ong and Ravin N. Bhatt, eds., *More Is Different: Fifty Years of Condensed Matter Physics* (Princeton, N.J.: Princeton University Press, 2001), 1–8, 7.

23. Bernard J. Baars, "The Double Life of B. F. Skinner: Inner Conflict, Dissociation and the Scientific Taboo against Consciousness," *Journal of Consciousness Studies* 10 (2003): 5–25.

24. Lenny Moss, "From Representational Preformationism to the Epigenesis of Openness to the World? Reflections on a New Vision of the Organism," in Linda Van Speybroeck, Dani de Waele, Gertrudis Van de Vijver, and Mitzi de Szereto, eds., *From Epigenesis to Epigenetics: The Genome in Context* (New York: New York Academy of Sciences, 2002), 219–30, 222.

25. Arthur T. Winfree, *When Time Breaks Down: The Three-Dimensional Dynamics of Electrochemical Waves and Cardiac Arrhythmias* (Princeton, N.J.: Princeton University Press, 1987); Walter J. Freeman, *How Brains Make Up Their Minds* (New York: Columbia University Press, 2001); C. Sonnenschein and A. M. Soto, *The Society of Cells: Cancer and Control of Cell Proliferation* (Oxford: Bios Scientific Publishers/New York: Springer, 1999); F. Eugene Yates and Laurel A. Benton, "Loss of Integration and Resiliency with Age: A Dissipative Destruction," in E. J. Masoro, ed., *Handbook of Physiology—Aging* (Oxford: Oxford University Press, 1993), 591–610.

26. Alfred North Whitehead, "Nature and Life," in Alfred North Whitehead, *Modes of Thought* (New York: Free Press, 1968), 127–69; 148. (Originally published separately by the University of Chicago Press in 1934.)

27. I would like to thank William A. Dembski, Ellen F. Hall, and Mark McCulley for their comments on the manuscript. I would also like to express my heartfelt gratitude to them, together with Stephen J. Anderson, Celica Milovanovic, Lenny Moss, and Aron Zysow, for their friendship. Not only would this essay not exist without all of their support, both moral and material—neither would I.

11. WHY EVOLUTION FAILS THE TEST OF SCIENCE
Cornelius G. Hunter

1. National Academy of Sciences, *Science and Creationism: A View from the National Academy of Sciences*, 2nd ed. (Washington: National Academy Press, 1999), 6.

2. Carl Zimmer, *Evolution* (New York: HarperCollins, 2001), 104.

3. Charles Darwin, *The Origin of Species*, 6th ed. (1872; repr. London: Collier Macmillan, 1962), 136.

4. D. Penny, L. R. Foulds, M. D. Hendy, "Testing the Theory of Evolution by Comparing Phylogenetic Trees Constructed from Five Different Protein Sequences," *Nature* 297 (1982): 197–200.

5. "I should without hesitation adopt [evolution], even if it were unsupported by other facts or arguments." Charles Darwin, *Origin*, 457.

6. Gavin de Beer, *Atlas of Evolution*, (London: Nelson, 1964), 16.

7. Elizabeth Pennisi, "Charting a Genome's Hills and Valleys," *Science* 296 (2002): 1601–03.
8. Michael Balter, "Morphologists Learn to Live With Molecular Upstarts," *Science* 276 (1997): 1032–34.
9. Carl Zimmer, *Evolution*, 325.
10. Isaac Asimov, *Asimov's New Guide to Science* (New York: Basic, 1984).
11. D. H. Erwin, "Macroevolution Is More than Repeated Rounds of Microevolution," *Evolution & Development* 2 (2000): 61–62.
12. T. S. Kemp, *Fossils and Evolution* (Oxford: Oxford University Press, 1999), 16. See also: Robert Carroll, *Patterns and Processes of Vertebrate Evolution* (Cambridge: Cambridge University Press, 1997), 8–10.
13. Ernst Mayr, *What Evolution Is*, (New York: Basic, 2001), 272.
14. Stephen Jay Gould, "Hooking Leviathan by Its Past," *Natural History* (May 1994).
15. J. G. M. Thewissen et al., "Fossil Evidence for the Origin of Aquatic Locomotion in Archaeocete Whales," *Science* 263 (1994): 210–12.
16. Laurie R. Godfrey, "Creationism and Gaps in the Fossil Record," in *Scientists Confront Creationism* (New York: Norton, 1983), 199.
17. Douglas Futuyma, *Science on Trial*; quoted in Phillip Johnson, *Darwin on Trial* (Downers Grove, Ill.: InterVarsity, 1991), 76.
18. Henry Gee, *Deep Time: Cladistics, The Revolution in Evolution* (London: Fourth Estate, 2000), 1–2.
19. *Harper's Magazine* (February 1985), 60.
20. Carl Zimmer, *Evolution*, 138.
21. Robert Carroll, *Patterns and Processes of Vertebrate Evolution* (Cambridge: Cambridge University Press, 1997), 8–10.
22. Mark Ridley, *Evolution* (Boston: Blackwell Scientific, 1993), 49.
23. Johannes Schul, Slide 19, www.biology.missouri.edu/courses/Bio302_Schul/Evidence.htm
24. Quoted in Steve Jones, *Darwin's Ghost* (New York: Random House, 2000), 128.
25. James 1:2, NKJV.
26. Quoted in Stephen Jay Gould, *Ever Since Darwin, Reflections in Natural History*, (New York: Norton, 1973), 141–46.
27. Erasmus Darwin, *Zoonomia, or The Laws of Organic Life*, vol. I (London: J. Johnson, 1794), 509; quoted in George B. Dysan, "Darwin in Kansas." *Science* 285 (1999): 1355.
28. Quoted in Colin Brown, *Philosophy and the Christian Faith* (Downers Grove, Ill.: InterVarsity, 1968), 57.
29. Stephen Jay Gould, "The Panda's Thumb," in *The Panda's Thumb* (New York: Norton, 1980), 20.

30. I have documented the religious foundation of evolution, including the religious interpretation of empirical evidence, by today's evolutionists in my books *Darwin's God: Evolution and the Problem of Evil* (Grand Rapids, Mich.: Brazos, 2001) and *Darwin's Proof: The Triumph of Religion Over Science* (Grand Rapids, Mich.: Brazos, 2003).

12. DARWINIAN EVOLUTIONARY THEORY AND THE LIFE SCIENCES IN THE TWENTY-FIRST CENTURY
Roland F. Hirsch

1. I have been fortunate to hear lectures by, receive reports of advances in research from, and to have discussions with many leading scientists and colleagues in the disciplines relevant to this topic. Some of their work is referenced here, along with that of many others, though much more could have been included. I appreciate the many opportunities they have given me to learn about key developments in chemistry and biology. However, the interpretations in this essay of the research results are mine, and it should not be assumed that the scientists responsible for a particular discovery would agree with my assessment of its significance for Darwinian evolutionary theory. I also wish to credit the authors of the other essays in this volume for educating me by raising important questions in their writings over the past fifteen years. Their work has encouraged me to look closely at the justification for the Darwinian approach in light of the wealth of new knowledge about life that is being produced by the new technologies. Finally, this article is adapted in part from an address given in August 2000 for the American Chemical Society Division of Analytical Chemistry Award for Distinguished Service in the Advancement of Analytical Chemistry, sponsored by the Waters Corporation. I would like to thank the Division and the sponsors for this honor and for the opportunity to express my ideas about evolution in public for the first time.

    Most of the basic concepts in biology discussed in this essay are covered in recent textbooks. The references given here are examples of current developments in biological research, selected from a much larger number of similar advances, and offer a starting point for reading about a particular topic. In many cases, review articles were selected instead of the original research papers, as the reviews will be more easily understood and will give references back to the primary literature. These articles are generally limited to ones that the author has read, but there are other articles that would cover many of the topics equally well.

2. F. Dyson, *Imagined Worlds* (Cambridge, Mass.: Harvard University Press, 1997), 49ff.

3. In addition to the articles referenced below, see, for example, R. F. Hirsch, "Analytical Chemistry and the Life Sciences," *Analytical Chemistry* 73 (2001): 117A; J. Handley, C. M. Harris, "Great Ideas of a Decade: Analytical Chemists Recall the Birth of What Are Now Key Fields of Research," *Analytical Chemistry* 73 (2001): 660A–666A; R. A. Keller, et al., "Analytical Applications of Single-Molecule Detection," *Analytical Chemistry* 74 (2002): 316A–324A; S. A. Hu, N. J. Dovichi, "Capillary Electrophoresis for the Analysis of Biopolymers," *Analytical Chemistry* 74 (2002): 2833–50; D. M. Cannon, Jr., N. Winograd, A. G. Ewing, "Quantitative Chemical Analysis of Single Cells," *Annual Review of Biophysics and Biomolecular Structure* 29 (2000): 239–63; "Synchrotron Supplement," *Nature Structural Biology* 5 (August 1998): 614–56.

4. E. Zubritsky, "How Analytical Chemists Saved the Human Genome Project . . . Or At Least Gave It a Helping Hand," *Analytical Chemistry* 74 (2002): 23A–26A.

5. Resources at The Institute for Genomic Research: www.tigr.org/tigr-scripts/CMR2/CMRHomePage.spl; resources at the National Center for Biotechnology Information: for eukaryotes: www.ncbi.nlm.nih.gov/PMGifs/Genomes/EG_T.html; for archaea and bacteria: www.ncbi.nlm.nih.gov/PMGifs/Genomes/micr.html for plants: www.ncbi.nlm.nih.gov/PMGifs/Genomes/PlantList.html

6. *Teaching about Evolution and the Nature of Science* (Washington: National Academy Press, 1998).

7. That horizontal gene transfer existed was known for some time (see Syvanen, M., "Molecular Clocks and Evolutionary Relationships: Possible Distortions Due to Horizontal Gene Flow," *Journal of Molecular Evolution* 26 [1987]: 16–23), but the pervasiveness was obviously unexpected by those who wrote the National Academy of Sciences book.

8. W. F. Doolittle, "Phylogenetic Classification and the Universal Tree," *Science* 284 (1999): 2124–28. W. F. Doolittle, "Uprooting the Tree of Life," *Scientific American* (February 2000): 90–95.

9. C. R. Woese, "On the Evolution of Cells," *Proceedings of the National Academy of Sciences, USA* 99 (2002): 8742–47. C. R. Woese, "Interpreting the Universal Phylogenetic Tree," *Proceedings of the National Academy of Sciences, USA* 97 (2000): 8392–96. W. F. Doolittle, "The Nature of the Universal Ancestor and the Evolution of the Proteome," *Current Opinion in Structural Biology* 10 (2000): 355–58.

10. R. L. Charlebois, R. G. Beiko, and Ragan, M. A. "Microbial Phylogenetics: Branching Out," *Nature* 421 (2003): 217–18.

11. J. Raymong, O. Zhaxybayeva, J. P. Gogarten, S. Y. Gerdes, and R. E. Blankenship, "Whole-Genome Analysis of Photosynthetic Prokaryotes," *Science* 298 (2002): 1616–20; E. Pennisi, "Bacteria Shared Photosynthesis Genes," *Science* 298 (2002): 1538–39.

12. J. O. Andersson, A. M. Sjogren, L. A. Davis, T. M. Embley, and A. J. Roger, "Phylogeneic Analyses of Diplomonad Genes Reveal Frequent Lateral Gene Transfers Affecting Eukaryotes," *Current Biology* 13, no. 2 (2003): 94–104. J. O. Andersson and A. J. Roger, "Evolution of Glutamate Dehydrogenase Genes: Evidence for Lateral Gene Transfer within and between Prokaryotes and Eukaryotes," *BioMed Central Evolutionary Biology* 3 (2003): article 14.

13. E. Bergthorsson, K. L. Adams, B. Thomason, and J. D. Palmer, "Widespread Horizontal Transfer of Mitochondrial Genes in Flowering Plants," *Nature* 424 (2003): 197–201.

14. J. M. Archibald, M. B. Rogers, M. Toop, K. Ishida, and P. J. Keeling, "Lateral Gene Transfer and the Evolution of Plastid-Targeted Proteins in the Secondary Plastid-Containing Alga *Bigelowiella natans,*" *Proceedings of the National Academy of Sciences, USA* 100 (2003): 7678–83.

15. U. L. Rosewich and H. C. Kistler "Role of Horizontal Gene Transfer in the Evolution of Fungi," *Annual Review of Phytopathology* 38 (2000): 325–63.

16. E. H. Scholl, J. L. Thorne, J. P. McCarter, D. M. Bird, "Horizontally Transferred Genes in Plant-Parasitic Nematodes: A High-Throughput Genomic Approach," *Genome Biology* 4 (2003): paper R39.

17. A. Mira, H. Ochman, and N. A. Moran, "Deletional Bias and the Evolution of Bacterial Genomes," *Trends in Genetics* 17 (2001): 589–96.

18. C. Dennis, "Mouse Genome: A Forage in the Junkyard," *Nature* 420 (2002): 458–59.

19. J. A. Shapiro, "Repetitive DNA, Genome System Architecture and Genome Reorganization," *Research in Microbiology* 153 (2002): 447–53.

20. M. Szymanski and J. Barciszewski, "Beyond the Proteome: Non-Coding Regulatory RNAs," *Genome Biology* 3 (2002): 0005.1–0005.8.

21. J. Hasty, D. McMillen, and J. J. Collins,. "Engineered Gene Circuits," *Nature* 420 (2002): 224–30.

22. E. H. Davidson, D. R. McClay, and L. Hood, "Regulatory Gene Networks and the Properties of the Developmental Process," *Proceedings of the National Academy of Sciences, USA* 100 (2003): 1475–80; www.its.caltech.edu/~mirsky/endomes.htm

23. C. Dennis, "Altered States," *Nature* 421 (2003): 686–88. A.P. Feinberg, "Cancer Epigenetics Takes Center Stage," *Proceedings of the National Academy of Sciences, USA* 98 (2001): 392–94. M. A. Goldman, "The

Epigenetics of the Cell," *Genome Biology* 4 (2003): 309. J. A. Shapiro, "Genome Organization and Reorganization in Evolution: Formatting for Computation and Function," *Annals of the New York Academy of Sciences* 981 (2002): 111–34.

24. Y. O. Chernoff, "Mutation Processes at the Protein Level: Is Lamarck back?" *Mutation Research/Reviews in Mutation Research* 488 (2001): 39–64.

25. W. S. Hancock, "The Challenges Ahead," *Journal of Proteome Research* 1 (2002): 9. D. F. Hunt, "Personal Commentary on Proteomics," *Journal of Proteome Research* 1 (2002): 15–19. R. Aebersold, "Constellations in a Cellular Universe," *Nature* 422 (2003): 115–16. B. Marte, "Proteomics," *Nature* 422 (2003): 191, and the review articles that follow.

26. M. S. Lipton, et al., "Global Analysis of the Deinococcus Radiodurans Proteome by Using Accurate Mass Tags," *Proceedings of the National Academy of Sciences, USA* 99 (2002): 11049–54. Y. Shen, et al., "Packed Capillary Reversed-Phase Liquid Chromatography with High-Performance Electrospray Ionization Fourier Transform Ion Cyclotron Resonance Mass Spectrometry for Proteomics," *Analytical Chemistry* 73 (2001): 1766–75. J. Rappsilber and M. Mann, "Is Mass Spectrometry Ready for Proteome-wide Protein Expression Analysis?" *Genome Biology* 3 (2002), comment 2008.

27. H. J. McCune and A. D. Donaldson, "DNA Replication: Telling Time with Microarrays," *Genome Biology* 4 (2002): 204. R. W. Ye, T. Wang, L. Bedzyk, and K. M. Croker, "Applications of DNA Microarrays in Microbial Systems," *Journal of Microbiological Methods* 47 (2001): 257–72. M. T. Laub, H. H. McAdams, T. Feldblyum, C. M. Fraser, and L. Shapiro, "Global Analysis of the Genetic Network Controlling a Bacterial Cell Cycle," *Science* 290 (2000): 2144–48. A. T. Revel, A. M. Talaat, and M. V. Norgard, "DNA Microarray Analysis of Differential Gene Expression in *Borrelia burgdorferi*, the Lyme Disease Spirochete," *Proceedings of the National Academy of Sciences, USA* 99 (2002): 1562–67.

28. M. J. MacCoss, et al., "Shotgun Identification of Protein Modifications from Protein Complexes and Lens Tissue," *Proceedings of the National Academy of Sciences, USA* 99 (2002): 7900–05.

29. An experimental study is found in E. Rhoades, E. Gussakovsky, and G. Haran, "Watching Proteins Fold One Molecule at a Time," *Proceedings of the National Academy of Sciences, USA* 100 (2003; published online on February 28, 2003).

30. P. Wittung-Stafshede, "Role of Cofactors in Protein Folding," *Accounts of Chemical Research* 35 (2002): 201–08.

31. J. Hou, G. E. Sims, C. Zhang, and S. H. Kim, "A Global Representation of the Protein Fold Space," *Proceedings of the National Academy of Sciences, USA* 100 (2003): 2386–90.

32. J. W. H. Schymkowitz, F. Rousseau, and L. Serrano, "Surfing on Protein Folding Energy Landscapes," *Proceedings of the National Academy of Sciences, USA* 99 (2002): 15846–48.

33. S. M. Uptain and S. Lindquist, "Prions as Protein-Based Genetic Elements," *Annual Reviews of Microbiology* 56 (2002): 703-41.

34. R. D. Vale, "The Molecular Motor Toolbox for Intracellular Transport," *Cell* 112 (2003): 467–80.

35. B. Alberts, "The Cell as a Collection of Protein Machines: Preparing the Next Generation of Molecular Biologists," *Cell* 92 (1998): 291–94.

36. A. Yonath, "The Search and Its Outcome: High-Resolution Structures of Ribosomal Particles from Mesophilic, Thermophilic, and Halophilic Bacteria at Various Functional States," *Annual Reviews of Biophysics and Biomolecular Structure* 31 (2002): 257–73. V. Ramakrishnan, "Ribosome Structure and the Mechanism of Translation," *Cell* 108 (2002): 557–72. J. Frank, "The Ribosome—A Macromolecular Machine Par Excellence," *Chemistry & Biology* 7 (2000): R133–R141. H. F. Noller and A. Baucom, "Structure of the 70S Ribosome: Implications for Movement," *Biochemical Society Transactions* 30 (2002): 1159–61. P. B. Moore and T. A. Steitz, "After the Ribosome Structures: How Does Peptidyl Transferase Work?" *RNA* 9 (2003): 155–59. J. A. Doudna and V. L. Rath, "Structure and Function of the Eukaryotic Ribosome: The Next Frontier," *Cell* 109 (2002): 153–56.

37. J. R. Warner, "Nascent Ribosomes," *Cell* 107 (2001): 133–36.

38. P. Cramer, D. A. Bushnell, and R. D. Kornberg, "Structural Basis of Transcription: RNA Polymerase II at 2.8 Ångstrom Resolution," *Science* 292 (2001): 1863–76. A. L. Gnatt, P. Cramer, J. Fu, D. A. Bushnell, and R. D. Kornberg, "Structural Basis of Transcription: An RNA Polymerase II Elongation Complex at 3.3 Ångstrom Resolution," *Science* 292 (2001):1876–82. A. Klug, "A Marvelous Machine for Making Messages," *Science* 292 (2001): 1844–46.

39. S. Walter and J. Buchner, "Molecular Chaperones—Cellular Machines for Protein Folding," *Angewandte Chemie International Edition in English* 41 (2002): 1098–1113. F. U. Hartl and M. Hayer-Hartl, "Molecular Chaperones in the Cytosol: From Nascent Chain to Folded Protein," *Science* 295 (2002): 1852–58. D. Thirumalai and G. H. Lorimer, "Chaperonin-Mediated Protein Folding," *Annual Review of Biophysics and Biomolecular Structure* 30 (2001): 245–69.

40. R. I. Morimoto, "Dynamic Remodeling of Transcription Complexes by Molecular Chaperones," *Cell* 110 (2002): 281–84.

41. P. J. Muchowski, "Protein Misfolding, Amyloid Formation, and Neurodegeneration: A Critical Role for Molecular Chaperones?" *Neuron* 35 (2002): 9–12.

42. M. Rouhi, "No Pools of Free Zinc in Cells," *Chemical & Engineering News* 79 (September 17, 2001): 53. H. M. Baker, B. F. Anderson and E. N. Baker, "Dealing with Iron: Common Structural Principles in Proteins that Transport Iron and Heme," *Proceedings of the National Academy of Sciences, USA* 100 (2003; published online, March 17, 2003).

43. A. C. Rosenzweig, "Copper Delivery by Metallochaperone Proteins," *Accounts of Chemical Research* 34 (2001): 119–28.

44. N. Kondo, et al., "Genome Fragment of *Wolbachia* Endosymbiont Transferred to X Chromosome of Host Insect," *Proceedings of the National Academy of Sciences, USA* 99 (2002): 14280–85.

45. M. E. Davey and G. A. O'Toole, "Microbial Biofilms: From Ecology to Molecular Genetics," *Microbiology and Molecular Biology Reviews* 64 (2000): 847–67.

46. R. M. Donal and J. W. Costerson, "Biofilms: Survival Mechanisms of Clinically Relevant Microorganisms," *Clinical Microbiology Reviews* 15 (2002): 167–93.

47. K. Lewis, "Riddle of Biofilm Resistance," *Antimicrobial Agents and Chemotherapy* 45 (2001): 999–1007.

48. B. L. Bassler, "Small Talk: Cell-to-Cell Communication in Bacteria," *Cell* 109 (2002): 421–24. M. B. Miller and B. L. Bassler, "Quorum Sensing in Bacteria," *Annual Reviews of Microbiology* 55 (2001): 165–99.

49. D. L. Erickson, et al., "*Pseudomonas aeruginosa* Quorum-Sensing Systems May Control Virulence Factor Expression in the Lungs of Patients with Cystic Fibrosis," *Infection and Immunity* 70 (2002): 1783–90.

50. P. E. Kolenbrander, et al., "Communication among Oral Bacteria," *Microbiology and Molecular Biology Reviews* 66 (2002): 486–505.

51. See for example L. E. Orgel, "The Origin of Life—A Review of Facts and Speculations," *Trends in Biochemical Sciences* 23 (1998): 491–95. G. Wächterhäuser, "The Origin of Life and Its Methodological Challenge," *Journal of Theoretical Biology* 187 (1997): 483–694. C. de Duve, *Vital Dust* (New York: Basic, 1995).

52. H. Huber, et al., "A New Phylum of Archaea Represented by a Nanosized Hyperthermophylic Symbiont," *Nature* 417 (2002): 63–67.

53. R. Gil, et al., "Extreme Genome Reduction in *Buchnera* spp.: Toward the Minimal Genome Needed for Symbiotic Life," *Proceedings of the*

National Academy of Sciences, USA 99 (2002): 4454–58; R. C. H. J. van Ham, et al., "Reductive Genome Evolution in *Buchnera Aphidicola*," *Proceedings of the National Academy of Sciences, USA* 100 (2003): 581–86.

54. C. A. Hutchinson, et al., "Global Transposon Mutagenesis and a Minimal Mycoplasma Genome," *Science* 286 (1999): 2165–69.

55. R. L. Carroll, "Towards a New Evolutionary Synthesis," *TRENDS in Evolution and Ecology* 15 (2000): 27–32; 205–06.

56. A. S. Wilkins, "Evolutionary Processes: A Special Issue," *BioEssays* 22 (2000): 1051–52.

57. L. Hood, "A Personal View of Molecular Technology and How It Has Changed Biology," *Journal of Proteome Research* 1 (2002): 399–409. See also the web site of the Institute for Systems Biology, www.systemsbiology.org/.

13. CHEATING THE MILLENNIUM
Christopher Michael Langan

1. "Meaning" entails recognition, referring specifically to a recognizable and therefore informational relationship among related entities. Since information is abstract, so is recognition, and so is meaning (whether or not the related entities are themselves physical and concrete). *Naturalism*, of which the theory of evolution is an example, is an essentially materialistic viewpoint that denies or disregards abstract modes of existence, thus limiting meaning to "material" drives and instincts. But where the abstract contains the physical, capturing its structure in the form of meaningful informational patterns called "laws of nature", abstraction and meaning are plainly essential to both science and nature.

2. Charles Darwin, *The Origin of Species* (New York: Bantam Classic, [1859] 1999).

3. Science is a two-step, two-level process concerned with (1) formulating hypotheses about nature, and (2) proving or disproving these hypotheses to some degree of confirmation. Relative to level 1, level 2 requires a higher level of discourse incorporating truth-functional criteria independent of any particular falsifiable hypothesis. Because maintaining this distinction helps to insure that false hypotheses do not figure in their own "validation," purportedly falsifiable (level 1) theories like neo-Darwinism should not be confused with the confirmational level of science.

4. Properly speaking, science includes both the empirical and mathematical sciences. Most of those who call themselves "scientists," as well as many proponents of ID theory, assume that scientific confirmation can only be

achieved by strict application of the scientific method and must thus be empirical. However, this is an oversimplification. The empirical sciences are not only mathematical in structure, but too heavily indebted to mathematical reasoning to exclude mathematical methods as possible means of confirming facts about nature. So with regard to the scientific status of ID theory, both empirical and mathematical methods of confirmation must be duly considered.

5. It can also be cogently argued that the design inference requires the establishment of means, motive and opportunity for a designer to act, and that meeting these requirements amounts to explaining the designer.

6. Theistic evolution is a simple conjunction of theism and Darwinism which pays no real attention to their mutual consistency or the model-theoretic implications of combining them.

7. B. Robinson, "Public Beliefs about Evolution and Creation," *Ontario Consultants on Religious Tolerance* [online, 1995]. Available at www.religioustolerance.org/ev_publi.htm

8. M. W. Ho and P. T. Saunders, "Beyond Neo-Darwinism—An Epigenetic Approach to Evolution," *Journal of Theoretical Biology* 78 (1978): 573–91. See 574: ". . . neo-Darwinism exhibits a great power of assimilation, incorporating any opposing viewpoint as yet another 'mechanism' in the grand 'synthesis.' But a real synthesis should begin by identifying conflicting elements in the theory, rather than in accommodating contradictions as quickly as they arise."

9. David Hume, *Enquiries Concerning Human Understanding* and *Concerning the Principles of Morals*, ed. by L. A. Selby-Bigge, 3rd revised ed., ed. by P. H. Nidditch, (Oxford: Oxford University Press, 1975).

10. Immanuel Kant, *The Critique of Pure Reason*, trans. Norman Kemp Smith. (New York: St. Martin's Press, 1929, 1965). Available: URL: www.arts.cuhk.edu.hk/Philosophy/Kant/cpr.

11. While material and efficient causation are superficially physical and can be described in more or less materialistic terms, formal and final causation are more abstract. Francis Bacon, who strongly influenced scientific methodology, classified these abstract modes of causation as *metaphysics* rather than *physics*. See Francis Bacon, *Thoughts on the Nature of Things* (Kessinger Publishing, 1997)]

12. These questions about *laws* of causality address the nature and origin of causality itself, and are thus metacausal analogues of Aristotle's questions about causality. The answers presented in this paper—roughly, that laws are elements of syntax of the language of nature, that they are composed of telesis and self-transducing metainformation, that they reside in syntactic (space-time-object) operators whose states they govern,

that they arose through the metacausal self-configuration of the language of nature, that their properties include closure, comprehensiveness, consistency and coherence, and that their functionality and maintenance rely on intrinsic features of the language of nature—are thus metacausally analogous to Aristotle's modes of causation.

13. For example, there is the gap between mind and matter; the gap between abstract and concrete existence; the gap between causality and generative cosmogony; the gap between classical and quantum mechanics, and so on. Because these gaps are serious, there is no reason to think that causality can be adequately explained as long as they exist.

14. Alfred North Whitehead, *Process and Reality* (New York: The Free Press, 1985).

15. Michael Behe, *Darwin's Black Box* (New York: The Free Press, 1996).

16. William A. Dembski, *The Design Inference: Eliminating Chance Through Small Probabilities* (Cambridge: Cambridge University Press, 1998).

17. M. Pigliucci, "Methodological vs. philosophical naturalism, or why we should be skeptical of religion," in *Tales of the Rational: Skeptical Essays About Nature and Science* (Atlanta Freethought Society, 2000). Available: URL: http://fp.bio.utk.edu/skeptic/Essays/ methodological_naturalism.htm

18. At the time that Charles Darwin made this observation and formulated his natural selection thesis, it was still obscured by centuries of teleological dominance.

19. The canonical *principle of indifference* (or *insufficient reason*) states that where there is no positive reason for assigning different probabilities to competing statistical or predictive assertions, e.g. different possible mutations weighted by relative frequency, equal probabilities must be assigned to all. Since this is essentially how neo-Darwinism calculates its random distributions of mutations and other events, it is just a biological variant of the principle of indifference.

20. Kant, *The Critique of Pure Reason*, 83: "Things which we see are not by themselves what we see. . . . It remains completely unknown to us what the objects may be by themselves and apart from the receptivity of our senses. We know nothing but our manner of perceiving them." Or again, 147: "We ourselves introduce that order and regularity in the appearance which we entitle 'nature'. We could never find them in appearances had we not ourselves, by the nature of our own mind, originally set them there."

21. Ibid., 93: "Thoughts without content are empty, intuitions without concepts are blind."

22. For cognitive (and thus for theoretical and scientific) purposes, *reality*

consists of perception plus the abstract cognitive apparatus required to generate, support, and sustain it.

23. It makes no difference that scientific theories are based on "objective" empirical observations; the key point is that scientific observation and theorization require subjectively conscious agents called "scientists," and that there exists no possible means of ruling out subjectivity on the part of any other kind of observer-theorist. Whatever reality "might have been without us," our presence immediately implies that it possesses a subjective dimension.

24. *Property dualism* asserts that the properties *mental* and *physical*, while essentially different, apply to the same objects. Dual aspect monism asserts that these two properties together characterize the fundamental "substance" of nature.

25. The *Church-Turing Thesis* asserts that the class of recursive functions and the class of effectively computable functions are the same. This is generally taken to imply an isomorphism between the formal, abstract realm of recursive functions and the physical, mechanical realm in which abstract Turing machines are instantiated. For theoretical purposes, this isomorphism must be taken for granted; without it, theoretical instances of recursion could not be model-theoretically interpreted in physical reality, and physical reality could not be scientifically explained.

26. This is the case even if what gets iterated is a "continuous" function representing motion in a differentiable manifold.

27. Scientific methodology conforms to the *scientific method*, which prescribes that nature be treated as if it were everywhere both discernable and replicable, and the related doctrine of falsifiability, which asserts that science is concerned only with hypotheses that are conceivably false and susceptible to empirical disproof. However, *nature* cannot be meaningfully defined in such a way that these criteria always hold within it. For example, no full description of nature can exclude references to universal, unconditional and therefore unfalsifiable properties of nature, and such unfalsifiable properties need not be scientifically trivial.

28. In physics, spatial and spatiotemporal manifolds are usually constrained by the *locality principle*, according to which nothing travels faster than light. Locality can be more fundamentally defined as the condition that in relocating from one point to another in a metric space, an object must traverse the entire sequence of adjacent finite or infinitesimal intervals comprising some intervening path within the metric on which locality is being enforced. In other words, locality means "no sudden jumps from one point to another, through the space containing the points or any external space thereof." The bearing on causality is obvious.

29. Continuity is understood in terms of infinitesimal displacements. Several approaches exist to the topic of infinitesimals, some more controversial than others. The most common is the Cauchy-Weierstrass epsilon-delta formalism based on series and limits; the most sophisticated is that of which A. Robinson's *nonstandard analysis* is the earliest and most successful representative.

30. Perhaps the most fashionable discrete model universe is explicitly based on a computational paradigm, the cellular automaton. An encyclopedic account of this paradigm can be found in S. Wolfram, *A New Kind of Science* (Champaign, Ill.: Wolfram Media, 2002).

31. This means "extrinsic to the object affected by causality." For example, consider the problem of the origin of the *real universe*. Where the real universe is defined to contain all that is perceptible and/or of relevance to that which is perceptible, anything sufficiently real to have originated, caused or influenced it is contained within it by definition. Thus, extrinsic causality (standard determinacy) cannot be invoked to explain the origin of the real universe. Because every instance of causation *within* the real universe ultimately leads back to the origin of reality by causal regression, standard determinacy fails as a causal paradigm.

32. This particular formulation of the "physical causal closure thesis" is due to the contemporary philosopher Jaegwon Kim. See J. Kim, *Mind in a Physical World* (Cambridge, Mass.: MIT Press, 2000). By the mathematical definition of closure, causal closure implies reflexive self-determinism. Because the physical causal closure thesis instead relies on standard determinism, it is conceptually deficient and powerless to effect causal closure.

33. *Physical* is a rather ambiguous term that currently means "of or relating to matter and energy or the sciences dealing with them, especially physics." It thus refers to a relationship of unspecified extent, namely, the extended relational plexus generated by the concepts of *matter* and *energy*. While causality does indeed relate to matter and energy, it is an abstract principle that is more general and cohesive than its physical instantiations, in contrast to which it can be neither held in the hand nor converted to heat. Because it thus bears description as neither matter nor energy, it resides elsewhere in this extended relationship. It follows that causality is more than physical. Where *physical* is further defined as "belonging to the class of phenomena accessible to the scientific method," only those levels of causality which are both discernable and replicable may be called "physical."

34. In any case, the self-containment of the real universe is implied by the following contradiction: if there were any *external* entity or influence that

were sufficiently real to affect the real universe, then by virtue of its reality, it would by definition be *internal* to the real universe.

35. Metacausality is the causal principle or agency responsible for the origin or "causation" of causality itself (in conjunction with state). This makes it responsible for its own origin as well, ultimately demanding that it self-actualize from an ontological groundstate consisting of unbound ontic potential.

36. Where time is defined on physical change, metacausal processes that affect potentials without causing actual physical changes are by definition atemporal.

37. *Telesis* is a convergent metacausal generalization of law and state, where law relates to state roughly as the syntax of a language relates to its expressions through generative grammar, but with the additional stipulation that as a part of syntax, generative grammar must in this case generate itself along with state. Feedback between syntax and state may thus be called *telic feedback*.

38. Beyond a certain level of specificity, no detailed knowledge of state or law is required in order to undertake a generic logical analysis of telesis.

39. To achieve causal closure with respect to final causation, a metacausal agency must self-configure in such a way that it relates to itself as the ultimate utility, making it the *agency, act* and *product* of its own self-configuration. This 3-way coincidence, called *triality*, follows from self-containment and implies that self-configuration is intrinsically utile, thus explaining its occurrence in terms of intrinsic utility.

40. It might be objected that the term "rationality" has no place in the discussion; in other words, that there is no reason to assume that the universe has sufficient self-recognitional coherence or "consciousness" to be "rational." However, since the universe does indeed manage to consistently self-recognize and self-actualize in a certain objective sense, and these processes are to some extent functionally analogous to human self-recognition and self-actualization, we can in this sense and to this extent justify the use of terms like "consciousness" and "rationality" to describe them. This is very much in the spirit of such doctrines as physical reductionism, functionalism and eliminativism, which assert that such terms devolve or refer to objective physical or functional relationships. Much the same reasoning applies to the term *utility*.

41. In computation theory, *recognition* denotes the acceptance of a language by a transducer according to its programming or "transductive syntax." Because the universe coherently processes internal information and thus bears description as a "self-accepting transducer," this concept is not without meaning in physics and cosmology.

42. The concept of potential is an essential ingredient of physical reasoning. Where a *potential* is a set of possibilities from which something is *actualized*, potential is necessary to explain the existence of anything in particular (as opposed to some other partially equivalent possibility).

43. Possible constraints include locality, uncertainty, blockage, noise, interference, undecidability and other intrinsic features of the natural world.

44. Examples include the *atheism* and *materialism* riders often attached to neo-Darwinism, and the *biblical creationism* rider often mistakenly attached to ID theory.

45. This view was captured by the French astronomer and mathematician Pierre Simon Laplace (1749–1827) in his *Philosophical Essay on Probabilities* (1814): "An intellect which at any given moment knew all the forces that animate Nature and the mutual positions of the beings that comprise it, if this intellect were vast enough to submit its data to analysis, could condense into a single formula the movement of the greatest bodies of the universe and that of the lightest atom: for such an intellect nothing could be uncertain; and the future just like the past would be present before our eyes." This view, called *Laplacian determinism*, went virtually unchallenged until the first half of the twentieth century, when it was undermined by such new concepts as quantum uncertainty and theoretic undecidability. But even though such problems seem to rule out an explicit calculation of the sort that Laplace envisioned, his ideal is still very much a driving force in science.

46. The scientific method mandates a constructive relationship between empirical observation and rational theorization that is designed for the investigation of phenomena possessing two criteria, *discernability* and *replicability*. That is, it confines scientific attention to that which can be exclusively and repeatedly observed under similar conditions anywhere in time or space; it does not cover any indiscernible or localized natural influence that is not conditionally (and thus falsifiably) distributed over space and time. Yet, indiscernables and unconditional universals must exist in order for nature to be stable—e.g., the universal, unconditional and intangible logical syntax which enforces consistency throughout the universe—and the exclusion of localized causal influences from nature is rationally insupportable.

47. In addition to other criteria, relations and properties are distinguished by *arity* and *order*. The arity (adicity, cardinality) of a relation is just the number of *relands* or things related, while its order depends on whether its relands are individual elements, relations of elements, relations of relations of elements, or so on. Similarly, a property (attribute, predicate)

is distinguished by whether it is attributed to individual elements, properties of elements, properties of properties of elements, or et cetera.

48. Some manifolds come with special provisions for motion and causality, e.g. *metrics* defining the notion of distance, *derivatives* defining the notion of movement, and *affine connections* permitting the parallel transport of vectors through space.

49. The bottom-up thesis is insidious in the way it carries the apparent randomness of experimental distributions of mutation events upward from low-order to high-order relationships, all the way to the phenotypic and social realms. This is what encourages many neo-Darwinists (and those whom they influence) to view mankind, and life in general, as "random" and "purposeless."

50. Within a given set of constraints, many possible future states of a physical system may be causally compatible with a single present state, and many alternative present states may be causally compatible with a single future state. Thus, higher-order and lower-order causal relationships describing the same system need not uniquely determine each other by top-down and bottom-up causation respectively. The physical situation is suggestive of formal model-theoretic ambiguity as captured by, for example, the *Duhem-Quine thesis*, according to which a given set of observations may be consistent with multiple theories of causation, and a single Laplacian snapshot can result in many possible predictions or retrodictions depending on the causal influences that are physically active or theoretically presumed to be active. Dual-aspect monism ultimately transforms model-theoretic ambiguity into causal freedom, revealing nature as its own creative theoretician and physical modeler and thereby effecting causal closure.

51. These extensions are to some extent mutually incompatible. In order to reconcile the outstanding conflicts and conceptual dissonances between General Relativity and quantum mechanics, yet another metatheoretic extension is now required.

52. C. M. Langan, "The Cognitive-Theoretic Model of the Universe: A New Kind of Reality Theory," *Progress in Complexity, Information and Design* I.2/1.3 (2002).

53. C. M. Patton and J. A. Wheeler, "Is Physics Legislated by Cosmogony?" in *Quantum Gravity*, ed. by Isham, Penrose, and Sciama, (Clarendon Press, Oxford, 1975), 538–605. In this paper, the term *pregeometry* is used in reference to "something deeper than geometry, that underlies both geometry and particles. . . . [N]o perspective seems more promising than the view that it must provide the Universe with a way to come into being." The SCSPL extension of physical reality fits this description.

54. Where laws of nature incorporate not only observables but the abstractions relating them, bringing physical states and natural laws into coincidence reduces the set of physical (observable) properties to a subset of the set of abstract properties. Thus, the abstract is recognized as a *natural* generalization of the concrete.

55. *Telic recursion* is a quantum metaprocess based on a generalized form of recursion maximizing intrinsic utility over entire (pregeometric) regions of spacetime through telic feedback under the guidance of coherent metacausal invariants called *telons*.

56. SCSPL is developed by adjoining to (propositional and predicate) logic a limiting form of model theory from which it acquires certain necessary high-level properties of any possible valid theory of reality at large. Thus, its syntactic and semantic validity can be logically established. By its method of construction, SCSPL is classified as a metaphysical tautology or *supertautology*.

57. Inflationary cosmology, membrane theory and various other theories have been assumed to require external extensions of physical reality. In contrast, SCSPL conspansive duality permits the extension mandated by SCSPL, as well as all other valid extensions of physical reality, to be physically internalized in a certain specific sense relating to conspansiive duality.

58. See www.teleologic.org for a description of teleologic evolution.

59. Human psycho-intellectual, sociopolitical and technological modes of evolution may also be distinguished on various levels of aggregation.

60. In the CTMU, instances of irreducible and specified complexity are metacausally generalized to dynamic syntax-state relationships called *telons* which self-actualize by telic recursion.

14: THE DENIABLE DARWIN
David Berlinski

1. A. S. Romer's *Vertebrate Paleontology,* 3rd ed. (Chicago: University of Chicago Press, 1966) may be consulted with profit.

2. The details have been reported in the *New York Times* and in *Science*: evidence that at least some entomologists have a good deal of time on their hands.

3. Schützenberger's comments were made at a symposium held in 1966. The proceedings were edited by Paul S. Moorhead and Martin Kaplan and published as *Mathematical Challenges to the Neo-Darwinian Interpretation of Evolution* (Wistar Institute Press, 1967). Schützenberger's remarks, together with those of the physicist Murray Eden at the same

symposium, constituted the first significant criticism of evolutionary doctrine in recent decades.

4. Murray Eden is, as usual, perceptive: "It is as if," he writes, "some pre-Newtonian cosmologist had proposed a theory of planetary motion which supposed that a natural force of unknown origin held the planets in their courses. The supposition is right enough and the idea of a force between two celestial bodies is a very useful one, but it is hardly a theory."

5. *Black Mischief: Language, Life, Logic and Luck* (1986).

6. The same pattern of intellectual displacement is especially vivid in Daniel Dennett's description of natural selection as a force subordinate to what he calls "the principle of the accumulation of design." Sifting through the debris of chance, natural selection, he writes, occupies itself by "thriftily conserving the design work . . . accomplished at each stage." But there is *no* such principle. Dennett has simply assumed that a sequence of conserved advantages will converge to an improvement in design; the assumption expresses a *non sequitur*.

7. It is absurdly easy to set up a sentence-searching algorithm obeying purely Darwinian constraints. The result, however, is always the same—gibberish.

8. "The Spandrels of San Marco and the Panglossian Paradigm: A Critique of the Adaptationist Programme," *Proceedings of the Royal Society* B205 (1979).

CONTRIBUTORS

JAMES BARHAM

was trained in classics at the University of Texas at Austin and in history of science at Harvard University. He is an independent scholar who has published articles on evolutionary epistemology, the philosophy of mind, and the philosophy of biology in both print and electronic journals, including *BioSystems, Evolution and Cognition, Rivista di Biologia,* and Metanexus.net. Barham was born in Dallas, Texas, in 1952, and raised conventionally as a Southern Baptist. A childhood fascination with astronomy and physics led him to question his religious upbringing at an early age. Russell's *Why I Am Not a Christian* influenced him profoundly, as it has so many provincial youth, and by the seventh grade he was a defiant (not to say, village) atheist. Barham always had an equal attraction to the sciences and the humanities, but for many years felt no contradiction between the world of purpose, meaning, and value revealed through literature, music, and the visual arts, and the tough-minded reductionism endorsed, as he supposed, by science. Gradually, however, Barham became increasingly troubled by the tension between the two incompatible sides of his personal worldview. Finally, in the late 1980s he discovered the literature of nonlinear dynamics, which led directly to his second loss of faith—in metaphysical Darwinism. Since then, he has been laboring to develop a theory of purpose, meaning, and value as objective realities and emergent properties of the *sui generis* dynamics of the living state of matter, as well as to trace some of the implications of this theory for our understanding of human nature. In this vein he is working on a book to be called *Neither Ghost nor Machine.*

MICHAEL J. BEHE

was born in 1952 and grew up in Harrisburg, Pennsylvania. In 1974 he graduated from Drexel University in Philadelphia with a Bachelor of Science degree in Chemistry. He did his graduate studies in biochemistry at the University of Pennsylvania and was awarded the Ph.D. in 1978 for his dissertation research on sickle-cell disease. From 1978 to 1982 he was a Jane Coffin Childs postdoctoral fellow at the National Institutes of Health where he investigated DNA structure. From 1982 to 1985 Behe was Assistant Professor of Chemistry at Queens College in New York City, where he was awarded a Research Career Development Award from the National Institutes of Health. In 1985 he moved to Lehigh University where he is currently Professor of Biochemistry. Behe has authored over forty technical papers and one book, *Darwin's Black Box: The Biochemical Challenge to Evolution*, which argues that living systems at the molecular level are best explained as being the result of deliberate intelligent design. *Darwin's Black Box* has been reviewed by the *New York Times, Nature, Philosophy of Science, Christianity Today*, and over 100 other periodicals. Behe and his wife reside near Bethlehem, Pennsylvania, with their eight children.

DAVID BERLINSKI

was born in New York City in 1942 and educated at the Bronx High School of Science, Columbia College, and Princeton University, from which he received his Ph.D. He taught philosophy and logic at Stanford University during the 1960s, and during the 1970s worked as a management consultant with McKinsey and Company and as a senior quantitative analyst for the City of New York. During the late 1970s, Berlinski served as a professor of mathematics at the Université de Paris at Jussieu, and thereafter held research positions at the Institute for Applied Systems Analysis in Austria, and the Institut des Hautes Etudes Scientifiques in France. Berlinski has taught mathematics and philosophy at a number of American universities. His books include *On Systems Analysis; Black Mischief: Language, Life, Logic, Luck; A Tour of the Calculus; The Advent of the Algorithm;* and *Newton's Gift*. He is also the author of three novels. Berlinski now lives in Paris.

J. BUDZISZEWSKI

(Ph.D. Yale, 1981) is professor of government and philosophy at the University of Texas at Austin. He is a political theorist and philosopher of natural law. His recent work focuses on the repression of moral knowledge—what we really know, how we tell ourselves that we don't know what we do, and what happens to the structures of conscience and moral judgment when we try. Presently he is writing a book on the momentum of evil. A fellow of the Wilberforce Forum as well as Discovery Institute's Center for Science and Culture, Budziszewski is also a member of the Board of Directors of the Institute on Religion and Democracy. His articles have appeared in journals of law, ethics, theology, public policy, and political theory, and his books include *The Resurrection of Nature: Political Theory and the Human Character; The Nearest Coast of Darkness: A Vindication of the Politics of Virtues; True Tolerance: Liberalism and the Necessity of Judgment; Written on the Heart: The Case for Natural Law; The Revenge of Conscience: Politics and the Fall of Man;* and *What We Can't Not Know: A Guide.*

WILLIAM A. DEMBSKI

is associate research professor in the conceptual foundations of science at Baylor University and a senior fellow with Discovery Institute's Center for Science and Culture in Seattle. He is also the executive director of the International Society for Complexity, Information, and Design (www.iscid.org). A graduate of the University of Illinois at Chicago where he earned a B.A. in psychology, an M.S. in statistics, and a Ph.D. in philosophy, he also received a doctorate in mathematics from the University of Chicago in 1988 and a master of divinity degree from Princeton Theological Seminary in 1996. He has held National Science Foundation graduate and postdoctoral fellowships. Dembski has published articles in mathematics, philosophy, and theology journals and is the author of several books. In *The Design Inference: Eliminating Chance through Small Probabilities* he examines the design argument in a post-Darwinian context and analyzes the connections linking chance, probability, and intelligent causation. The sequel to *The Design Inference,* titled *No Free Lunch: Why Specified Complexity Cannot Be Purchased without Intelligence,* appeared in 2002 and critiques Darwinian and other naturalistic accounts of evolution. Dembski is currently coediting a book with Michael Ruse for Cambridge University Press titled *Debating Design: From Darwin to DNA.*

MICHAEL JOHN DENTON

studied medicine at Bristol University. He was awarded a BSc in Physiology in 1964 and an MBChB degree in 1969. As a postgraduate he studied developmental biology at Kings College, London University where he gained a Ph.D. in 1974. He trained in Pathology at the Post Graduate Medical School, London and at the Hospital for Sick Children in Toronto. Since 1989 he has been a Senior Research Fellow in Human Genetics in the Biochemistry Department at the University of Otago, Dunedin, New Zealand. For the past 20 years Denton's main research focus has been on the genetics of human retinal disease. His group has made a major contribution to the field by identifying several new genes responsible for retinal diseases. He has had a longstanding interest in evolutionary biology and has written two books on the subject, *Evolution: A Theory in Crisis* and *Nature's Destiny.* He holds that the intrinsic properties of matter have played a significant role in directing the course of evolution. He has argued in recent publications that molecular forms such as the protein folds are determined by natural law not natural selection and that much of life's order is predicable in principle from physics. Denton was recently invited to present these views in *Nature* and in an article for the recently published *Encyclopedia of Evolution*. He has an article on the same subject in press in the *Journal of Theoretical Biology*.

ROLAND F. HIRSCH

is a program manager in the Office of Biological & Environmental Research in the Office of Science of the U.S. Department of Energy (DOE). His responsibilities include managing research in structural molecular biology, analytical chemistry, and genome sequencing instrumentation, and research supporting the cleanup on contamination at the Manhattan Project sites. He received his A.B. from Oberlin College (1961) and M.S. and Ph.D. (1965) from the University of Michigan. Prior to joining DOE, Hirsch was a health scientist administrator at the National Institutes of Health. He served on the faculty of Seton Hall University from 1965 to 1988, the last four years on leave with the Chemical Sciences Division of DOE. At Seton Hall he was chair of the Chemistry Department, Associate Dean of the college of Arts and Sciences, and mentor to six students receiving the Ph.D. in chemistry. He has served as chair of the 7500-member North Jersey Local Section of the American Chemical Society (ACS), as well as the 9000-member Division of Analytical Chemistry, and the ACS Committee on International Activities, and received the Award for Distinguished Service in the Advancement of Analytical Chemistry in 2000. His essay in this volume is based in part upon his award address.

CORNELIUS G. HUNTER

is a graduate of the University of Michigan where he earned a B.S and M.S. in aerospace engineering and the University of Illinois where he earned a Ph.D. in biophysics. He is the author of the award-winning *Darwin's God: Evolution and the Problem of Evil* and has recently completed its sequel, *Darwin's Proof: The Triumph of Religion Over Science.* He is currently senior scientist at a high-tech research firm and part-time postdoctoral researcher at the University of California at San Diego. Hunter's research interests include molecular biophysics, computational biology, and optimal estimation and control of nonlinear systems. He is currently developing a new method for describing the three-dimensional protein backbone structure and Bayesian methods for predicting protein local structure from the corresponding amino acid sequence. He is also investigating long-range signals in protein amino acid sequences and their correlation with tertiary structure. Hunter's interest in the theory of evolution involves both the scientific, historical, and theological aspects of the theory. His work has helped to expose the scientific weaknesses of evolution. He has shown that popular theological ideas motivated Darwin's development of evolution and that these ideas remain critical in today's defense of the theory.

PHILLIP E. JOHNSON

is the Jefferson Peyser Emeritus Professor of Law at the University of California at Berkeley. Johnson is a well-known speaker and writer on the philosophical significance of Darwinism. His books on this topic include *Darwin on Trial, Reason in the Balance, Defeating Darwinism by Opening Minds, The Wedge of Truth,* and *Asking the Right Questions.* After completing his law degree at the University of Chicago, Johnson was a law clerk for Chief Justice Earl Warren of the United States Supreme Court. Johnson taught law for over thirty years at the University of California at Berkeley. He is the author of two widely used textbooks on criminal law: *Criminal Law: Cases, Materials, and Text* and *Cases and Materials on Criminal Procedure.* Johnson entered the evolution controversy because he found the books defending Darwinism dogmatic and unconvincing. He is an advisor to Discovery Institute's Center for Science and Culture.

ROBERT C. KOONS

is Professor of Philosophy at the University of Texas at Austin. A graduate of Michigan State University, Oxford (B.A. First Class Honours, 1981), and UCLA (Ph.D. in philosophy, 1987), Koons was a Marshall Scholar, Danforth Fellow and a Richard M. Weaver Fellow. He is the author of *Paradoxes of Belief and Strategic Rationality* (Cambridge University Press, 1992), winner of the Gustave Arlt Award in the Humanities, and *Realism Regained: An Exact Theory of Causation, Teleology and the Mind* (Oxford University Press, 2000), as well as articles in such journals as *Mind, American Philosophical Quarterly*, and *Philosophical Studies*. He is a Senior Fellow of the Center for Science and Culture of the Discovery Institute, a faculty affiliate of the Intercollegiate Studies Institute, and a member of the American Philosophical Association, the Association for Symbolic Logic, the Society for Exact Philosophy, the National Association of Scholars, and the Society of Christian Philosophers. Koons's research is primarily in the areas of the philosophy of logic and mathematics, metaphysics, epistemology, metaethics, and philosophical theology. He is currently researching problems of mental and teleological causation and related questions in the metaphysics of events, time, substances, and the mind.

CHRISTOPHER MICHAEL LANGAN

is an independent researcher and reality theorist whose extraordinary intellect has not prevented him from living a rough, unsheltered, and exciting life. Challenged from early childhood with extreme poverty, inadequate schooling, and the responsibility of helping care for his younger siblings, he learned young to value brawn as highly as brains. After working as a cowboy, firefighter, construction worker, and bar bouncer in various nightclubs across the East End of Long Island, he came to the attention of the media in 1999 for combining one of the world's highest IQs with a bare-knuckled lifestyle and a lack of formal higher education. Having conducted original investigations in fields including mathematics, physics, cosmology, and the cognitive sciences over more than two decades, Langan has contributed articles on these and other topics to a number of alternative intellectual periodicals and has authored a collection of philosophical essays, *The Art of Knowing*. A fellow of the

International Society for Complexity, Information and Design, he recently published an intriguing account of his groundbreaking theory of reality, the Cognitive-Theoretic Model of the Universe, in its journal *Progress in Complexity, Information, and Design*. He is the co-founder and president of a nonprofit organization, the Mega Foundation, established to offer aid, support and camaraderie to the "severely gifted," a small and often-neglected population with whose plight he is intimately acquainted.

NANCY R. PEARCEY

is a senior fellow of Seattle's Discovery Institute and a free-lance writer. She studied under Francis Schaeffer at L'Abri Fellowship in Switzerland and went on to earn a master's degree from Covenant Theological Seminary, followed by graduate work in history of philosophy at the Institute for Christian Studies in Toronto. She also studied violin at Iowa State University and in Heidelberg, Germany. Pearcey has been writing and speaking on the relation between science and the Christian worldview since 1977. In 1991, she became the founding editor of BreakPoint, a daily radio commentary program, and was executive editor of the program for nearly nine years. During the same period, she was policy director and senior fellow of the Wilberforce Forum, and coauthored a monthly column in *Christianity Today*. Pearcey has served as managing editor of the journal *Origins & Design*, an editorial board member for Salem Communications Network, and a commentator on Public Square Radio. Her articles have appeared in *The Washington Times*, *Human Events*, *First Things*, *Books & Culture*, *World*, *The Human Life Review*, *Christianity Today*, and the *Regent University Law Review*. She is coauthor of the books *How Now Shall We Live?* and *The Soul of Science*.

MARCEL-PAUL SCHÜTZENBERGER

(1920–96) was Professor of the Faculty of Sciences at the University of Paris and a member of the French Academy of Sciences. He was trained as a mathematician and doctor of medicine. In 1966 Schützenberger participated in the Wistar Symposium on mathematical objections to neo-Darwinism. His arguments were subtle and often misunderstood by biologists. Darwin's theory and the interpretation of biological systems as formal objects were, he observed, at odds insofar as randomness is known to degrade meaning in formal contexts. But Schützenberger also argued that Darwin's theory logically required some active principle of coordination between the typographic space of the informational macromolecules (DNA and RNA) and the organic space of living creatures themselves—which Darwin's theory does not provide. In this January 1996 interview with the French science monthly *La Recherche*, he pursued these themes anew, finding inspiration for his ideas both in the mathematical ideas that he had pioneered and in the speculative tradition of French biological thought that stretched from Georges Cuvier to Lucien Cuenot. Schützenberger was a man of universal curiosity and great wit; throughout his life he was both joyful and unafraid.

EDWARD SISSON

is a partner at a large Washington D.C.–based international law firm, specializing in litigation arising out of multi-million dollar corporate acquisitions. He also maintains an extensive pro bono practice in the areas of international democracy, human rights, and the arts. Prior to becoming a lawyer, he spent nine years producing experimental avant-garde multi-media music theater performances, based in San Francisco and on tour across the US and Europe. His final production, "Actual Sho," was chosen by the US State Department to represent the US at major avant-garde festivals in Belgrade, Yugoslavia, and Wroclaw, Poland, in 1987. Before becoming a theater producer he was an apprentice architect. He earned his law degree magna cum laude at Georgetown (1991) and earned his bachelor of science at the Massachusetts Institute of Technology, majoring in environmental design (1977); he also attended Pomona College, majoring in English and Philosophy (1973–75).

FRANK J. TIPLER

is Professor of Mathematical Physics at Tulane University in New Orleans. He is the coauthor of the acclaimed book *The Anthropic Cosmological Principle*, which takes as its subject the relationship between cosmology and intelligent life. He does research in two areas of physics: global general relativity and the physics of computation. Global general relativity deals with the structure of the cosmos on the largest scales, and computational physics is concerned with the limits on computers imposed by the laws of physics. Tipler's conclusion that there are no ultimate limits to computation (or to the biosphere) is discussed in his book *The Physics of Immortality*, which was on the German bestseller list for fifteen weeks. Selected by the *New York Times* as one of the Notable Books of 1994, *The Physics of Immortality* has been translated into four languages, and more than 200,000 copies are in print world-wide.

JOHN WILSON

is the founding editor of the bimonthly review *Books & Culture* and an editor at large for *Christianity Today* magazine. He has been the editor of the annual series *Best Christian Writing* since its inception; the latest volume, *Best Christian Writing 2004,* was recently published by Jossey-Bass with an introduction by Miroslav Volf. Wilson's essays and reviews appear regularly in a variety of publications.

INDEX